Toshiaki Iwashiro

I hope the cherry trees bloom soon!

Toshiaki Iwashiro was born December 11, 1977, in Tokyo and has the blood type of A. His debut manga was the popular *Mieru Hito*, which ran from 2005 to 2007 in Japan in *Weekly Shonen Jump*, where *Psyren* was also serialized.

PSYREN VOL. 10
SHONEN JUMP Manga Edition

STORY AND ART BY TOSHIAKI IWASHIRO

Translation/Camellia Nieh
Lettering/Annaliese Christman
Design/Matt Hinrichs
Editor/Joel Enos

PSYREN © 2007 by Toshiaki Iwashiro
All rights reserved.
First published in Japan in 2007 by SHUEISHA Inc., Tokyo.
English translation rights arranged by SHUEISHA Inc.

The rights of the author(s) of the work(s) in this publication to be so
identified have been asserted in accordance with the Copyright, Designs
and Patents Act 1988. A CIP catalogue record for this book is available
from the British Library.

Printed in the U.S.A.

Published by VIZ Media, LLC
P.O. Box 77010
San Francisco, CA 94107

10 9 8 7 6 5 4 3 2 1
First printing, May 2013

www.viz.com

PARENTAL ADVISORY
RATED T FOR TEEN
PSYREN is rated T for Teen and is
recommended for ages 13 and up.
This volume contains fantasy violence.
ratings.viz.com

THE WORLD'S
MOST POPULAR MANGA
SHONEN JUMP
www.shonenjump.com

SHONEN JUMP MANGA EDITION

10

ALIEN SKY

Story and Art by
Toshiaki Iwashiro

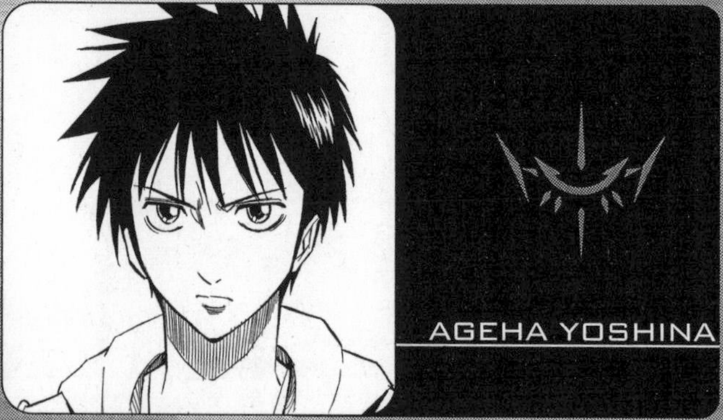
AGEHA YOSHINA

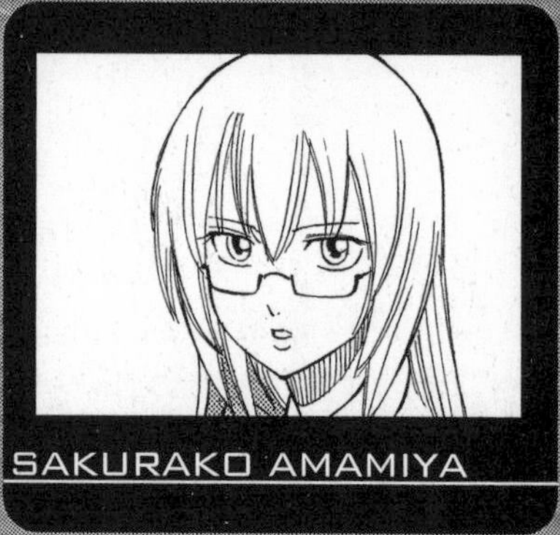
SAKURAKO AMAMIYA

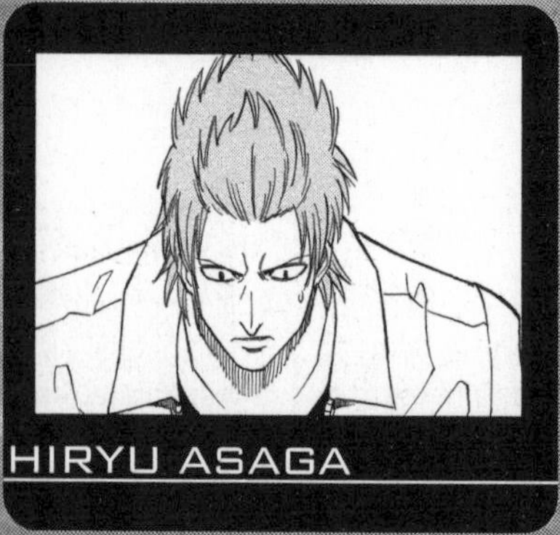
HIRYU ASAGA

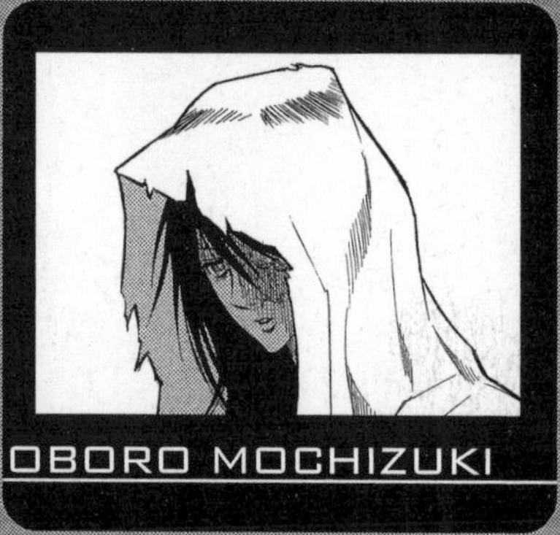
OBORO MOCHIZUKI

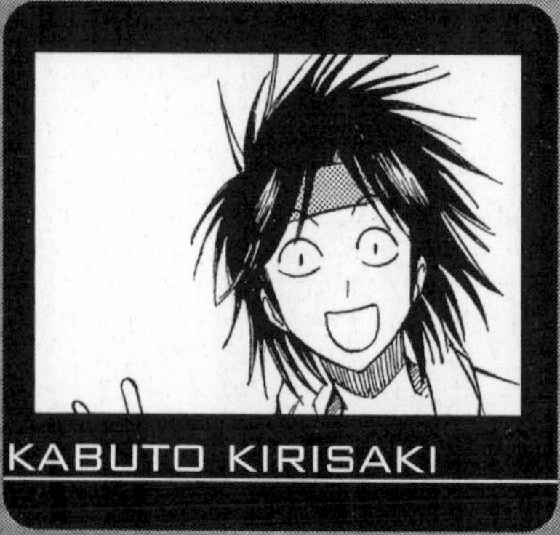
KABUTO KIRISAKI

Characters

MIROKU AMAGI

THE ELMORE WOOD GANG

NEMESIS Q

Story

WHILE SEARCHING FOR HIS MISSING FRIEND SAKURAKO, HIGH-SCHOOLER AGEHA YOSHINA HAPPENS UPON A RED PHONE CARD EMBLAZONED WITH THE WORD *PSYREN* THAT SETS HIM UP AS A PLAYER IN A LIFE-OR-DEATH GAME IN THE BIZARRE PSYREN WORLD.

THE MYSTERIOUS NEMESIS Q SHOWS UP SEEKING HELP FOR ITS AILING CREATOR. AGEHA, KYLE AND COMPANY SET OUT FOR DREAMEATER ISLAND. THERE THEY ENCOUNTER THE NEO-AMAKUSA GROUP, WHO ARE OUT TO DESTROY Q'S CREATOR! THE LEADER OF THE GROUP IS USUI, THE PHONY COP AGEHA ENCOUNTERED BACK IN PRESENT-DAY JAPAN. WITH THE HELP OF THEIR FRIENDS, AGEHA AND SAKURAKO MANAGE TO TRIUMPH OVER THE NEO-AMAKUSA, EVADING USUI'S MEMORY-ERASING PSI ATTACK. FINALLY, THEY FIND THEMSELVES FACE-TO-FACE WITH Q'S CREATOR!

PSYREN

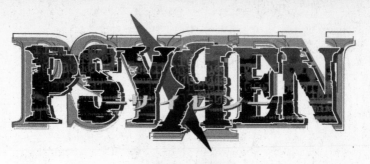

VOL. 10
ALIEN SKY
CONTENTS

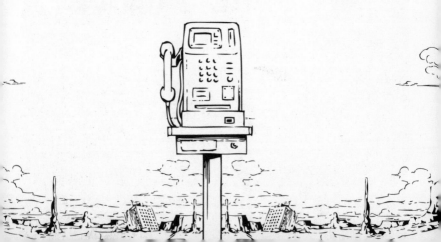

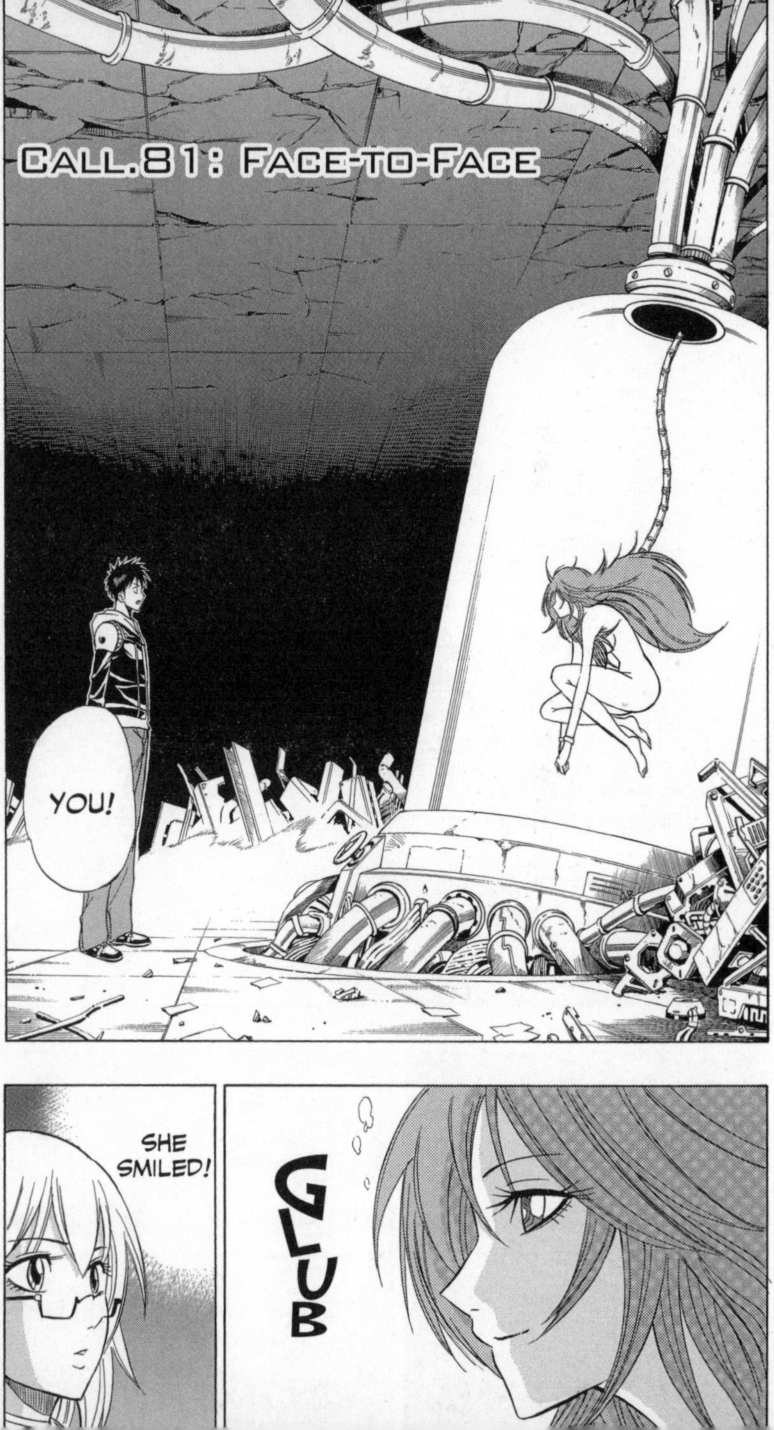
CALL.81: FACE-TO-FACE
YOU!
GLUB
SHE SMILED!

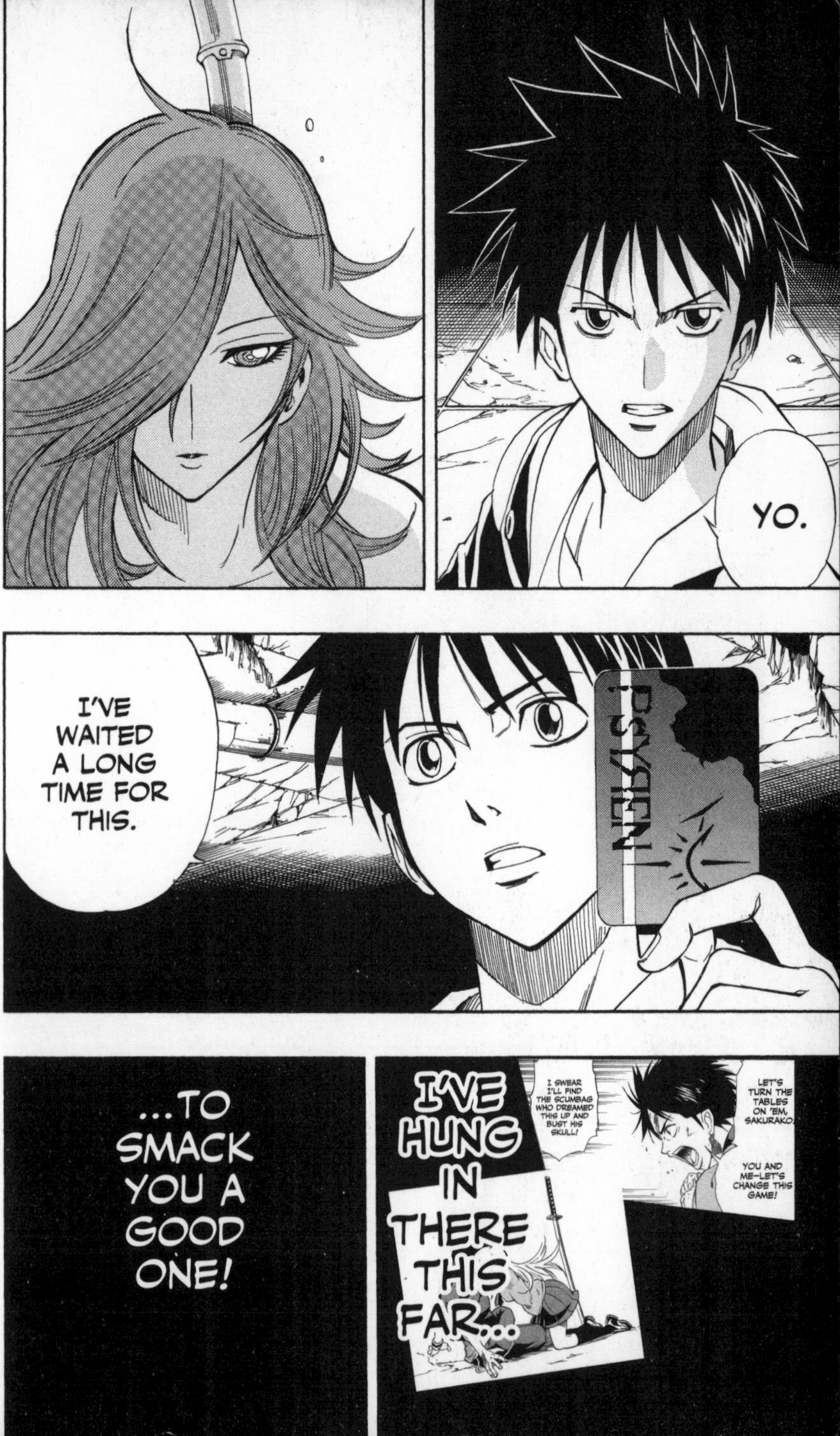
YO.
I'VE WAITED A LONG TIME FOR THIS.
PSYREN
LET'S TURN THE TABLES ON 'EM, SAKURAKO.
I SWEAR I'LL FIND THE SCUMBAG WHO DREAMED THIS UP AND BUST HIS SKULL!
YOU AND ME—LET'S CHANGE THIS GAME!
I'VE HUNG IN THERE THIS FAR...
...TO SMACK YOU A GOOD ONE!

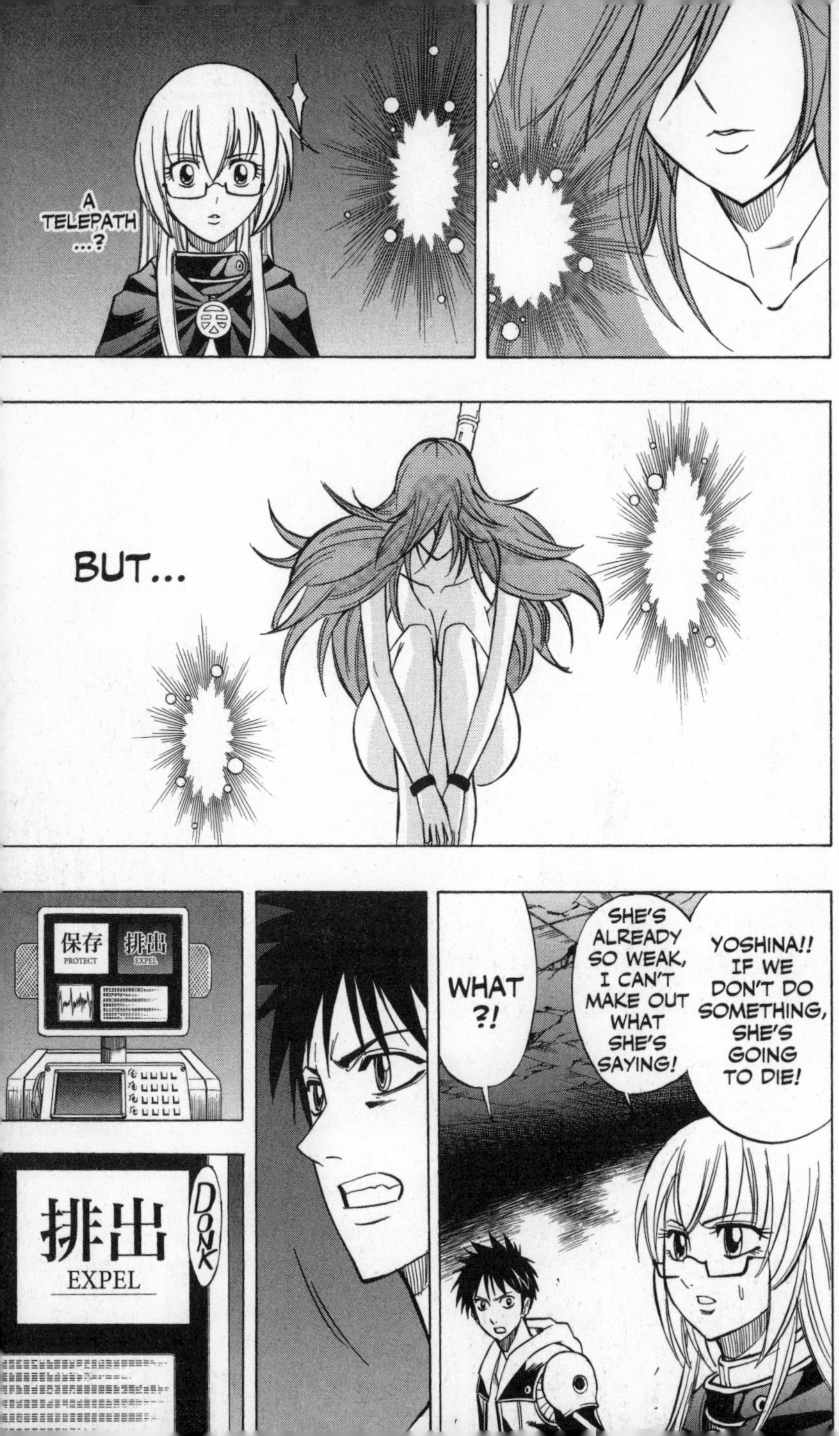

A TELEPATH ...?
BUT...
YOSHINA!! IF WE DON'T DO SOMETHING, SHE'S GOING TO DIE!
SHE'S ALREADY SO WEAK, I CAN'T MAKE OUT WHAT SHE'S SAYING!
WHAT ?!
保存 PROTECT
排出 EXPEL
排出 EXPEL
DONK

SH LOOP

K CH UNG

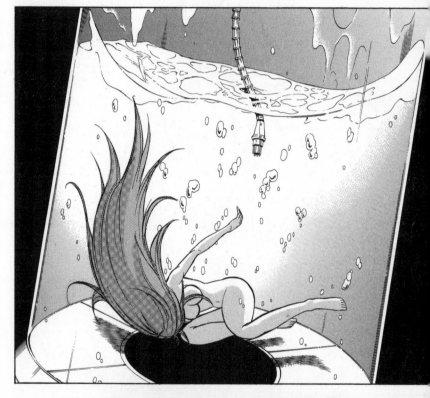

WE'VE GOT TO GET HER OUT OF THERE!

OH NO! WHAT NOW?

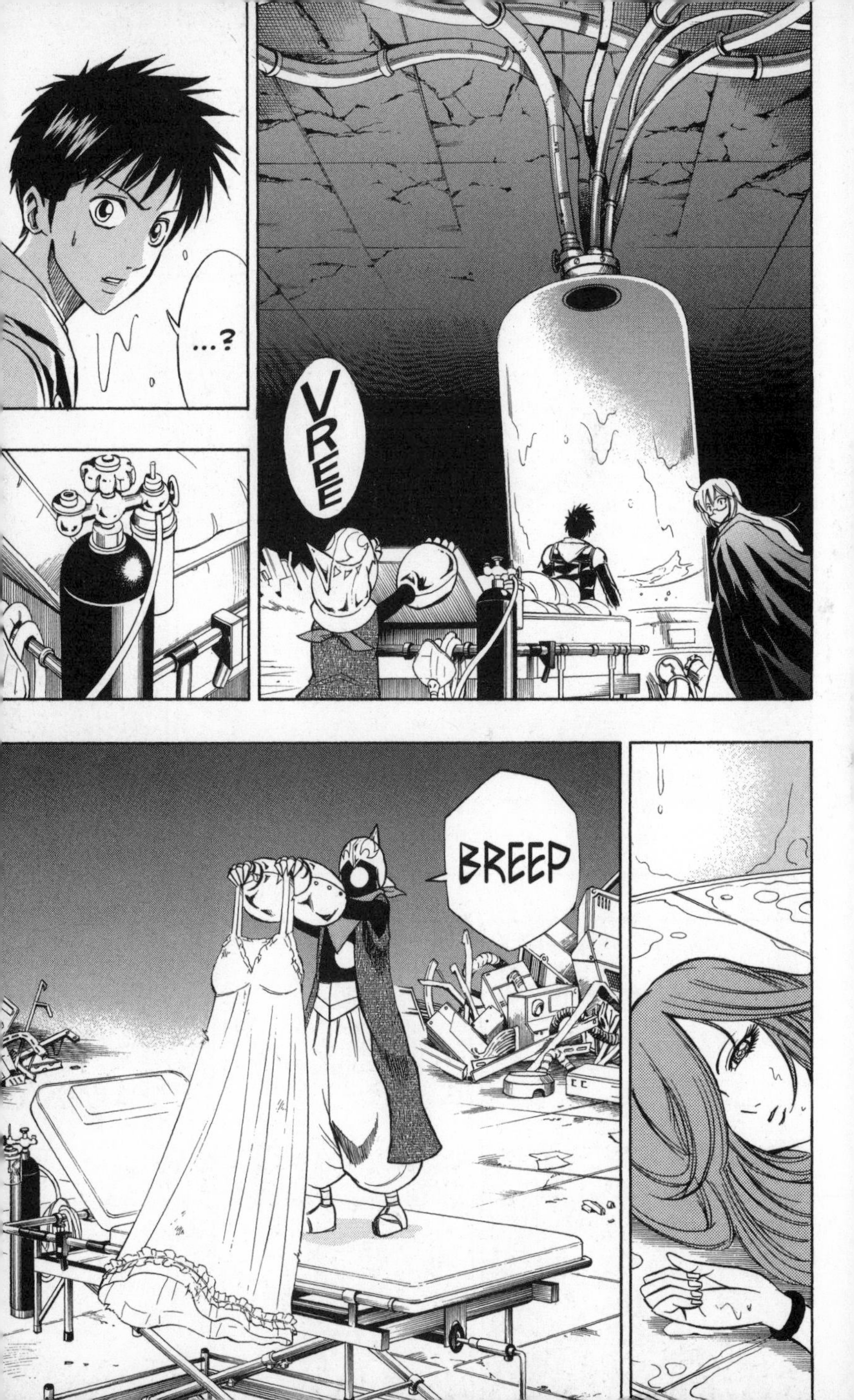
VREE
...?
BREEP

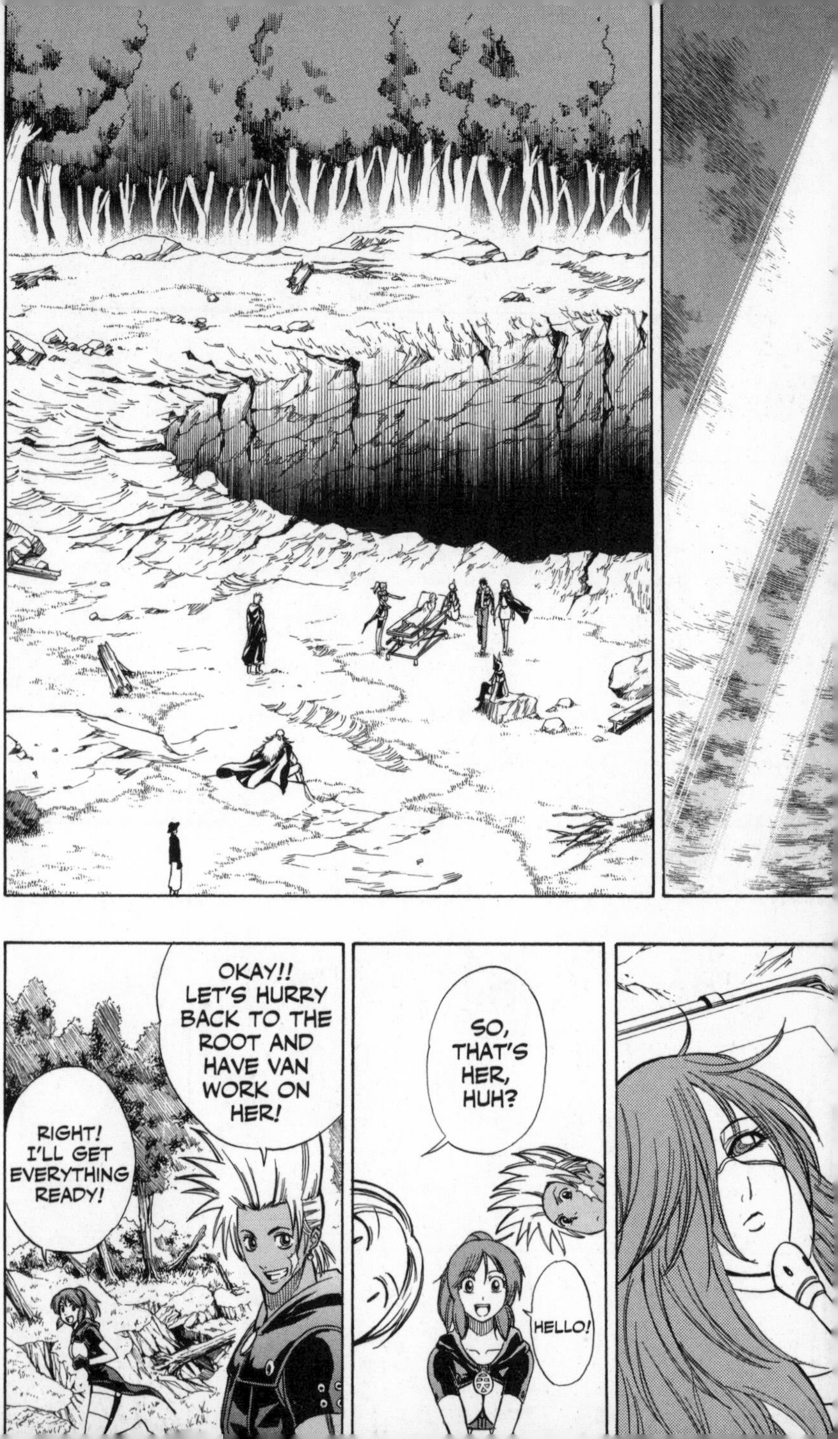
SO, THAT'S HER, HUH?
HELLO!
OKAY!! LET'S HURRY BACK TO THE ROOT AND HAVE VAN WORK ON HER!
RIGHT! I'LL GET EVERYTHING READY!

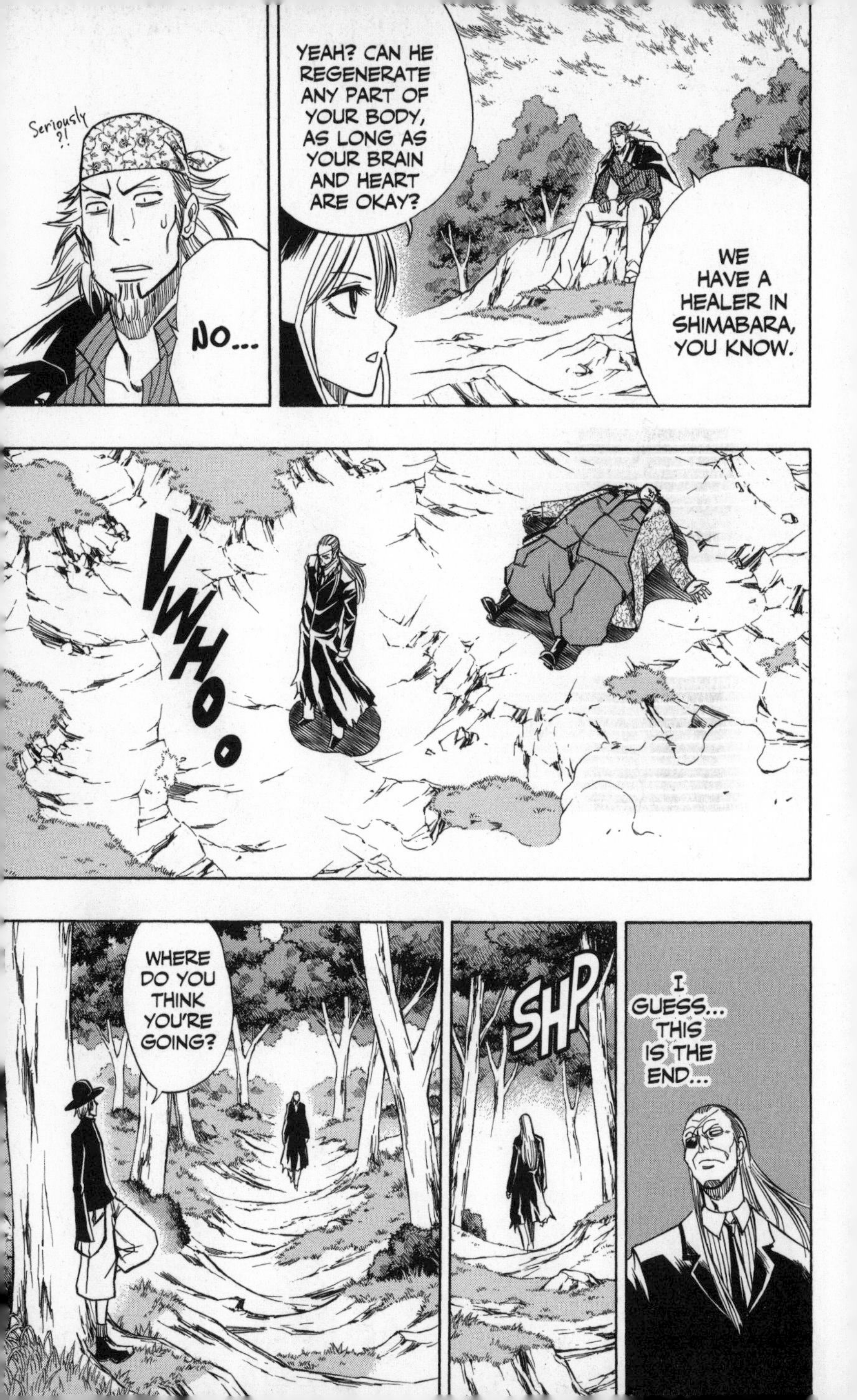
WE HAVE A HEALER IN SHIMABARA, YOU KNOW.
YEAH? CAN HE REGENERATE ANY PART OF YOUR BODY, AS LONG AS YOUR BRAIN AND HEART ARE OKAY?
Seriously?!
NO...
VWHOOO
I GUESS... THIS IS THE END...
SHP
WHERE DO YOU THINK YOU'RE GOING?

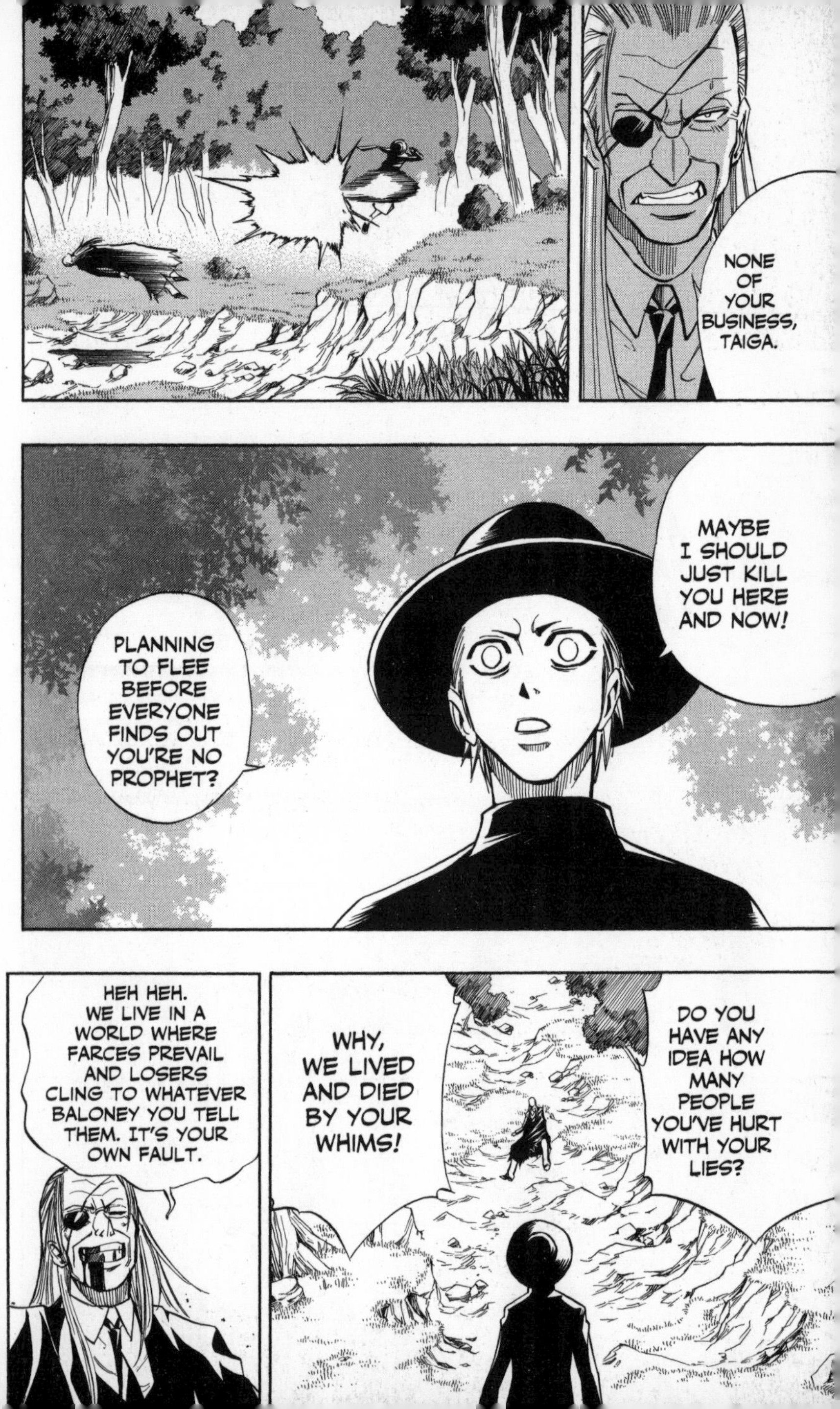
NONE OF YOUR BUSINESS, TAIGA.
MAYBE I SHOULD JUST KILL YOU HERE AND NOW!
PLANNING TO FLEE BEFORE EVERYONE FINDS OUT YOU'RE NO PROPHET?
DO YOU HAVE ANY IDEA HOW MANY PEOPLE YOU'VE HURT WITH YOUR LIES?
WHY, WE LIVED AND DIED BY YOUR WHIMS!
HEH HEH. WE LIVE IN A WORLD WHERE FARCES PREVAIL AND LOSERS CLING TO WHATEVER BALONEY YOU TELL THEM. IT'S YOUR OWN FAULT.

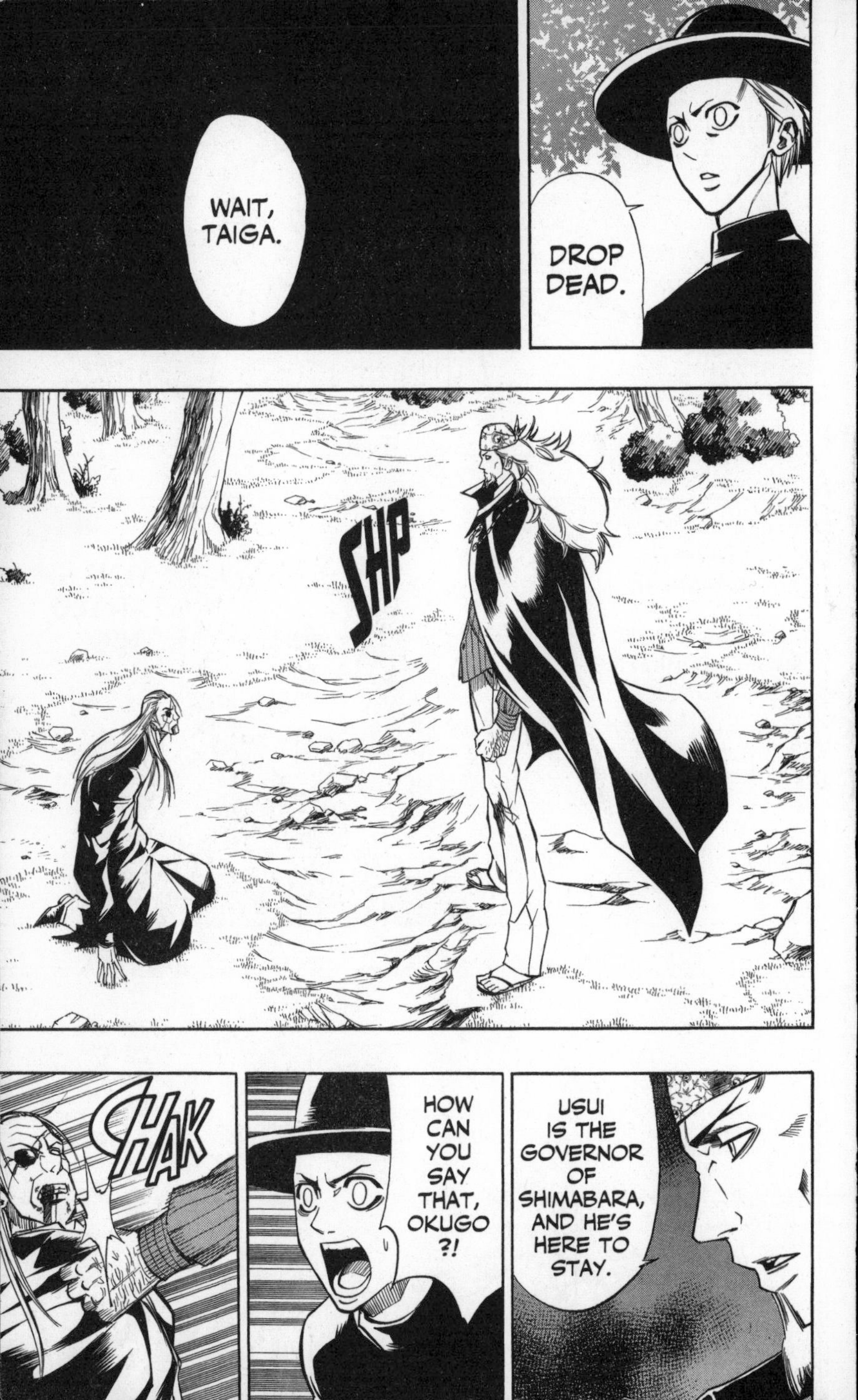
DROP DEAD.
WAIT, TAIGA.
SHP
USUI IS THE GOVERNOR OF SHIMABARA, AND HE'S HERE TO STAY.
HOW CAN YOU SAY THAT, OKUGO?!
CHAK

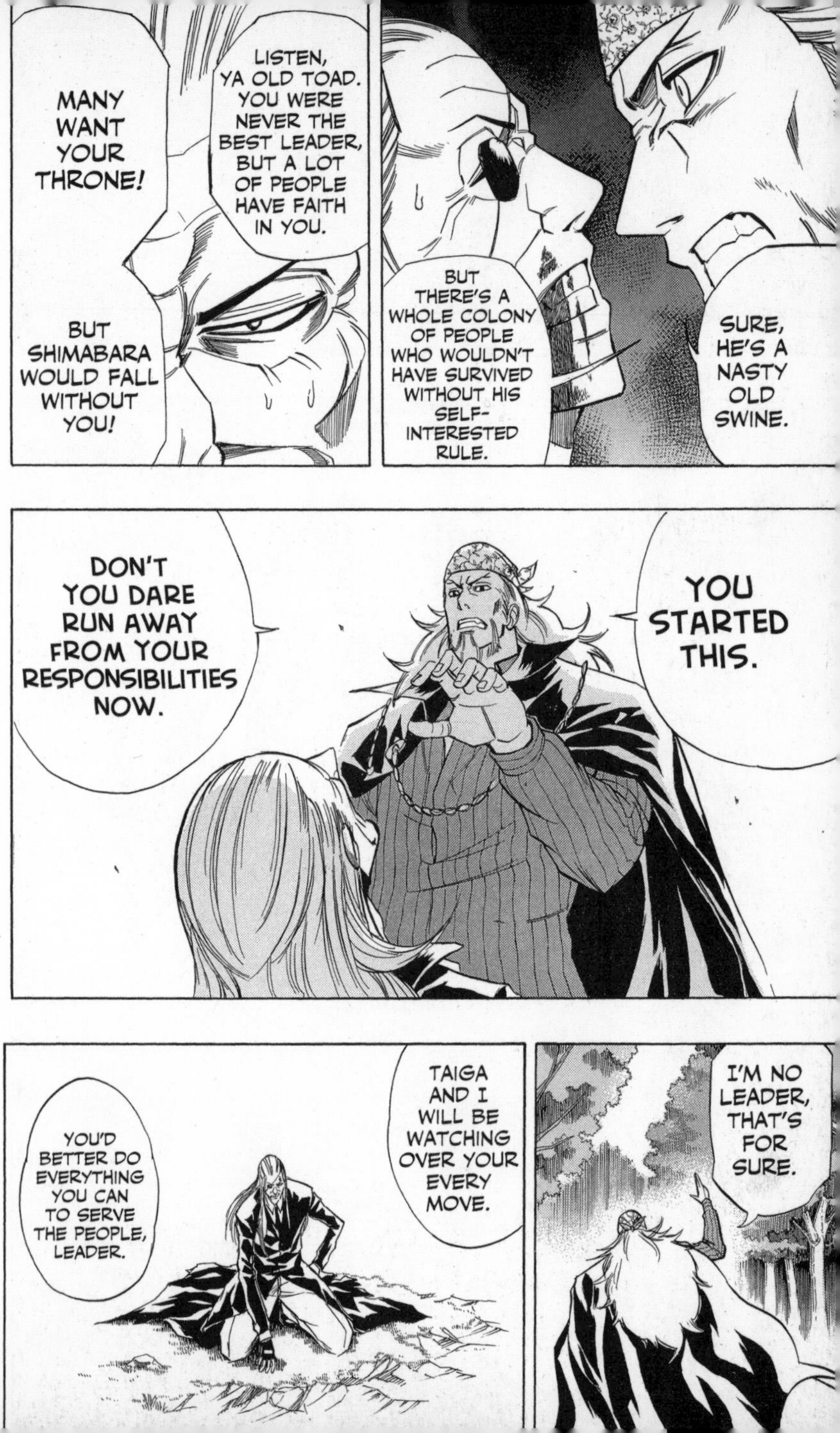
SURE, HE'S A NASTY OLD SWINE.
BUT THERE'S A WHOLE COLONY OF PEOPLE WHO WOULDN'T HAVE SURVIVED WITHOUT HIS SELF-INTERESTED RULE.
LISTEN, YA OLD TOAD. YOU WERE NEVER THE BEST LEADER, BUT A LOT OF PEOPLE HAVE FAITH IN YOU.
MANY WANT YOUR THRONE!
BUT SHIMABARA WOULD FALL WITHOUT YOU!
YOU STARTED THIS.
DON'T YOU DARE RUN AWAY FROM YOUR RESPONSIBILITIES NOW.
I'M NO LEADER, THAT'S FOR SURE.
TAIGA AND I WILL BE WATCHING OVER YOUR EVERY MOVE.
YOU'D BETTER DO EVERYTHING YOU CAN TO SERVE THE PEOPLE, LEADER.

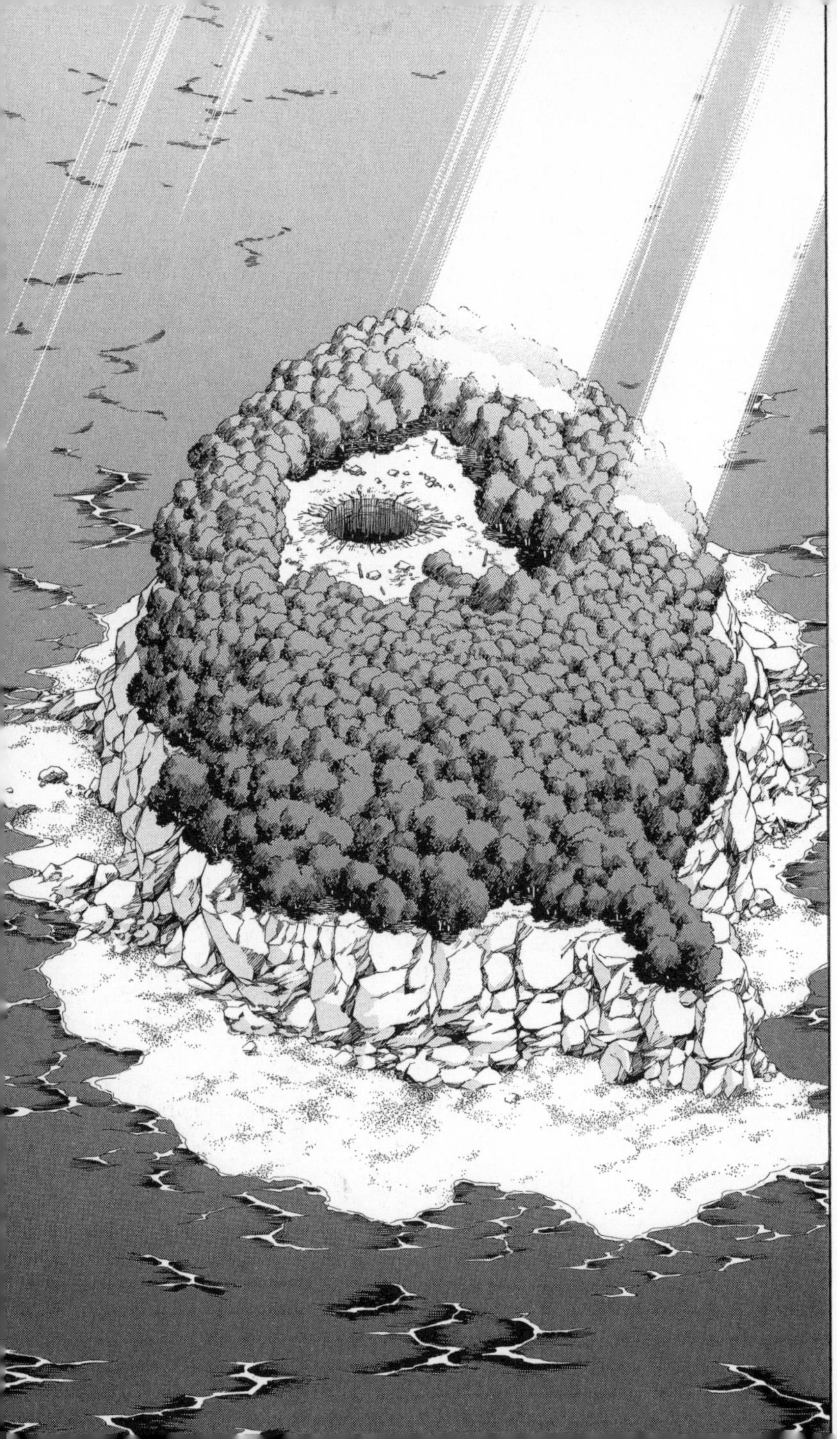

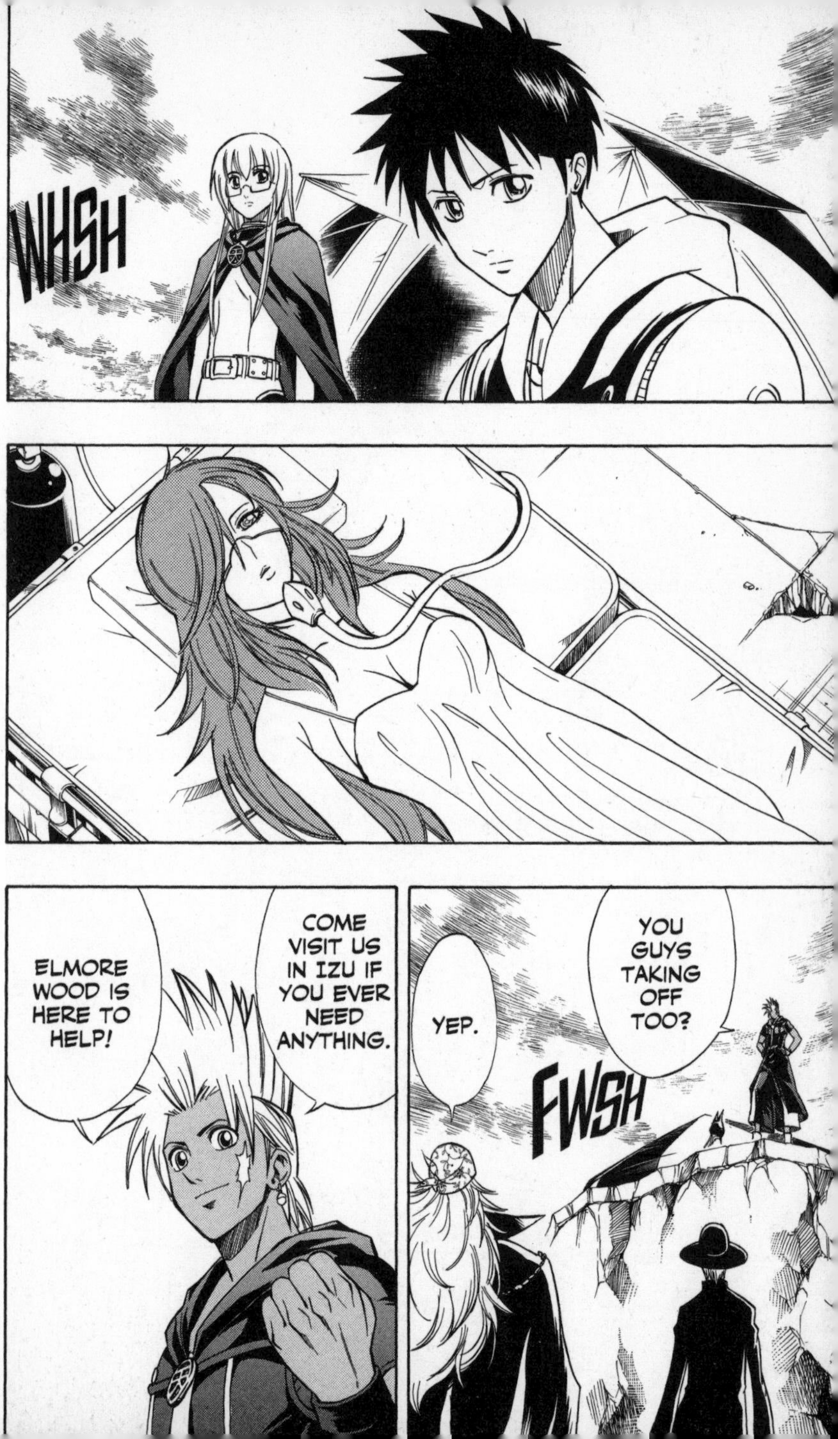
WHSH
YOU GUYS TAKING OFF TOO?
YEP.
FWSH
COME VISIT US IN IZU IF YOU EVER NEED ANYTHING.
ELMORE WOOD IS HERE TO HELP!

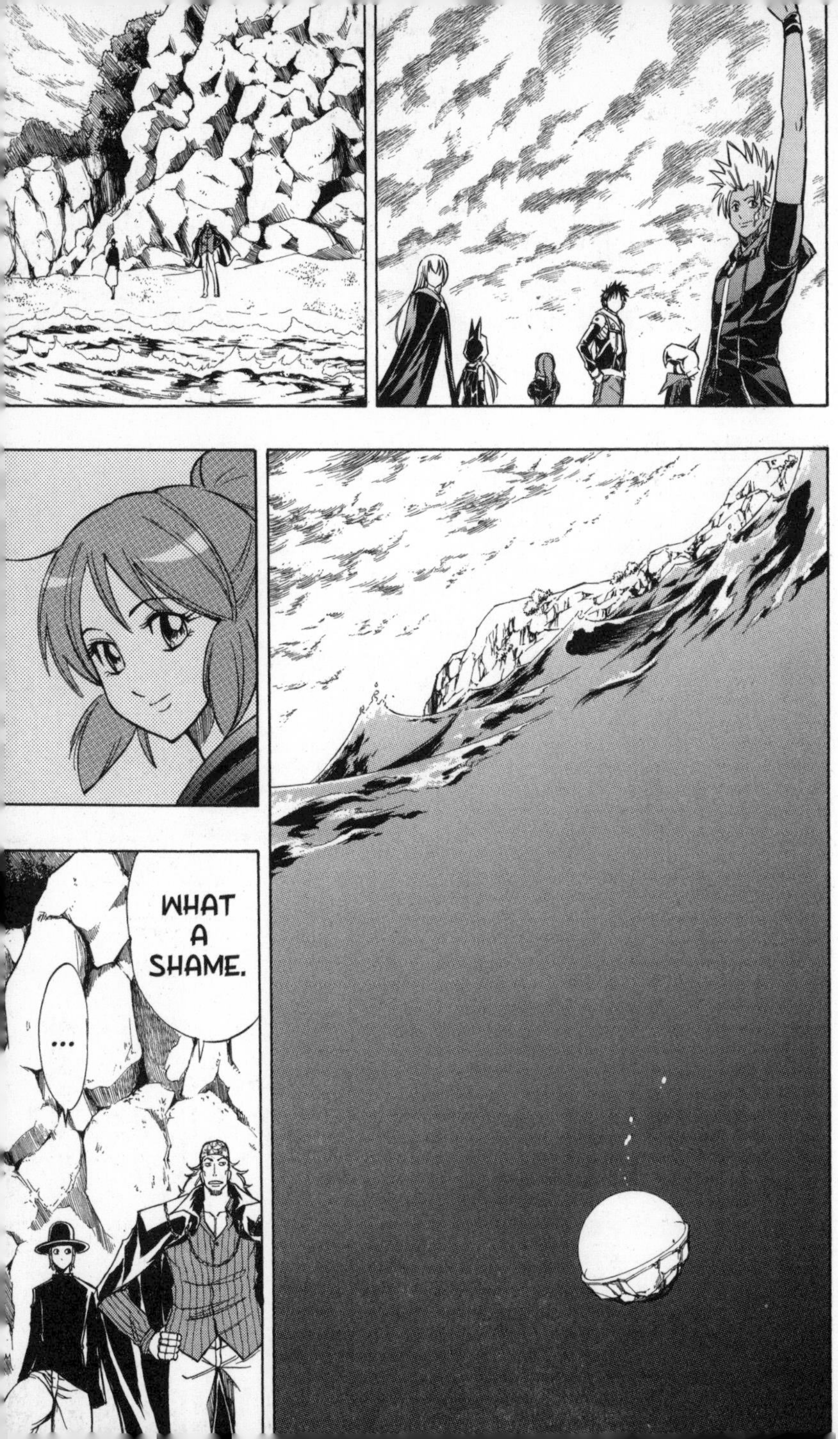
WHAT A SHAME.
...

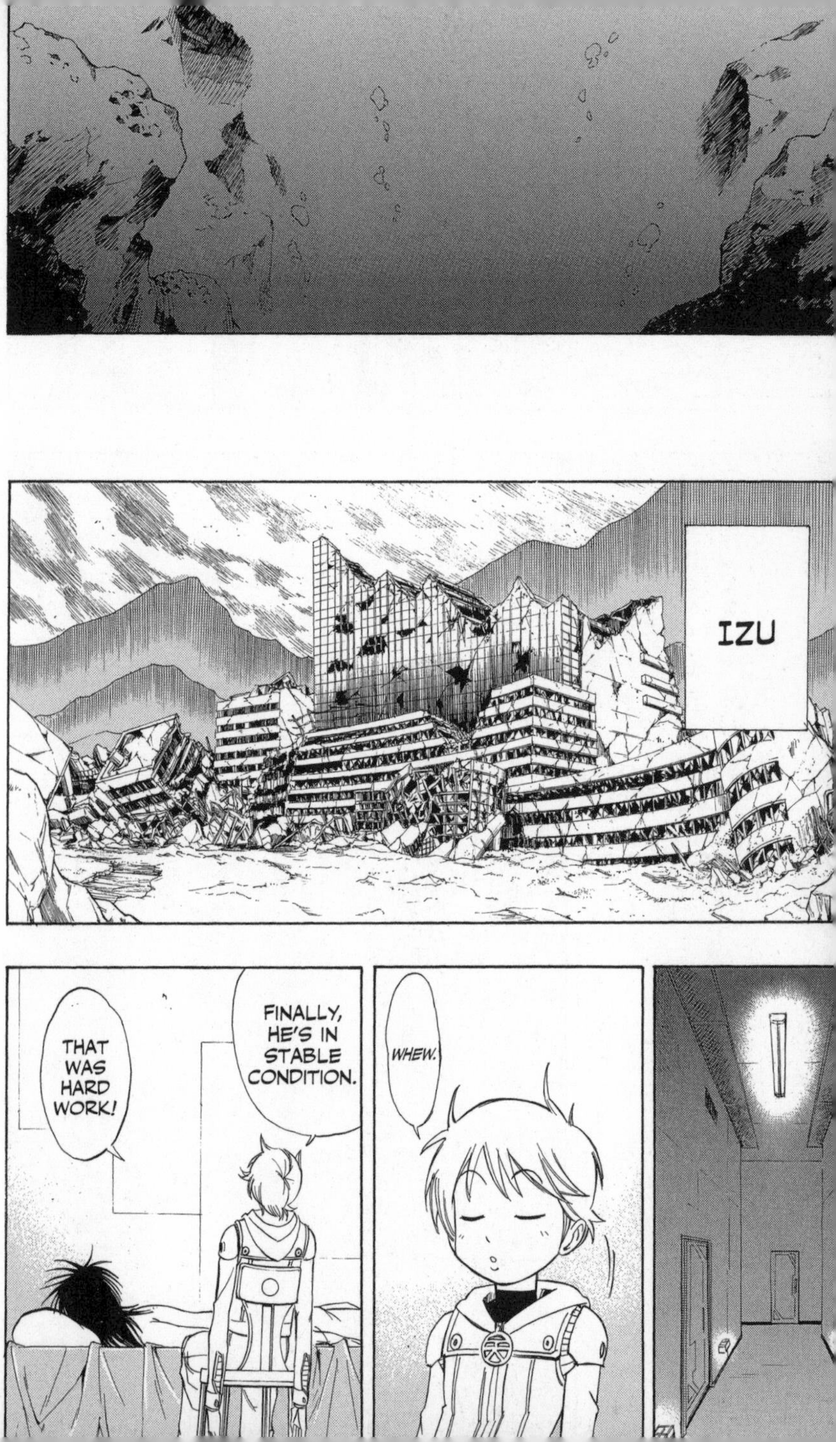
IZU
WHEW.
FINALLY, HE'S IN STABLE CONDITION.
THAT WAS HARD WORK!

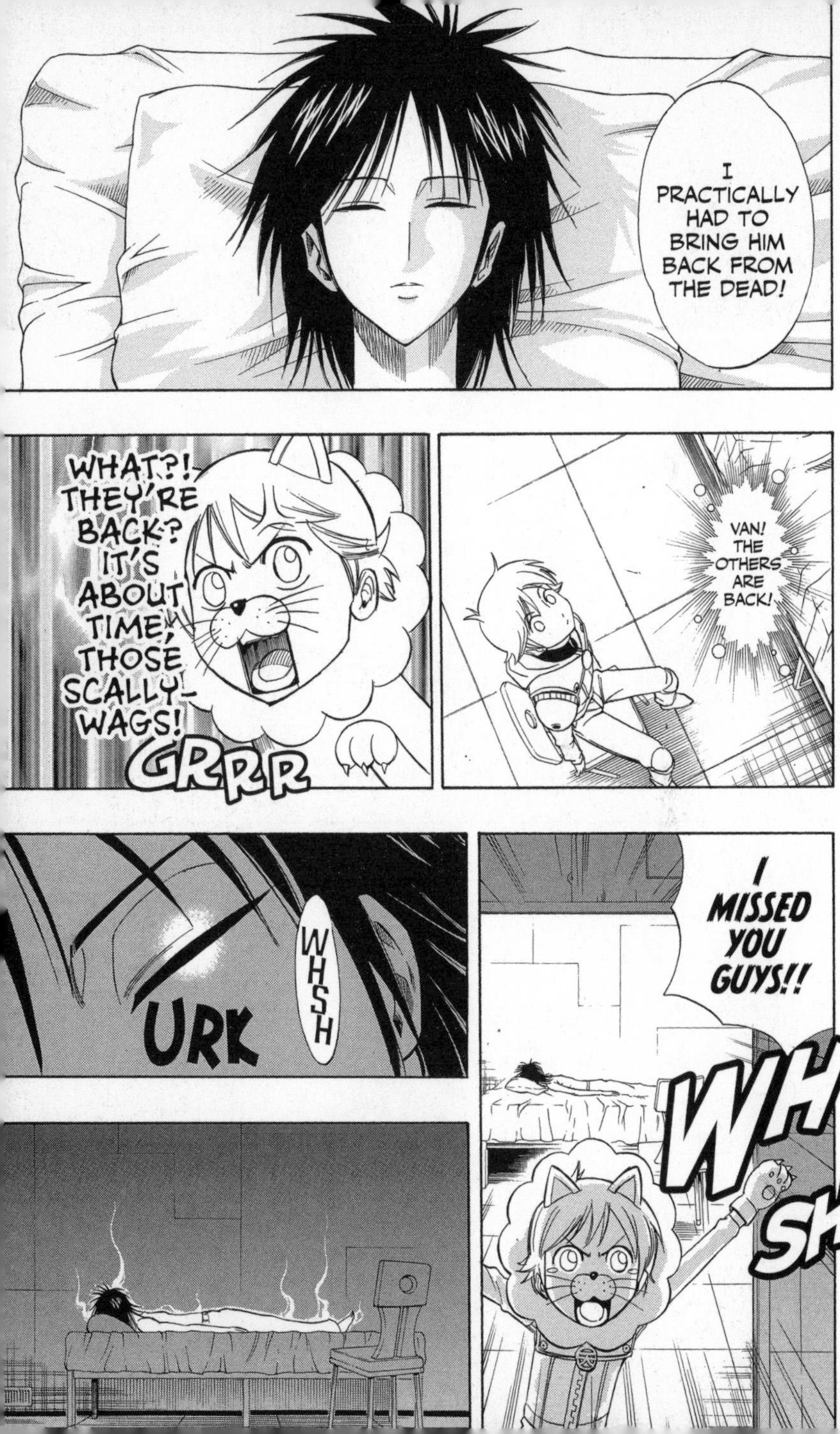
I PRACTICALLY HAD TO BRING HIM BACK FROM THE DEAD!
VAN! THE OTHERS ARE BACK!
WHAT?! THEY'RE BACK? IT'S ABOUT TIME, THOSE SCALLY-WAGS!
GRRR
I MISSED YOU GUYS!!
WHSH
WHSH
URK

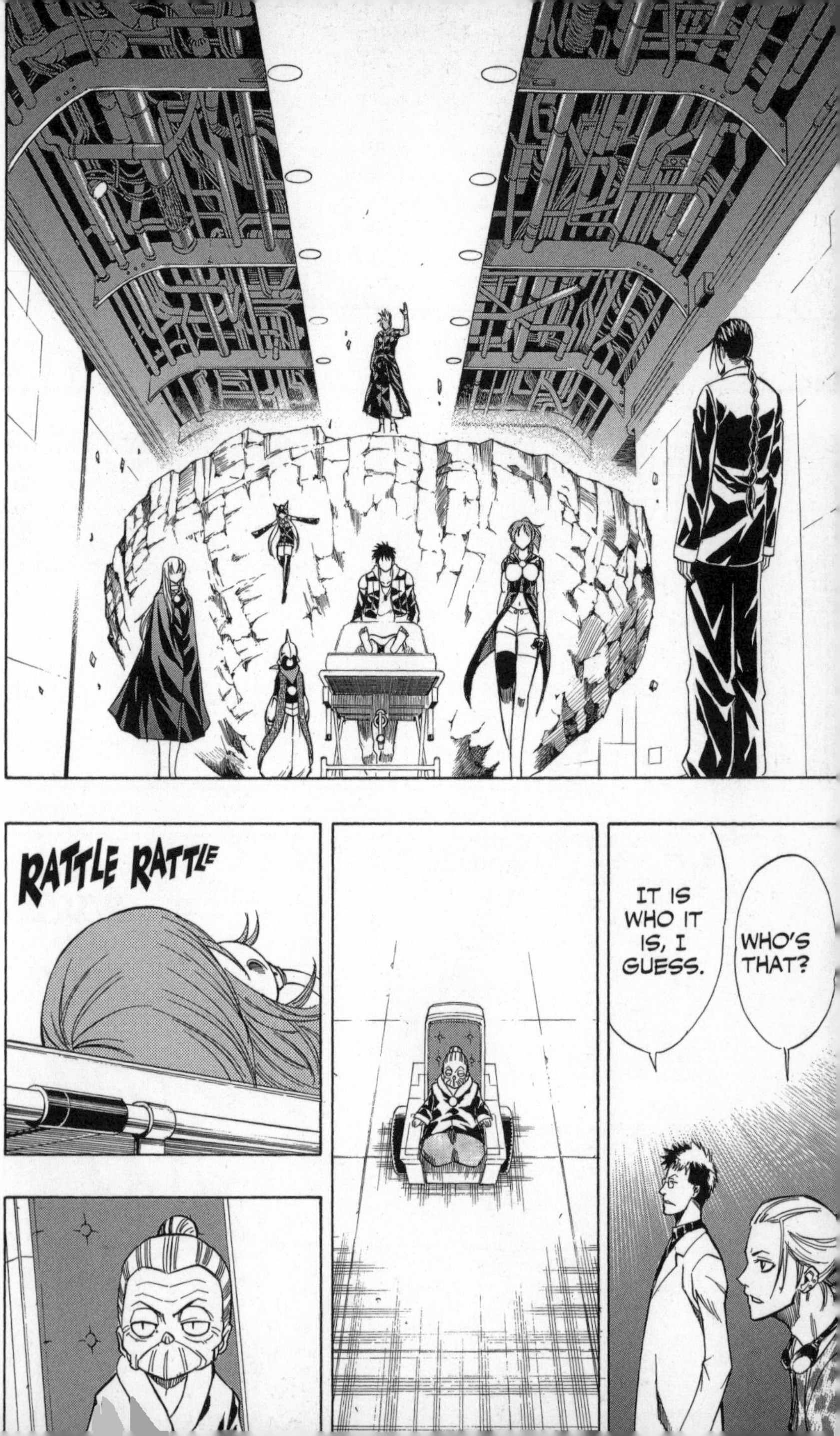
WHO'S THAT?
IT IS WHO IT IS, I GUESS.
RATTLE RATTLE

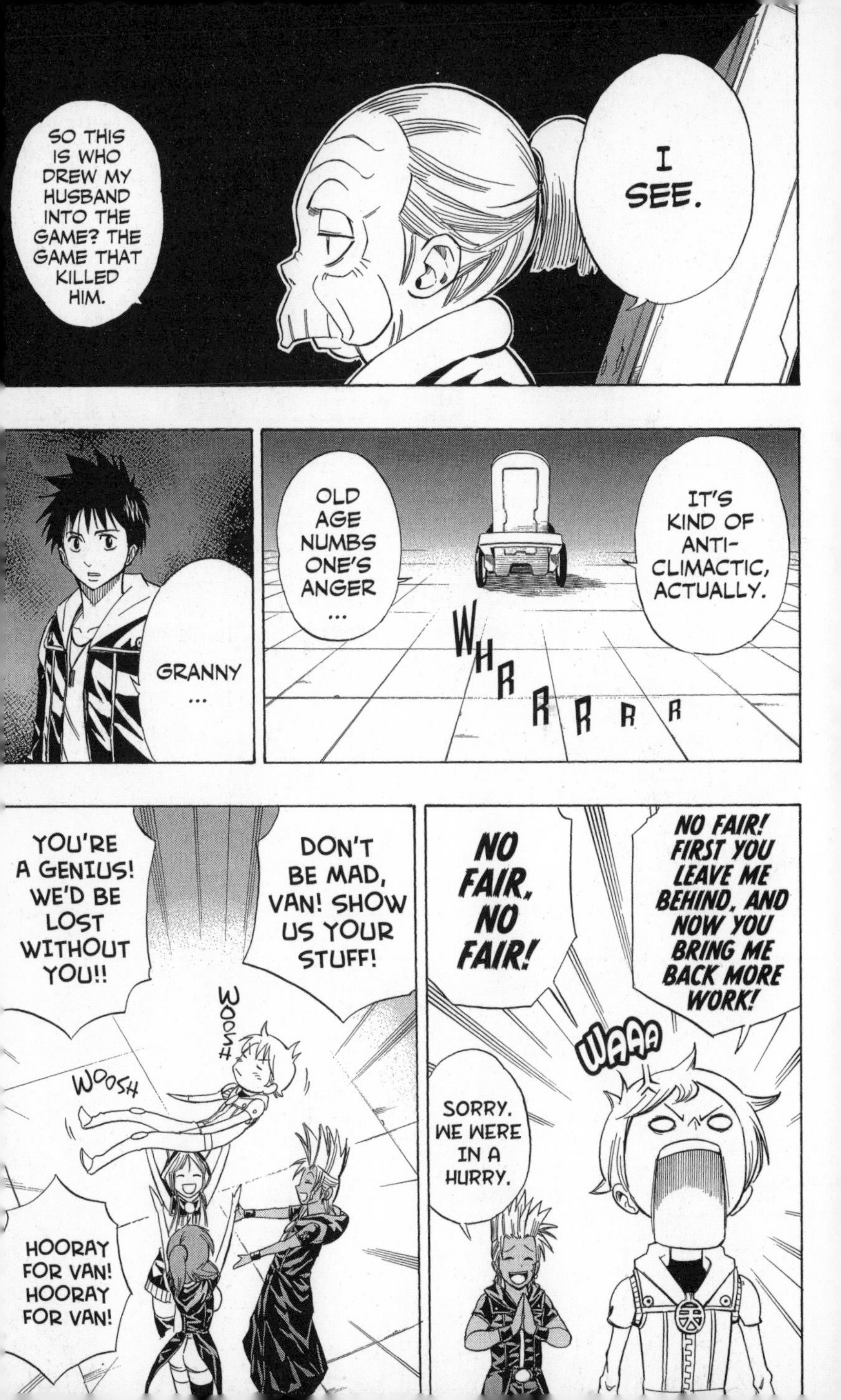
I SEE.
SO THIS IS WHO DREW MY HUSBAND INTO THE GAME? THE GAME THAT KILLED HIM.
IT'S KIND OF ANTI-CLIMACTIC, ACTUALLY.
OLD AGE NUMBS ONE'S ANGER ...
WHRRRRRR
GRANNY ...
NO FAIR! FIRST YOU LEAVE ME BEHIND, AND NOW YOU BRING ME BACK MORE WORK!
NO FAIR, NO FAIR!
WAAA
SORRY. WE WERE IN A HURRY.
DON'T BE MAD, VAN! SHOW US YOUR STUFF!
YOU'RE A GENIUS! WE'D BE LOST WITHOUT YOU!!
WOOSH
WOOSH
HOORAY FOR VAN! HOORAY FOR VAN!

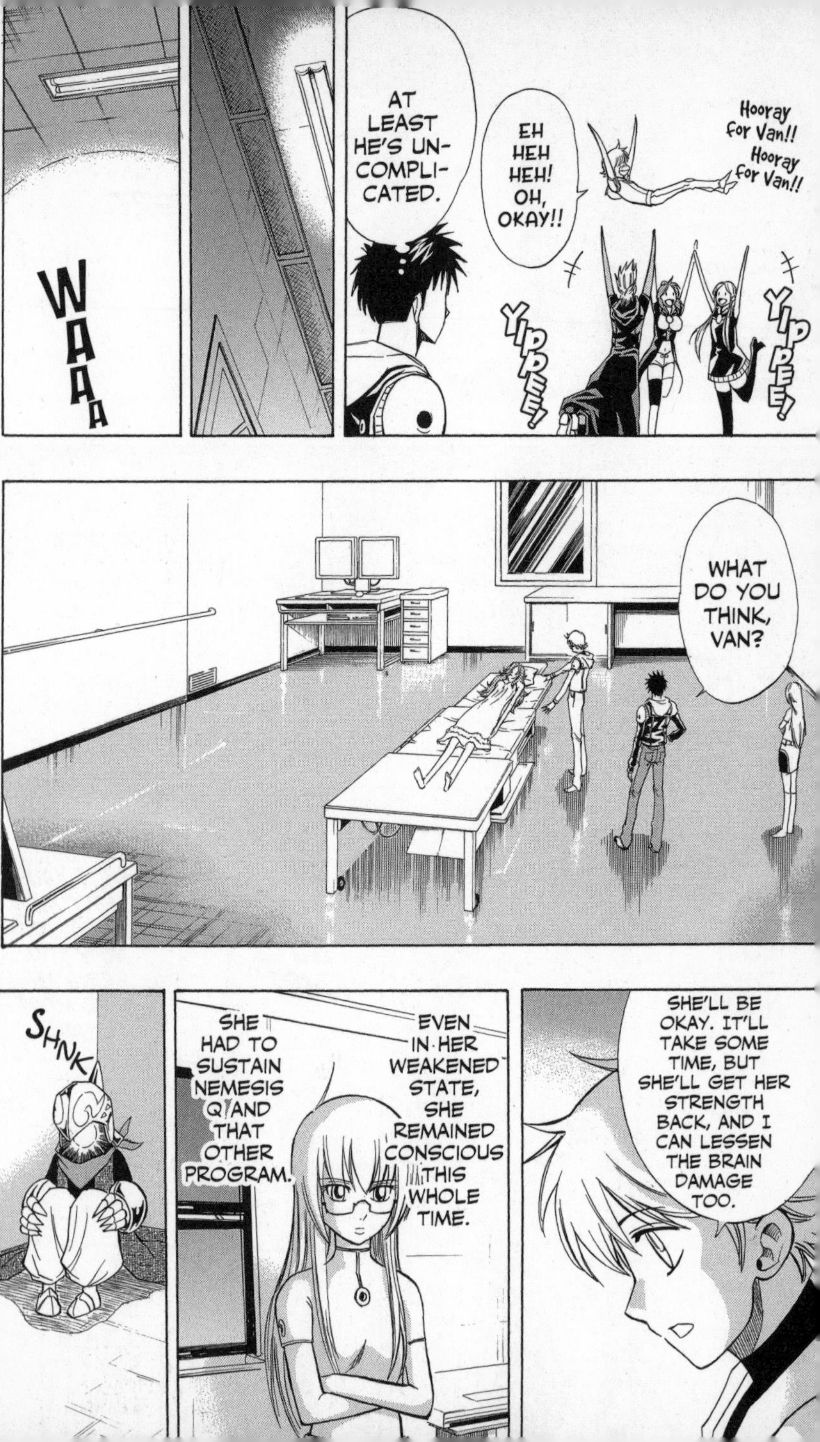
Hooray for Van!!
Hooray for Van!!
YIPPEE!
EH HEH HEH! OH, OKAY!!
YIPPEE!
AT LEAST HE'S UN-COMPLICATED.
WAAAA
WHAT DO YOU THINK, VAN?
SHE'LL BE OKAY. IT'LL TAKE SOME TIME, BUT SHE'LL GET HER STRENGTH BACK, AND I CAN LESSEN THE BRAIN DAMAGE TOO.
EVEN IN HER WEAKENED STATE, SHE REMAINED CONSCIOUS THIS WHOLE TIME.
SHE HAD TO SUSTAIN NEMESIS Q AND THAT OTHER PROGRAM.
SHNK

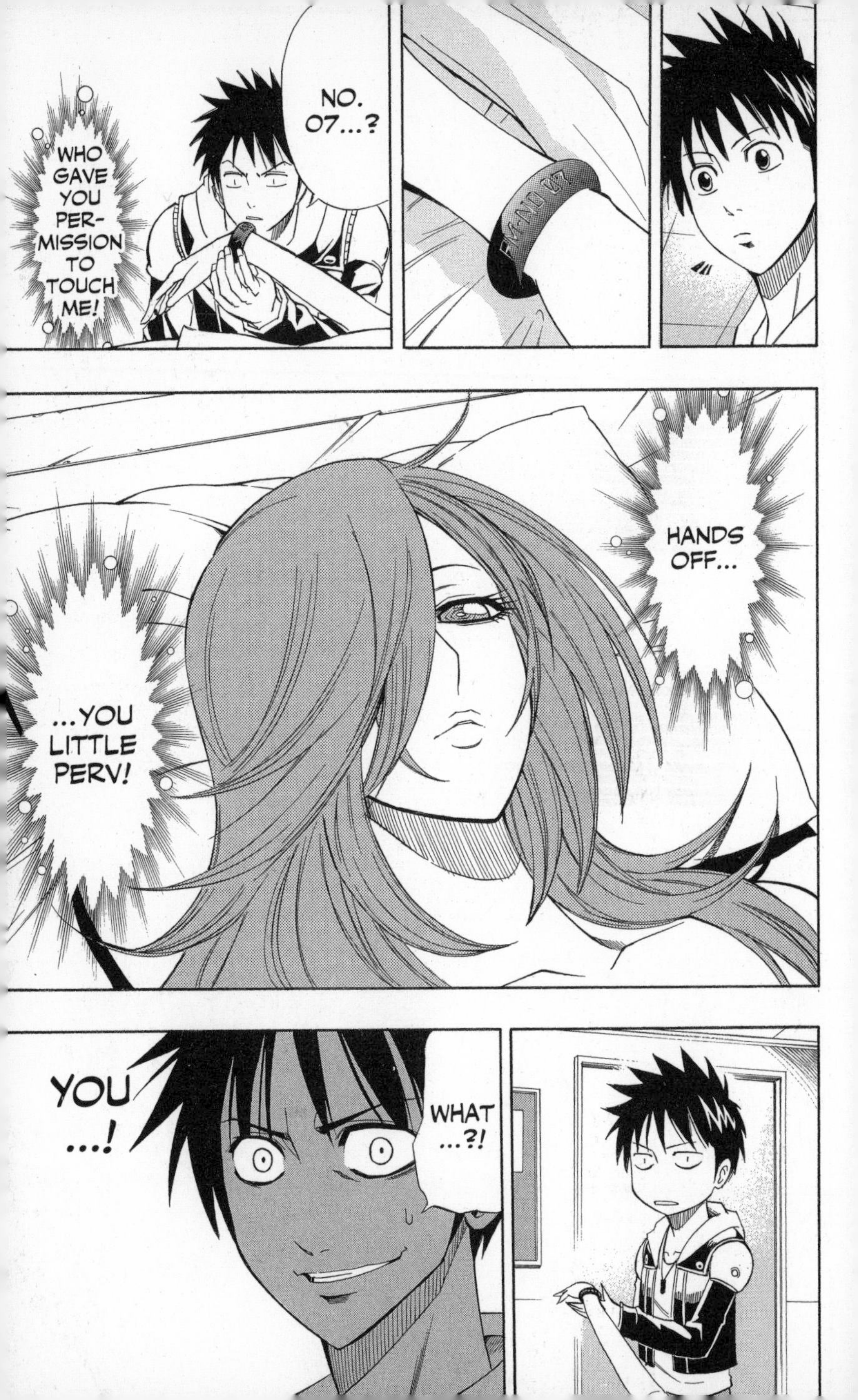
NO. 07...?
WHO GAVE YOU PER-MISSION TO TOUCH ME!
HANDS OFF...
...YOU LITTLE PERV!
WHAT ...?!
YOU ...!

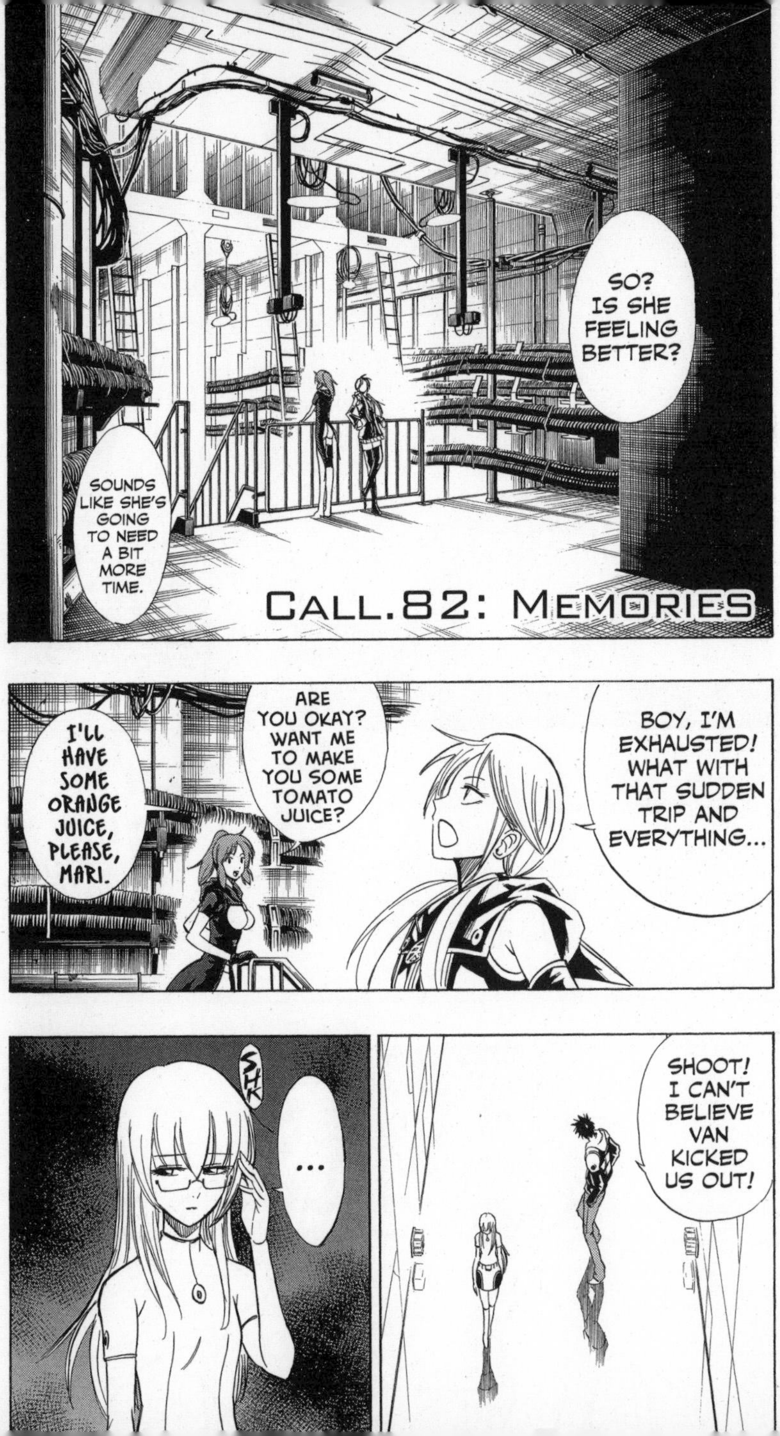
SO? IS SHE FEELING BETTER?
SOUNDS LIKE SHE'S GOING TO NEED A BIT MORE TIME.
CALL.82: MEMORIES
BOY, I'M EXHAUSTED! WHAT WITH THAT SUDDEN TRIP AND EVERYTHING...
ARE YOU OKAY? WANT ME TO MAKE YOU SOME TOMATO JUICE?
I'LL HAVE SOME ORANGE JUICE, PLEASE, MARI.
SHOOT! I CAN'T BELIEVE VAN KICKED US OUT!
SHK
...

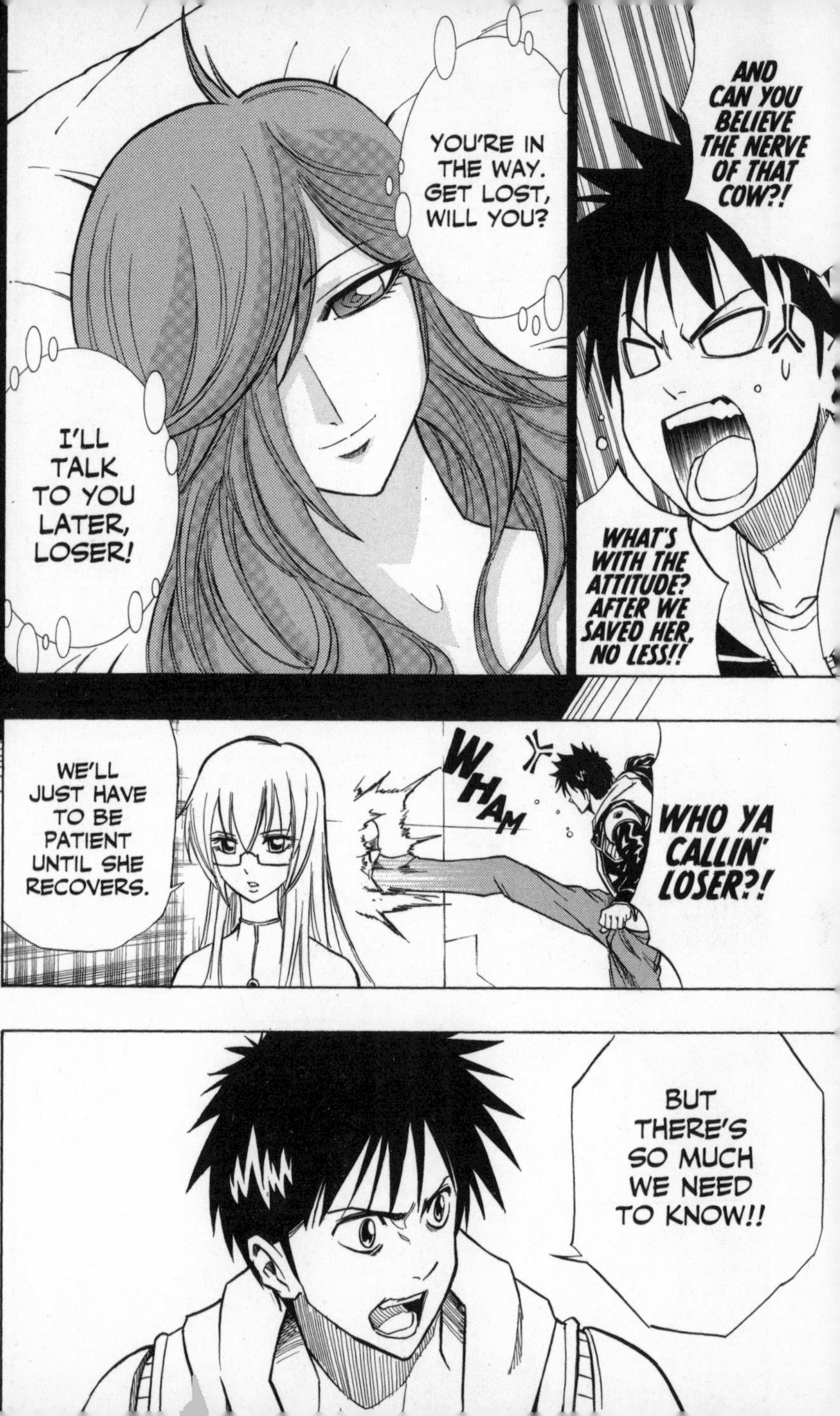
AND CAN YOU BELIEVE THE NERVE OF THAT COW?!
WHAT'S WITH THE ATTITUDE? AFTER WE SAVED HER, NO LESS!!
YOU'RE IN THE WAY. GET LOST, WILL YOU?
I'LL TALK TO YOU LATER, LOSER!
WHO YA CALLIN' LOSER?!
WHAM
WE'LL JUST HAVE TO BE PATIENT UNTIL SHE RECOVERS.
BUT THERE'S SO MUCH WE NEED TO KNOW!!

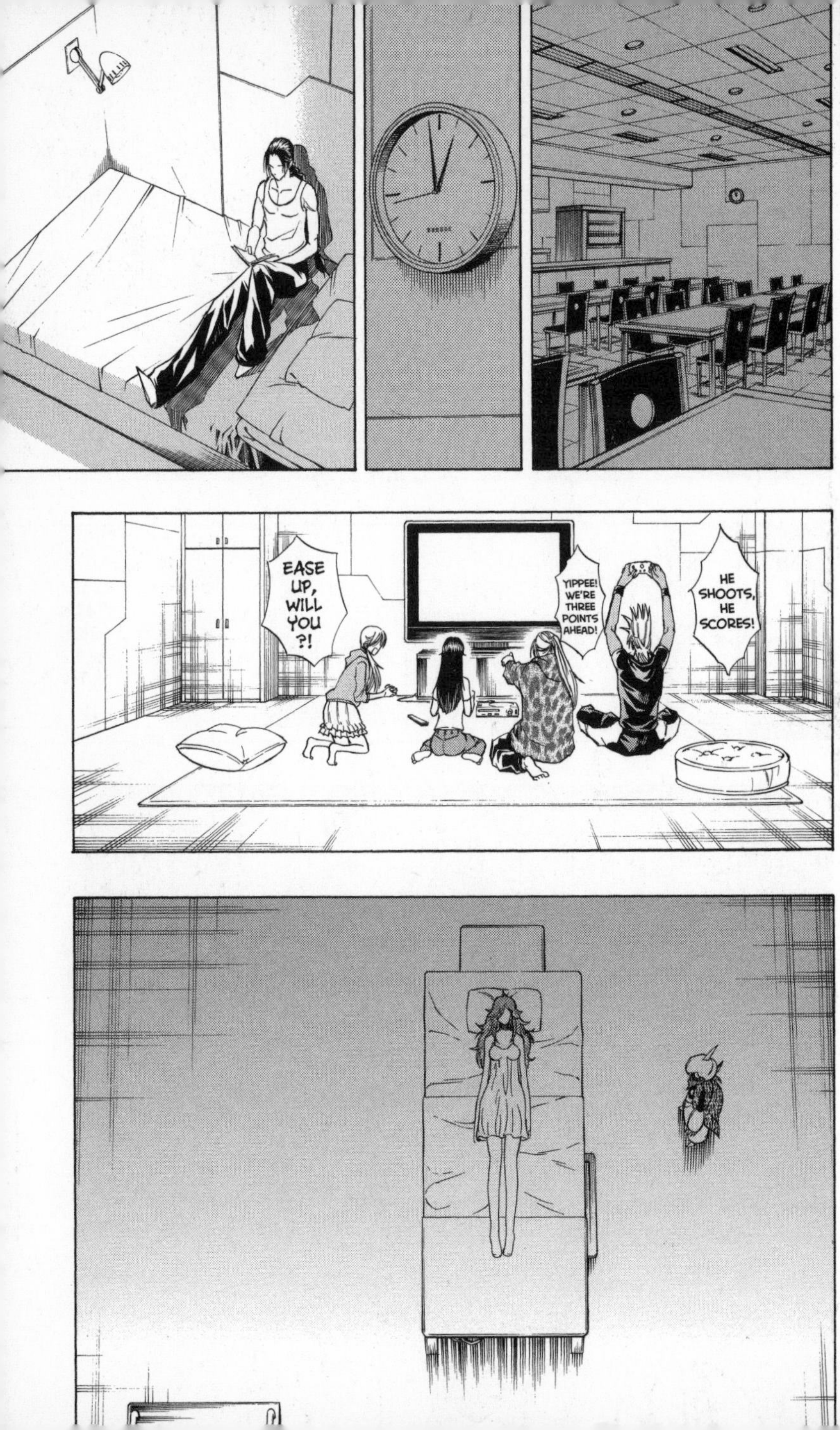
HE SHOOTS, HE SCORES!
YIPPEE! WE'RE THREE POINTS AHEAD!
EASE UP, WILL YOU?!

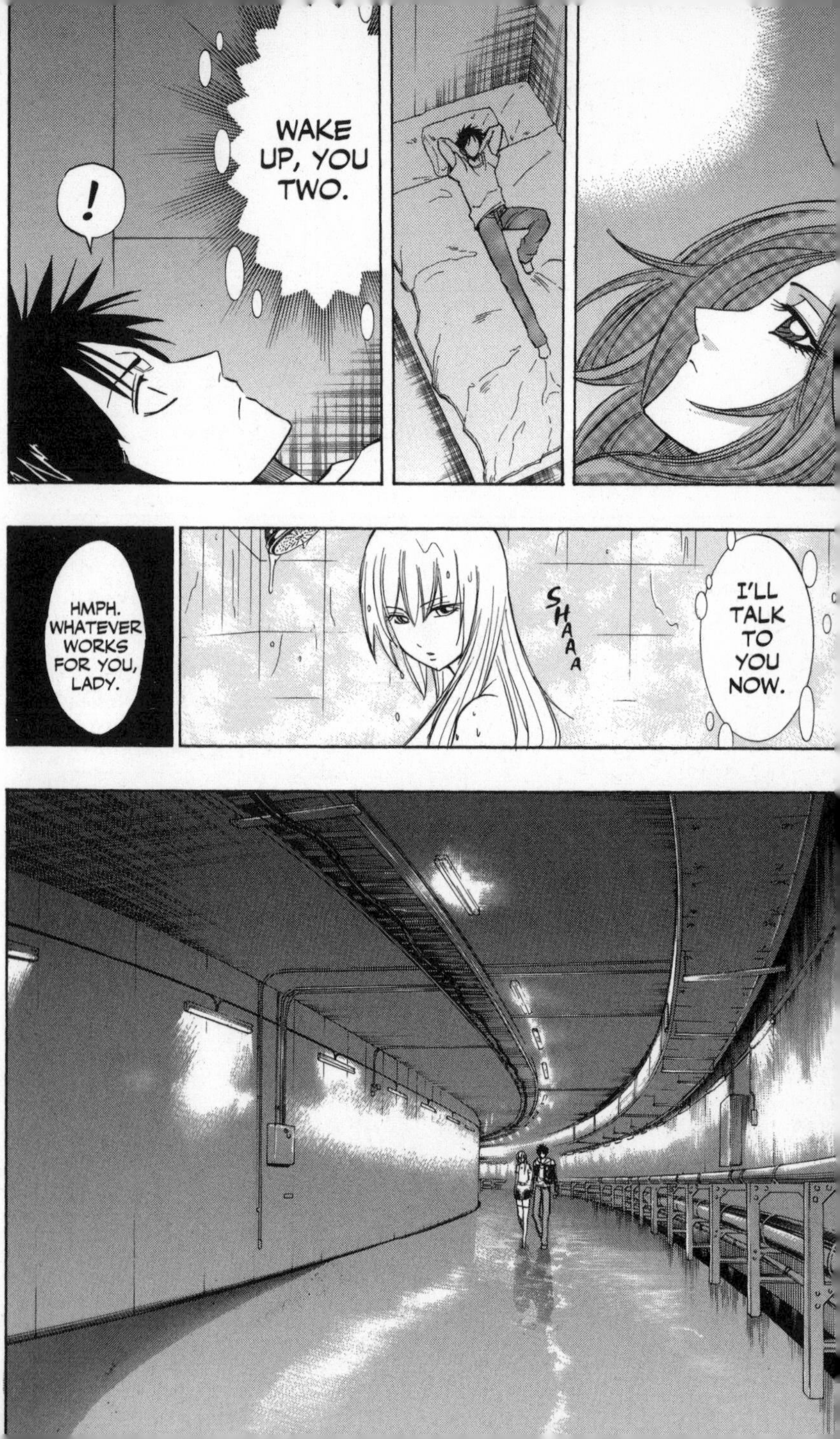
WAKE UP, YOU TWO.
!
I'LL TALK TO YOU NOW.
SHAAA
HMPH. WHATEVER WORKS FOR YOU, LADY.

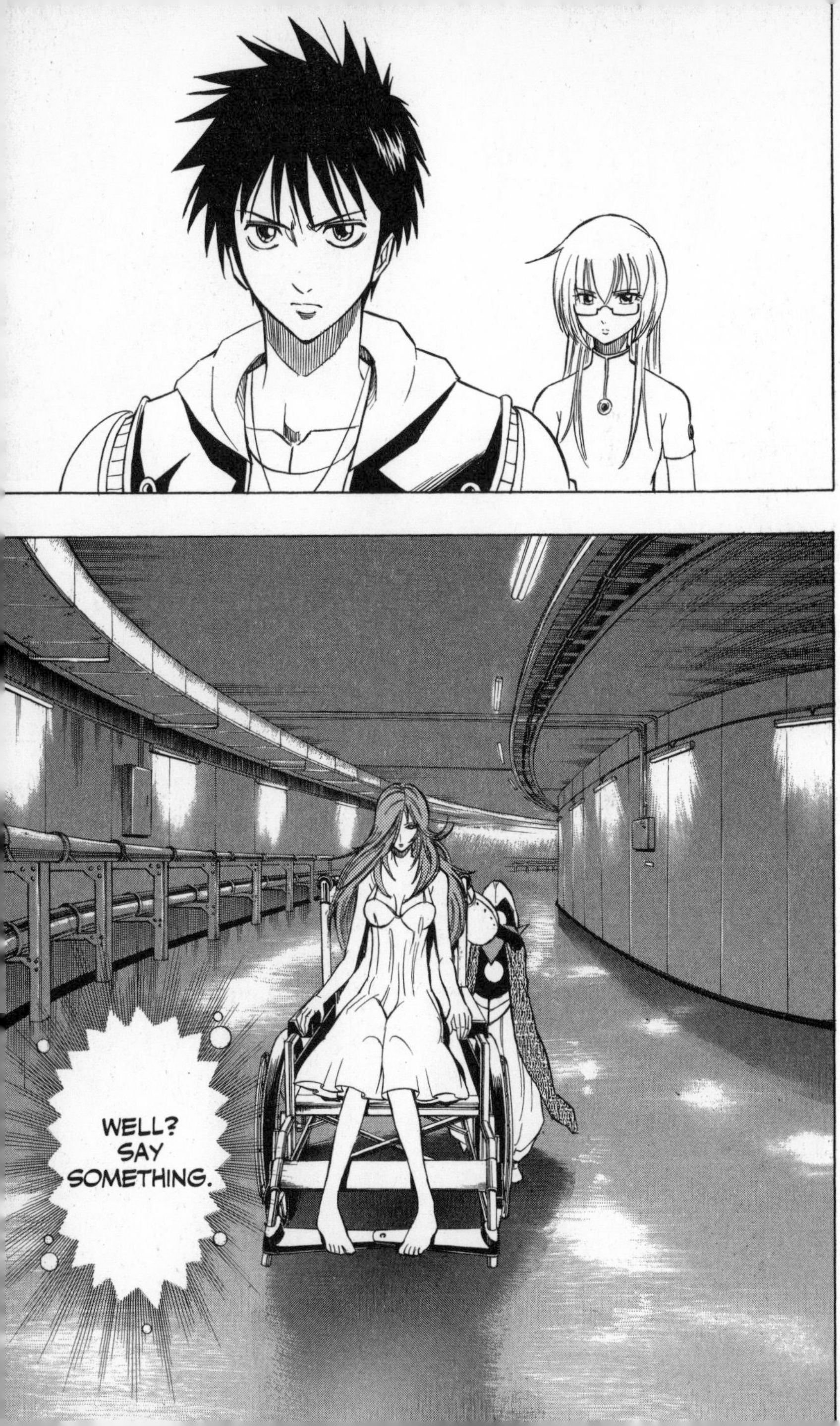
WELL? SAY SOMETHING.

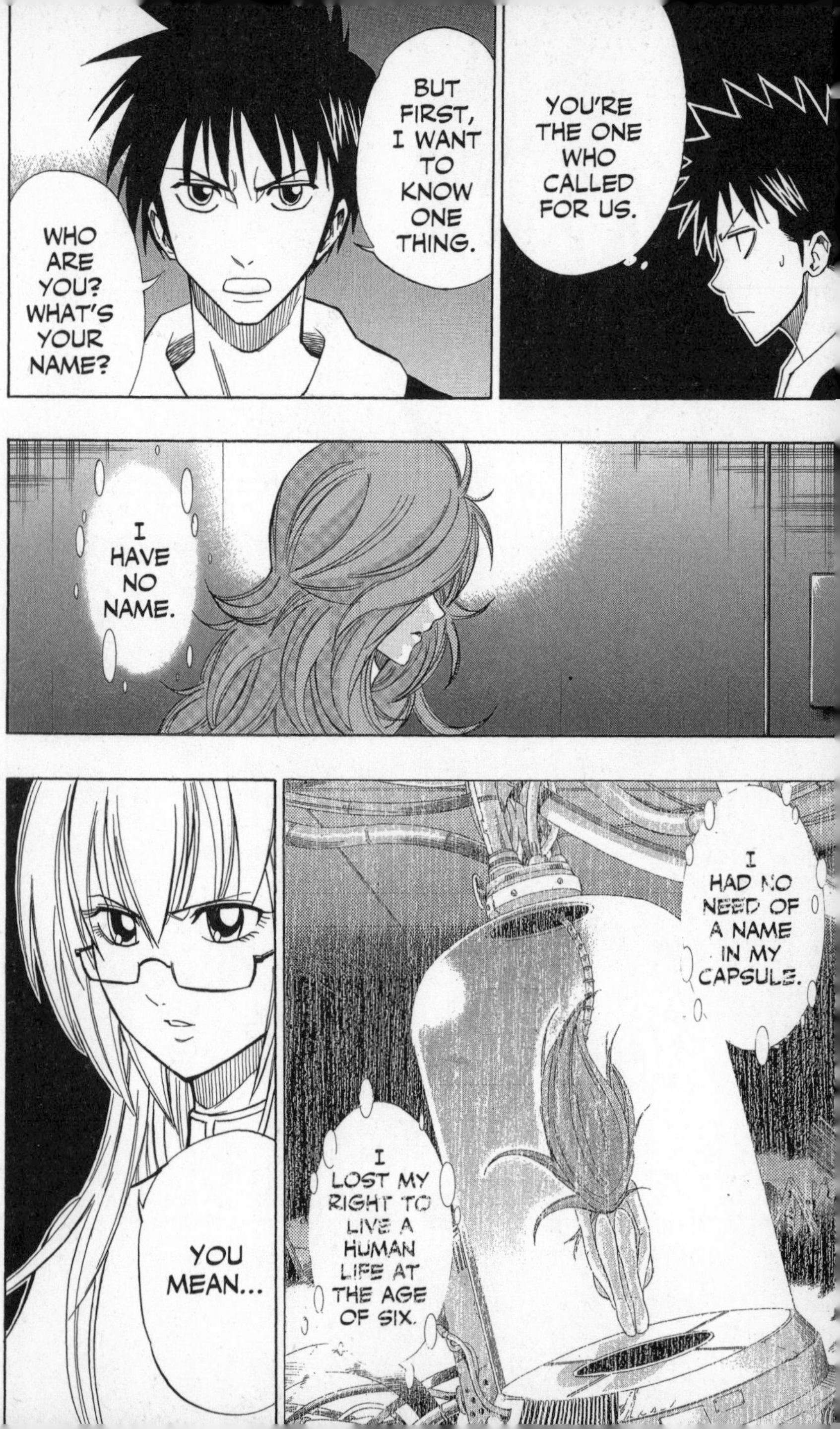
YOU'RE THE ONE WHO CALLED FOR US.
BUT FIRST, I WANT TO KNOW ONE THING.
WHO ARE YOU? WHAT'S YOUR NAME?
I HAVE NO NAME.
I HAD NO NEED OF A NAME IN MY CAPSULE.
I LOST MY RIGHT TO LIVE A HUMAN LIFE AT THE AGE OF SIX.
YOU MEAN...

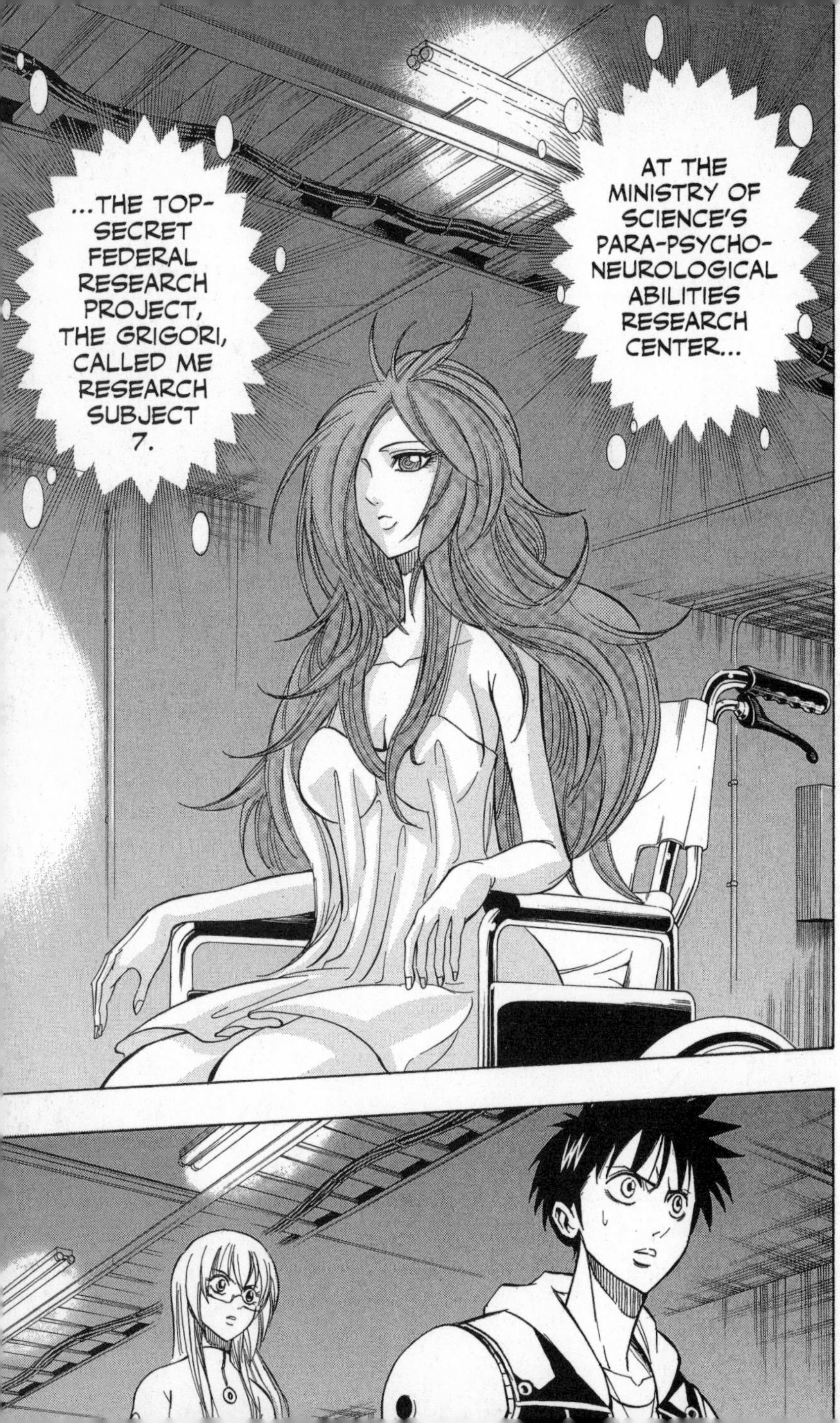
AT THE MINISTRY OF SCIENCE'S PARA-PSYCHO-NEUROLOGICAL ABILITIES RESEARCH CENTER...
...THE TOP-SECRET FEDERAL RESEARCH PROJECT, THE GRIGORI, CALLED ME RESEARCH SUBJECT 7.

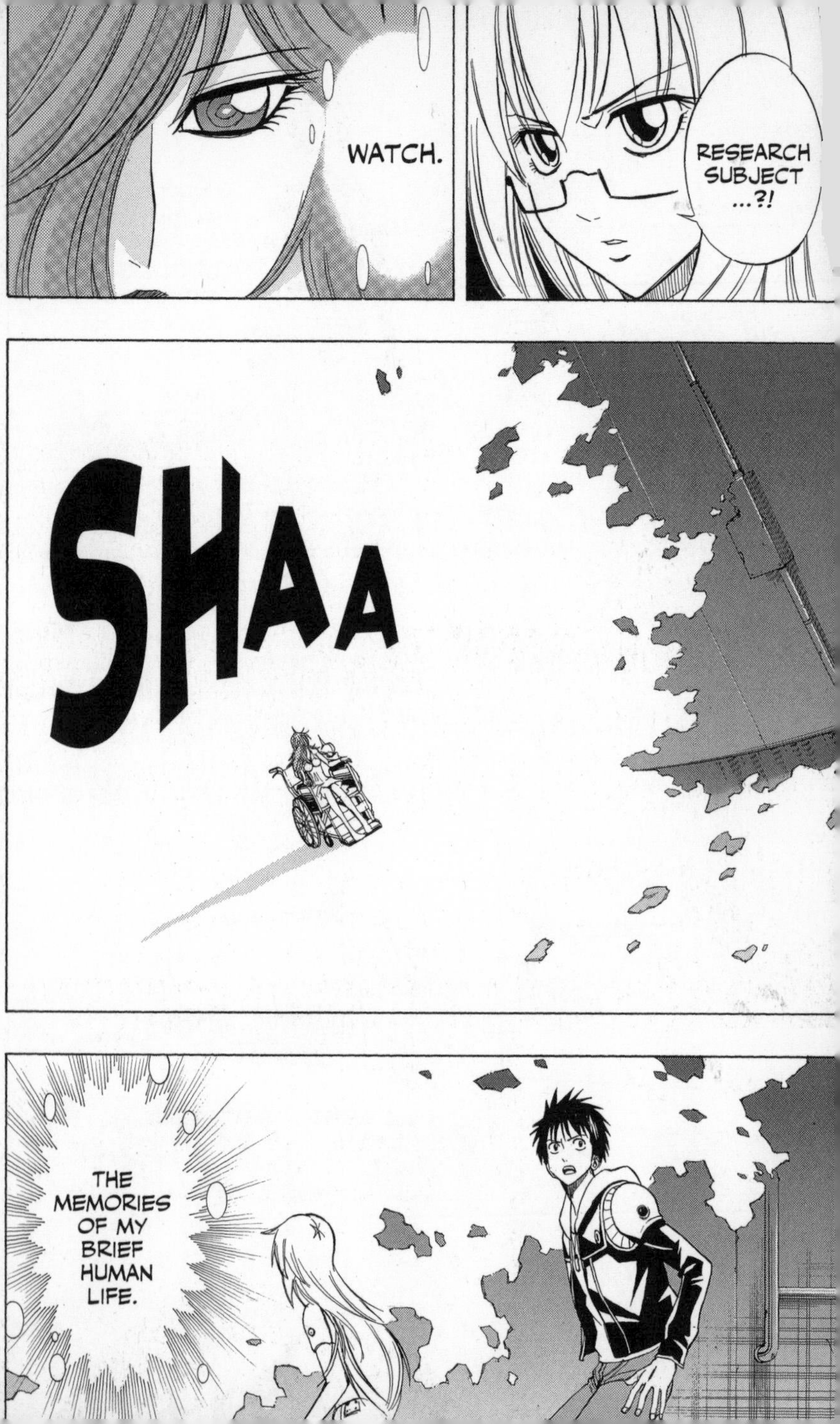
RESEARCH SUBJECT ...?!
WATCH.
SHAA
THE MEMORIES OF MY BRIEF HUMAN LIFE.

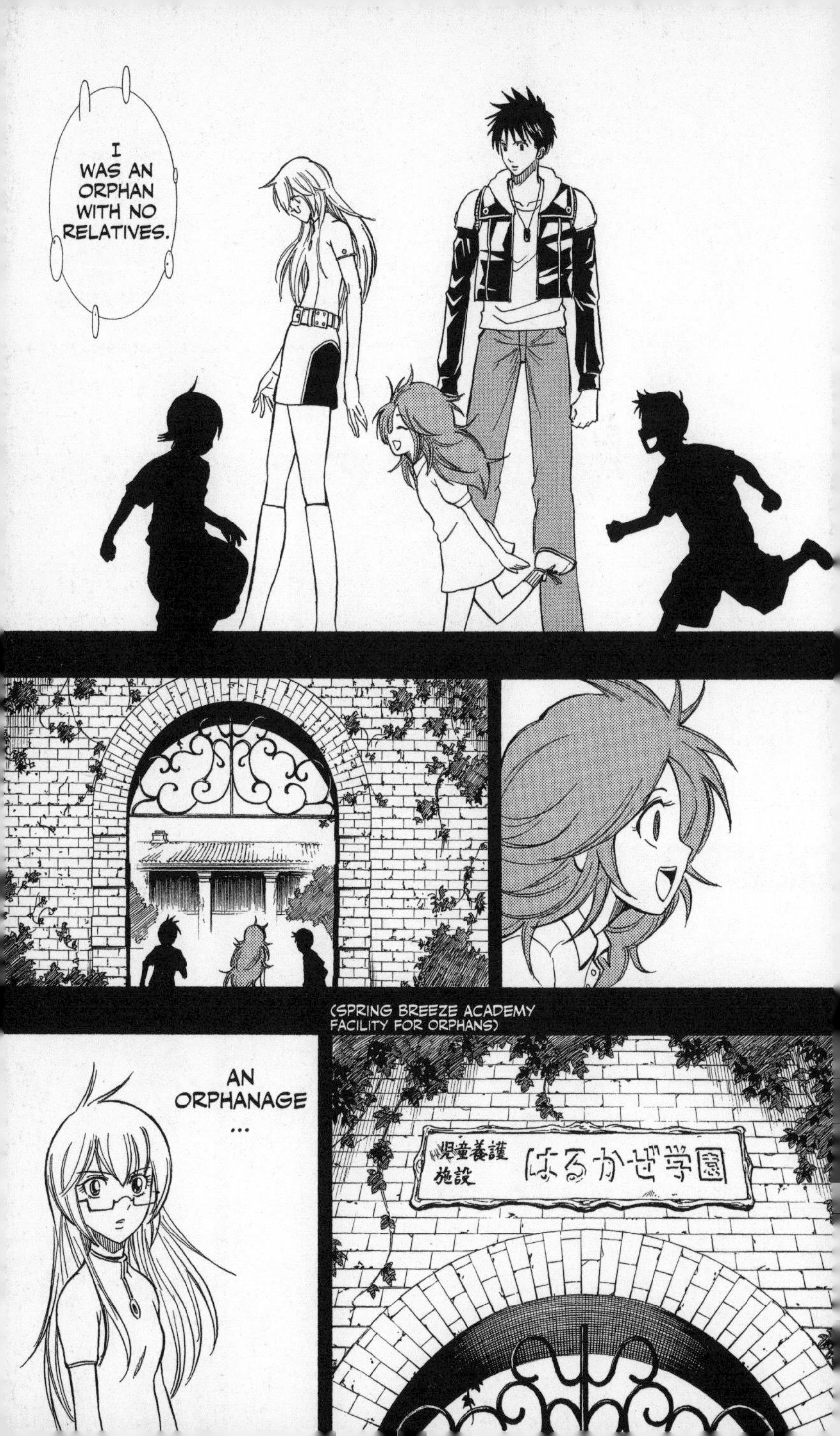
I WAS AN ORPHAN WITH NO RELATIVES.
(SPRING BREEZE ACADEMY FACILITY FOR ORPHANS)
児童養護施設 はるかぜ学園
AN ORPHANAGE ...

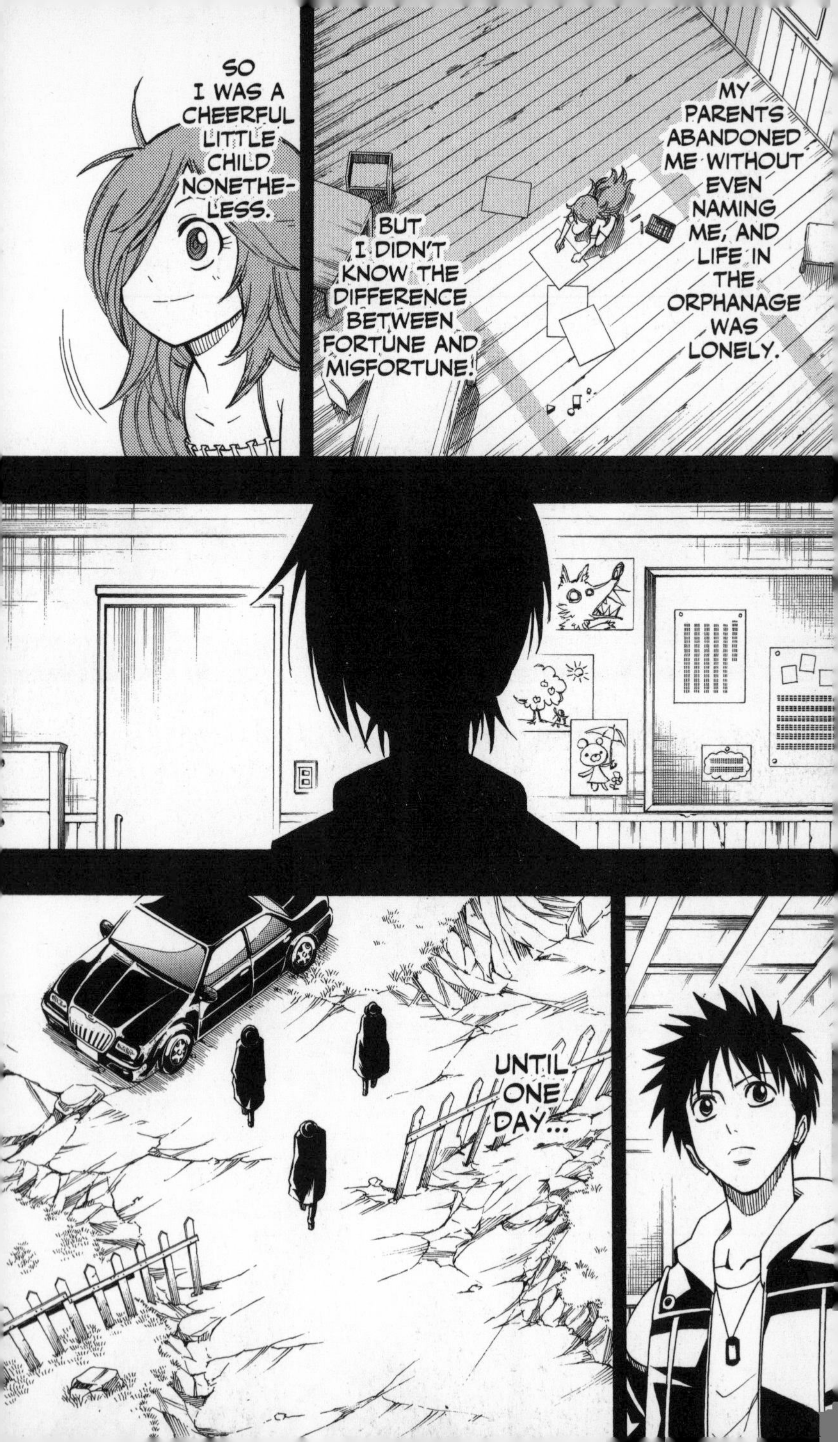
MY PARENTS ABANDONED ME WITHOUT EVEN NAMING ME, AND LIFE IN THE ORPHANAGE WAS LONELY.
BUT I DIDN'T KNOW THE DIFFERENCE BETWEEN FORTUNE AND MISFORTUNE!
SO I WAS A CHEERFUL LITTLE CHILD NONETHE-LESS.
UNTIL ONE DAY...

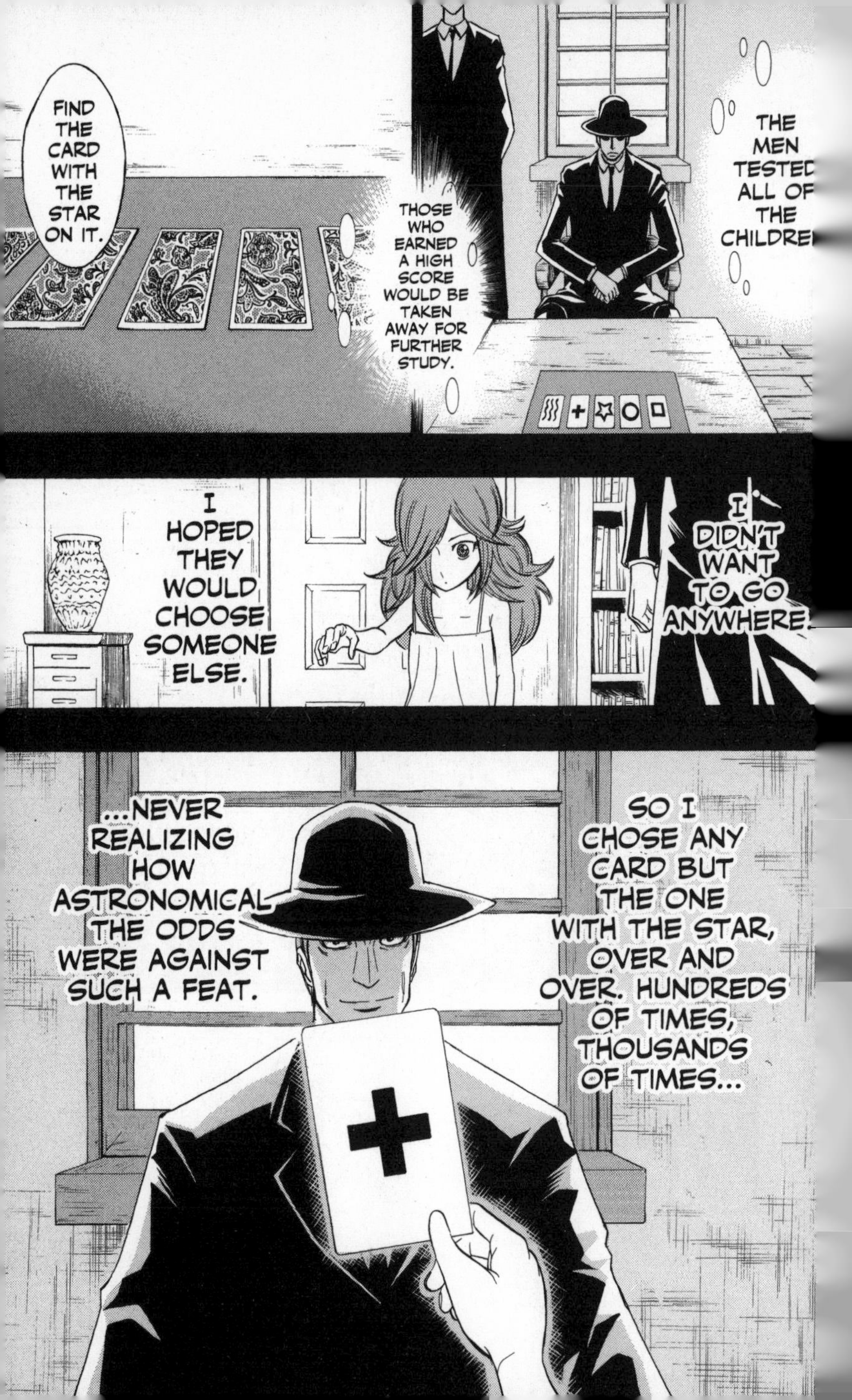
THE MEN TESTED ALL OF THE CHILDREN
THOSE WHO EARNED A HIGH SCORE WOULD BE TAKEN AWAY FOR FURTHER STUDY.
FIND THE CARD WITH THE STAR ON IT.
I DIDN'T WANT TO GO ANYWHERE.
I HOPED THEY WOULD CHOOSE SOMEONE ELSE.
SO I CHOSE ANY CARD BUT THE ONE WITH THE STAR, OVER AND OVER. HUNDREDS OF TIMES, THOUSANDS OF TIMES...
...NEVER REALIZING HOW ASTRONOMICAL THE ODDS WERE AGAINST SUCH A FEAT.

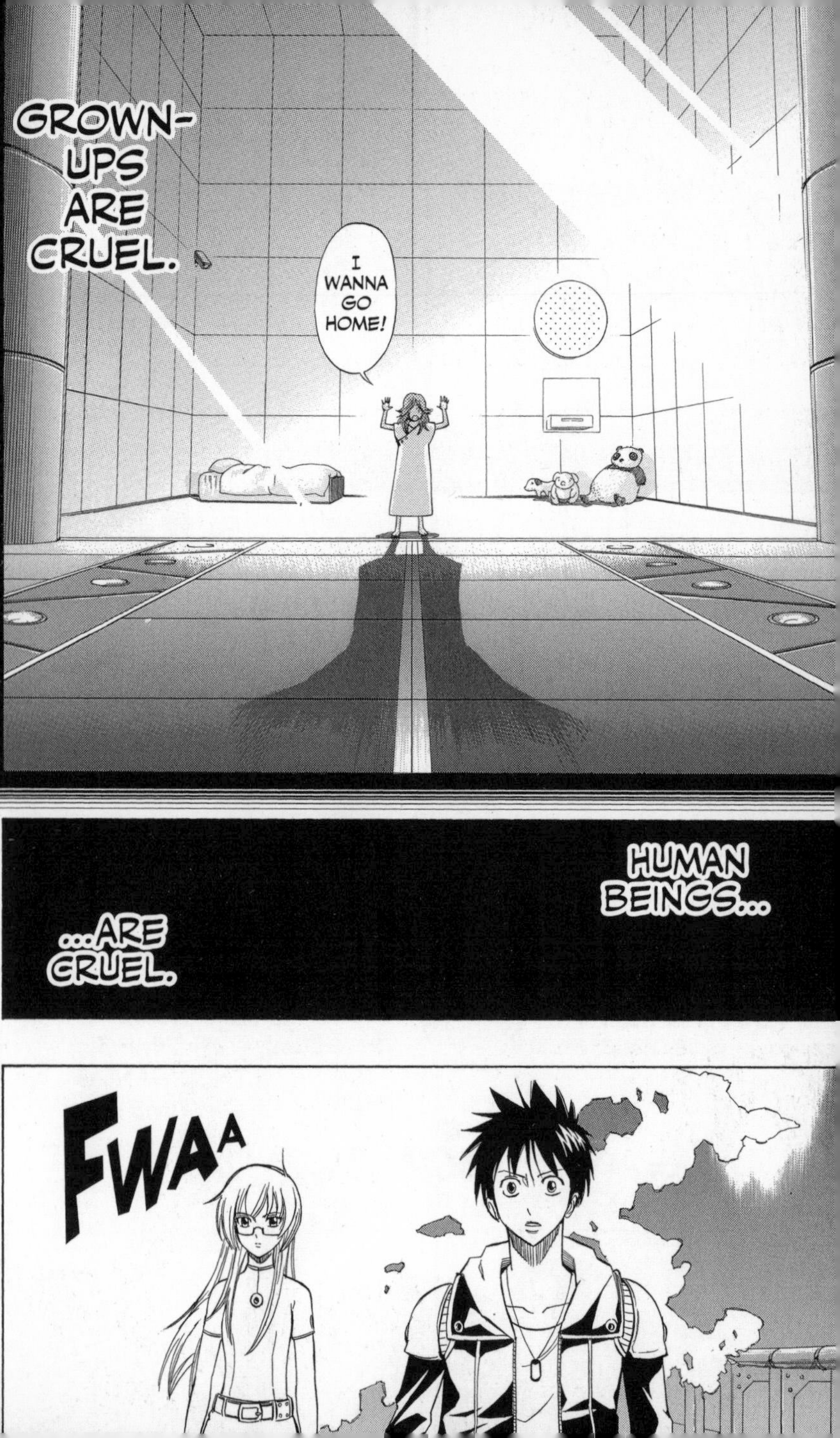
I WANNA GO HOME!
GROWN-UPS ARE CRUEL.
HUMAN BEINGS...
...ARE CRUEL.
FWAA

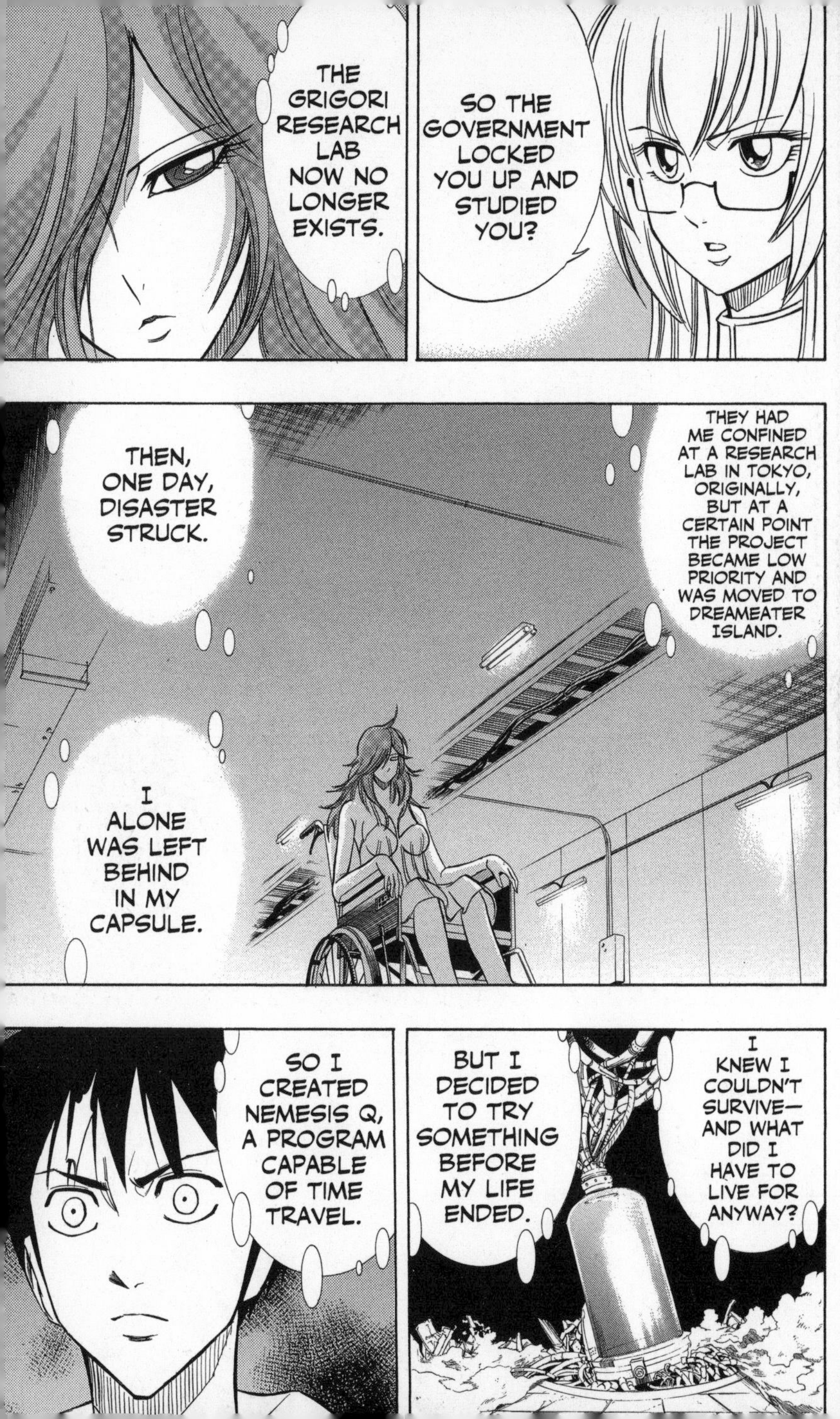
SO THE GOVERNMENT LOCKED YOU UP AND STUDIED YOU?
THE GRIGORI RESEARCH LAB NOW NO LONGER EXISTS.
THEY HAD ME CONFINED AT A RESEARCH LAB IN TOKYO, ORIGINALLY, BUT AT A CERTAIN POINT THE PROJECT BECAME LOW PRIORITY AND WAS MOVED TO DREAMEATER ISLAND.
THEN, ONE DAY, DISASTER STRUCK.
I ALONE WAS LEFT BEHIND IN MY CAPSULE.
I KNEW I COULDN'T SURVIVE— AND WHAT DID I HAVE TO LIVE FOR ANYWAY?
BUT I DECIDED TO TRY SOMETHING BEFORE MY LIFE ENDED.
SO I CREATED NEMESIS Q, A PROGRAM CAPABLE OF TIME TRAVEL.

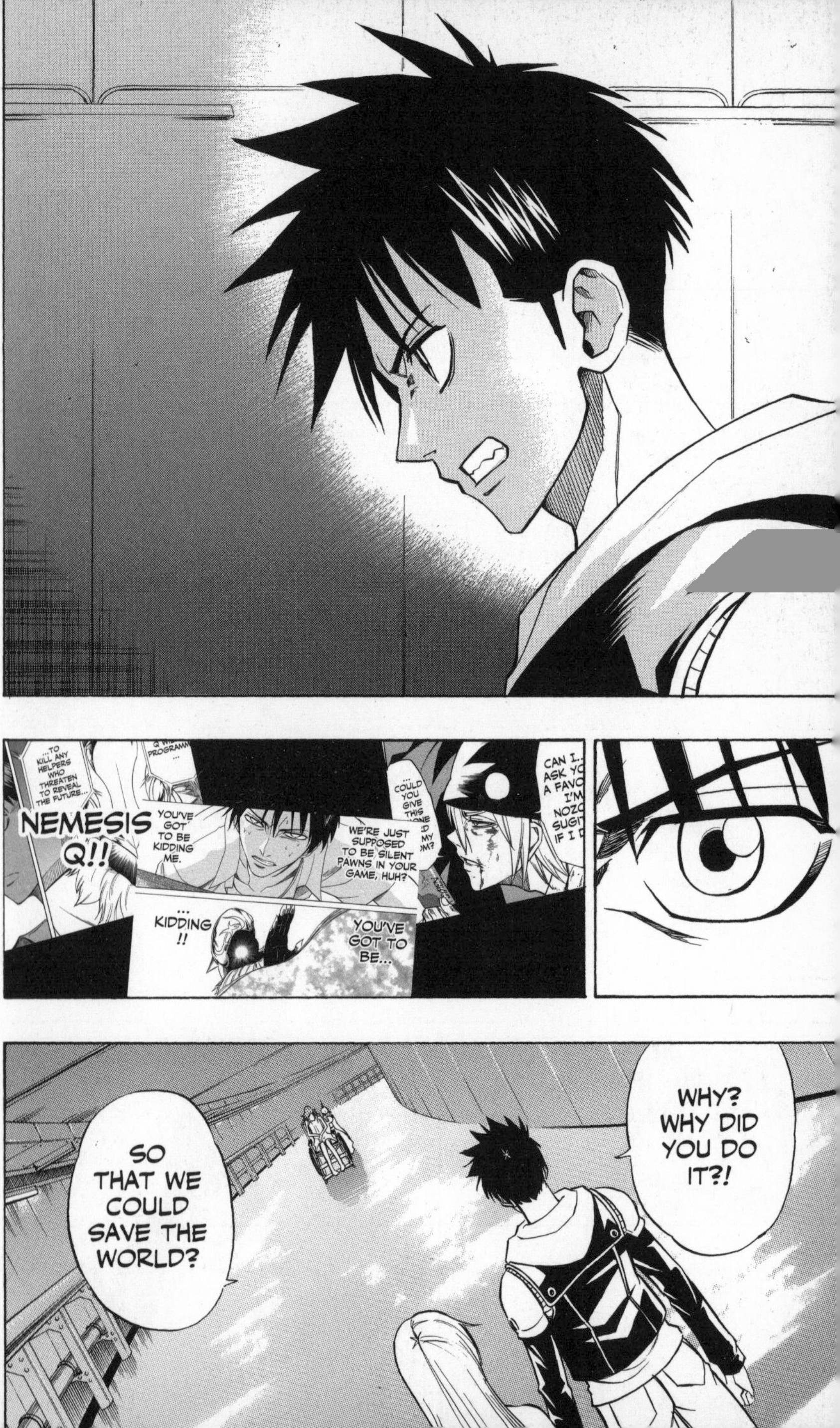
CAN I... ASK YO A FAVO I'M NOZO SUGIT IF I D
... COULD YOU GIVE THIS
WE'RE JUST SUPPOSED TO BE SILENT PAWNS IN YOUR GAME, HUH?
YOU'VE GOT TO BE KIDDING ME.
Q WI PROGRAMM
...TO KILL ANY HELPERS WHO THREATEN TO REVEAL THE FUTURE...
NEMESIS Q!!
YOU'VE GOT TO BE...
... KIDDING !!
WHY? WHY DID YOU DO IT?!
SO THAT WE COULD SAVE THE WORLD?

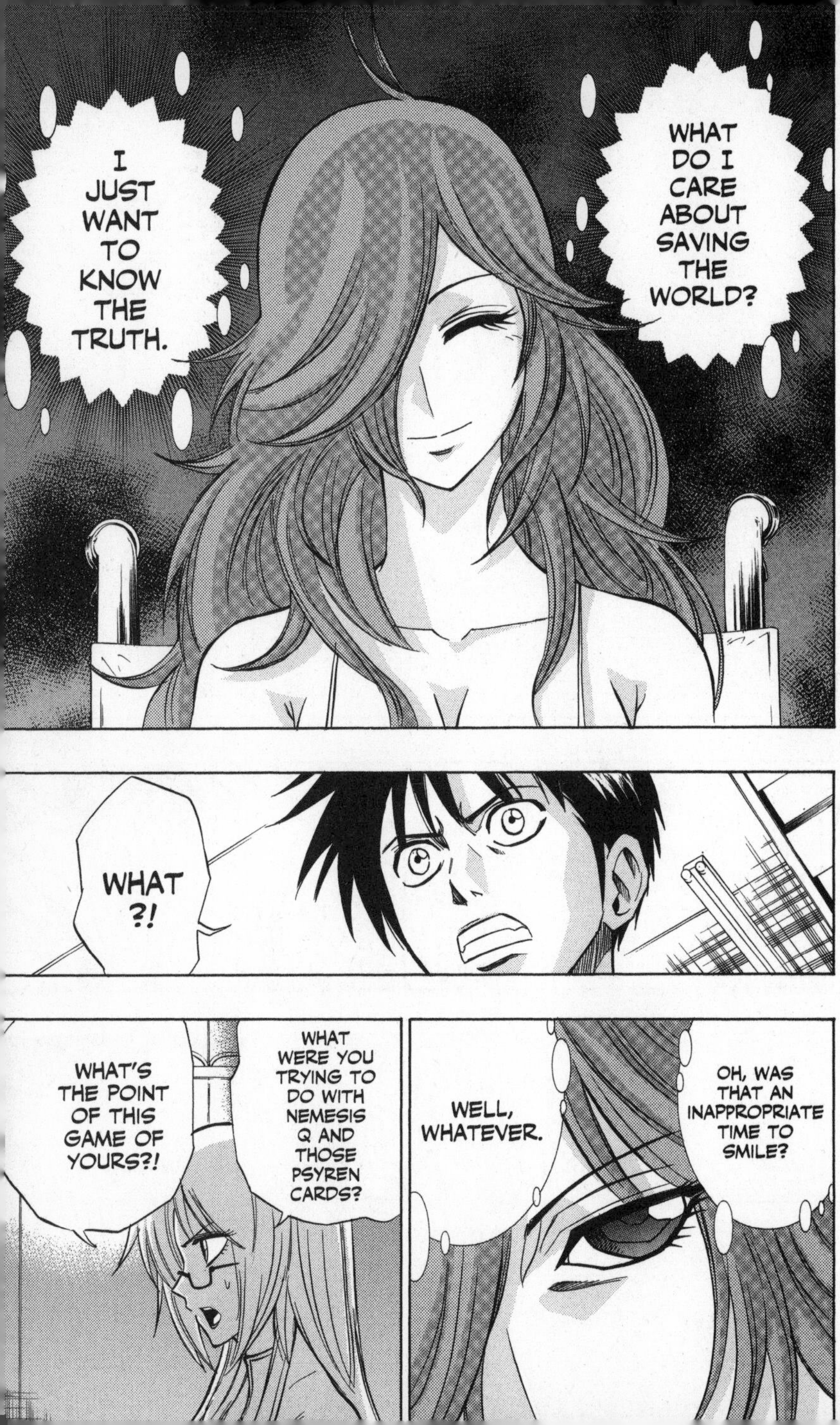
WHAT DO I CARE ABOUT SAVING THE WORLD?
I JUST WANT TO KNOW THE TRUTH.
WHAT ?!
OH, WAS THAT AN INAPPROPRIATE TIME TO SMILE?
WELL, WHATEVER.
WHAT WERE YOU TRYING TO DO WITH NEMESIS Q AND THOSE PSYREN CARDS?
WHAT'S THE POINT OF THIS GAME OF YOURS?!

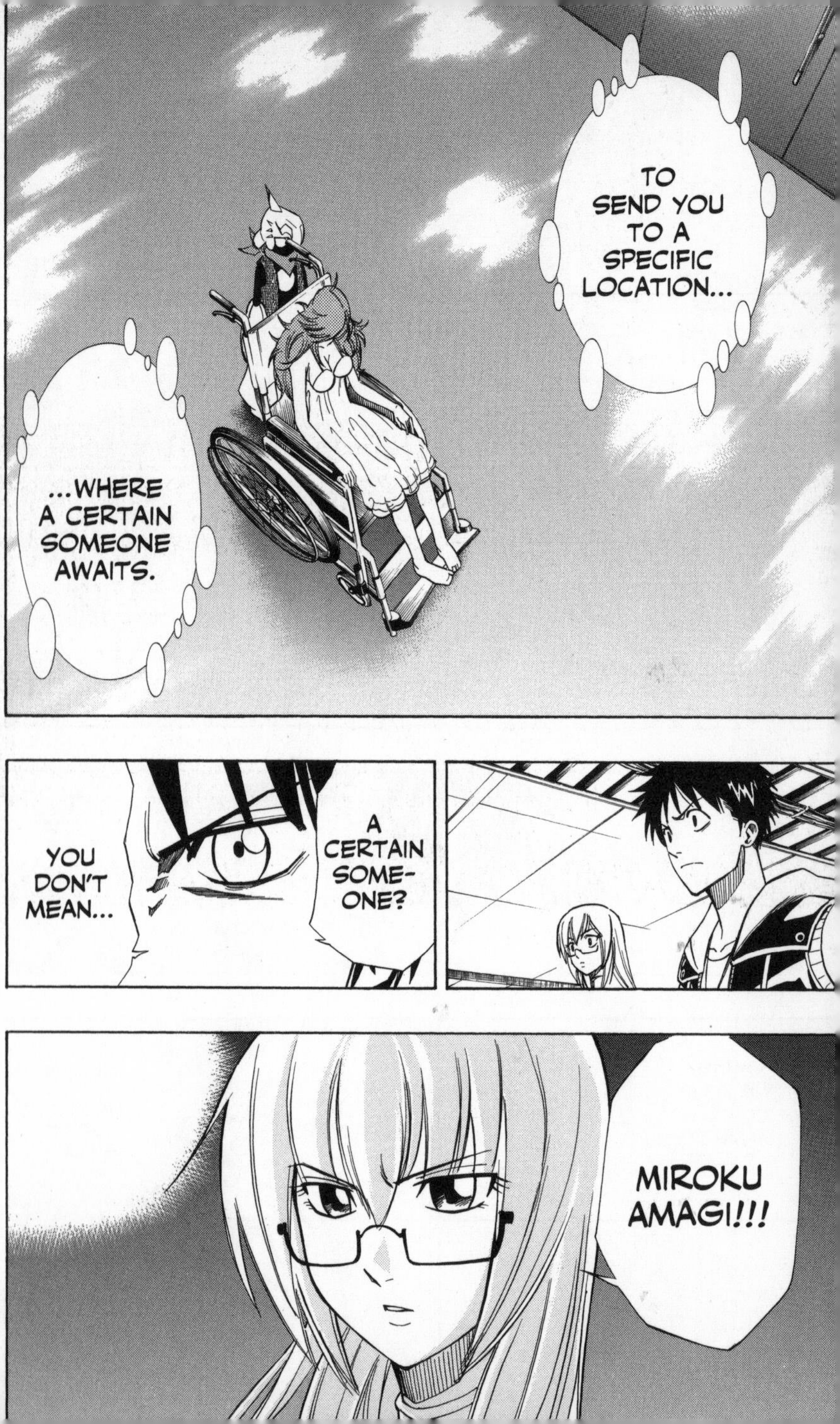
TO SEND YOU TO A SPECIFIC LOCATION...
...WHERE A CERTAIN SOMEONE AWAITS.
A CERTAIN SOME-ONE?
YOU DON'T MEAN...
MIROKU AMAGI!!!

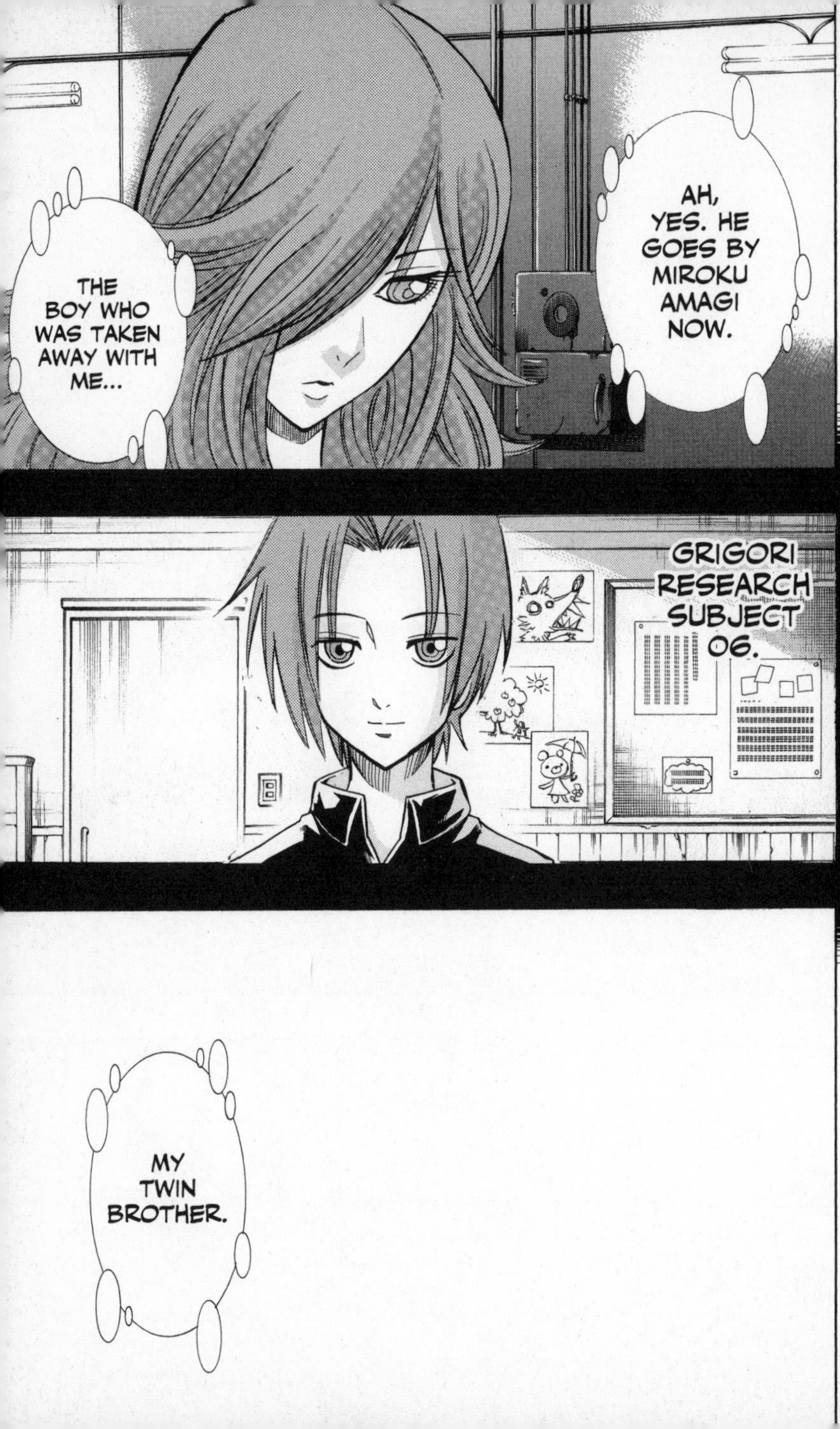
AH, YES. HE GOES BY MIROKU AMAGI NOW.
THE BOY WHO WAS TAKEN AWAY WITH ME...
GRIGORI RESEARCH SUBJECT 06.
MY TWIN BROTHER.

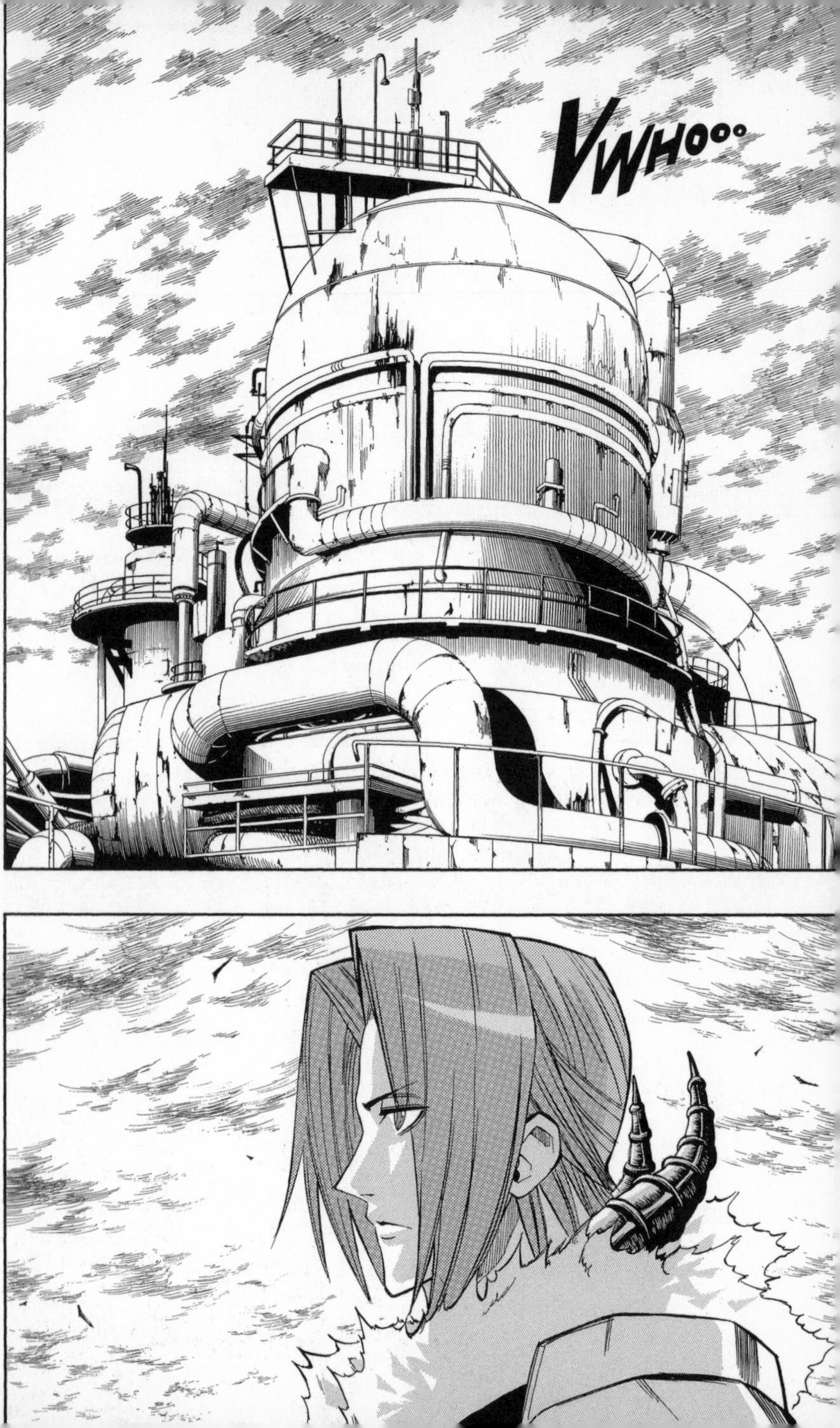
VWHOOO

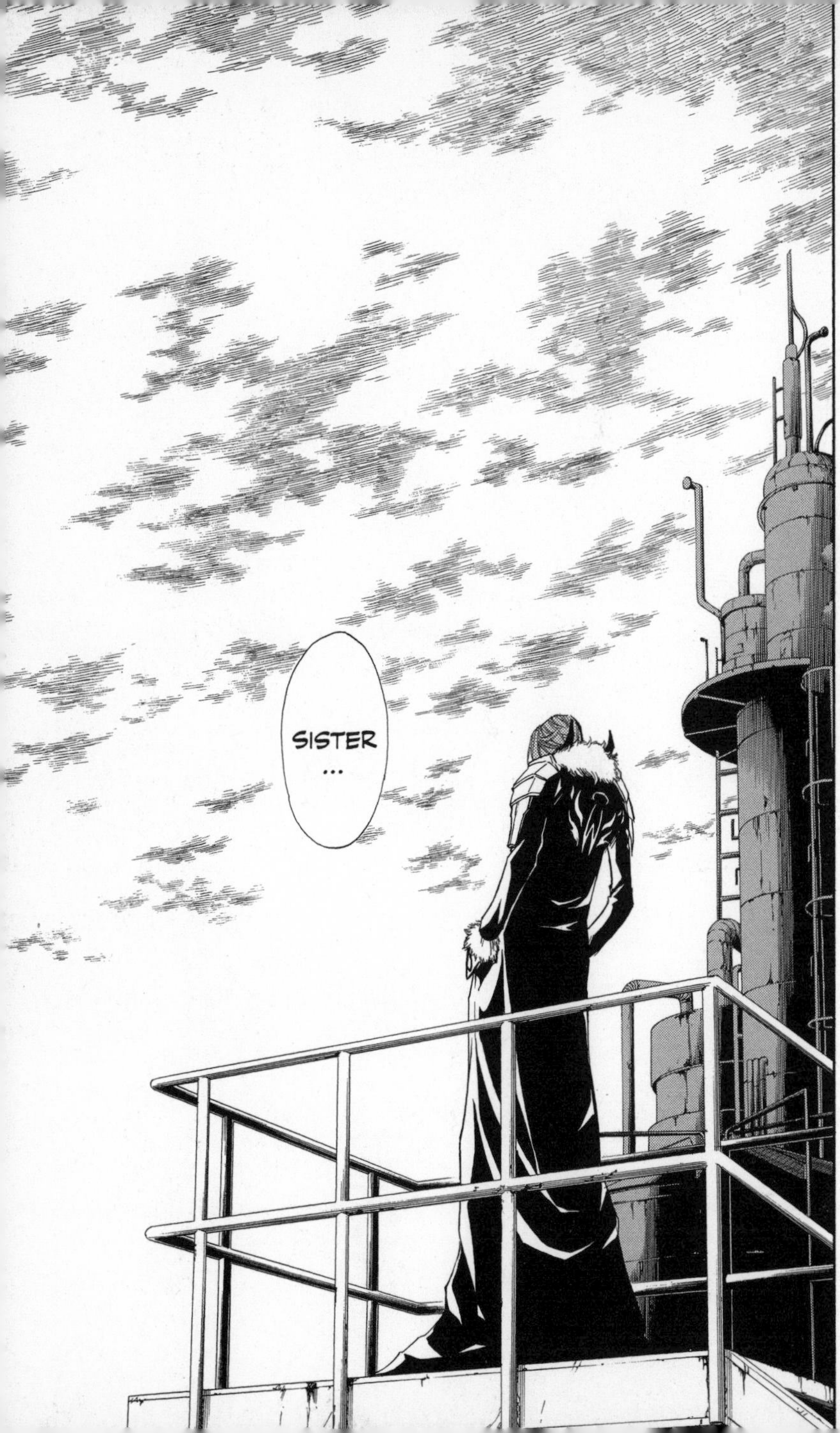
SISTER
...

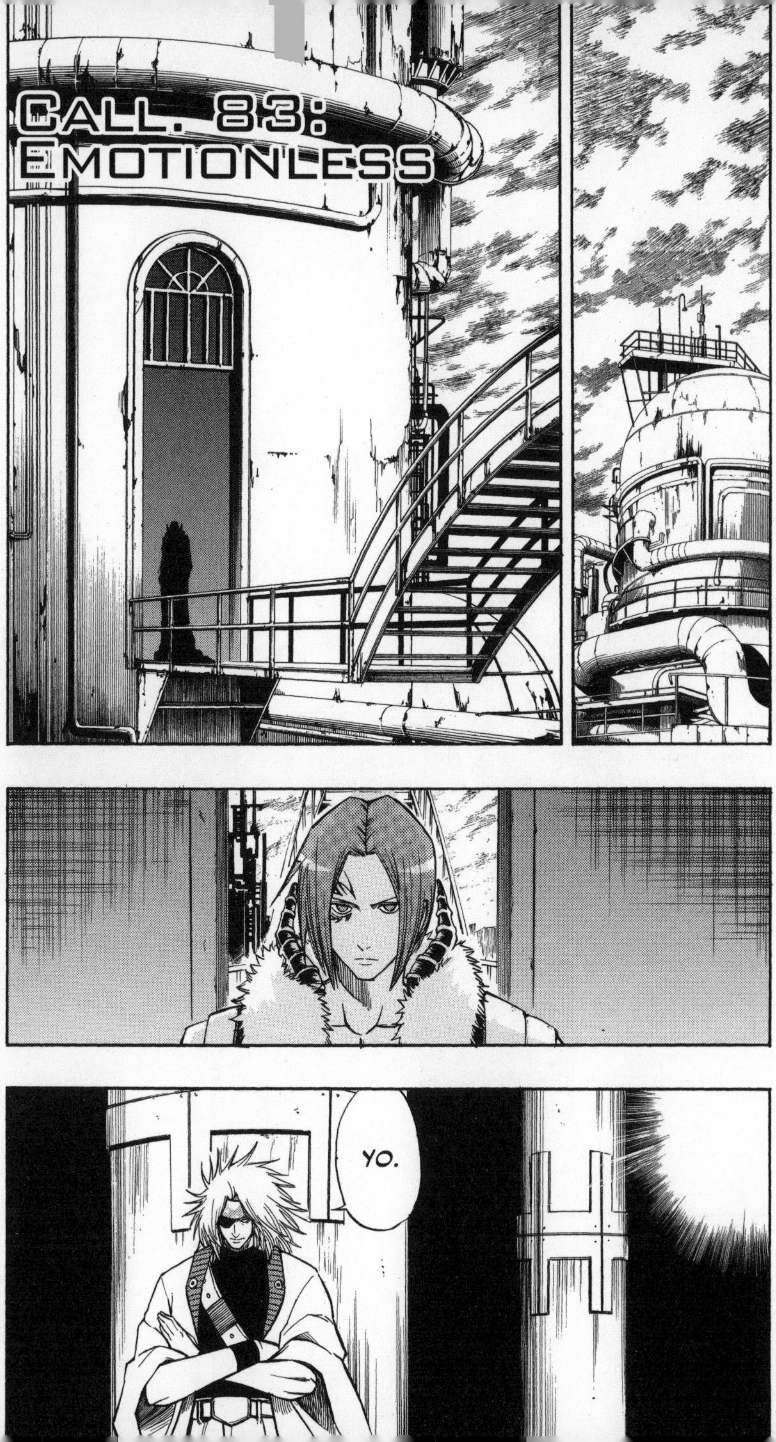
CALL. 83: EMOTIONLESS
YO.

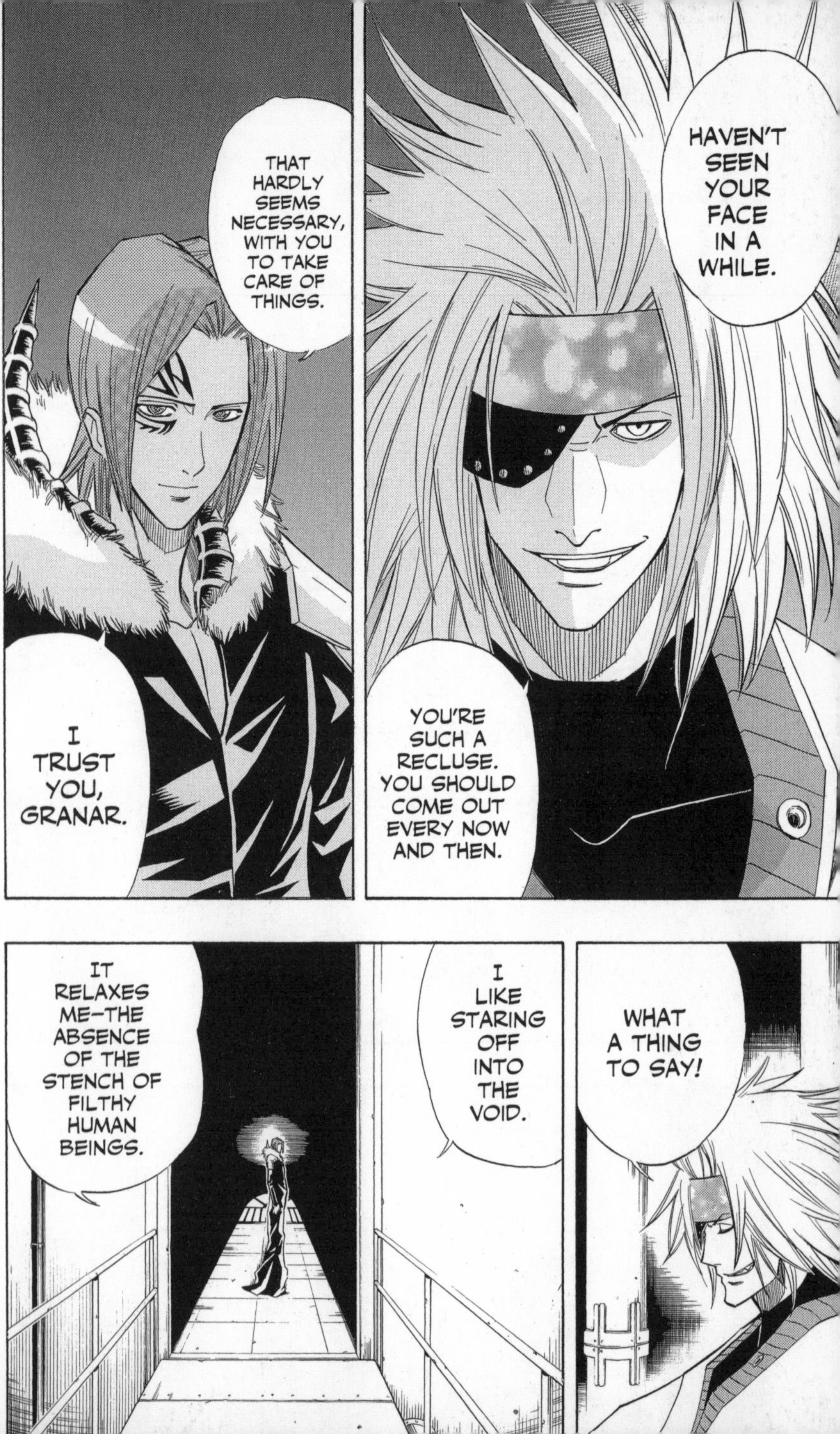
HAVEN'T SEEN YOUR FACE IN A WHILE.
YOU'RE SUCH A RECLUSE. YOU SHOULD COME OUT EVERY NOW AND THEN.
THAT HARDLY SEEMS NECESSARY, WITH YOU TO TAKE CARE OF THINGS.
I TRUST YOU, GRANAR.
WHAT A THING TO SAY!
I LIKE STARING OFF INTO THE VOID.
IT RELAXES ME—THE ABSENCE OF THE STENCH OF FILTHY HUMAN BEINGS.

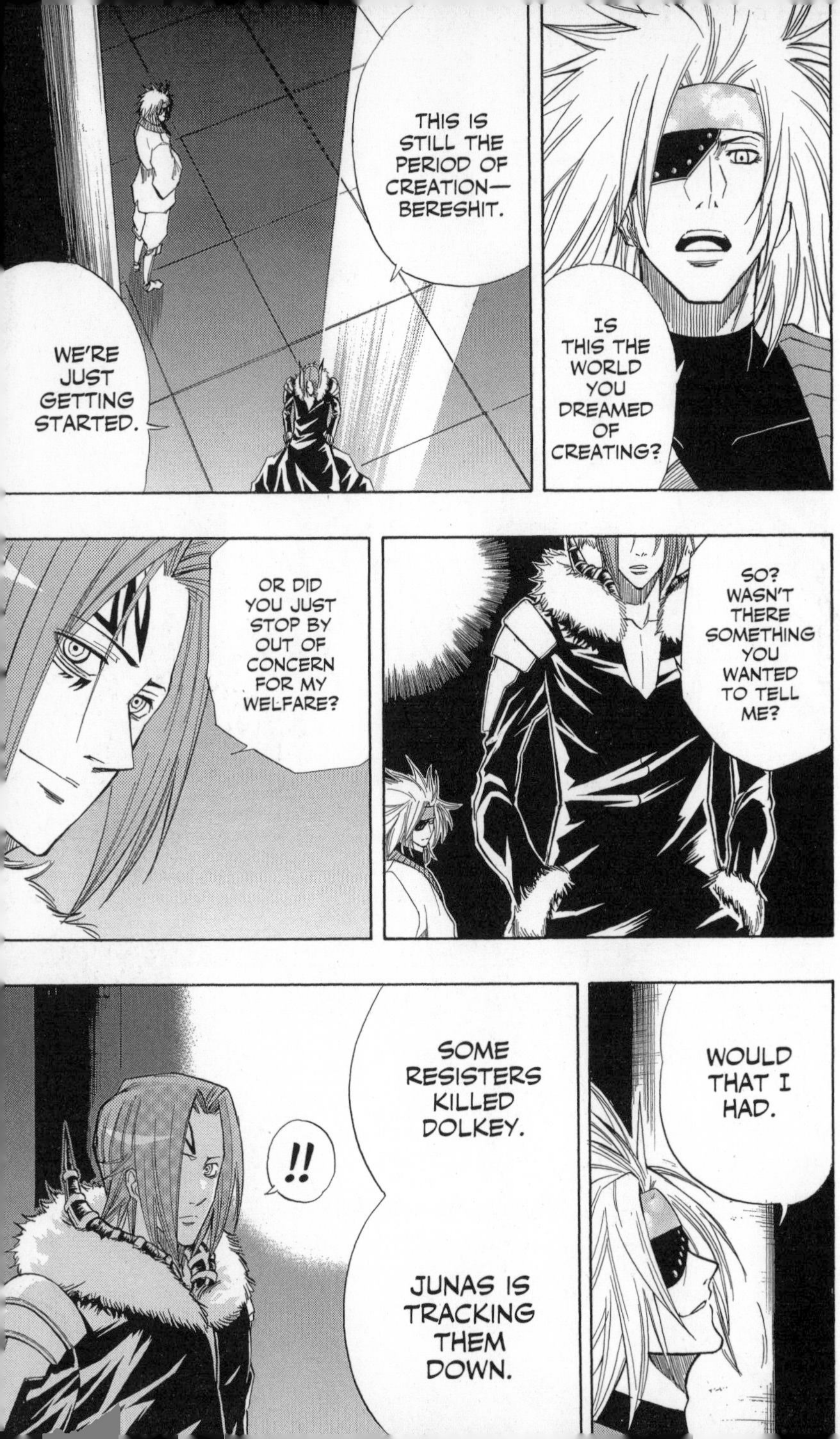
IS THIS THE WORLD YOU DREAMED OF CREATING?
THIS IS STILL THE PERIOD OF CREATION—BERESHIT.
WE'RE JUST GETTING STARTED.
SO? WASN'T THERE SOMETHING YOU WANTED TO TELL ME?
OR DID YOU JUST STOP BY OUT OF CONCERN FOR MY WELFARE?
WOULD THAT I HAD.
SOME RESISTERS KILLED DOLKEY.
!!
JUNAS IS TRACKING THEM DOWN.

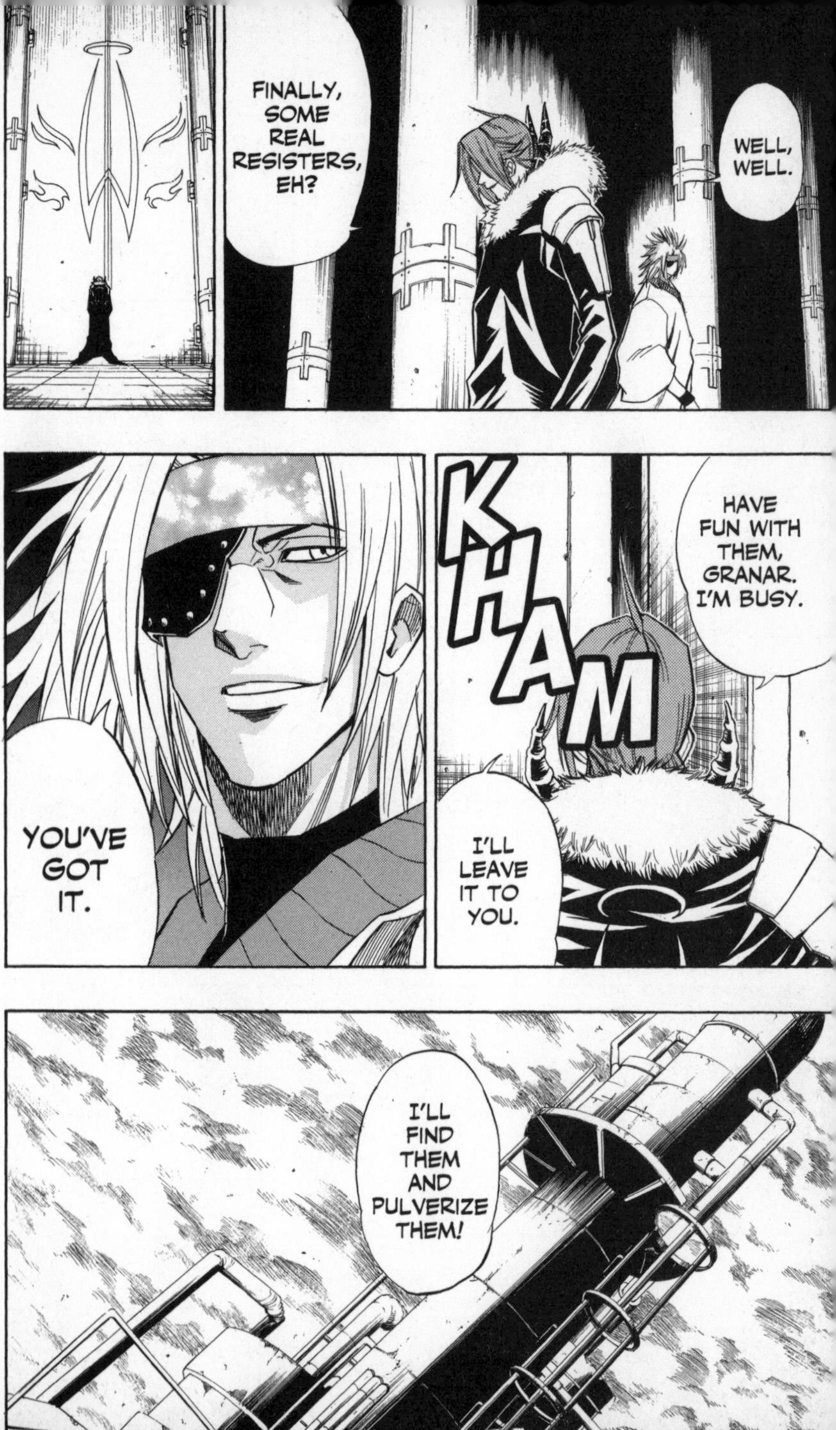
WELL, WELL.
FINALLY, SOME REAL RESISTERS, EH?
KHAM
HAVE FUN WITH THEM, GRANAR. I'M BUSY.
I'LL LEAVE IT TO YOU.
YOU'VE GOT IT.
I'LL FIND THEM AND PULVERIZE THEM!

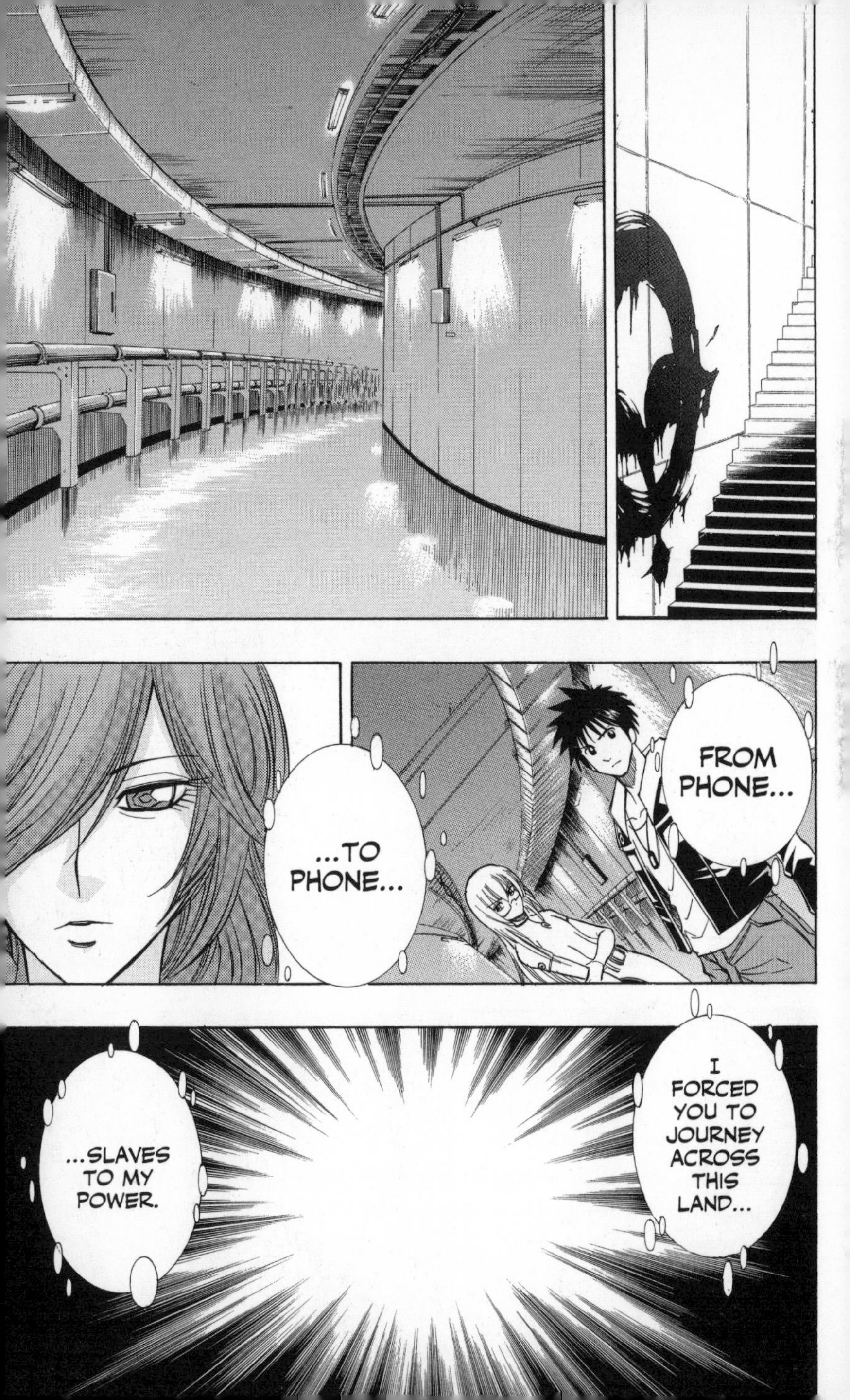
FROM PHONE...
...TO PHONE...
I FORCED YOU TO JOURNEY ACROSS THIS LAND...
...SLAVES TO MY POWER.

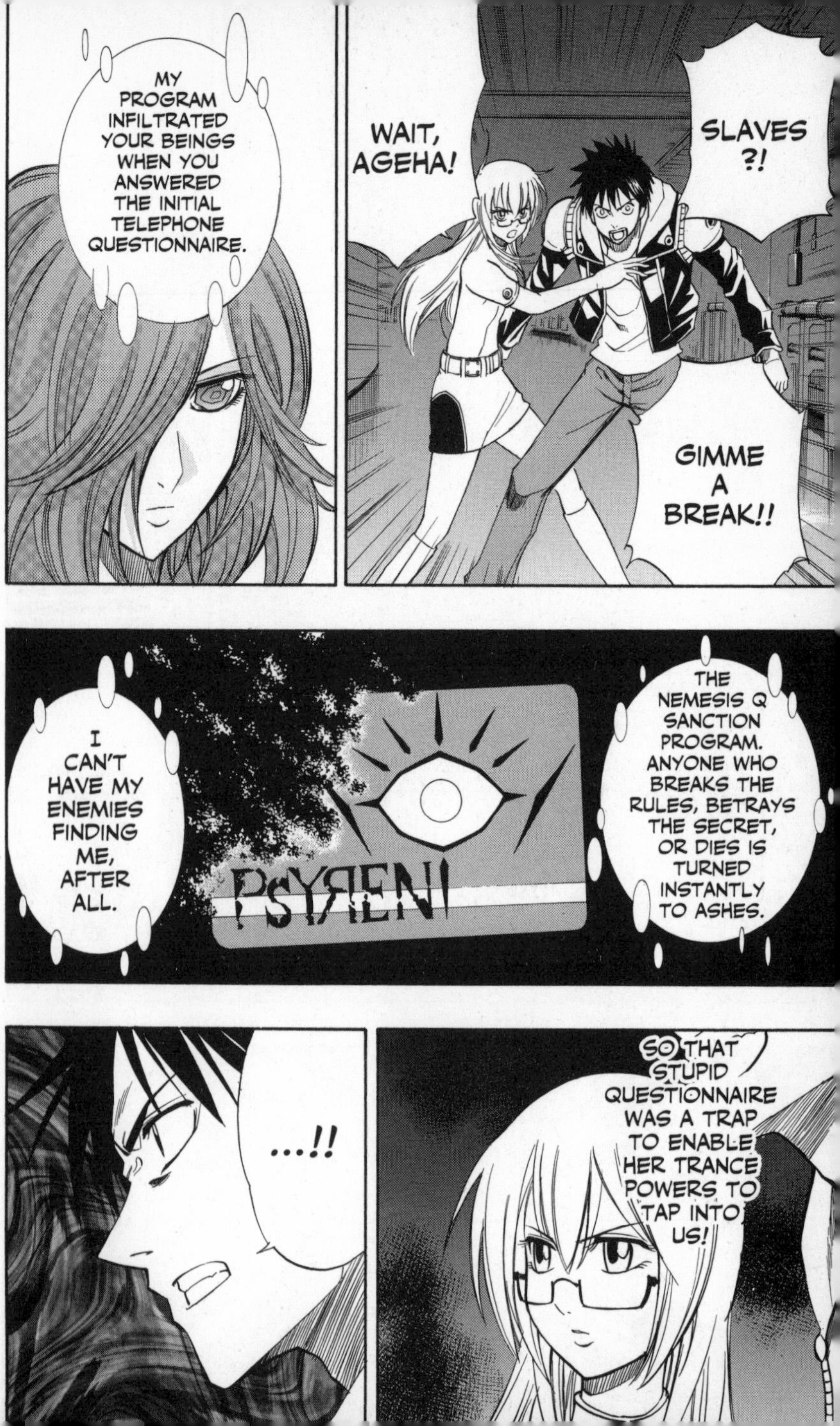
SLAVES ?!
WAIT, AGEHA!
GIMME A BREAK!!
MY PROGRAM INFILTRATED YOUR BEINGS WHEN YOU ANSWERED THE INITIAL TELEPHONE QUESTIONNAIRE.
THE NEMESIS Q SANCTION PROGRAM. ANYONE WHO BREAKS THE RULES, BETRAYS THE SECRET, OR DIES IS TURNED INSTANTLY TO ASHES.
PSYREN
I CAN'T HAVE MY ENEMIES FINDING ME, AFTER ALL.
SO THAT STUPID QUESTIONNAIRE WAS A TRAP TO ENABLE HER TRANCE POWERS TO TAP INTO US!
...!!

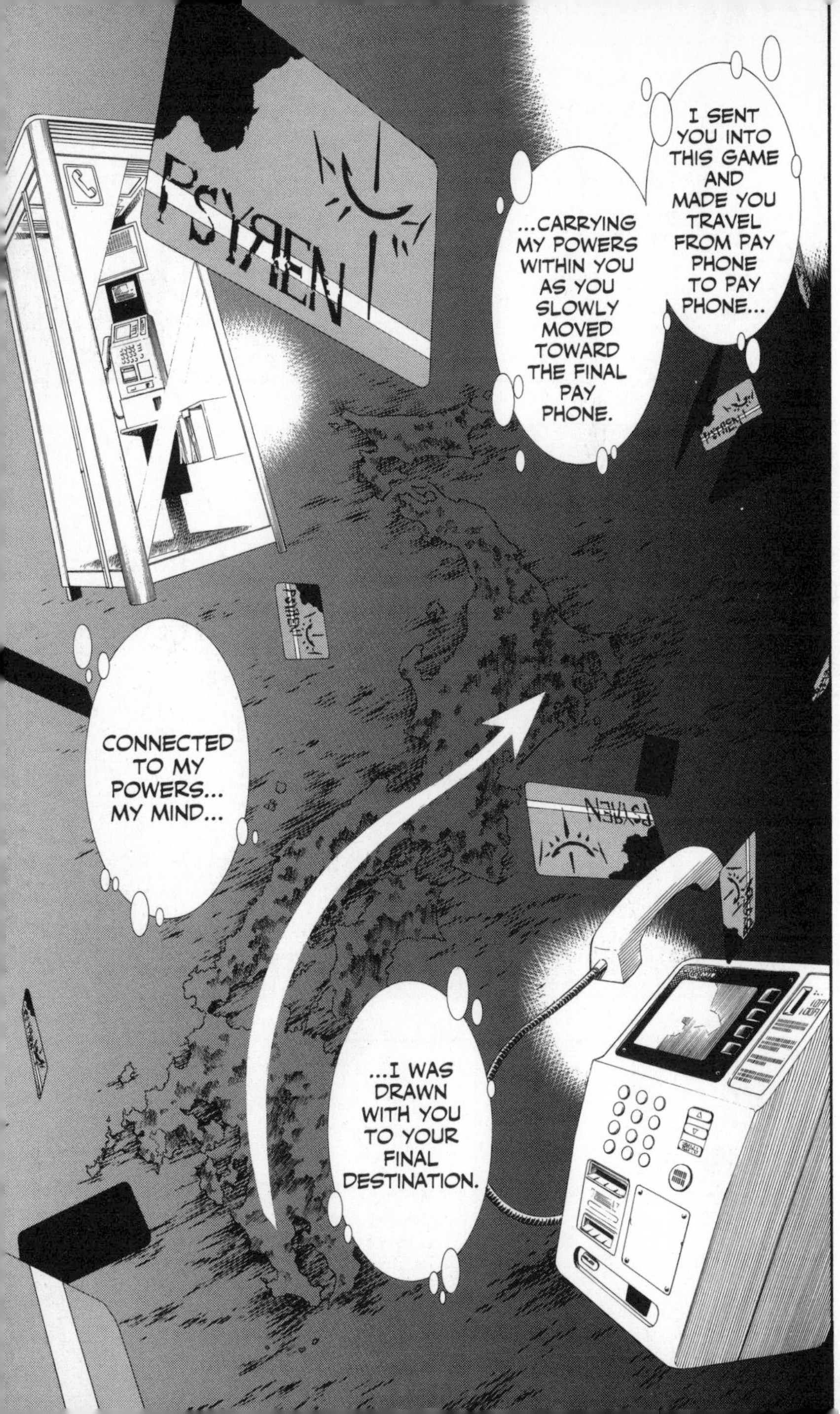
PSYREN
I SENT YOU INTO THIS GAME AND MADE YOU TRAVEL FROM PAY PHONE TO PAY PHONE...
...CARRYING MY POWERS WITHIN YOU AS YOU SLOWLY MOVED TOWARD THE FINAL PAY PHONE.
CONNECTED TO MY POWERS... MY MIND...
...I WAS DRAWN WITH YOU TO YOUR FINAL DESTINATION.
PSYREN

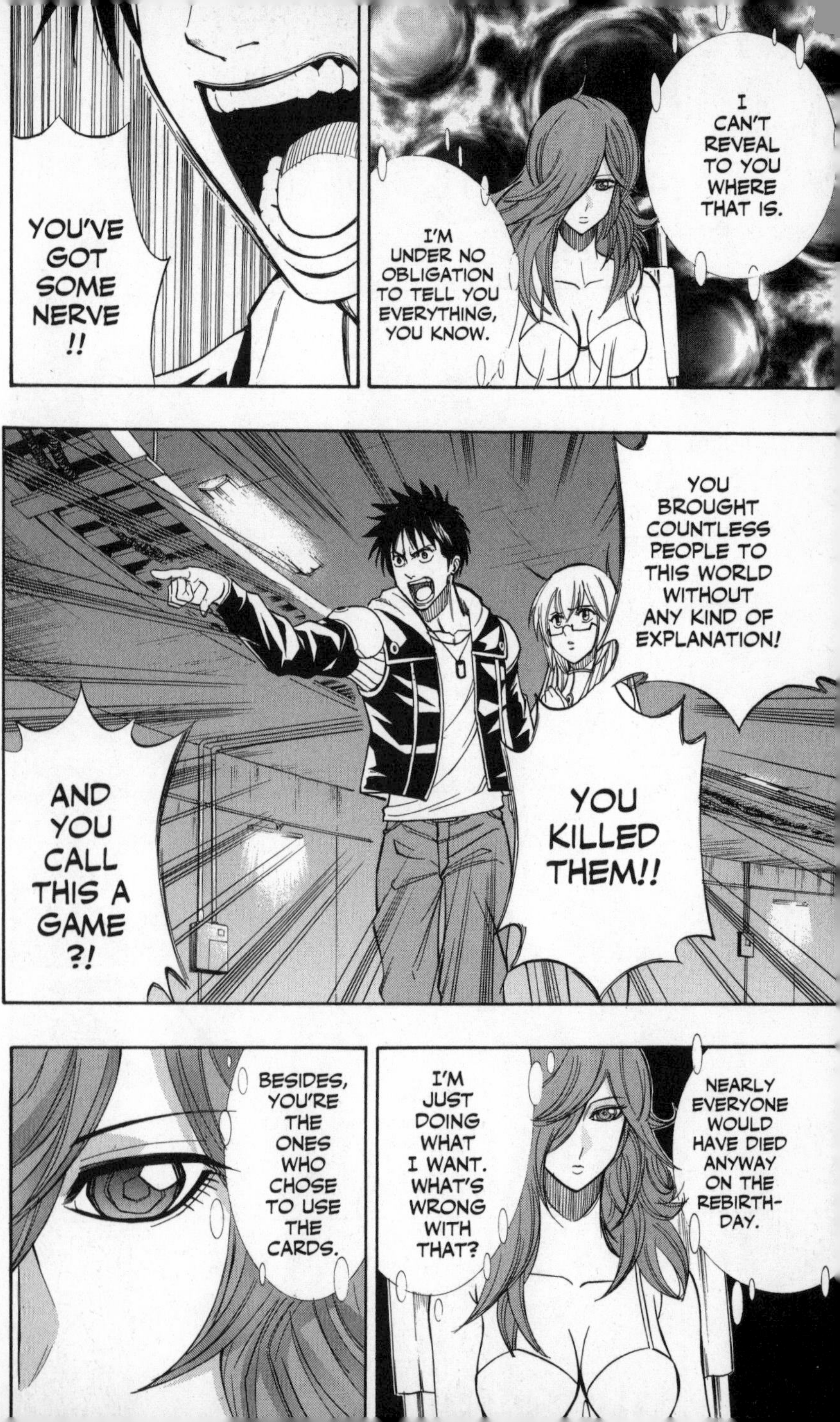
I CAN'T REVEAL TO YOU WHERE THAT IS.
I'M UNDER NO OBLIGATION TO TELL YOU EVERYTHING, YOU KNOW.
YOU'VE GOT SOME NERVE!!
YOU BROUGHT COUNTLESS PEOPLE TO THIS WORLD WITHOUT ANY KIND OF EXPLANATION!
YOU KILLED THEM!!
AND YOU CALL THIS A GAME?!
NEARLY EVERYONE WOULD HAVE DIED ANYWAY ON THE REBIRTH-DAY.
I'M JUST DOING WHAT I WANT. WHAT'S WRONG WITH THAT?
BESIDES, YOU'RE THE ONES WHO CHOSE TO USE THE CARDS.

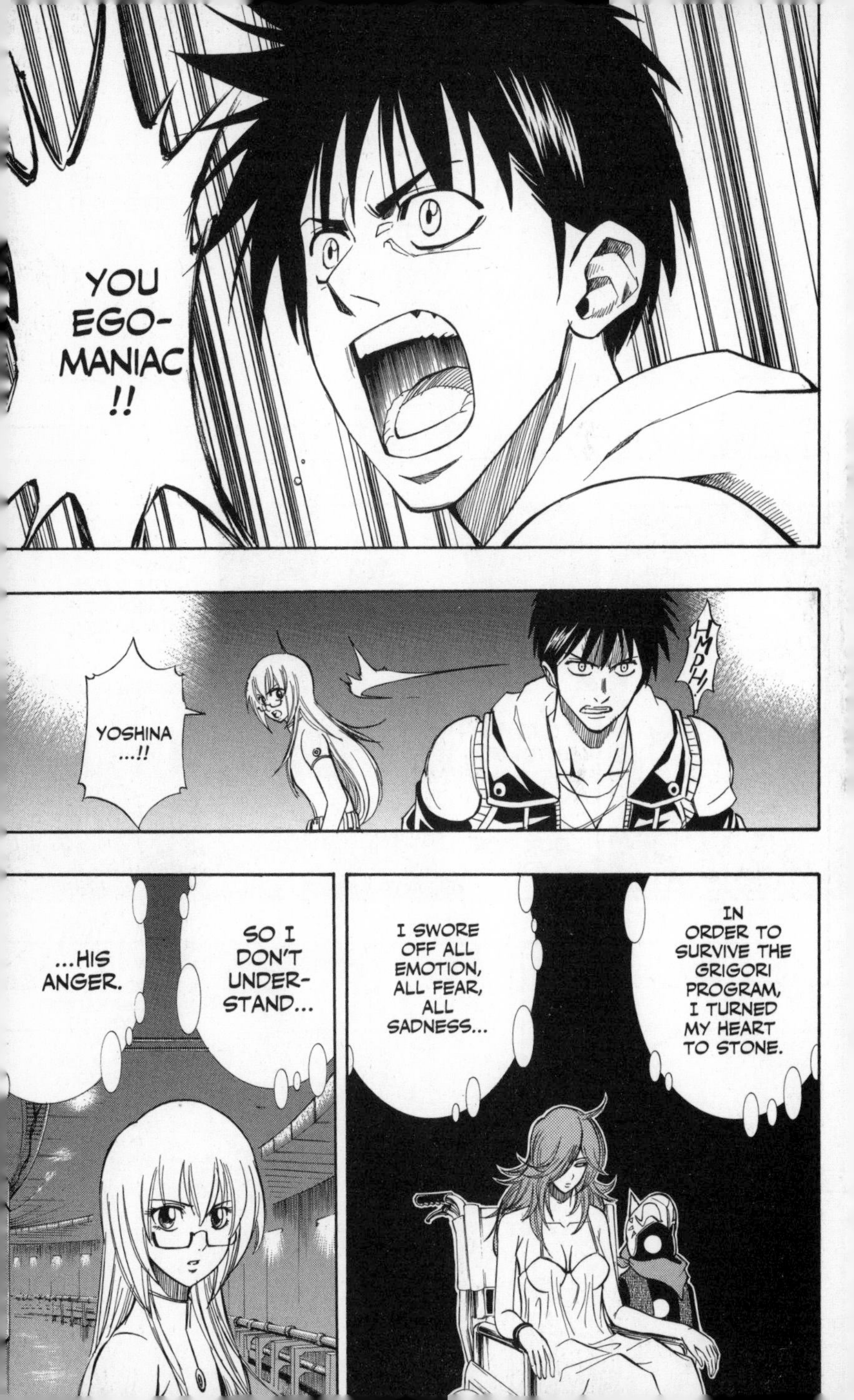
YOU EGO-MANIAC!!
HMPH!
YOSHINA...!!
IN ORDER TO SURVIVE THE GRIGORI PROGRAM, I TURNED MY HEART TO STONE.
I SWORE OFF ALL EMOTION, ALL FEAR, ALL SADNESS...
SO I DON'T UNDER-STAND...
...HIS ANGER.

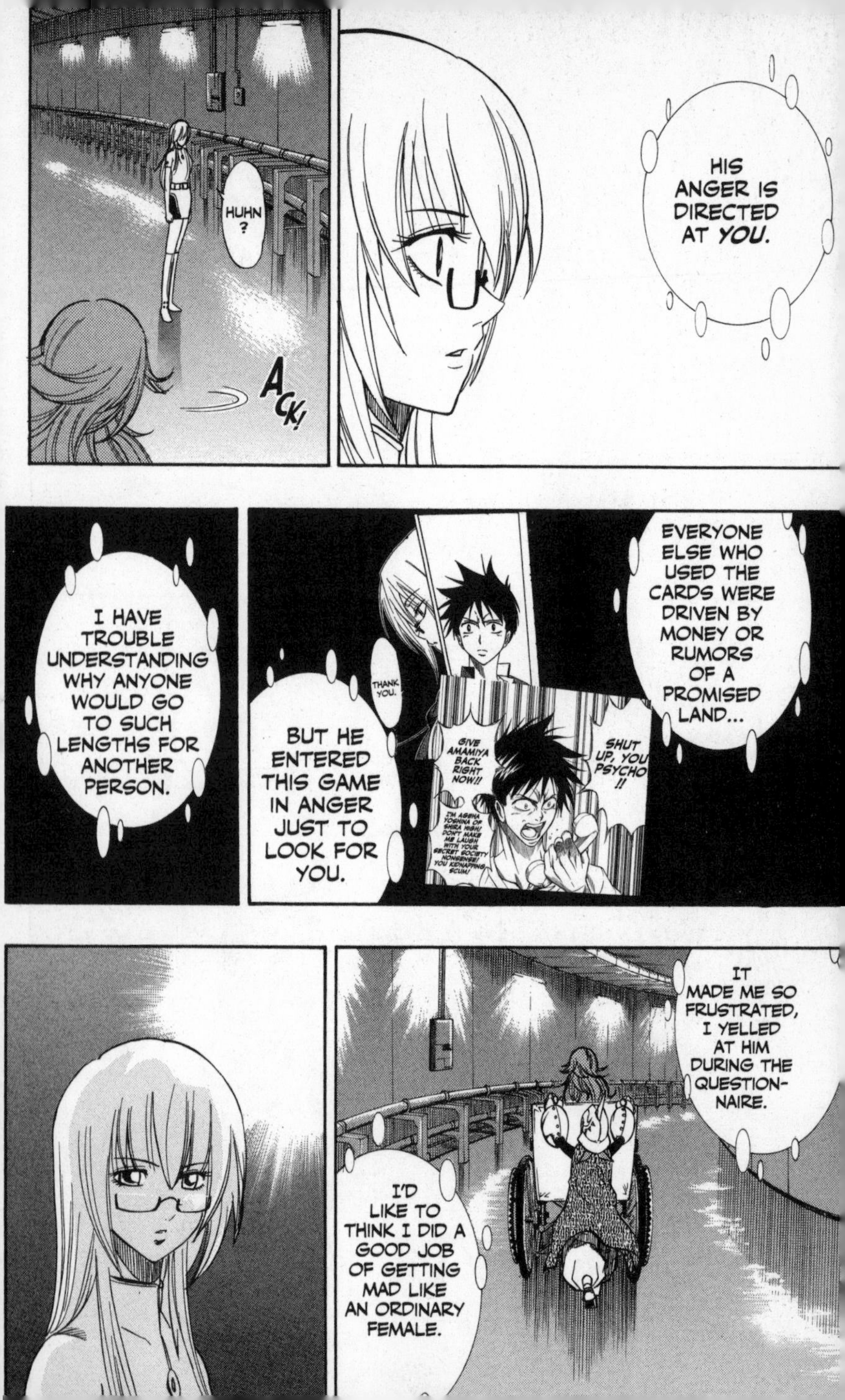
HIS ANGER IS DIRECTED AT *YOU*.
HUHN?
ACK!
EVERYONE ELSE WHO USED THE CARDS WERE DRIVEN BY MONEY OR RUMORS OF A PROMISED LAND...
SHUT UP, YOU PSYCHO!!
GIVE AMAMIYA BACK RIGHT NOW!!
I'M AGEHA YOSHINA OF SHIRA HIGH! DON'T MAKE ME LAUGH WITH YOUR SECRET SOCIETY NONSENSE! YOU KIDNAPPING SCUM!
THANK YOU.
BUT HE ENTERED THIS GAME IN ANGER JUST TO LOOK FOR YOU.
I HAVE TROUBLE UNDERSTANDING WHY ANYONE WOULD GO TO SUCH LENGTHS FOR ANOTHER PERSON.
IT MADE ME SO FRUSTRATED, I YELLED AT HIM DURING THE QUESTION-NAIRE.
I'D LIKE TO THINK I DID A GOOD JOB OF GETTING MAD LIKE AN ORDINARY FEMALE.

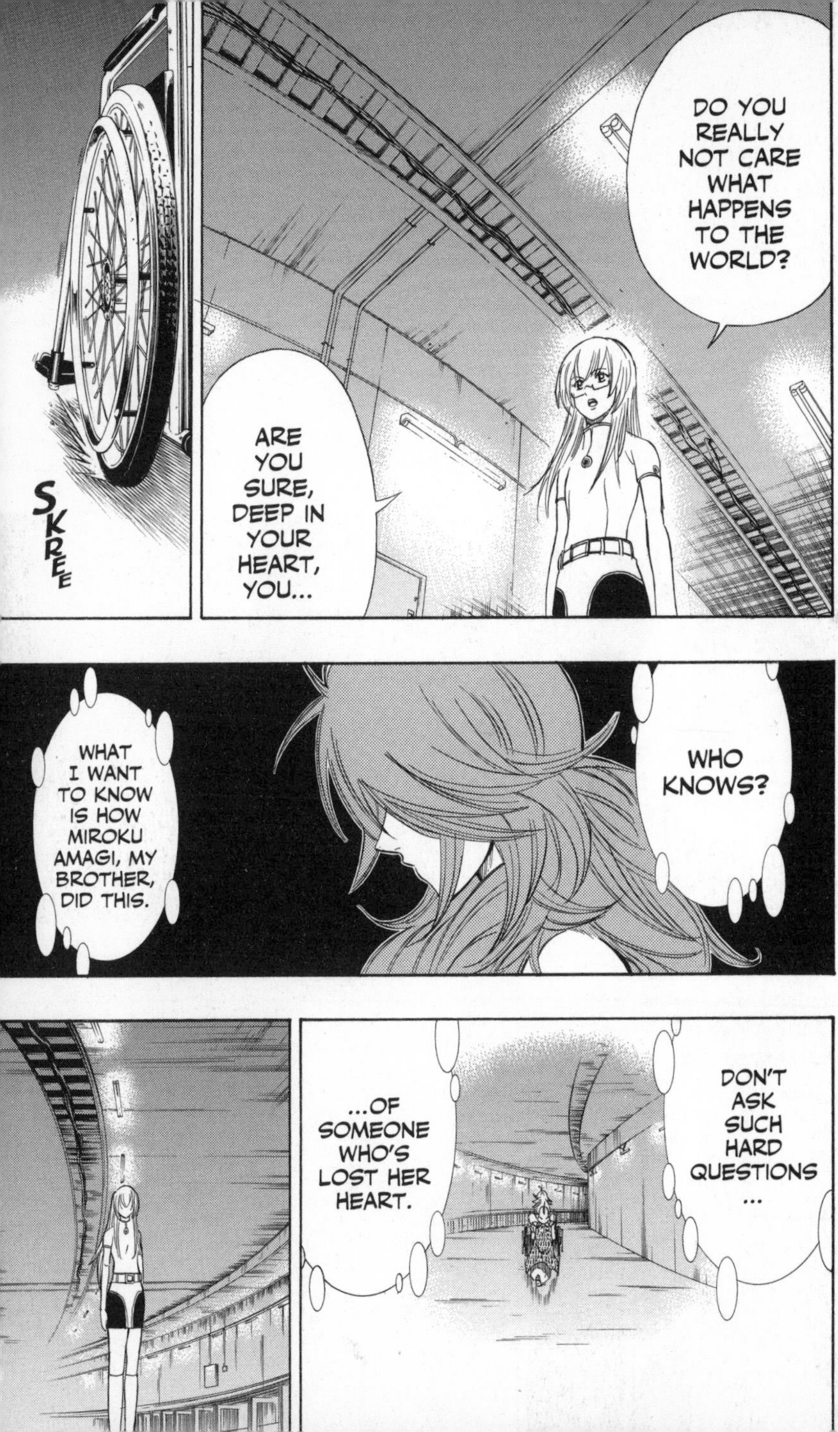
DO YOU REALLY NOT CARE WHAT HAPPENS TO THE WORLD?
ARE YOU SURE, DEEP IN YOUR HEART, YOU...
SKREE
WHO KNOWS?
WHAT I WANT TO KNOW IS HOW MIROKU AMAGI, MY BROTHER, DID THIS.
DON'T ASK SUCH HARD QUESTIONS...
...OF SOMEONE WHO'S LOST HER HEART.

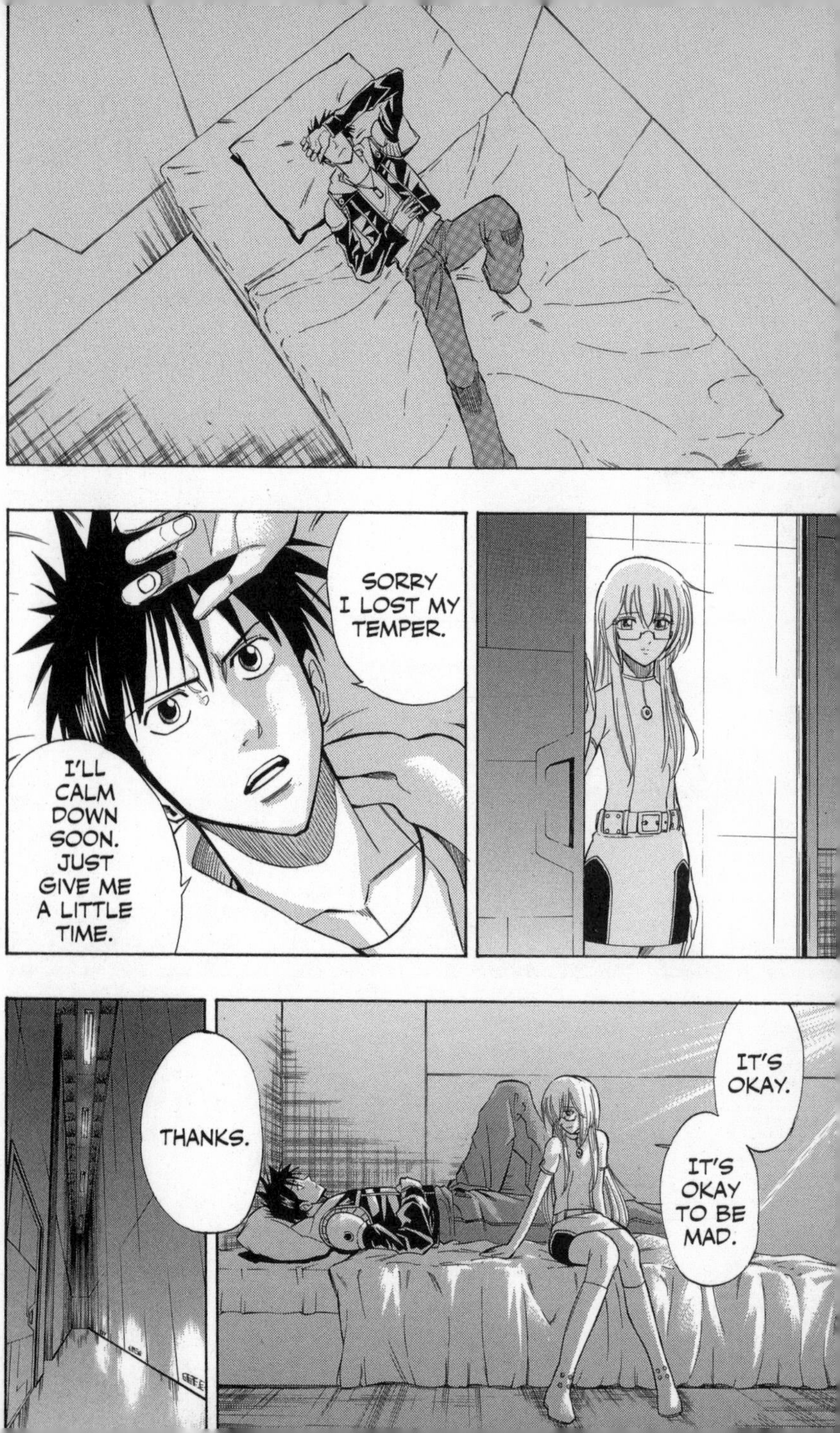
SORRY I LOST MY TEMPER.
I'LL CALM DOWN SOON. JUST GIVE ME A LITTLE TIME.
IT'S OKAY.
IT'S OKAY TO BE MAD.
THANKS.

FREDDY! YOU'RE SUPPOSED TO BE HELPING WITH THE CROPS!

I'm so sleepy...

sigh

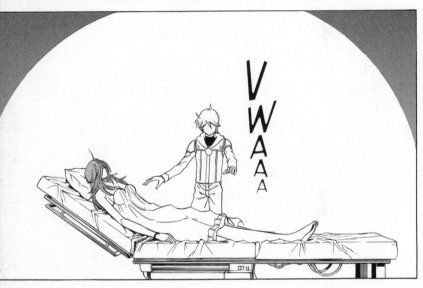

VWAAA

HERE TO DISTURB MY WORK AGAIN?

YO.

VEEEM

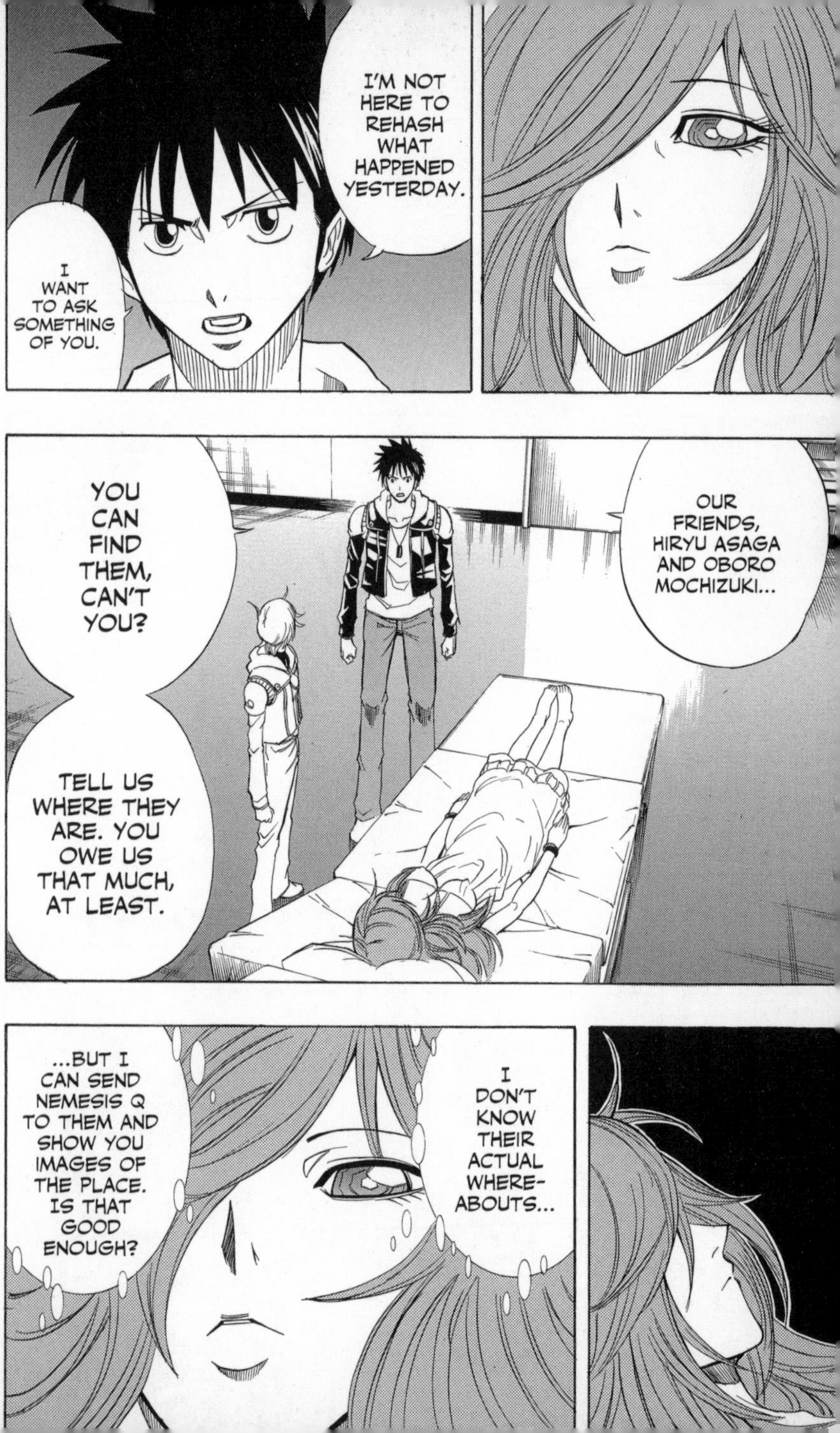
I'M NOT HERE TO REHASH WHAT HAPPENED YESTERDAY.
I WANT TO ASK SOMETHING OF YOU.
OUR FRIENDS, HIRYU ASAGA AND OBORO MOCHIZUKI...
YOU CAN FIND THEM, CAN'T YOU?
TELL US WHERE THEY ARE. YOU OWE US THAT MUCH, AT LEAST.
I DON'T KNOW THEIR ACTUAL WHERE-ABOUTS...
...BUT I CAN SEND NEMESIS Q TO THEM AND SHOW YOU IMAGES OF THE PLACE. IS THAT GOOD ENOUGH?

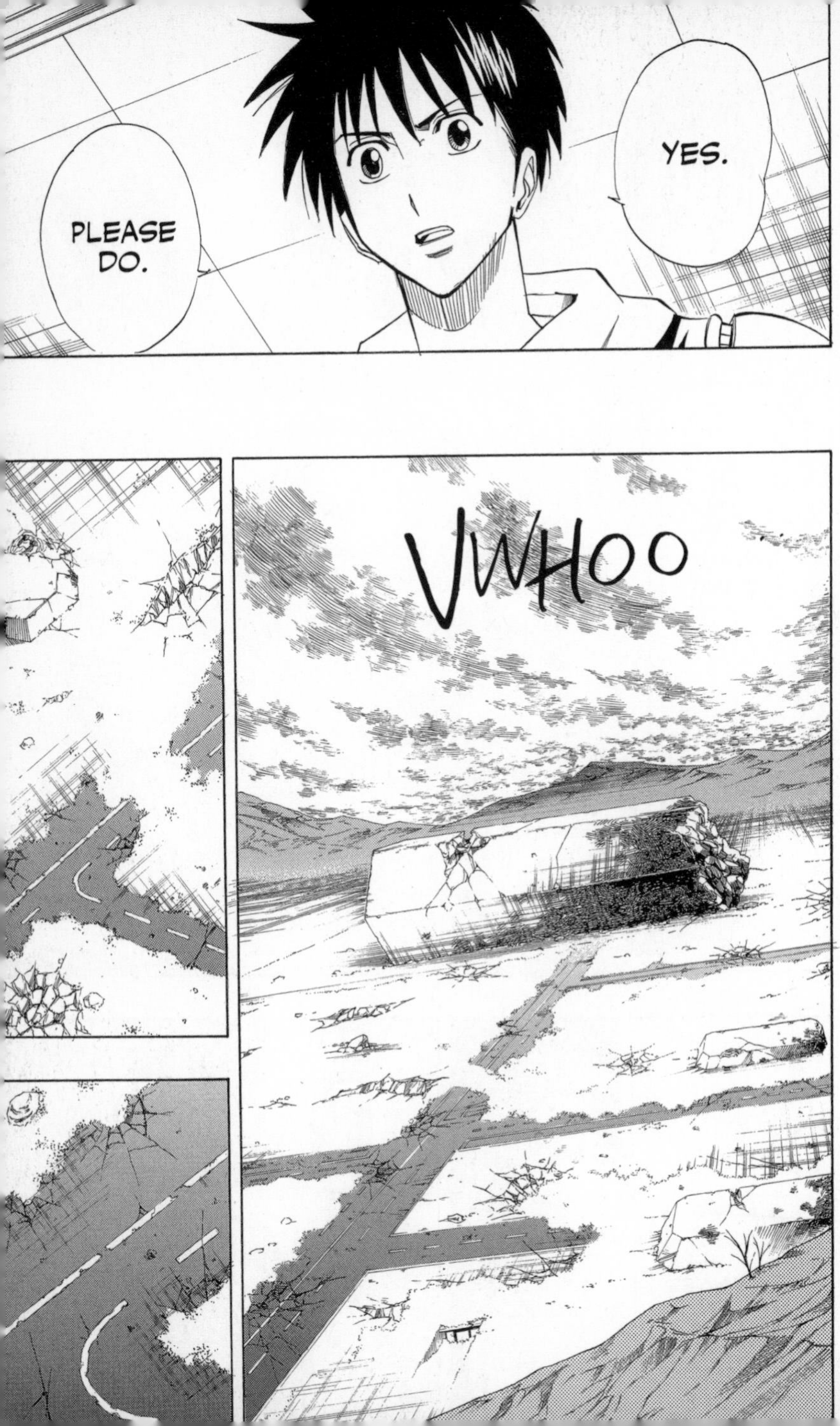
YES.
PLEASE DO.
VWHOO

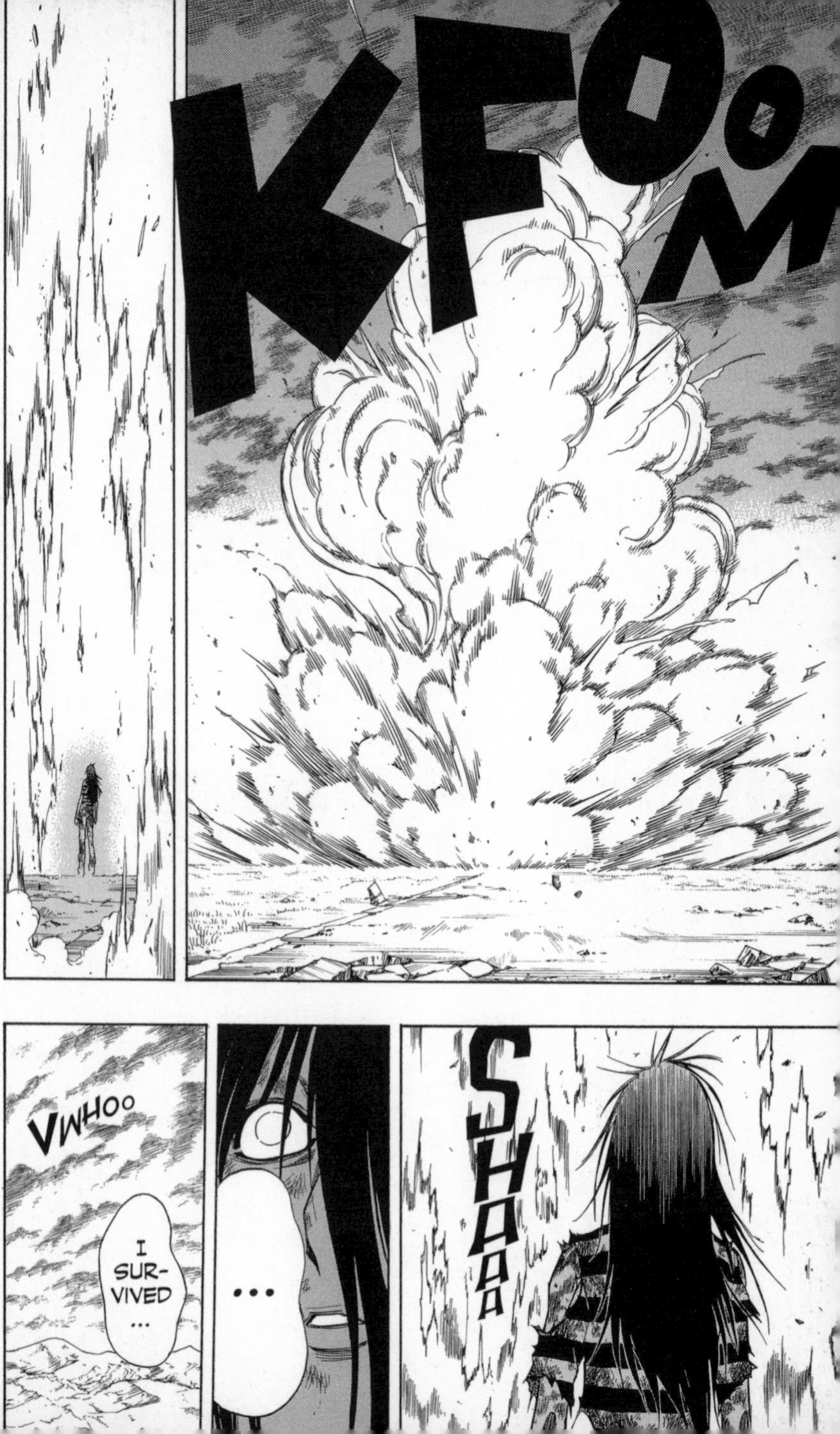
KFOOM
SHAAA
...
VWHOO
I SURVIVED ...

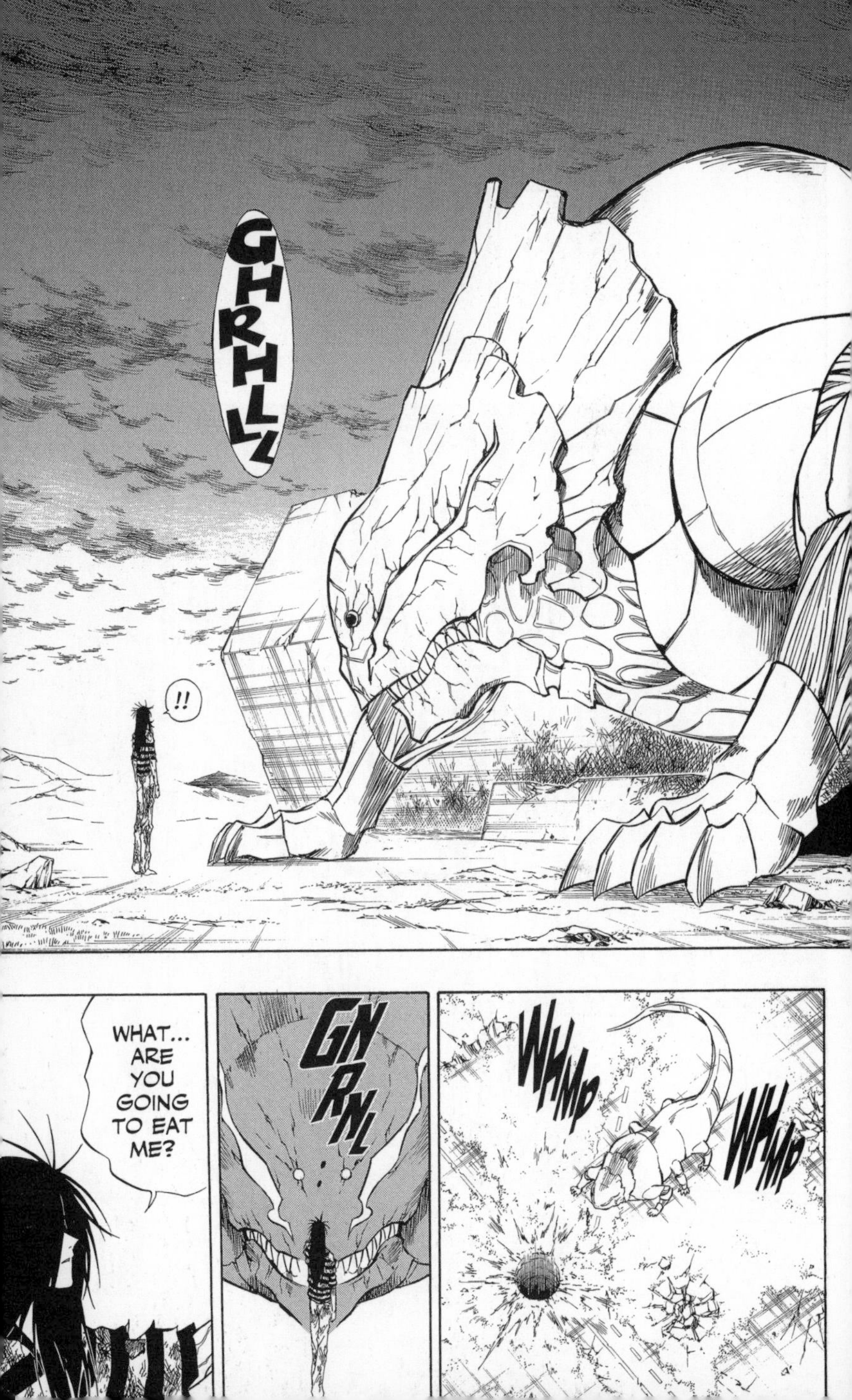
GHRHLL
!!
WHMP
WHMP
GNRNL
WHAT... ARE YOU GOING TO EAT ME?

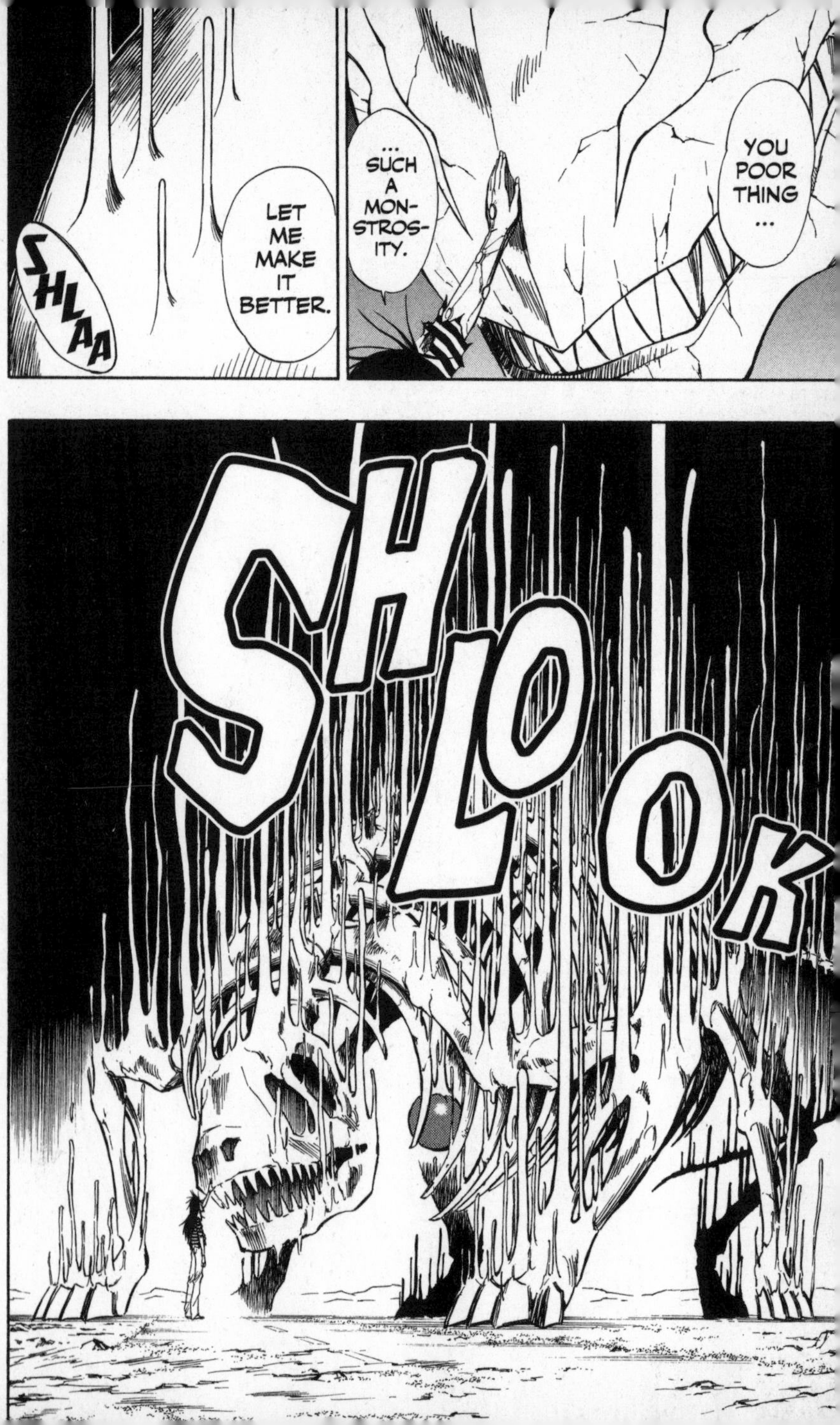
YOU POOR THING ...
... SUCH A MON-STROS-ITY.
LET ME MAKE IT BETTER.
SHLAA
SHLOOK

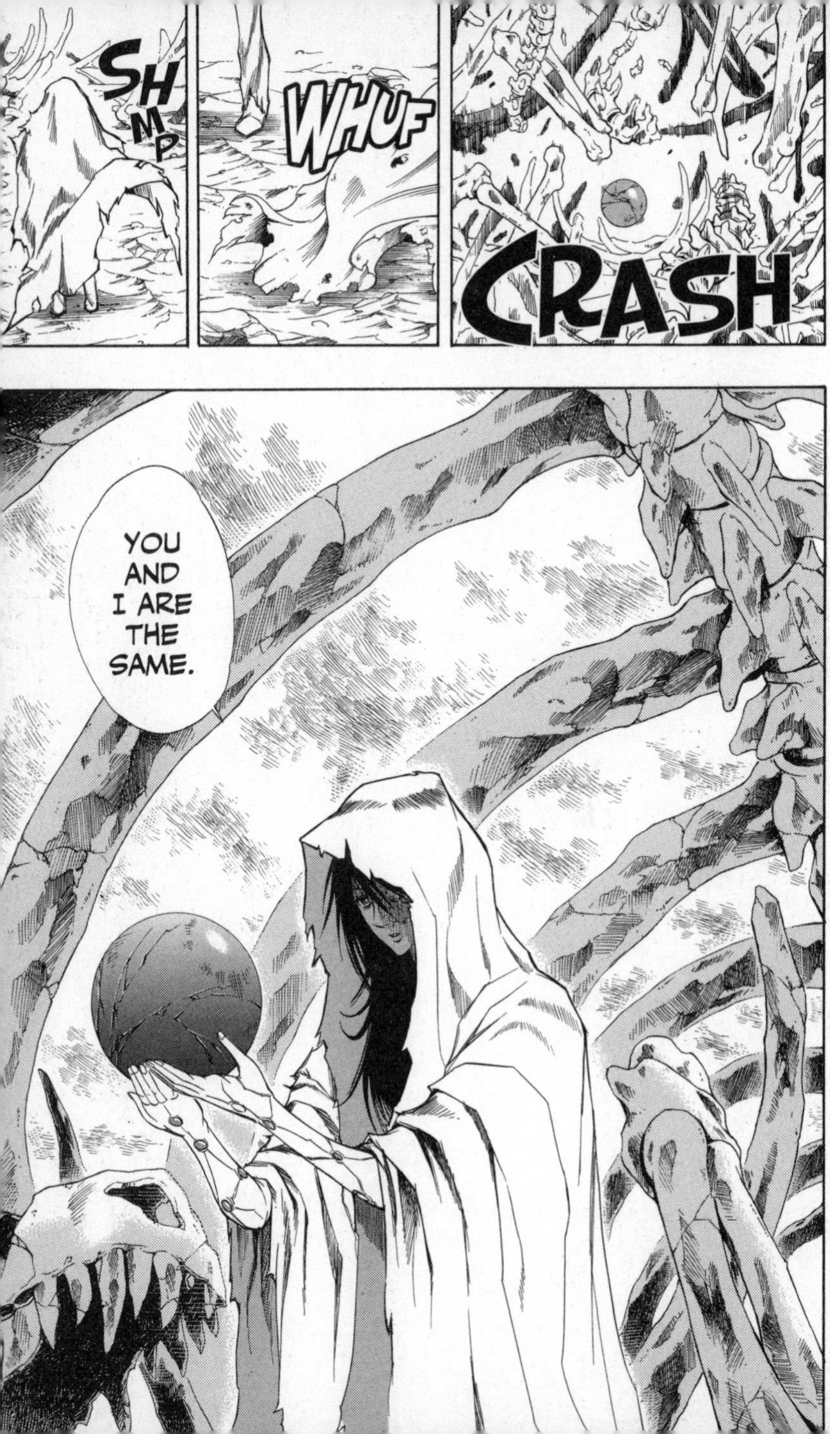
CRASH
WHUF
SHMP
YOU AND I ARE THE SAME.

Mutters and mumblings...

MOVIES I'VE SEEN RECENTLY

AVATAR – THE INITIAL IMPACT AND SATISFACTION WERE INCREDIBLE.
THE 3D MADE IT ALL THE MORE IMMERSIVE.
DISNEY'S A CHRISTMAS CAROL – BY CONTRAST, THE 3D ACTUALLY
DISTANCED THE AUDIENCE. A CHILDREN'S MOVIE THAT SCARES CHILDREN.
GOLDEN SLUMBER – THE PRODUCTION AND INTERPOLATION OF
FORESHADOWING WERE VERY MODERN AND BEAUTIFULLY DONE.
A MOVIE I'D LIKE TO SEE AGAIN.

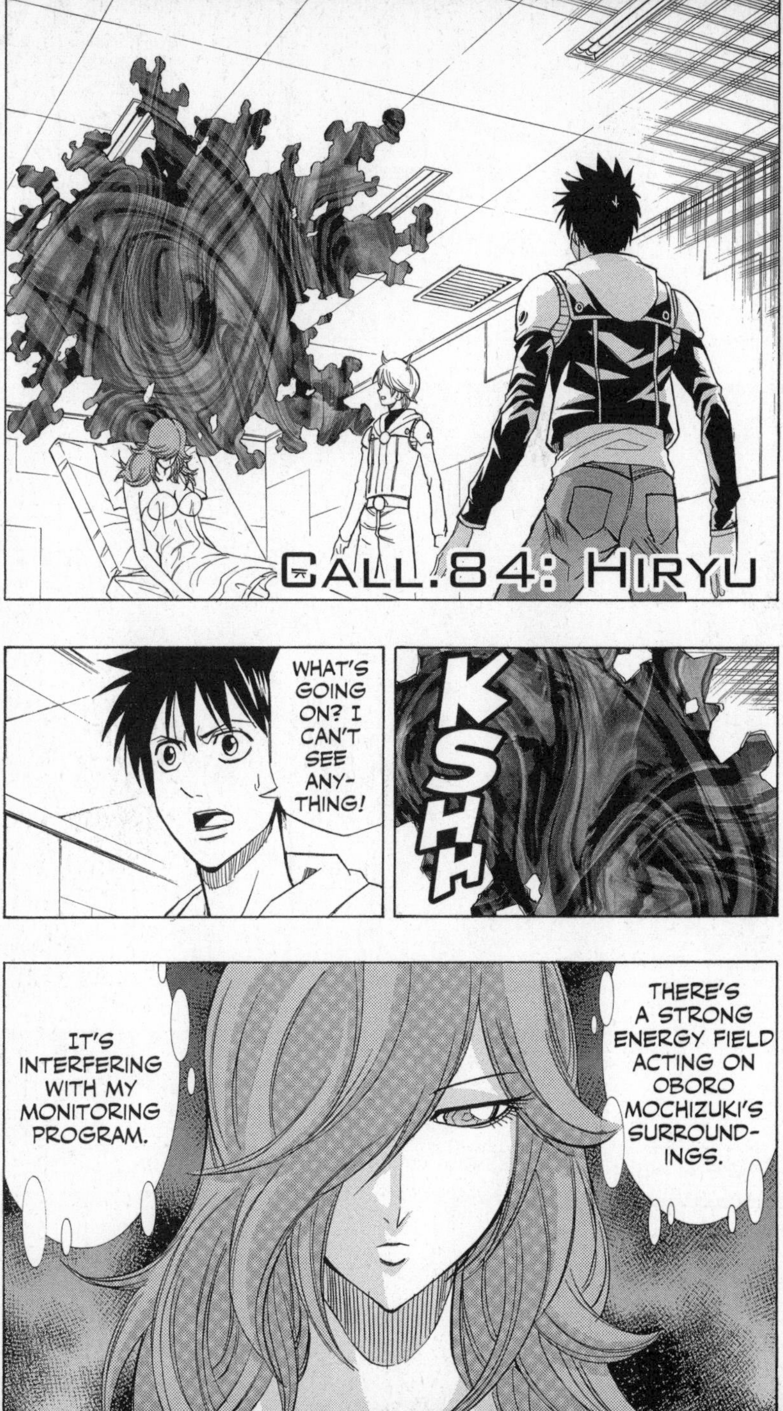
CALL.84: HIRYU
KSHH
WHAT'S GOING ON? I CAN'T SEE ANYTHING!
THERE'S A STRONG ENERGY FIELD ACTING ON OBORO MOCHIZUKI'S SURROUNDINGS.
IT'S INTERFERING WITH MY MONITORING PROGRAM.

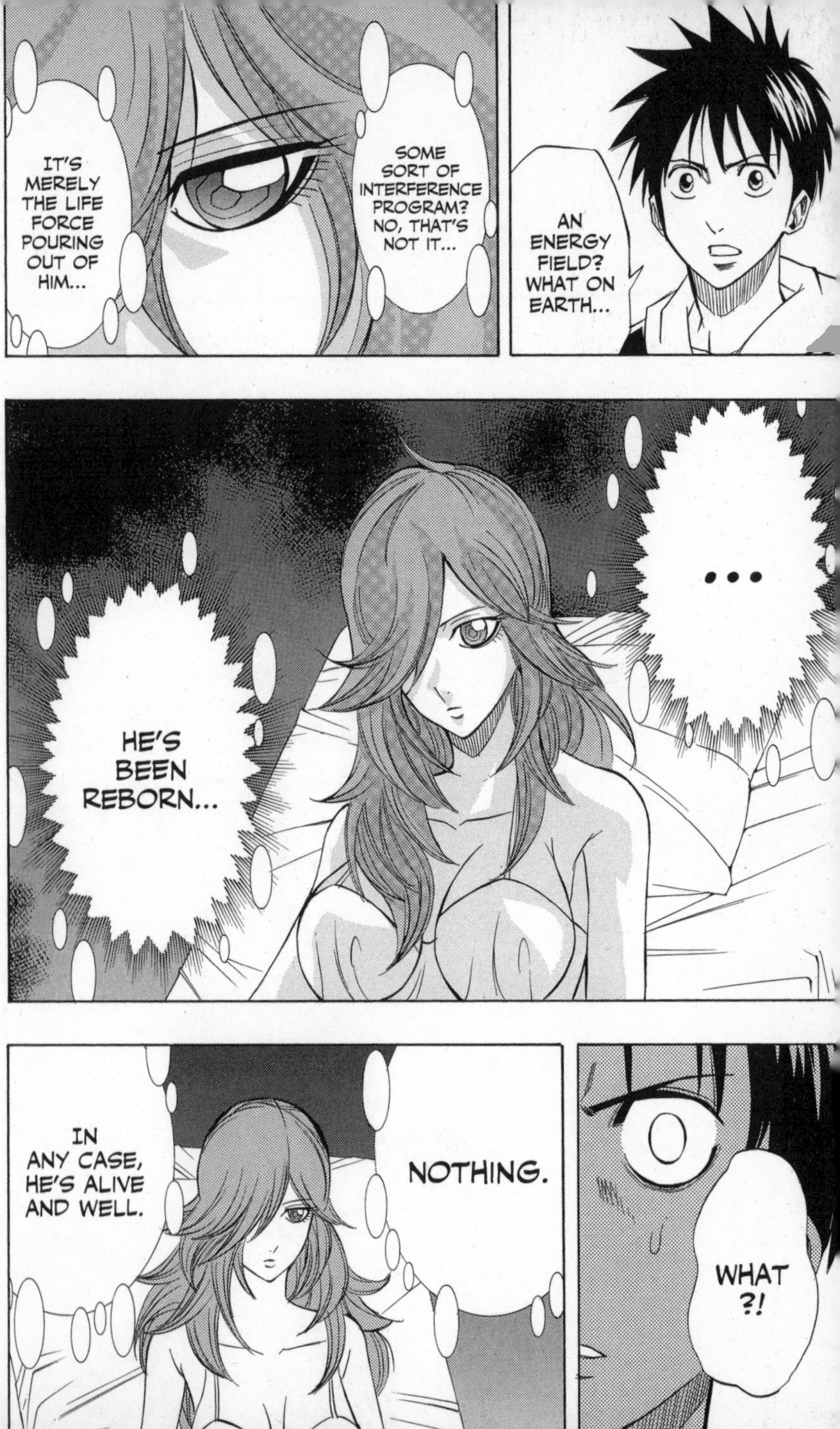
AN ENERGY FIELD? WHAT ON EARTH...
SOME SORT OF INTERFERENCE PROGRAM? NO, THAT'S NOT IT...
IT'S MERELY THE LIFE FORCE POURING OUT OF HIM...
...
HE'S BEEN REBORN...
WHAT ?!
NOTHING.
IN ANY CASE, HE'S ALIVE AND WELL.

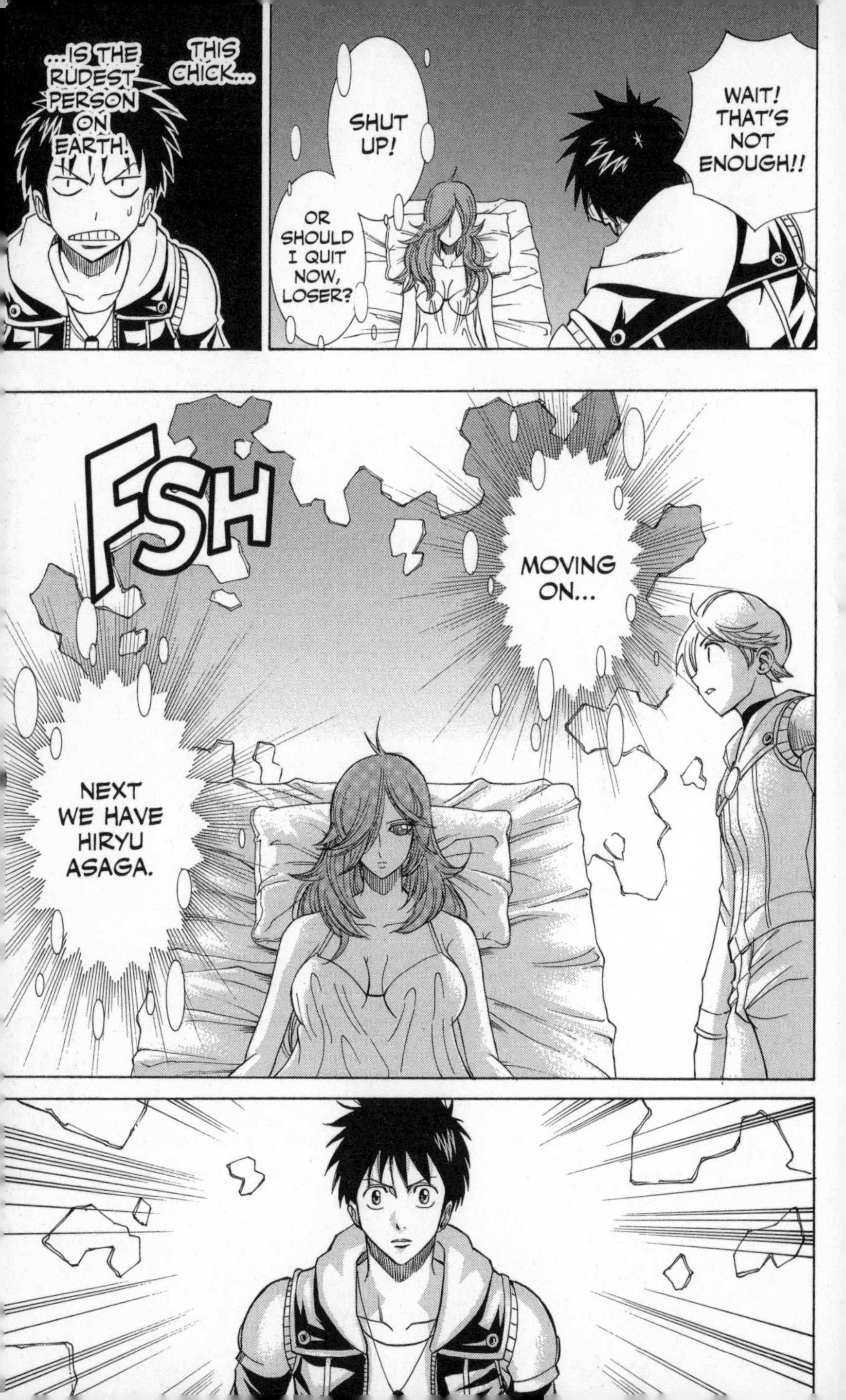
WAIT! THAT'S NOT ENOUGH!!
SHUT UP!
OR SHOULD I QUIT NOW, LOSER?
THIS CHICK...
...IS THE RUDEST PERSON ON EARTH!
FSH
MOVING ON...
NEXT WE HAVE HIRYU ASAGA.

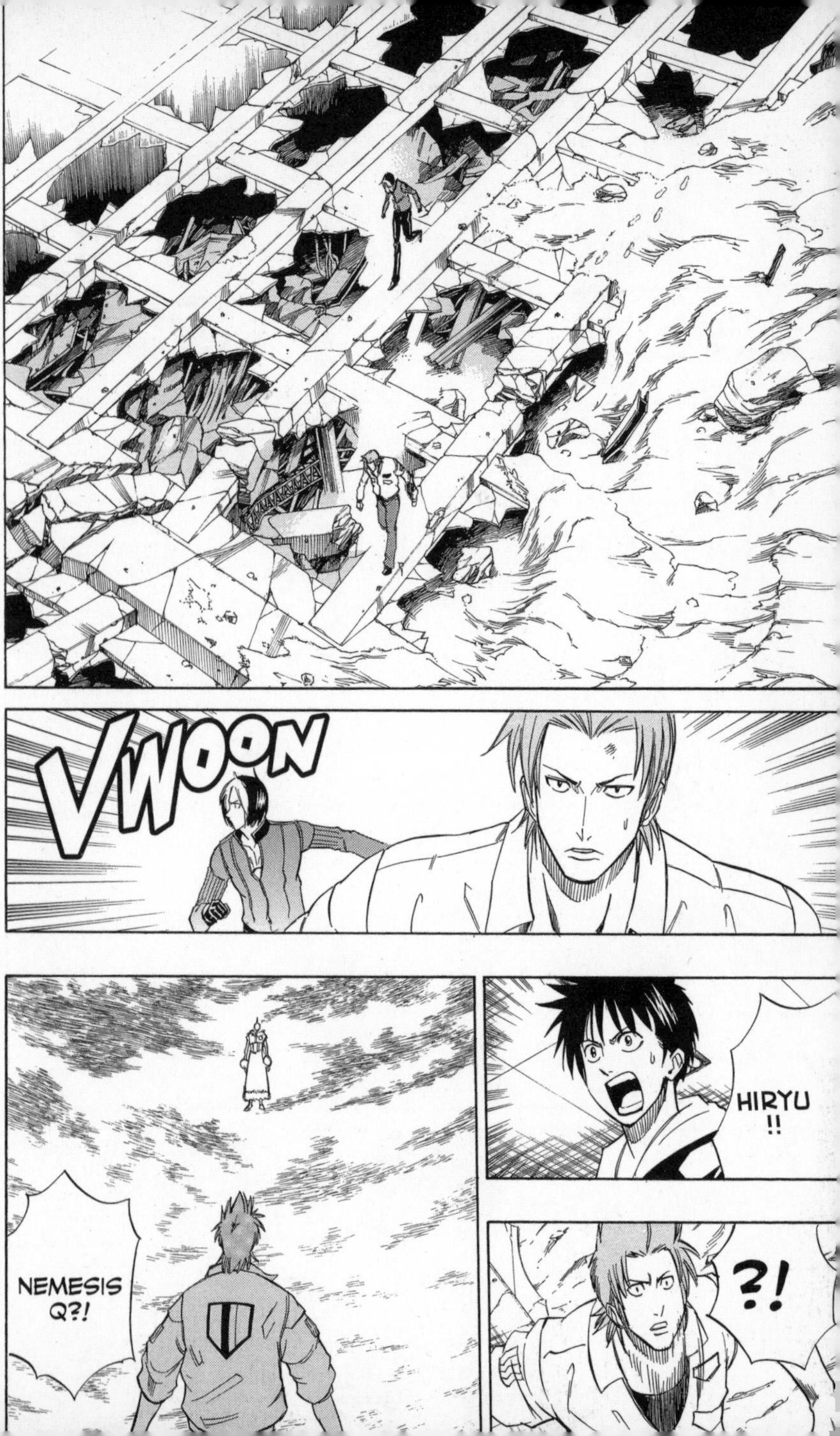
VWOON
HIRYU!!
?!
NEMESIS Q?!

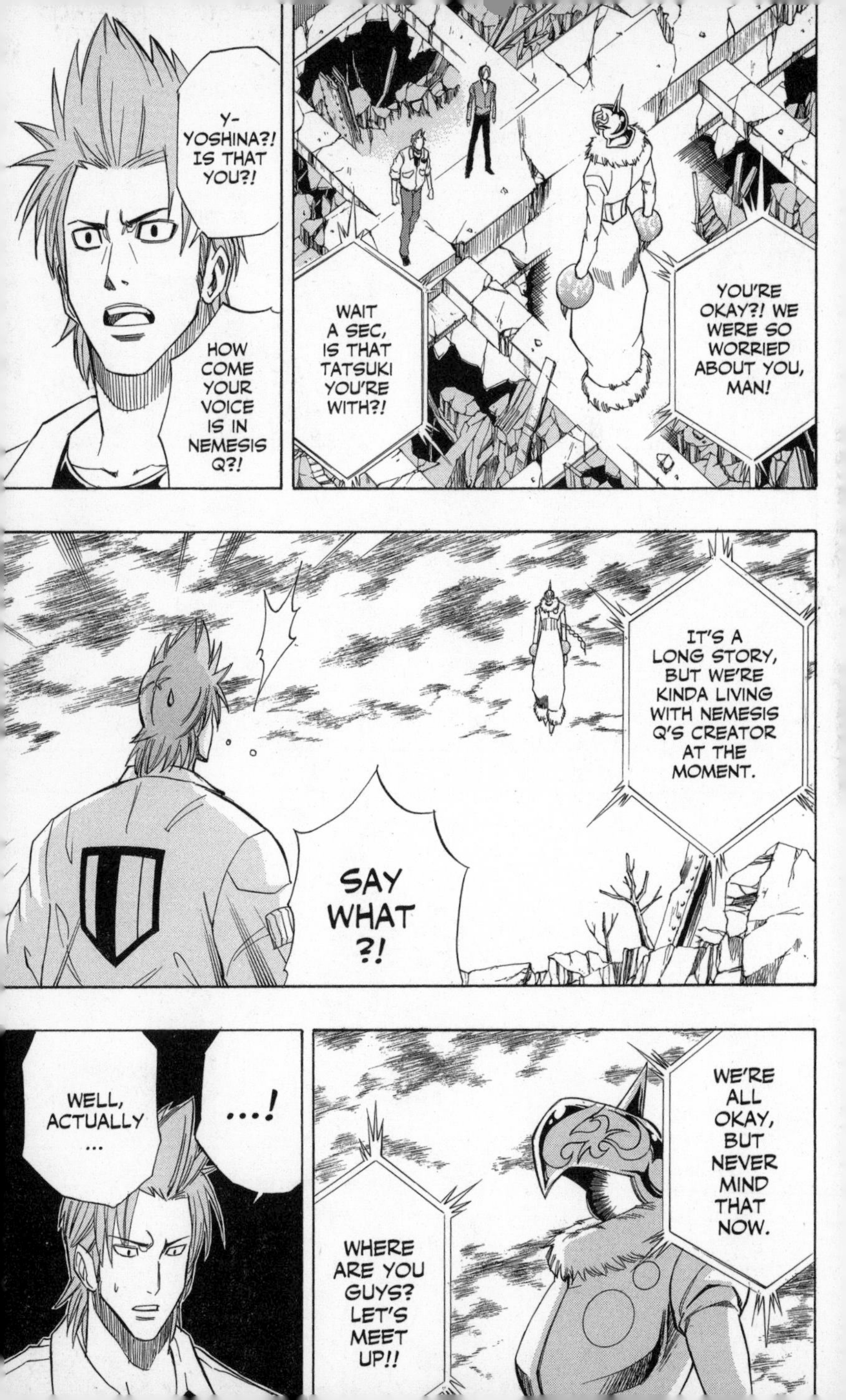
YOU'RE OKAY?! WE WERE SO WORRIED ABOUT YOU, MAN!
WAIT A SEC, IS THAT TATSUKI YOU'RE WITH?!
Y-YOSHINA?! IS THAT YOU?!
HOW COME YOUR VOICE IS IN NEMESIS Q?!
IT'S A LONG STORY, BUT WE'RE KINDA LIVING WITH NEMESIS Q'S CREATOR AT THE MOMENT.
SAY WHAT?!
WE'RE ALL OKAY, BUT NEVER MIND THAT NOW.
WHERE ARE YOU GUYS? LET'S MEET UP!!
...!
WELL, ACTUALLY ...

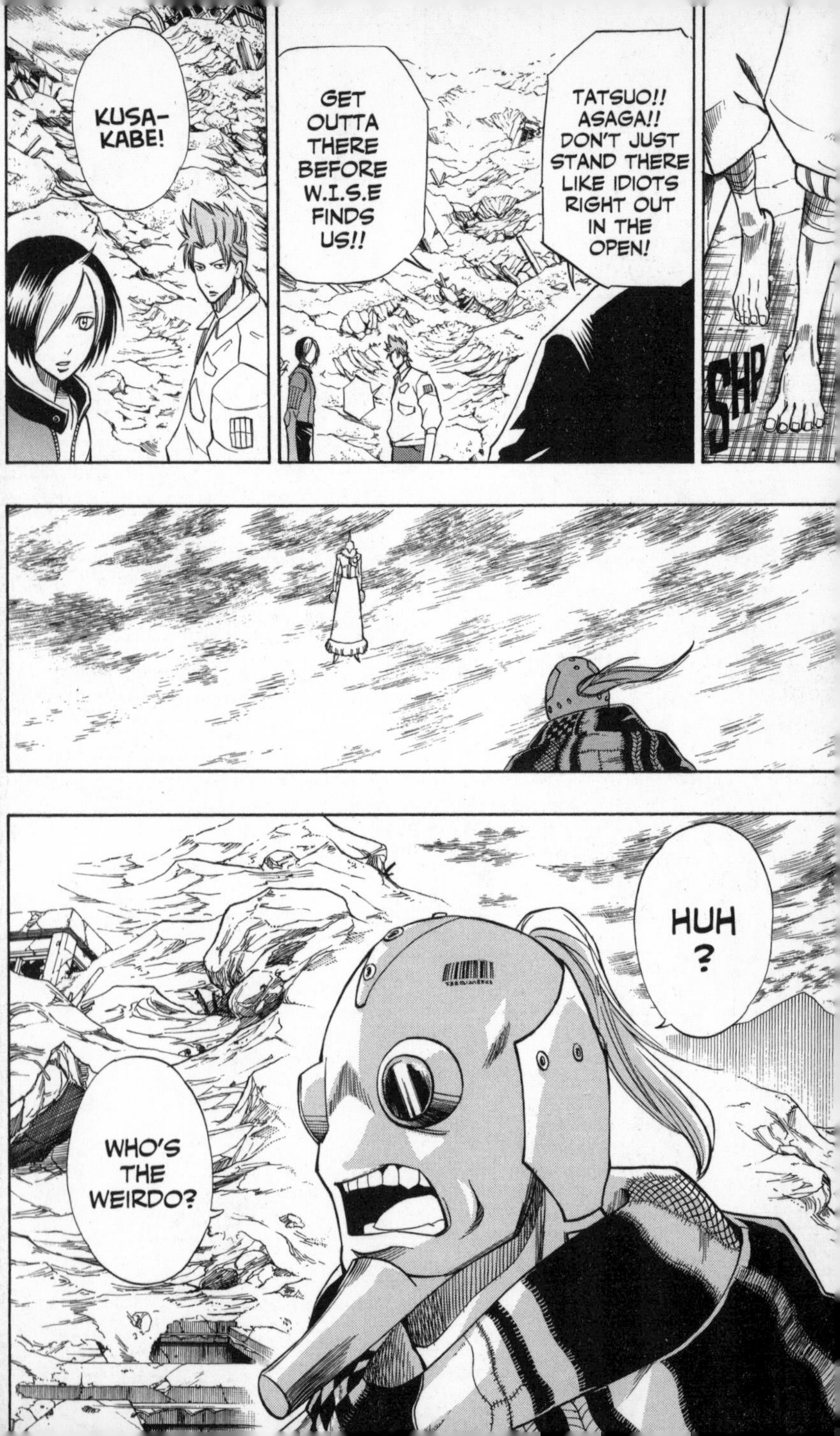
SHP
TATSUO!! ASAGA!! DON'T JUST STAND THERE LIKE IDIOTS RIGHT OUT IN THE OPEN!
GET OUTTA THERE BEFORE W.I.S.E FINDS US!!
KUSA-KABE!
HUH ?
WHO'S THE WEIRDO?

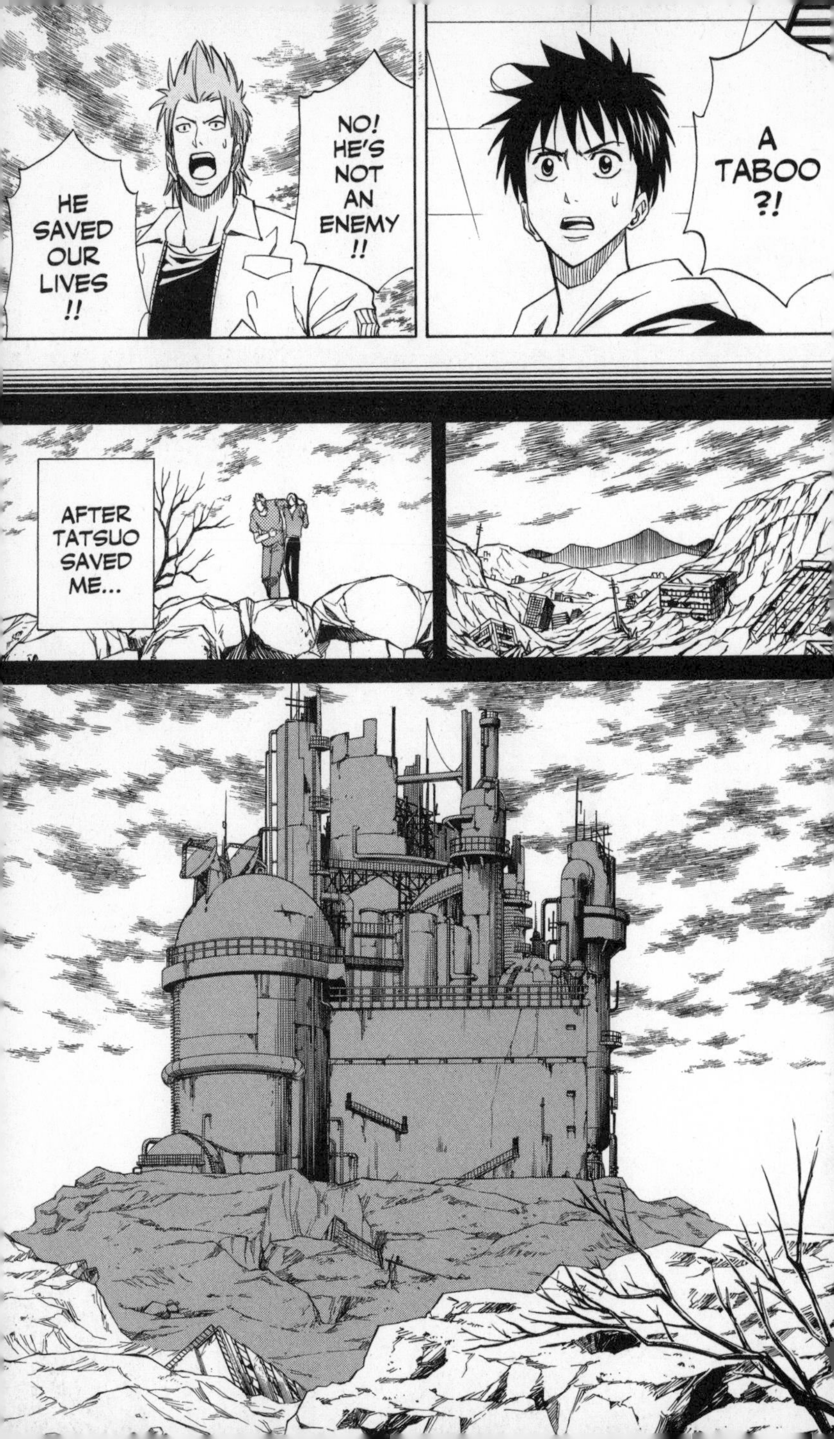
A TABOO ?!
NO! HE'S NOT AN ENEMY !!
HE SAVED OUR LIVES !!
AFTER TATSUO SAVED ME...

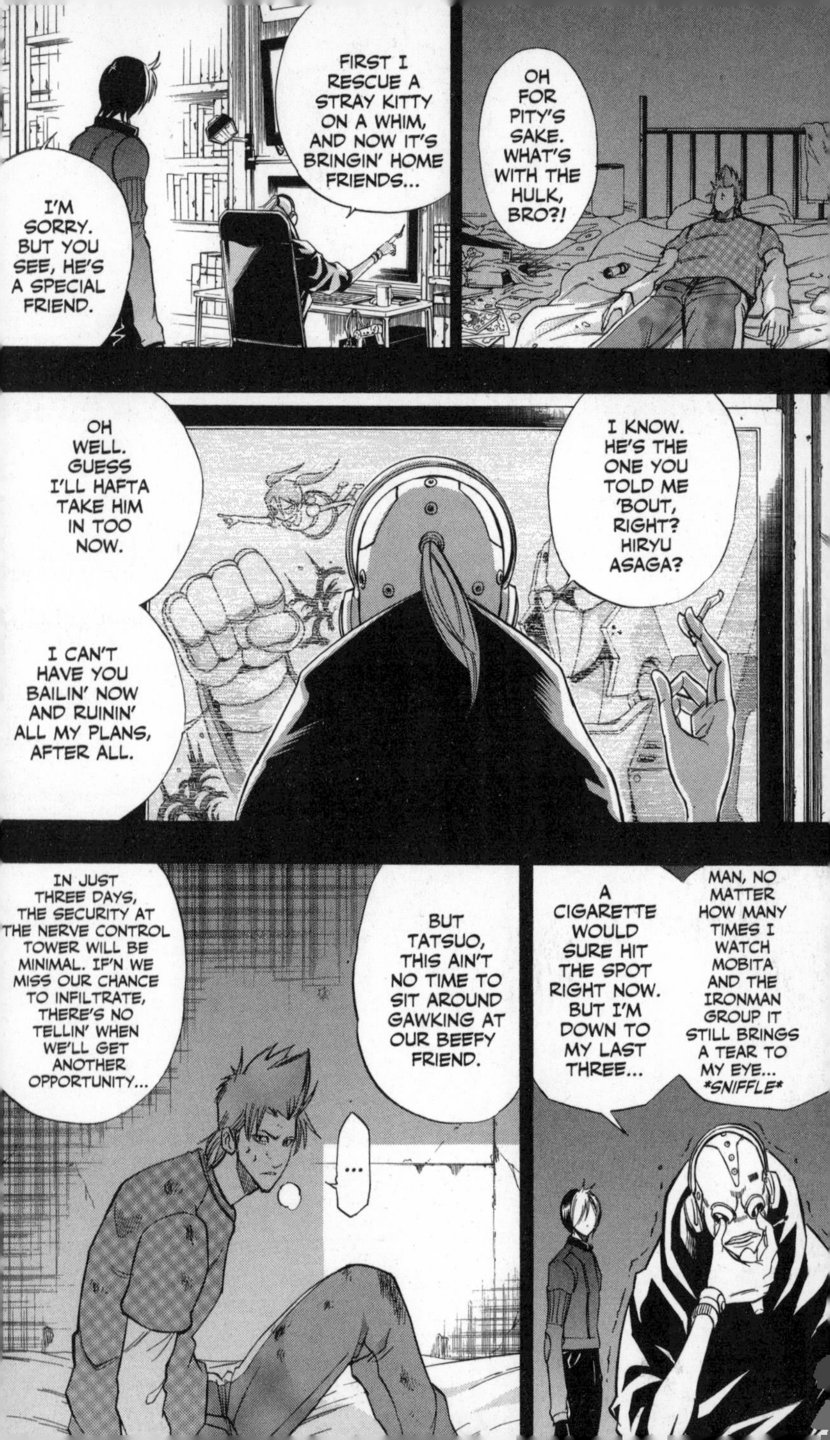
OH FOR PITY'S SAKE. WHAT'S WITH THE HULK, BRO?!
FIRST I RESCUE A STRAY KITTY ON A WHIM, AND NOW IT'S BRINGIN' HOME FRIENDS...
I'M SORRY. BUT YOU SEE, HE'S A SPECIAL FRIEND.
I KNOW. HE'S THE ONE YOU TOLD ME 'BOUT, RIGHT? HIRYU ASAGA?
OH WELL. GUESS I'LL HAFTA TAKE HIM IN TOO NOW.
I CAN'T HAVE YOU BAILIN' NOW AND RUININ' ALL MY PLANS, AFTER ALL.
MAN, NO MATTER HOW MANY TIMES I WATCH MOBITA AND THE IRONMAN GROUP IT STILL BRINGS A TEAR TO MY EYE... *SNIFFLE*
A CIGARETTE WOULD SURE HIT THE SPOT RIGHT NOW. BUT I'M DOWN TO MY LAST THREE...
BUT TATSUO, THIS AIN'T NO TIME TO SIT AROUND GAWKING AT OUR BEEFY FRIEND.
IN JUST THREE DAYS, THE SECURITY AT THE NERVE CONTROL TOWER WILL BE MINIMAL. IF'N WE MISS OUR CHANCE TO INFILTRATE, THERE'S NO TELLIN' WHEN WE'LL GET ANOTHER OPPORTUNITY...
...

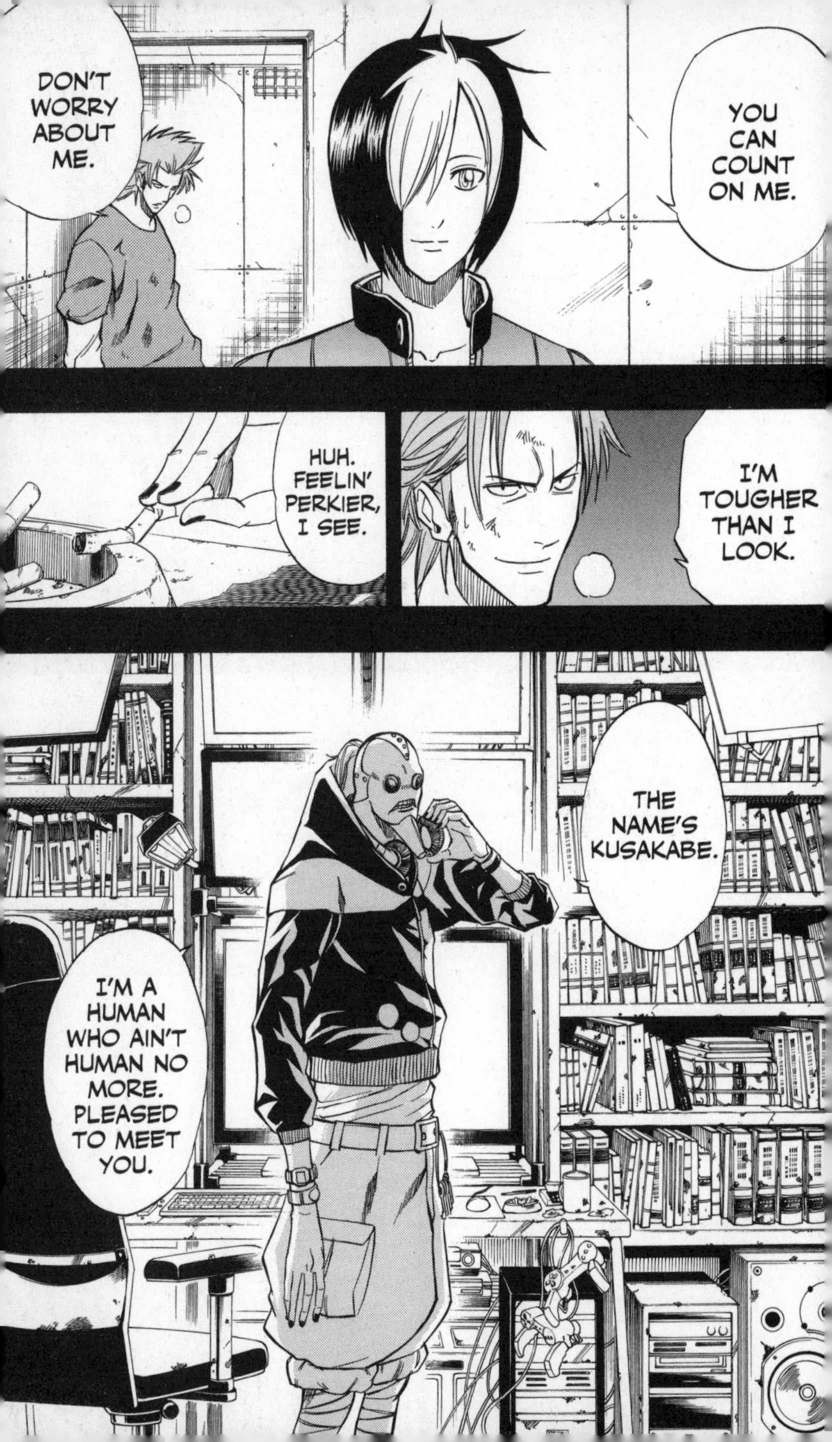
YOU CAN COUNT ON ME.
DON'T WORRY ABOUT ME.
I'M TOUGHER THAN I LOOK.
HUH. FEELIN' PERKIER, I SEE.
THE NAME'S KUSAKABE.
I'M A HUMAN WHO AIN'T HUMAN NO MORE. PLEASED TO MEET YOU.

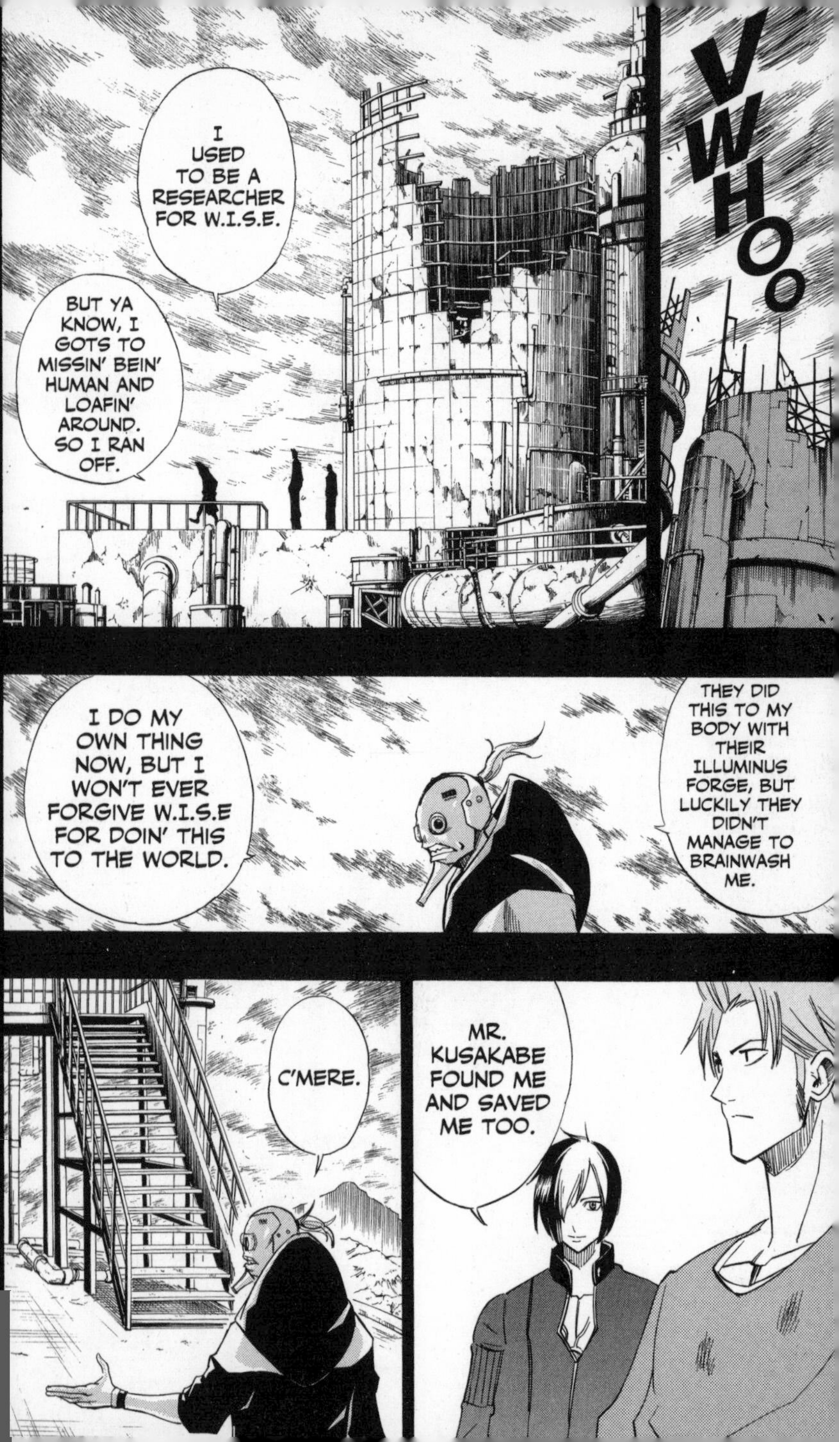
VWHOO
I USED TO BE A RESEARCHER FOR W.I.S.E.
BUT YA KNOW, I GOTS TO MISSIN' BEIN' HUMAN AND LOAFIN' AROUND. SO I RAN OFF.
THEY DID THIS TO MY BODY WITH THEIR ILLUMINUS FORGE, BUT LUCKILY THEY DIDN'T MANAGE TO BRAINWASH ME.
I DO MY OWN THING NOW, BUT I WON'T EVER FORGIVE W.I.S.E FOR DOIN' THIS TO THE WORLD.
MR. KUSAKABE FOUND ME AND SAVED ME TOO.
C'MERE.

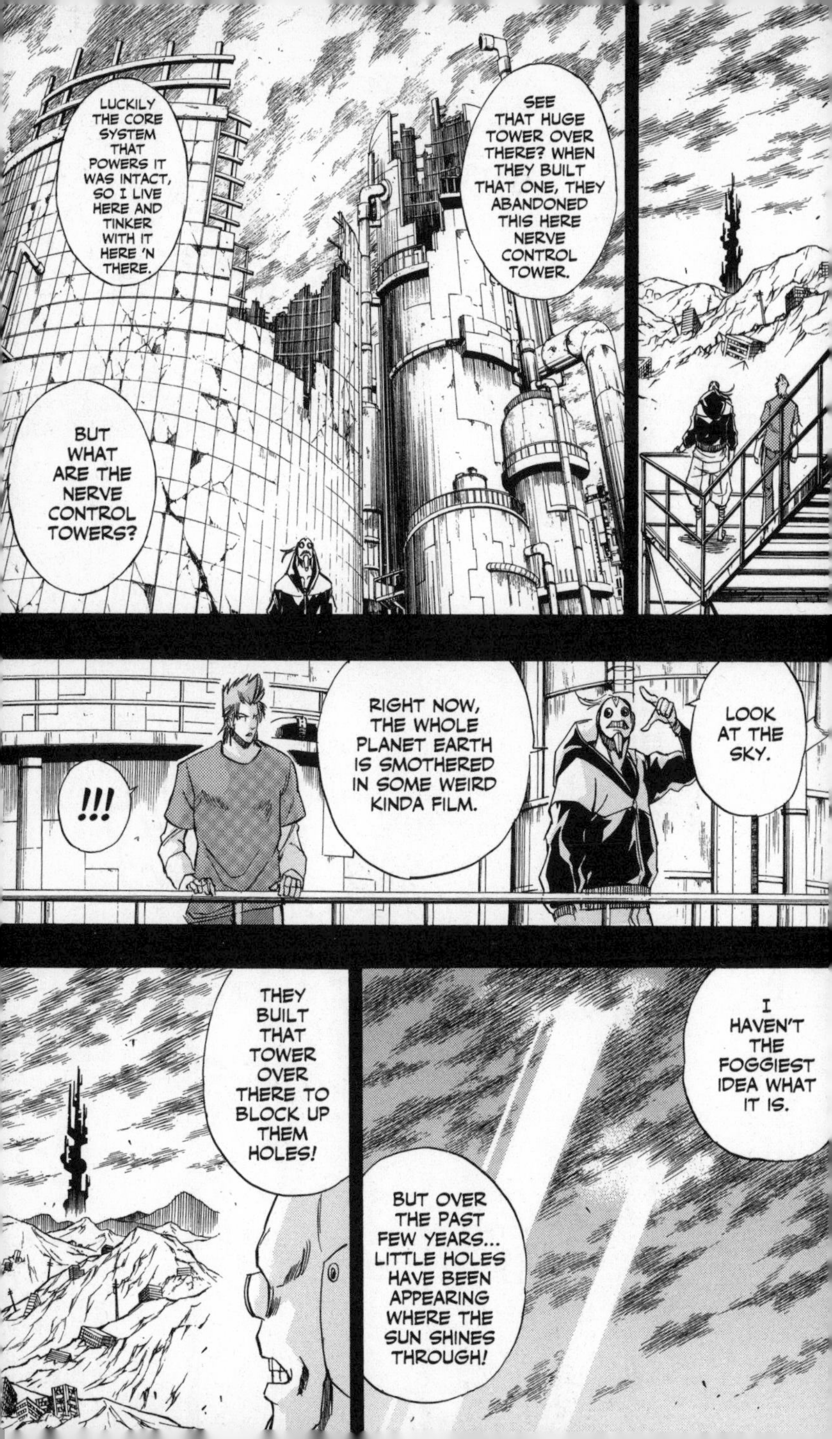
SEE THAT HUGE TOWER OVER THERE? WHEN THEY BUILT THAT ONE, THEY ABANDONED THIS HERE NERVE CONTROL TOWER.
LUCKILY THE CORE SYSTEM THAT POWERS IT WAS INTACT, SO I LIVE HERE AND TINKER WITH IT HERE 'N THERE.
BUT WHAT ARE THE NERVE CONTROL TOWERS?
LOOK AT THE SKY.
RIGHT NOW, THE WHOLE PLANET EARTH IS SMOTHERED IN SOME WEIRD KINDA FILM.
!!!
I HAVEN'T THE FOGGIEST IDEA WHAT IT IS.
BUT OVER THE PAST FEW YEARS... LITTLE HOLES HAVE BEEN APPEARING WHERE THE SUN SHINES THROUGH!
THEY BUILT THAT TOWER OVER THERE TO BLOCK UP THEM HOLES!

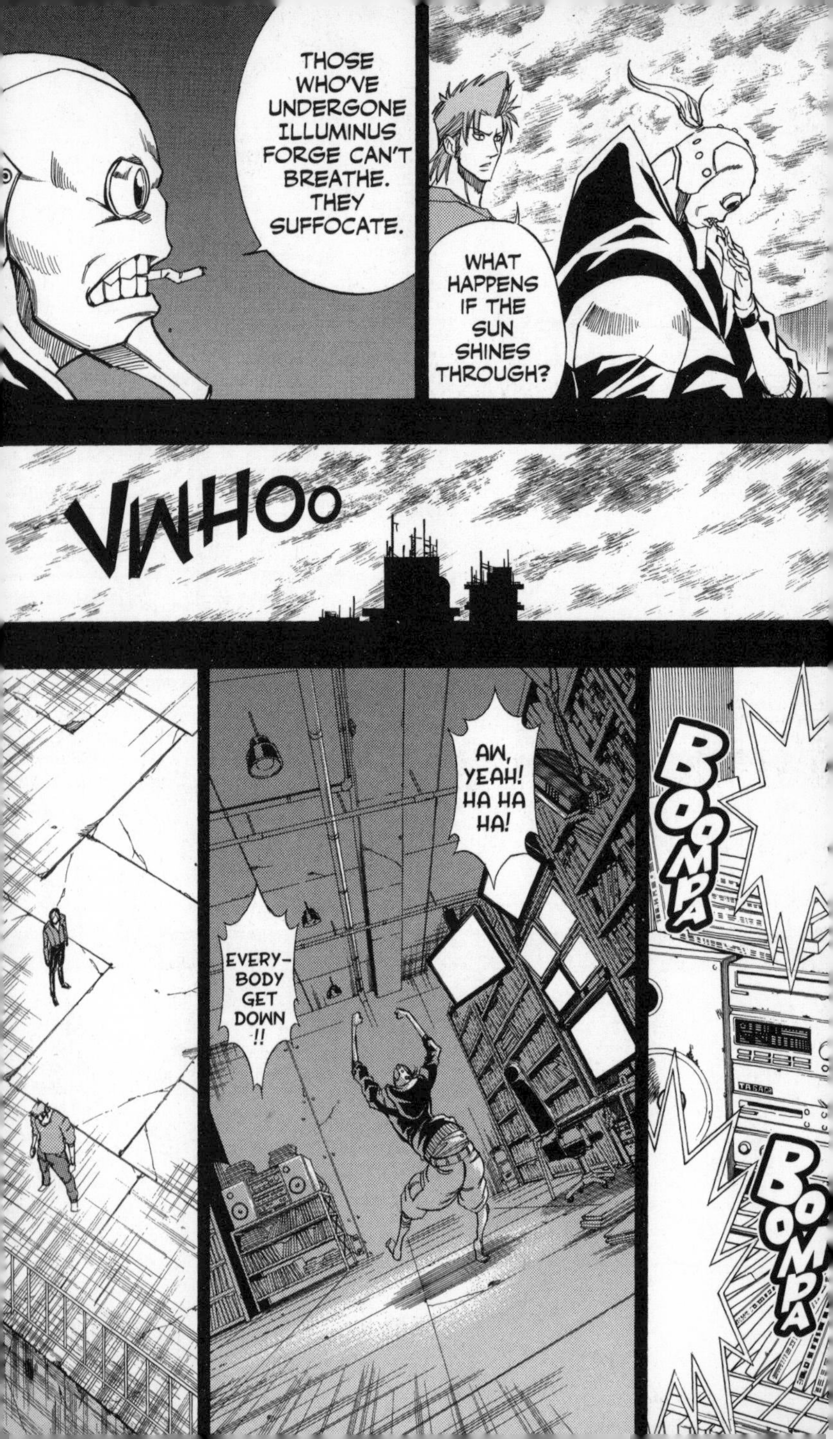
WHAT HAPPENS IF THE SUN SHINES THROUGH?
THOSE WHO'VE UNDERGONE ILLUMINUS FORGE CAN'T BREATHE. THEY SUFFOCATE.
VWHOO
BOOMPA
BOOMPA
AW, YEAH! HA HA HA!
EVERYBODY GET DOWN!!

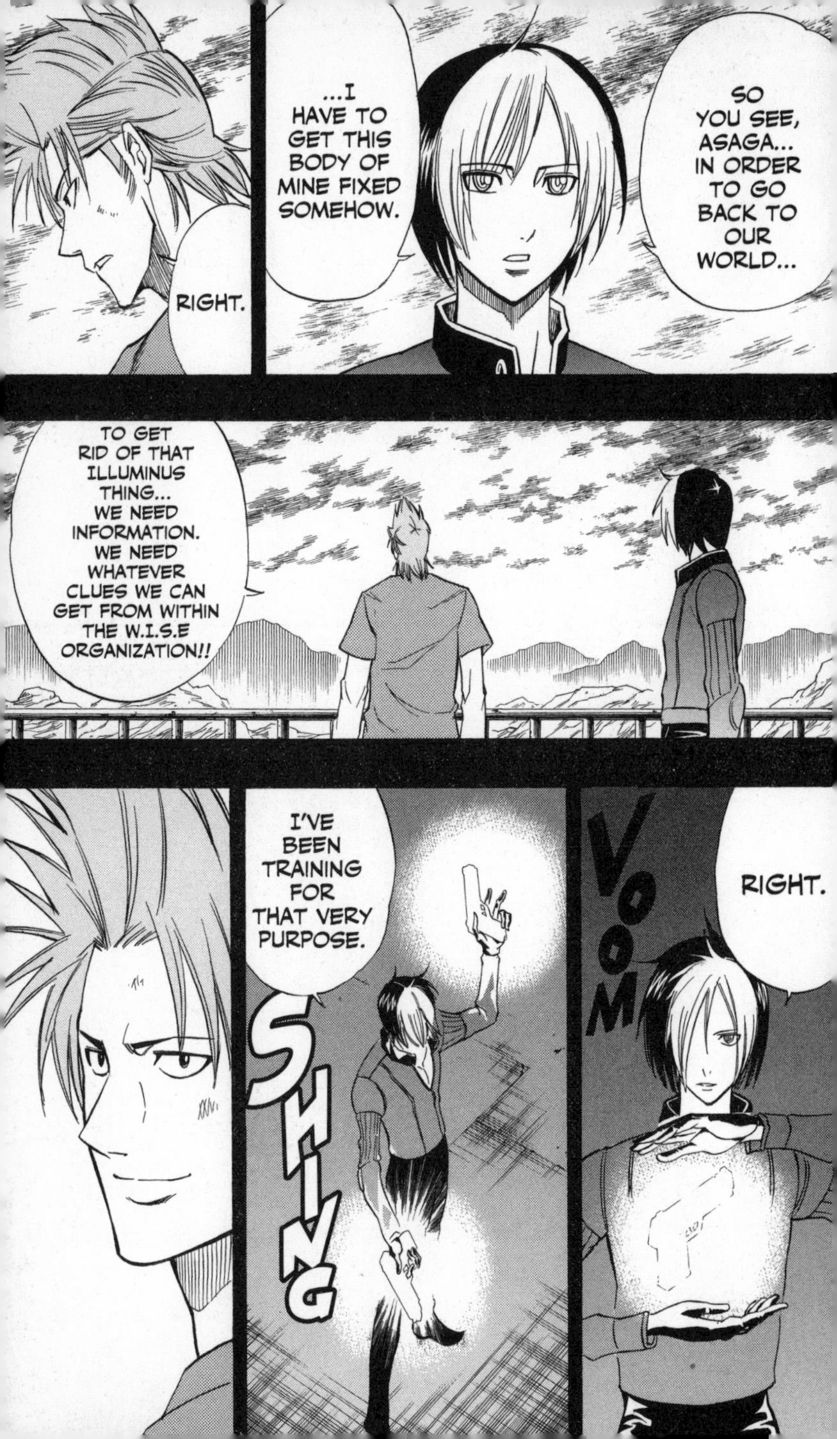
SO YOU SEE, ASAGA... IN ORDER TO GO BACK TO OUR WORLD...
...I HAVE TO GET THIS BODY OF MINE FIXED SOMEHOW.
RIGHT.
TO GET RID OF THAT ILLUMINUS THING... WE NEED INFORMATION. WE NEED WHATEVER CLUES WE CAN GET FROM WITHIN THE W.I.S.E ORGANIZATION!!
RIGHT.
VOOM
I'VE BEEN TRAINING FOR THAT VERY PURPOSE.
SHING

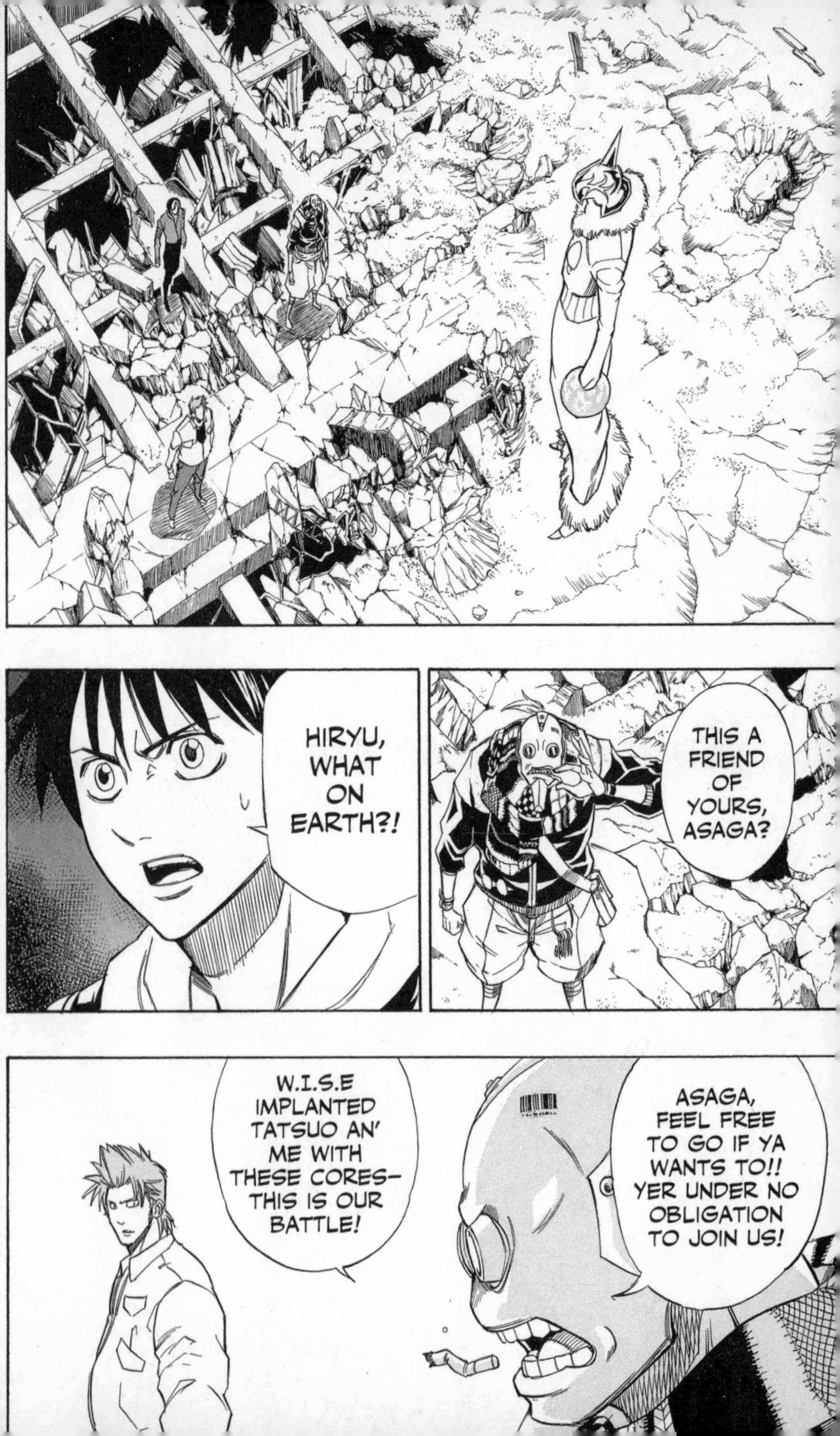
THIS A FRIEND OF YOURS, ASAGA?
HIRYU, WHAT ON EARTH?!
ASAGA, FEEL FREE TO GO IF YA WANTS TO!! YER UNDER NO OBLIGATION TO JOIN US!
W.I.S.E IMPLANTED TATSUO AN' ME WITH THESE CORES—THIS IS OUR BATTLE!

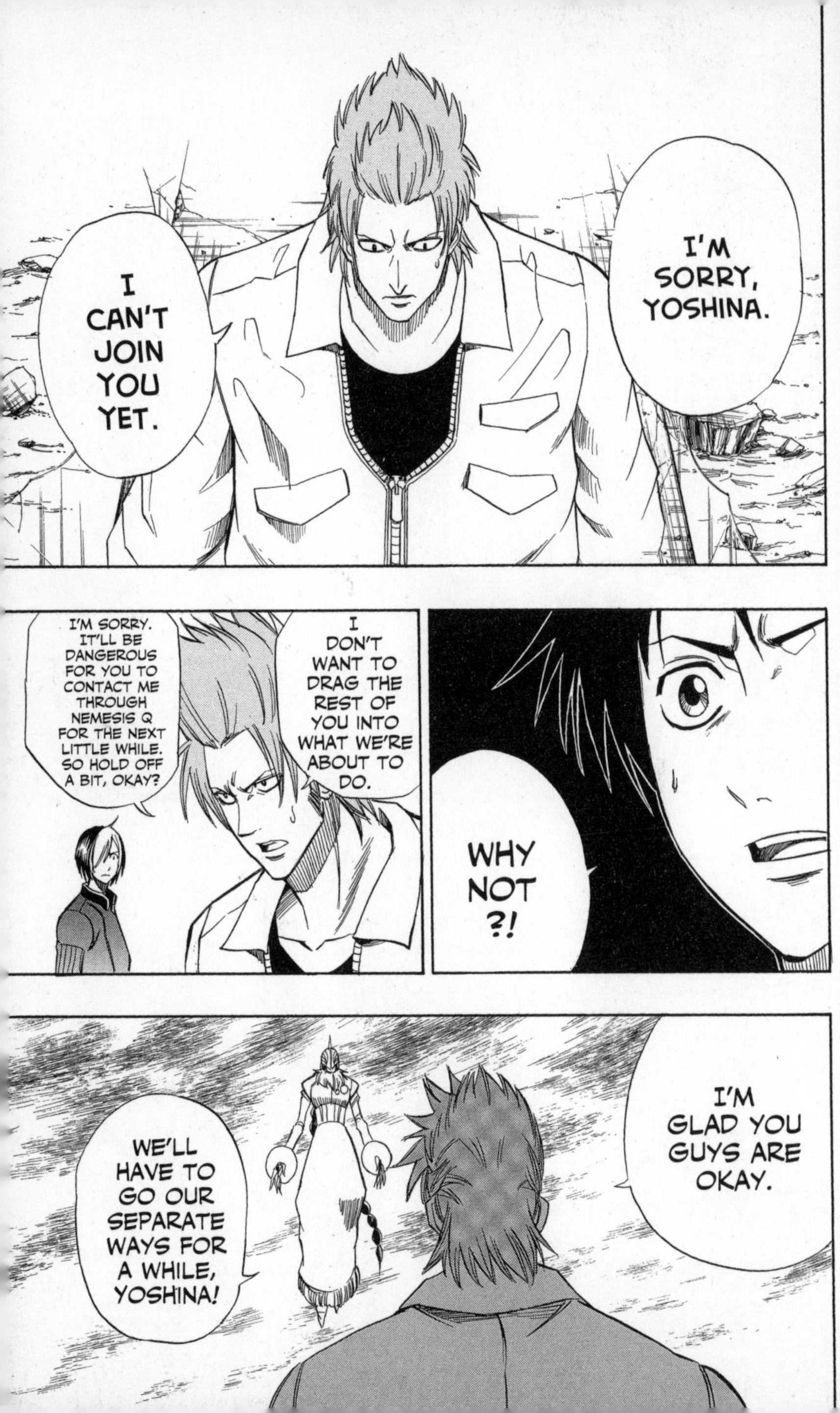
I'M SORRY, YOSHINA.
I CAN'T JOIN YOU YET.
WHY NOT?!
I DON'T WANT TO DRAG THE REST OF YOU INTO WHAT WE'RE ABOUT TO DO.
I'M SORRY. IT'LL BE DANGEROUS FOR YOU TO CONTACT ME THROUGH NEMESIS Q FOR THE NEXT LITTLE WHILE. SO HOLD OFF A BIT, OKAY?
I'M GLAD YOU GUYS ARE OKAY.
WE'LL HAVE TO GO OUR SEPARATE WAYS FOR A WHILE, YOSHINA!

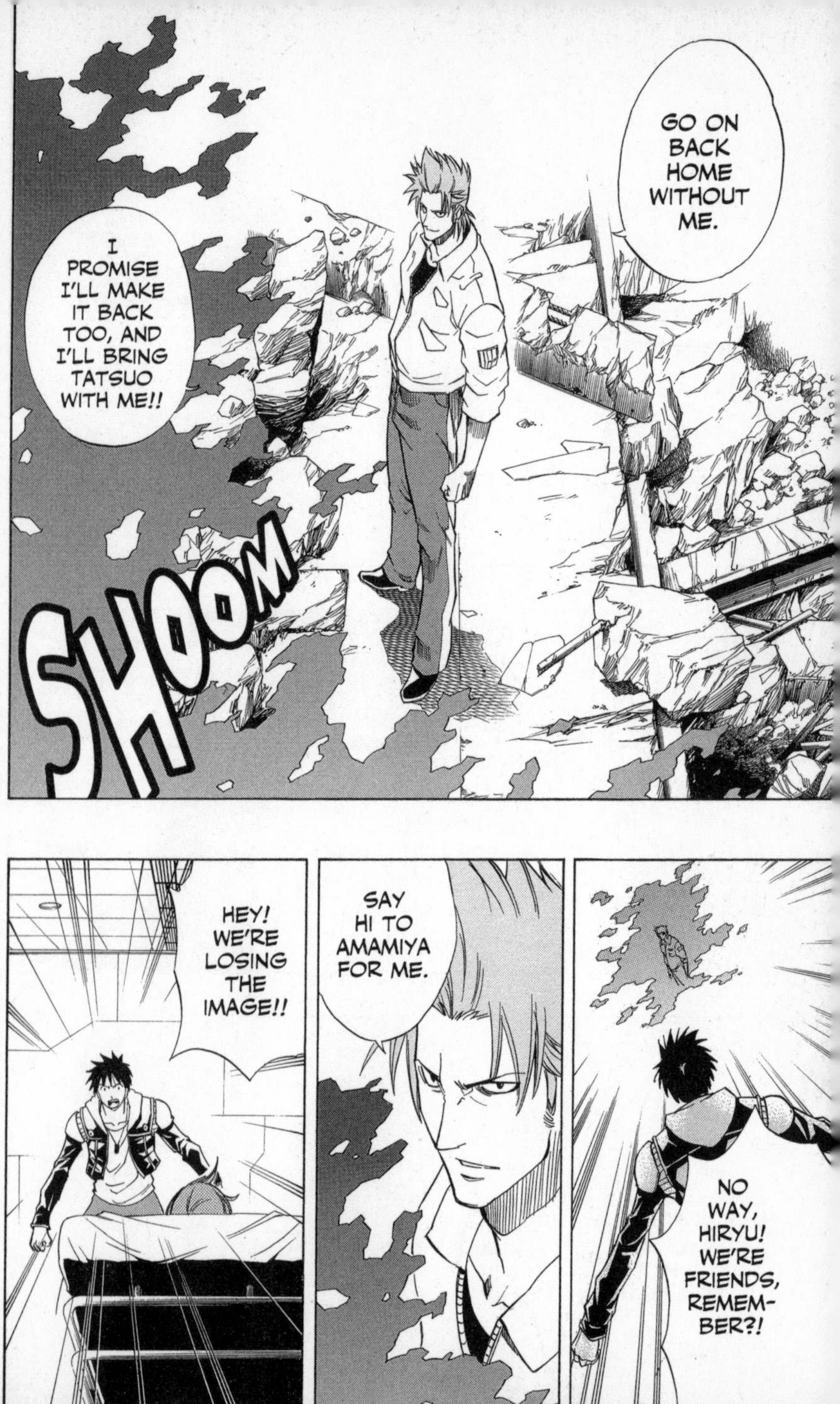
GO ON BACK HOME WITHOUT ME.
I PROMISE I'LL MAKE IT BACK TOO, AND I'LL BRING TATSUO WITH ME!!
SHOOM
NO WAY, HIRYU! WE'RE FRIENDS, REMEM-BER?!
SAY HI TO AMAMIYA FOR ME.
HEY! WE'RE LOSING THE IMAGE!!

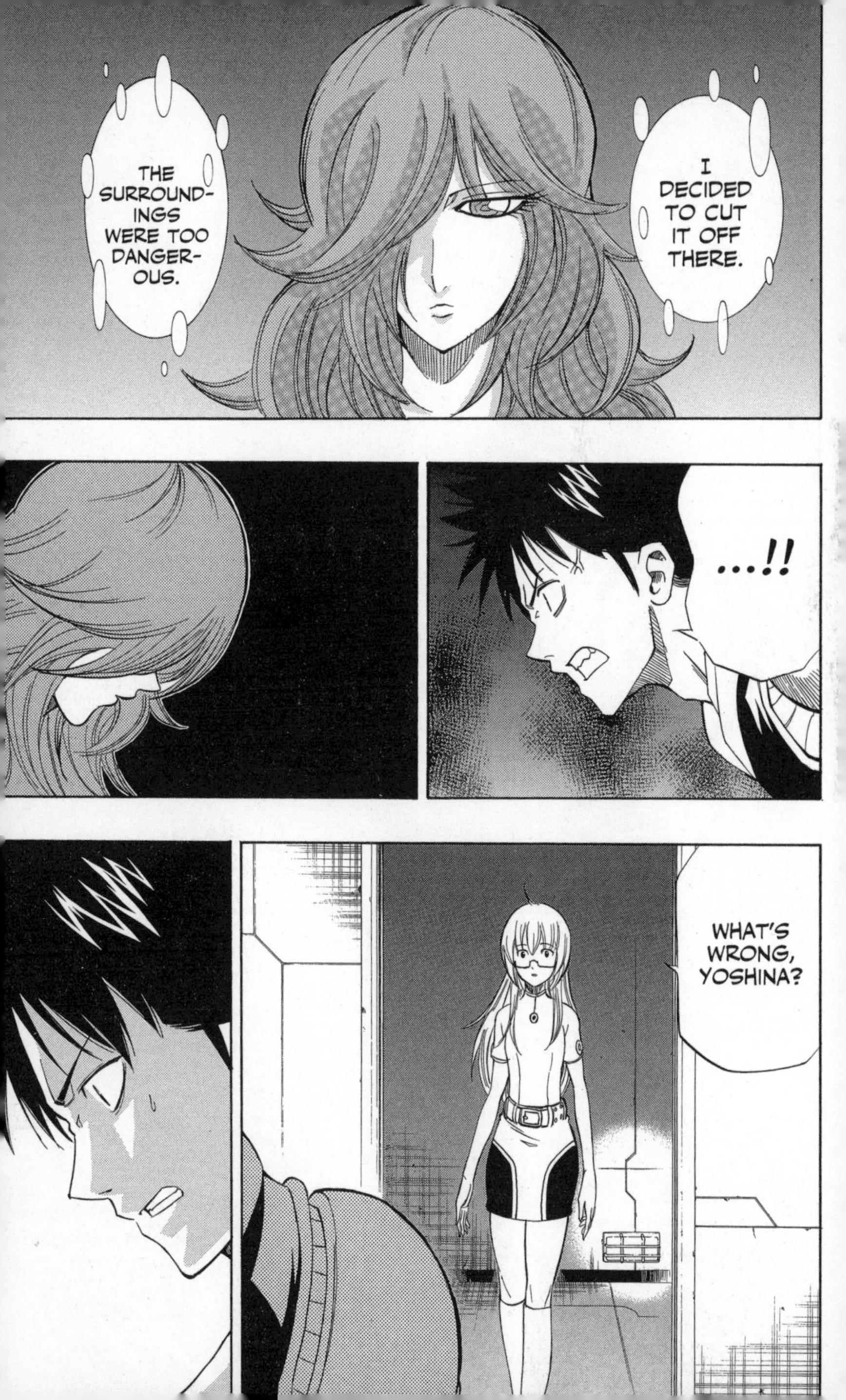
I DECIDED TO CUT IT OFF THERE.
THE SURROUNDINGS WERE TOO DANGEROUS.
...!!
WHAT'S WRONG, YOSHINA?

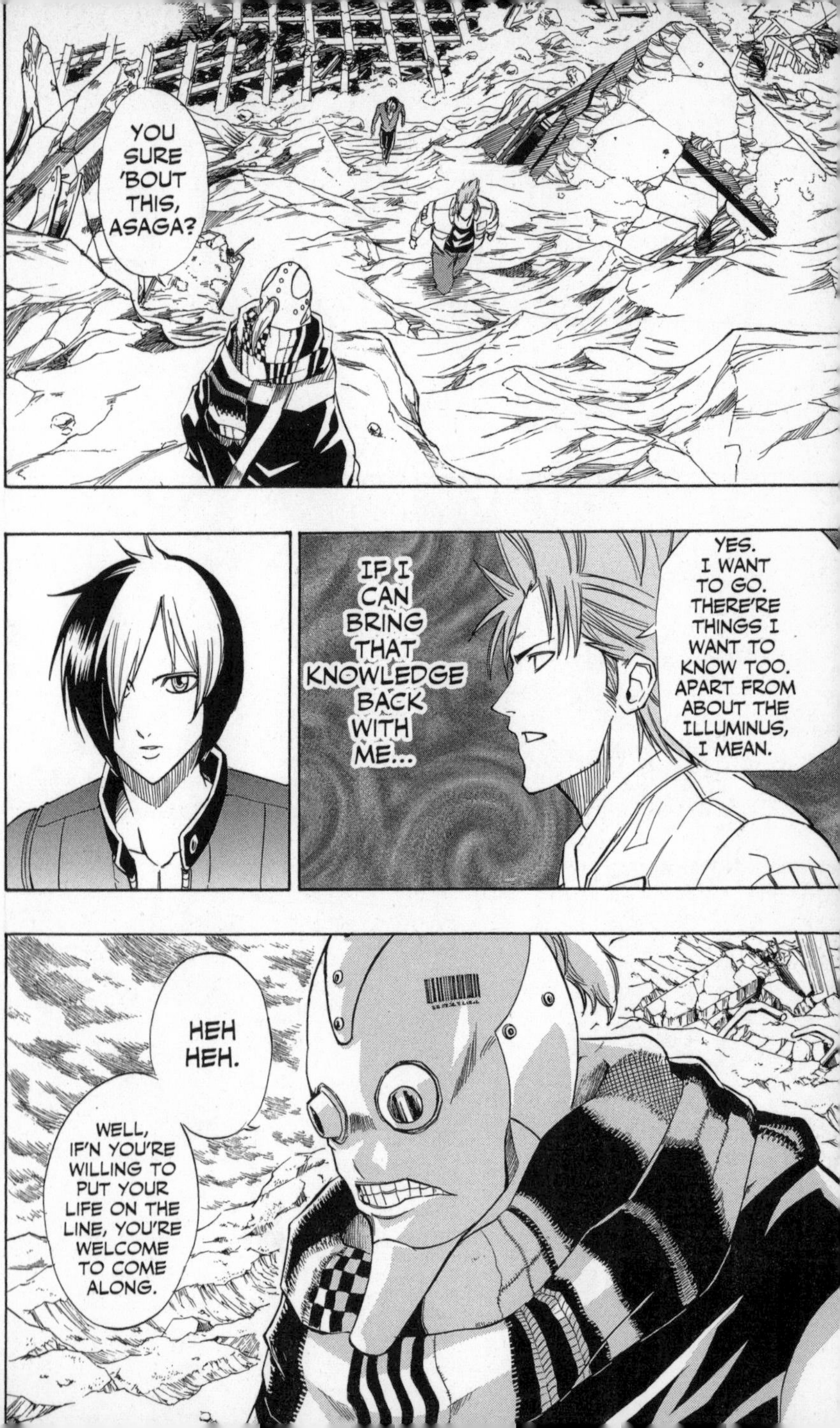
YOU SURE 'BOUT THIS, ASAGA?
YES. I WANT TO GO. THERE'RE THINGS I WANT TO KNOW TOO. APART FROM ABOUT THE ILLUMINUS, I MEAN.
IF I CAN BRING THAT KNOWLEDGE BACK WITH ME...
HEH HEH.
WELL, IF'N YOU'RE WILLING TO PUT YOUR LIFE ON THE LINE, YOU'RE WELCOME TO COME ALONG.

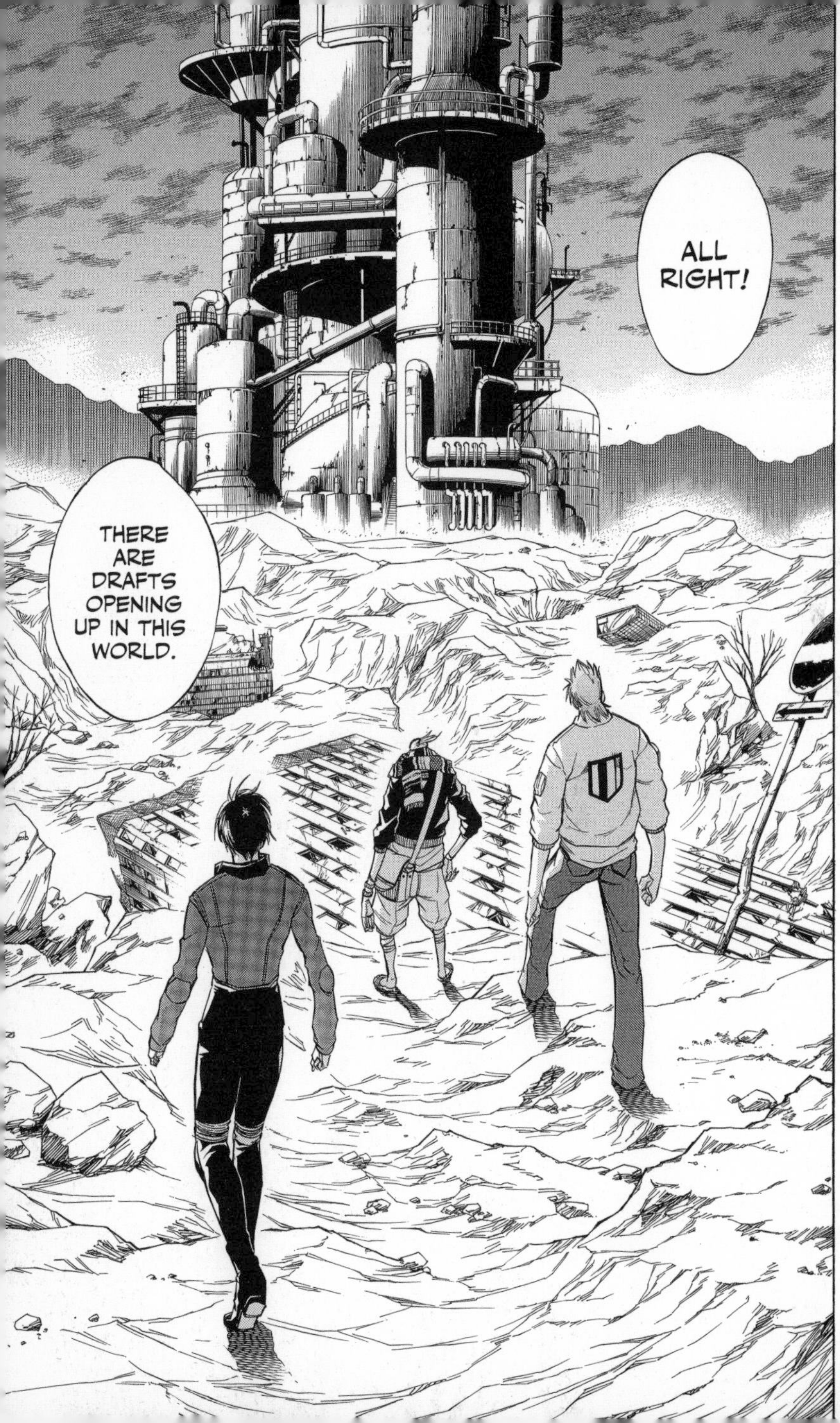
ALL RIGHT!
THERE ARE DRAFTS OPENING UP IN THIS WORLD.

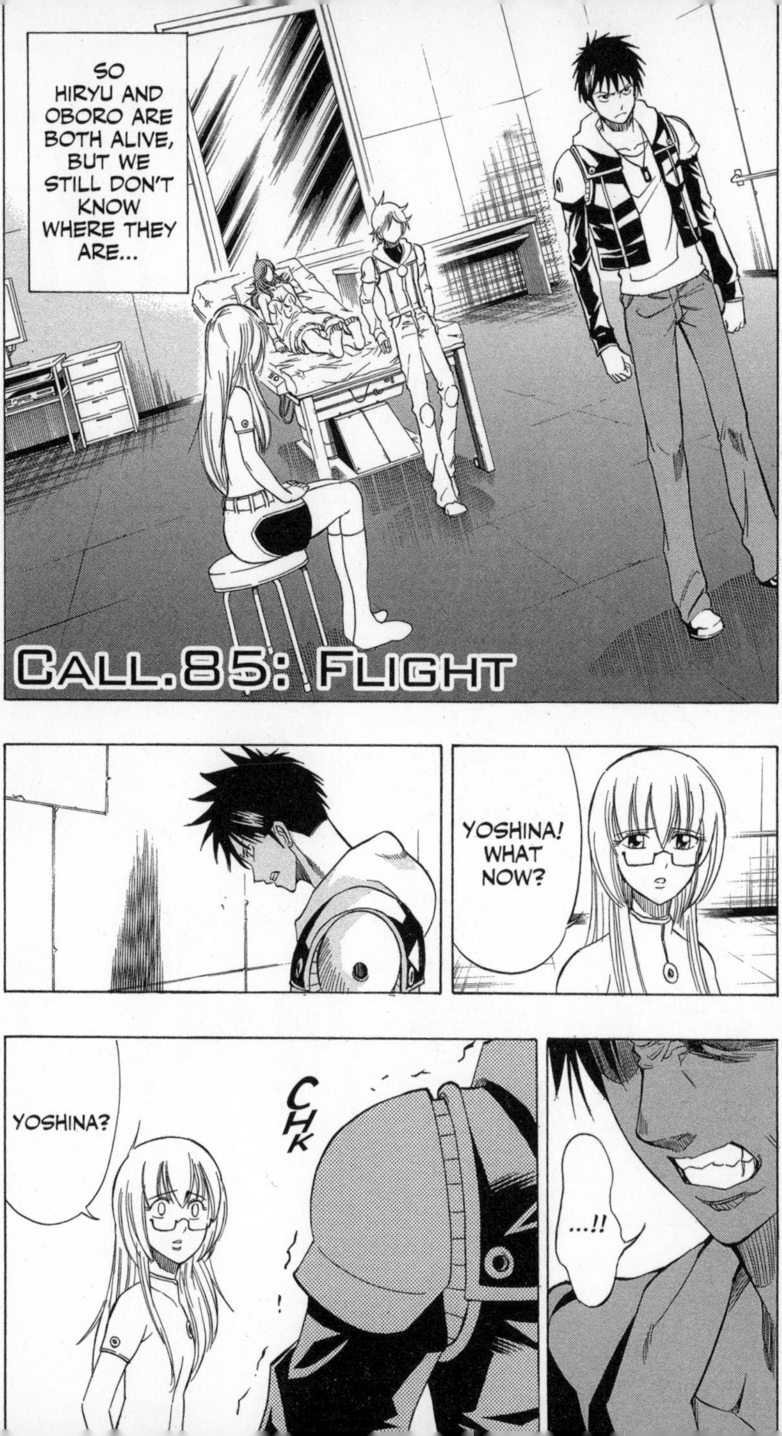
SO HIRYU AND OBORO ARE BOTH ALIVE, BUT WE STILL DON'T KNOW WHERE THEY ARE...
CALL.85: FLIGHT
YOSHINA! WHAT NOW?
...!!
CHK
YOSHINA?

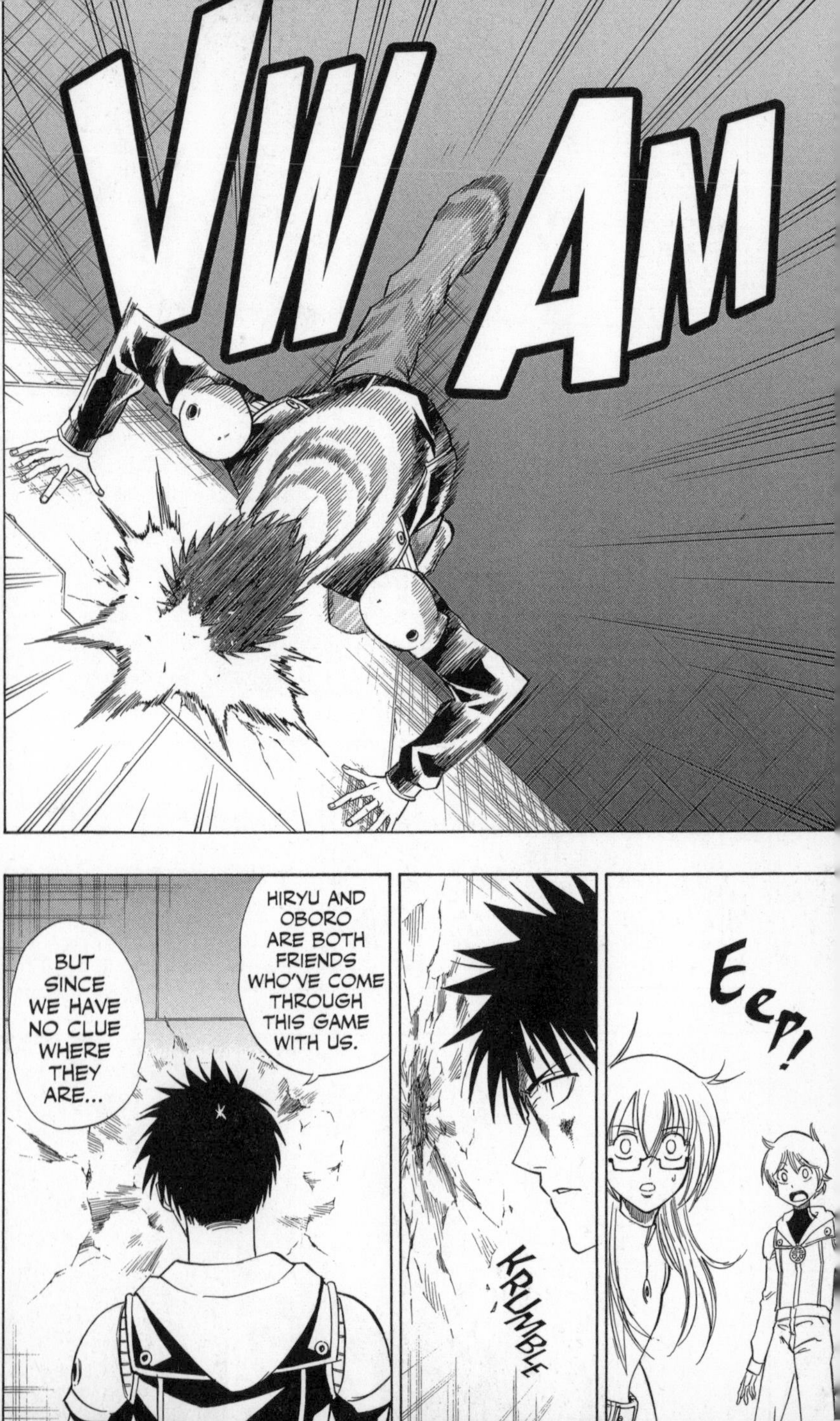
VWAM
Eep!
KRUMBLE
HIRYU AND OBORO ARE BOTH FRIENDS WHO'VE COME THROUGH THIS GAME WITH US.
BUT SINCE WE HAVE NO CLUE WHERE THEY ARE...

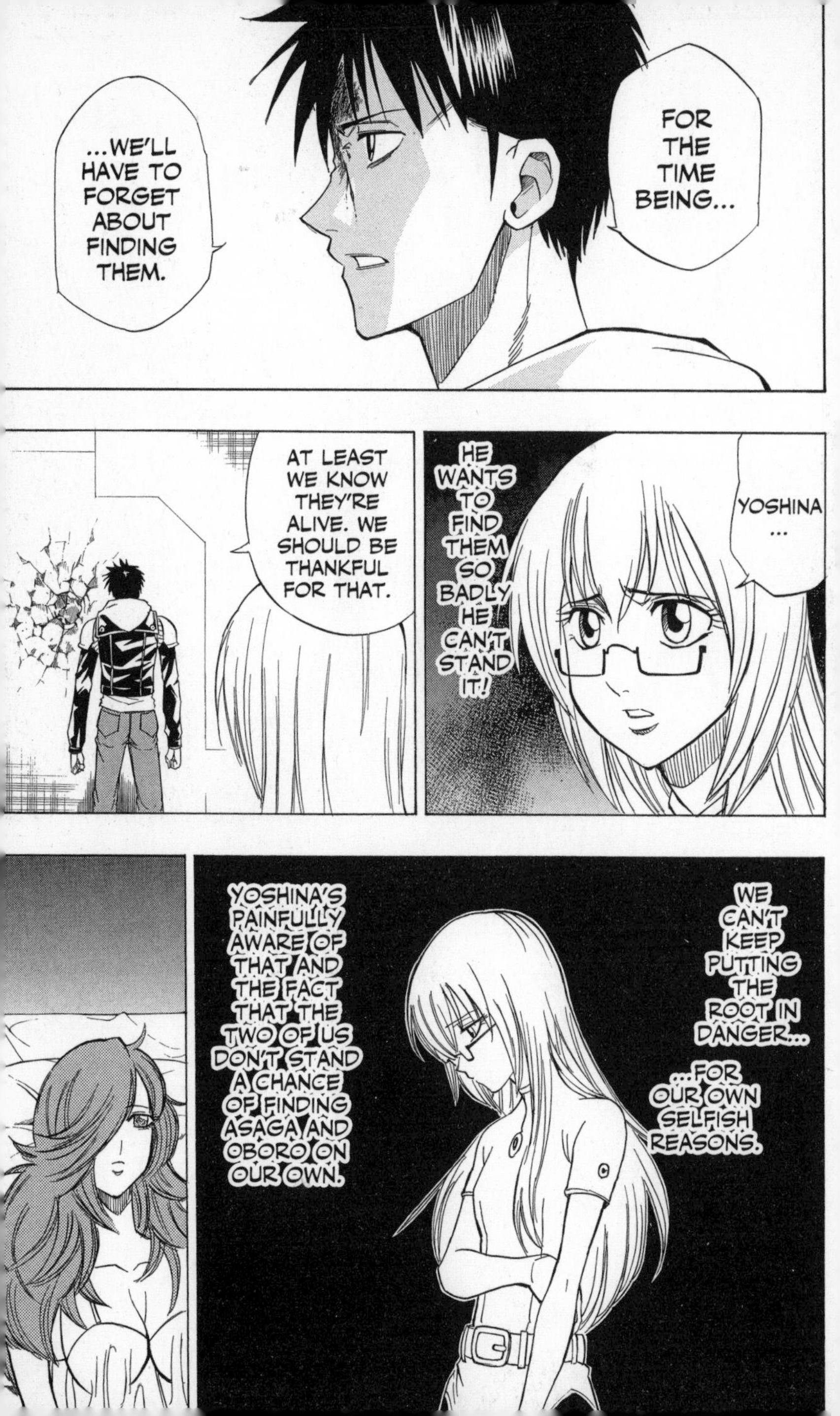
FOR THE TIME BEING...
...WE'LL HAVE TO FORGET ABOUT FINDING THEM.
YOSHINA ...
HE WANTS TO FIND THEM SO BADLY HE CAN'T STAND IT!
AT LEAST WE KNOW THEY'RE ALIVE. WE SHOULD BE THANKFUL FOR THAT.
WE CAN'T KEEP PUTTING THE ROOT IN DANGER...
...FOR OUR OWN SELFISH REASONS.
YOSHINA'S PAINFULLY AWARE OF THAT AND THE FACT THAT THE TWO OF US DON'T STAND A CHANCE OF FINDING ASAGA AND OBORO ON OUR OWN.

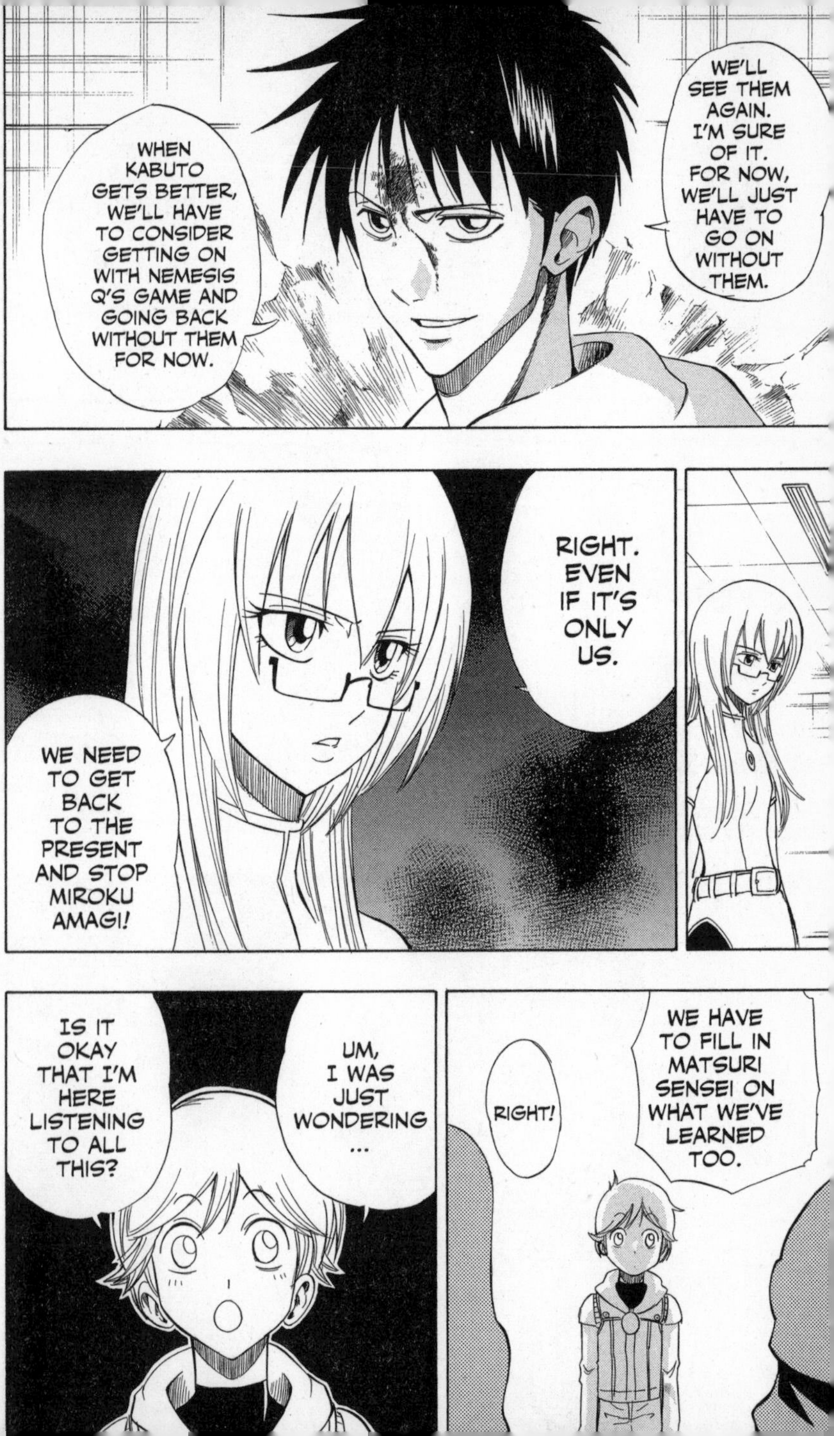
WE'LL SEE THEM AGAIN. I'M SURE OF IT. FOR NOW, WE'LL JUST HAVE TO GO ON WITHOUT THEM.
WHEN KABUTO GETS BETTER, WE'LL HAVE TO CONSIDER GETTING ON WITH NEMESIS Q'S GAME AND GOING BACK WITHOUT THEM FOR NOW.
RIGHT. EVEN IF IT'S ONLY US.
WE NEED TO GET BACK TO THE PRESENT AND STOP MIROKU AMAGI!
WE HAVE TO FILL IN MATSURI SENSEI ON WHAT WE'VE LEARNED TOO.
RIGHT!
UM, I WAS JUST WONDERING...
IS IT OKAY THAT I'M HERE LISTENING TO ALL THIS?

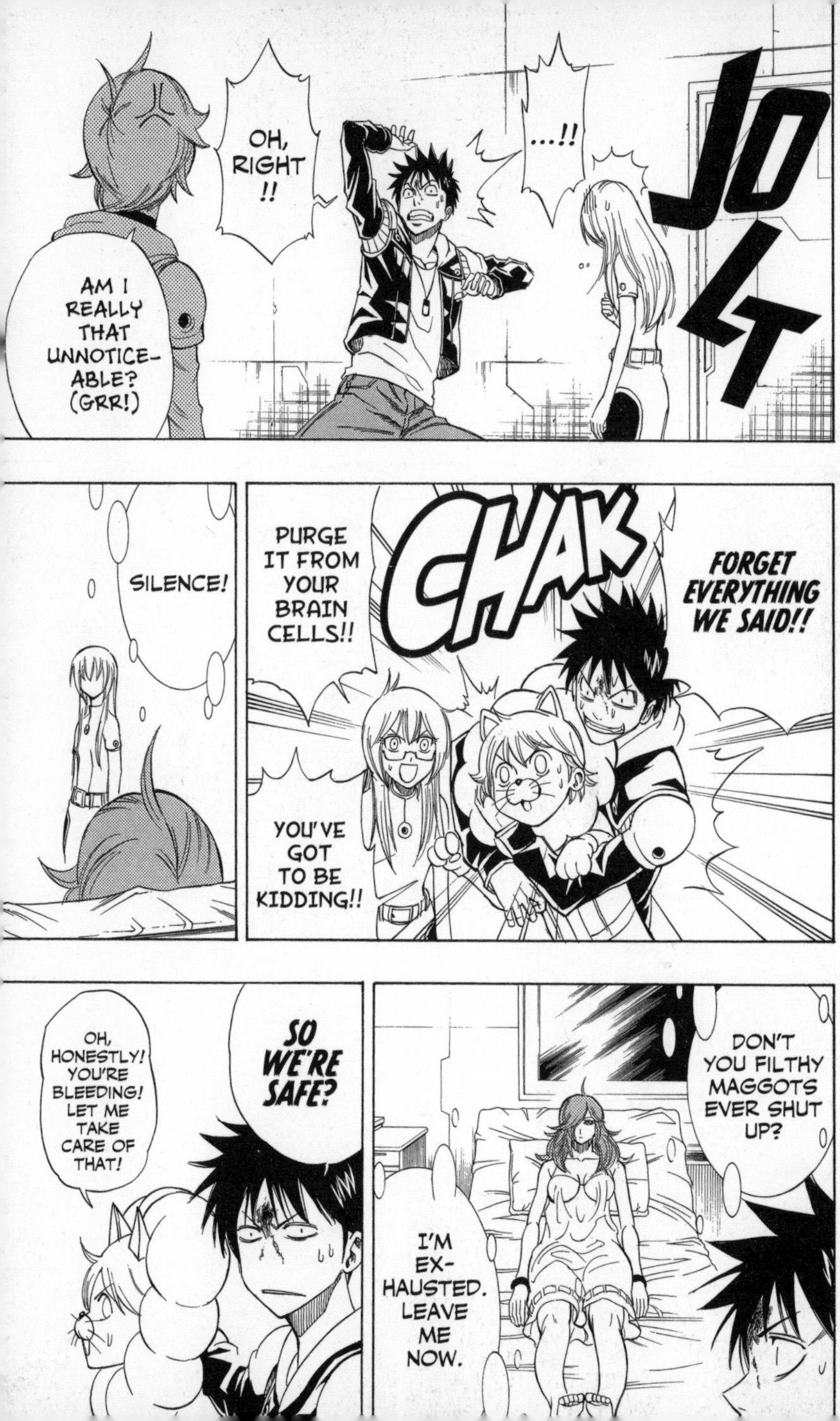
JOLT
...!!
OH, RIGHT!!
AM I REALLY THAT UNNOTICE-ABLE? (GRR!)
FORGET EVERYTHING WE SAID!!
CHAK
PURGE IT FROM YOUR BRAIN CELLS!!
YOU'VE GOT TO BE KIDDING!!
SILENCE!
DON'T YOU FILTHY MAGGOTS EVER SHUT UP?
I'M EX-HAUSTED. LEAVE ME NOW.
SO WE'RE SAFE?
OH, HONESTLY! YOU'RE BLEEDING! LET ME TAKE CARE OF THAT!

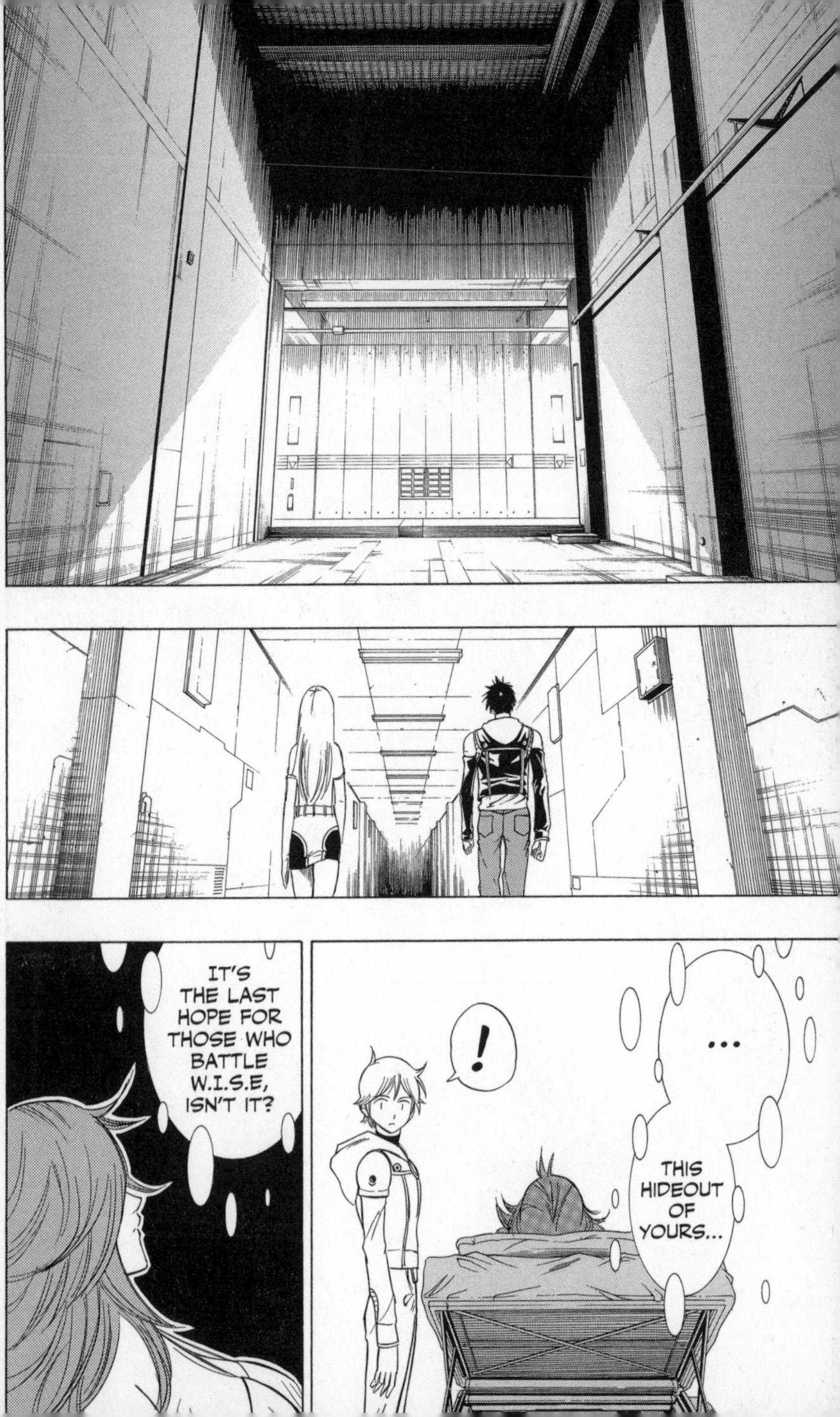
...
THIS HIDEOUT OF YOURS...
!
IT'S THE LAST HOPE FOR THOSE WHO BATTLE W.I.S.E, ISN'T IT?

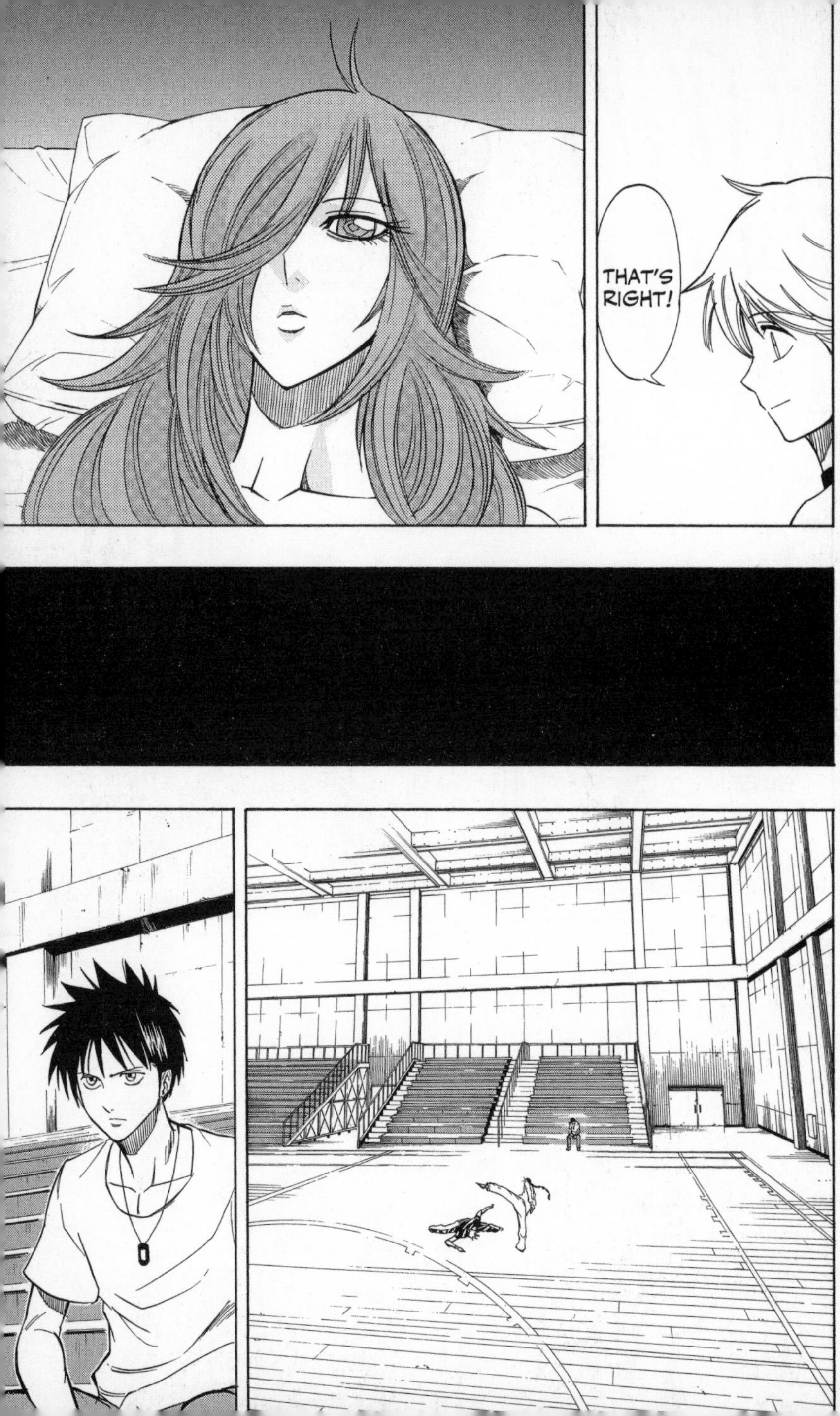
THAT'S RIGHT!

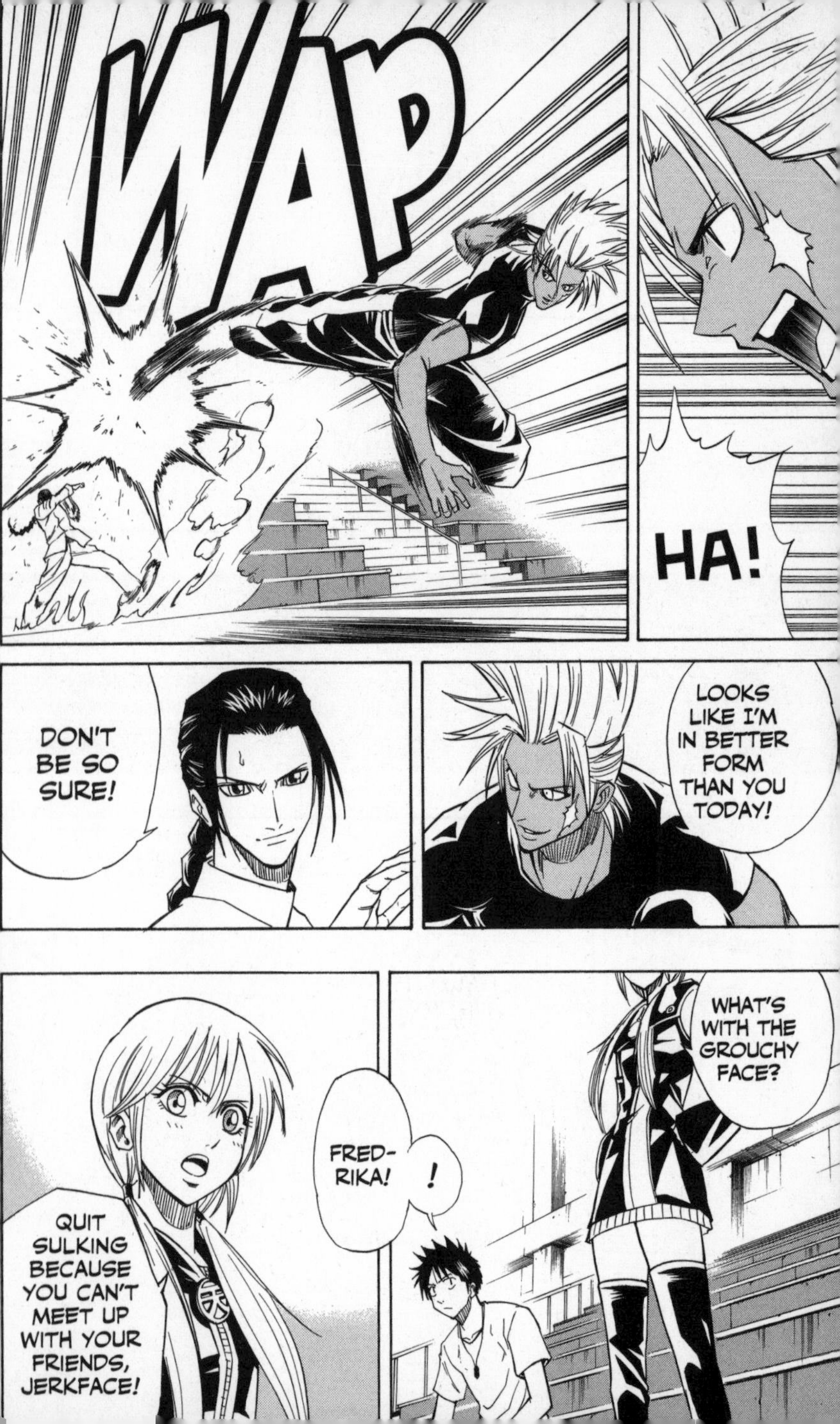

HA!
WAP
LOOKS LIKE I'M IN BETTER FORM THAN YOU TODAY!
DON'T BE SO SURE!
WHAT'S WITH THE GROUCHY FACE?
!
FRED-RIKA!
QUIT SULKING BECAUSE YOU CAN'T MEET UP WITH YOUR FRIENDS, JERKFACE!

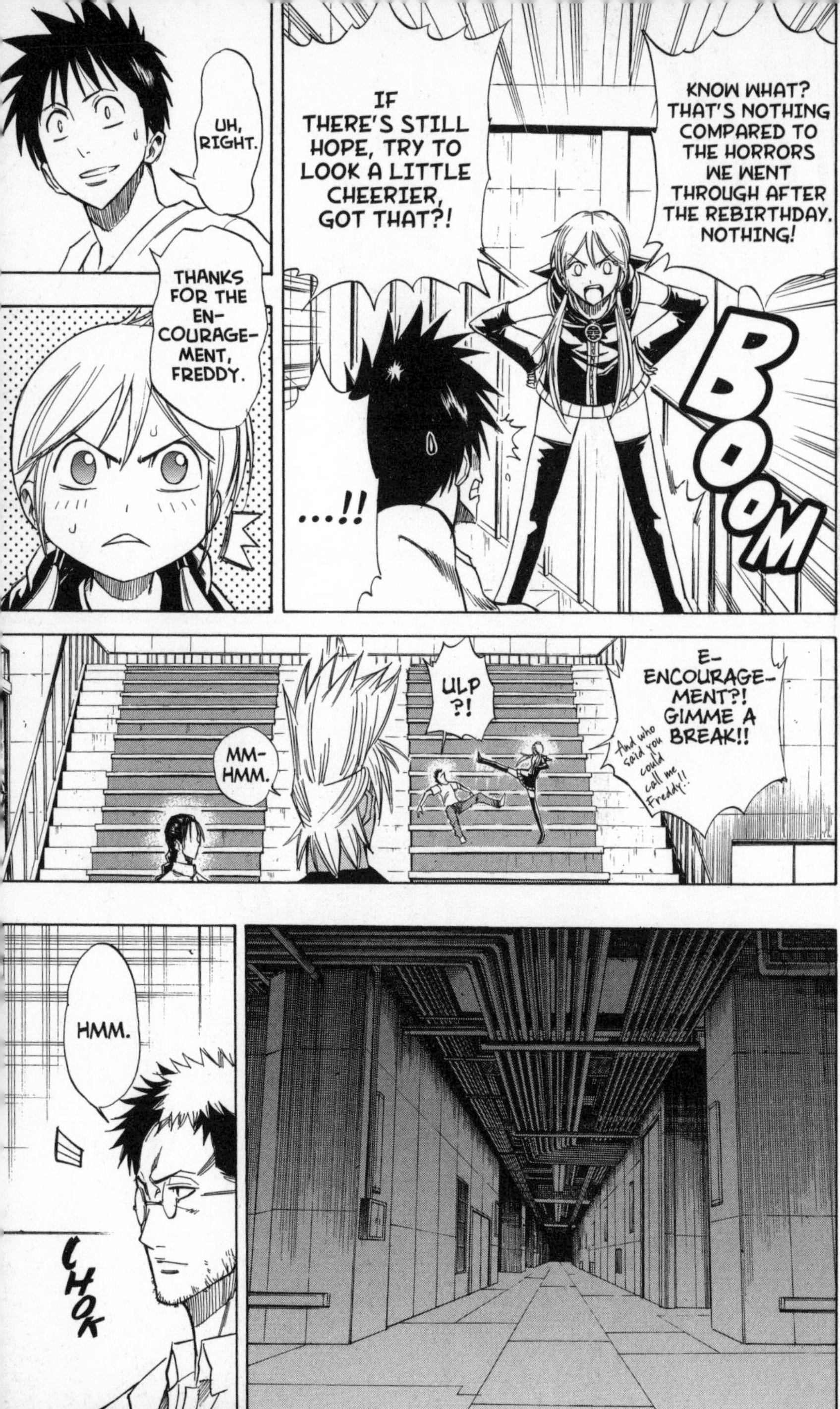
KNOW WHAT? THAT'S NOTHING COMPARED TO THE HORRORS WE WENT THROUGH AFTER THE REBIRTHDAY. NOTHING!
IF THERE'S STILL HOPE, TRY TO LOOK A LITTLE CHEERIER, GOT THAT?!
BOOM
...!!
UH, RIGHT.
THANKS FOR THE EN-COURAGE-MENT, FREDDY.
E-ENCOURAGE-MENT?! GIMME A BREAK!!
And who said you could call me Freddy!!
ULP?!
MM-HMM.
HMM.
CHOK

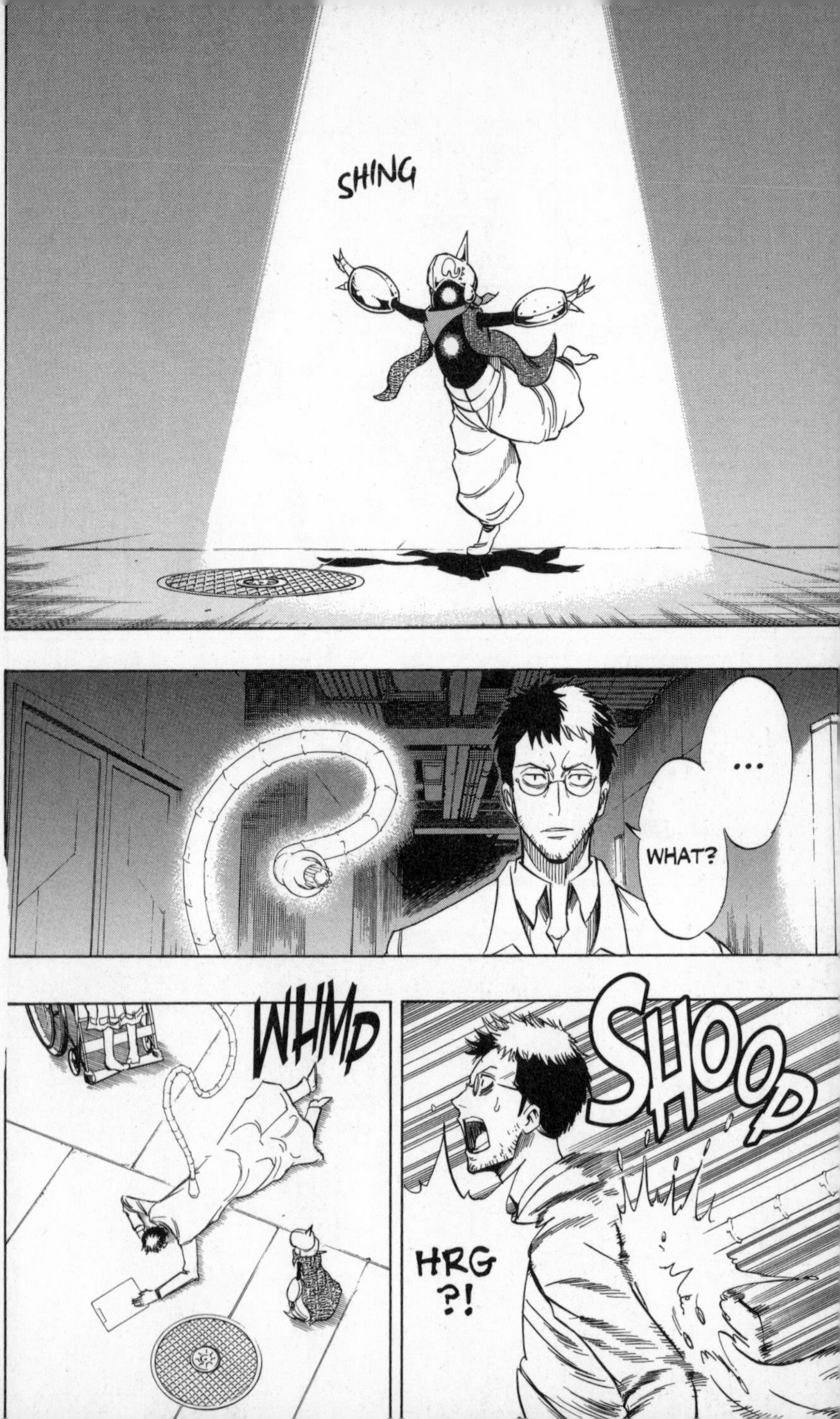
SHING
...
WHAT?
SHOOP
HRG ?!
WHMP

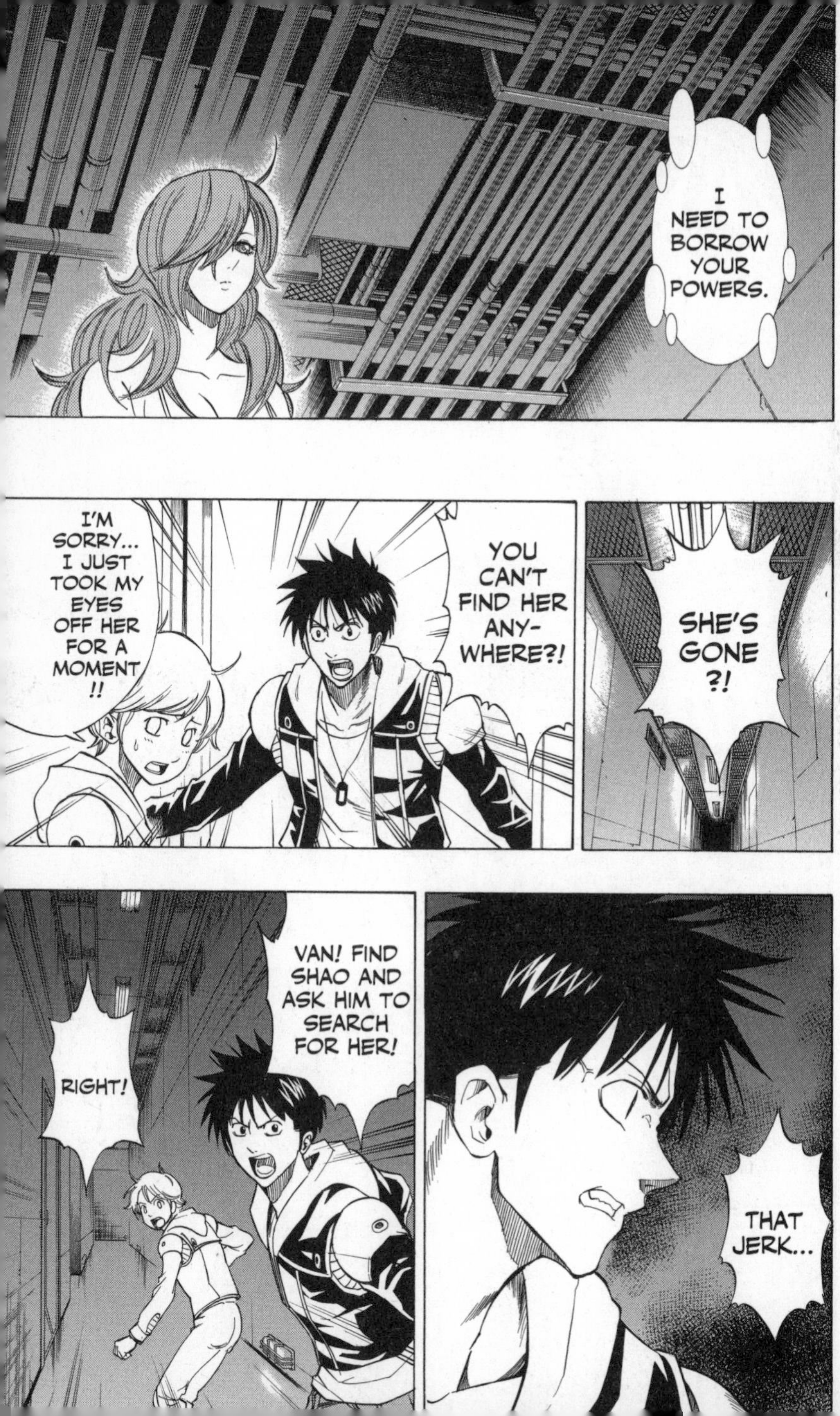
I NEED TO BORROW YOUR POWERS.
SHE'S GONE?!
YOU CAN'T FIND HER ANY-WHERE?!
I'M SORRY... I JUST TOOK MY EYES OFF HER FOR A MOMENT!!
THAT JERK...
VAN! FIND SHAO AND ASK HIM TO SEARCH FOR HER!
RIGHT!

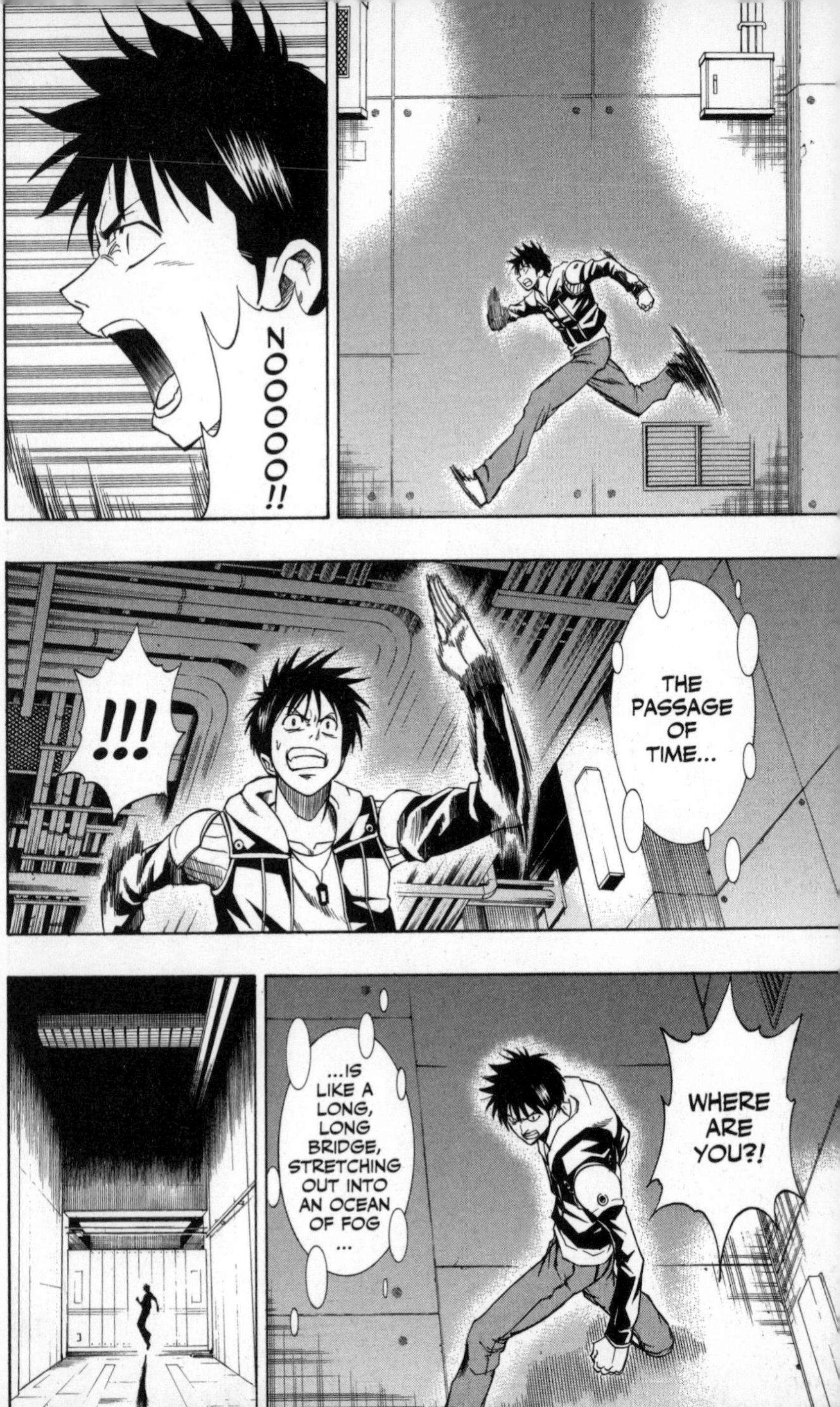
NOOOOOO!!
THE PASSAGE OF TIME...
!!!
WHERE ARE YOU?!
...IS LIKE A LONG, LONG BRIDGE, STRETCHING OUT INTO AN OCEAN OF FOG ...

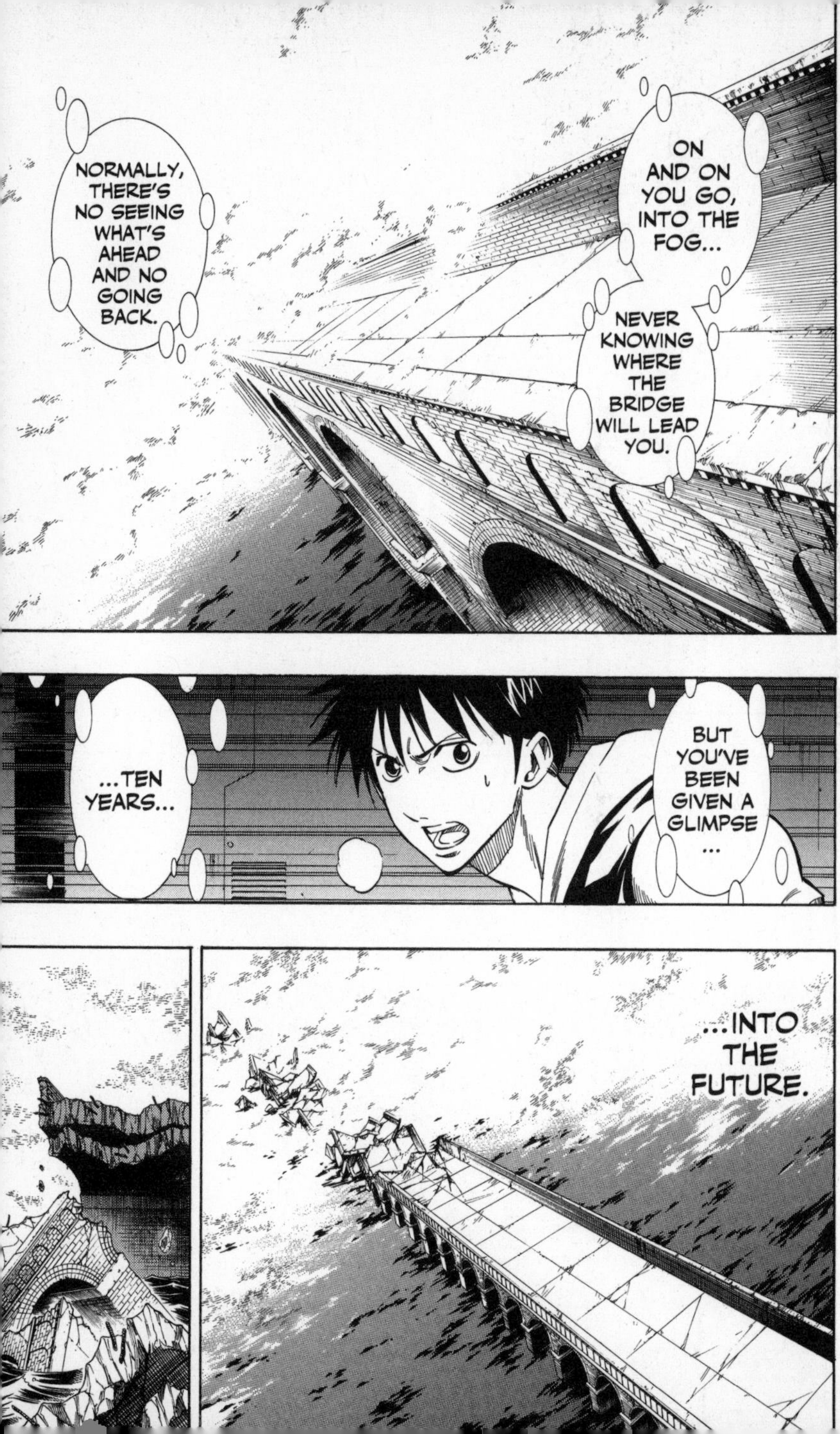
ON AND ON YOU GO, INTO THE FOG...
NEVER KNOWING WHERE THE BRIDGE WILL LEAD YOU.
NORMALLY, THERE'S NO SEEING WHAT'S AHEAD AND NO GOING BACK.
BUT YOU'VE BEEN GIVEN A GLIMPSE ...
...TEN YEARS...
...INTO THE FUTURE.

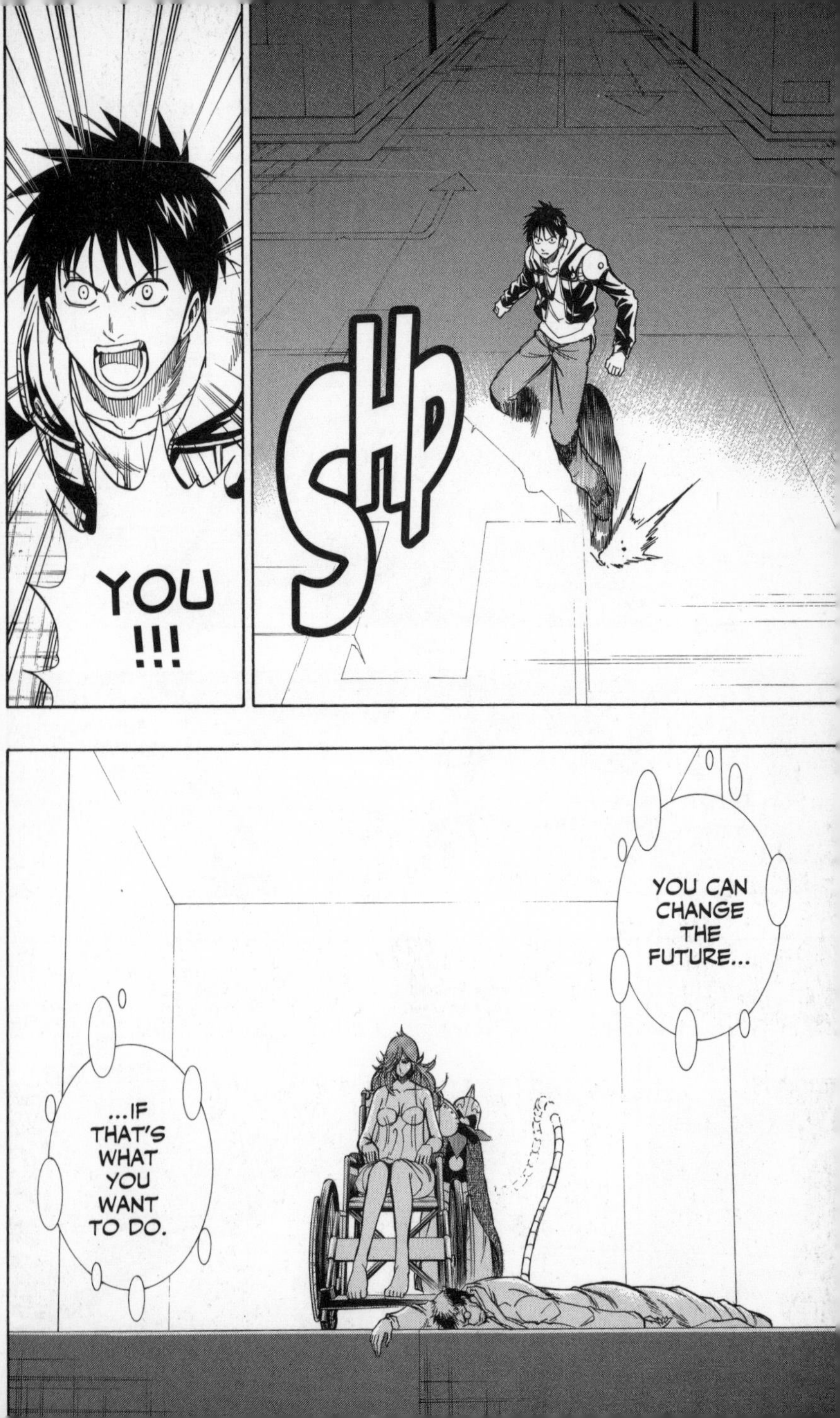
SHP
YOU !!!
YOU CAN CHANGE THE FUTURE...
...IF THAT'S WHAT YOU WANT TO DO.

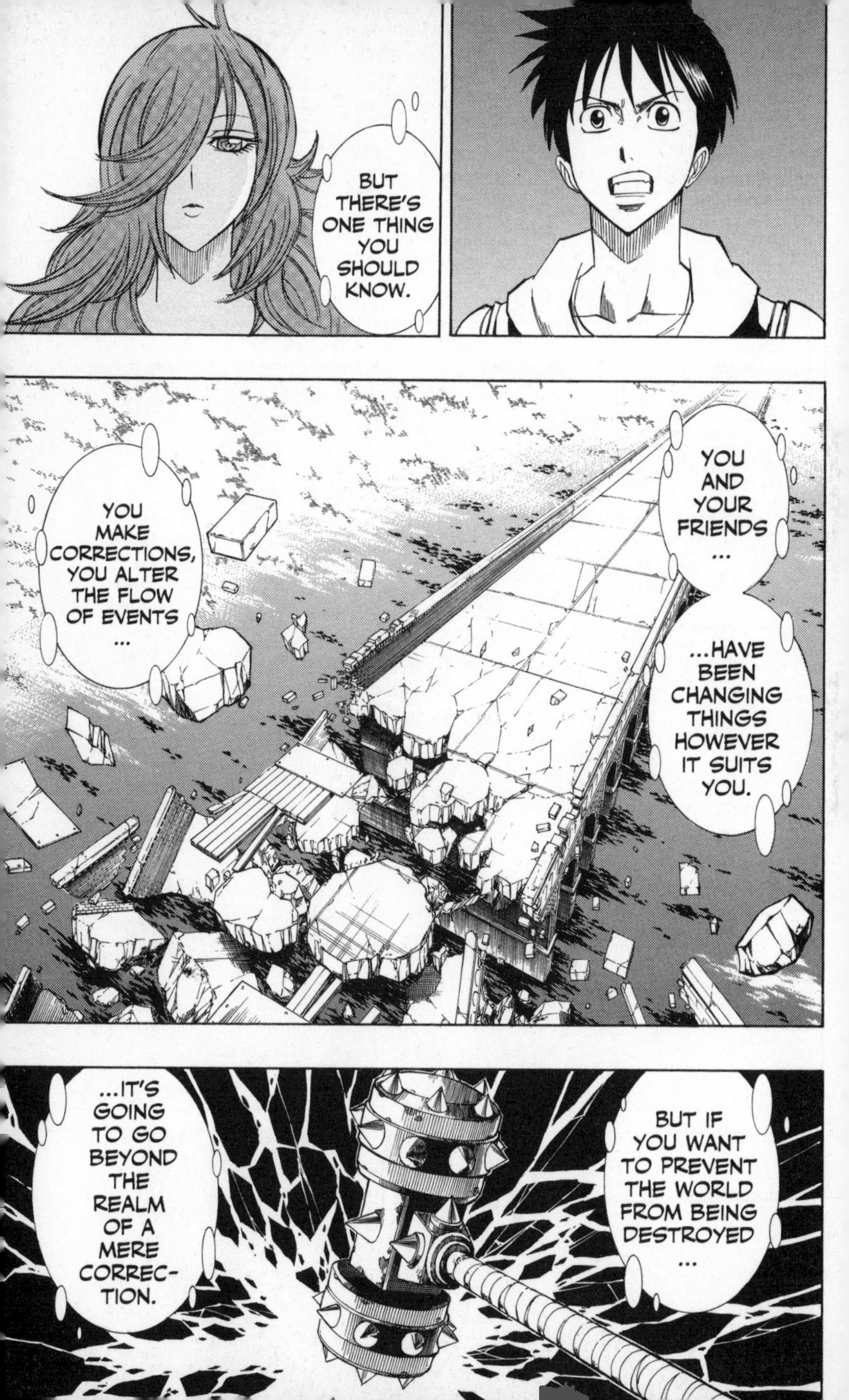
BUT THERE'S ONE THING YOU SHOULD KNOW.
YOU AND YOUR FRIENDS ...
...HAVE BEEN CHANGING THINGS HOWEVER IT SUITS YOU.
YOU MAKE CORRECTIONS, YOU ALTER THE FLOW OF EVENTS ...
BUT IF YOU WANT TO PREVENT THE WORLD FROM BEING DESTROYED ...
...IT'S GOING TO GO BEYOND THE REALM OF A MERE CORRECTION.

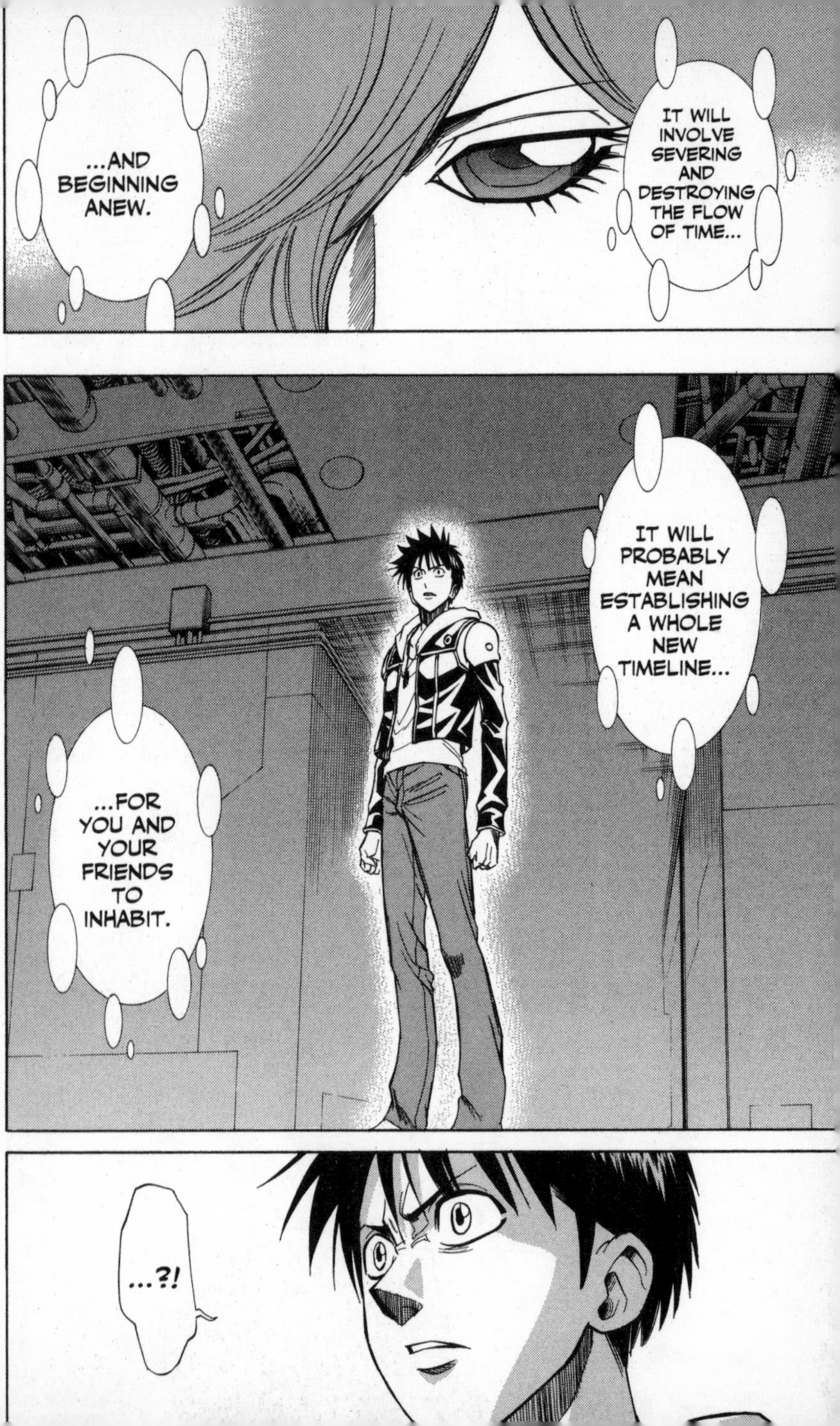
IT WILL INVOLVE SEVERING AND DESTROYING THE FLOW OF TIME...
...AND BEGINNING ANEW.
IT WILL PROBABLY MEAN ESTABLISHING A WHOLE NEW TIMELINE...
...FOR YOU AND YOUR FRIENDS TO INHABIT.
...?!

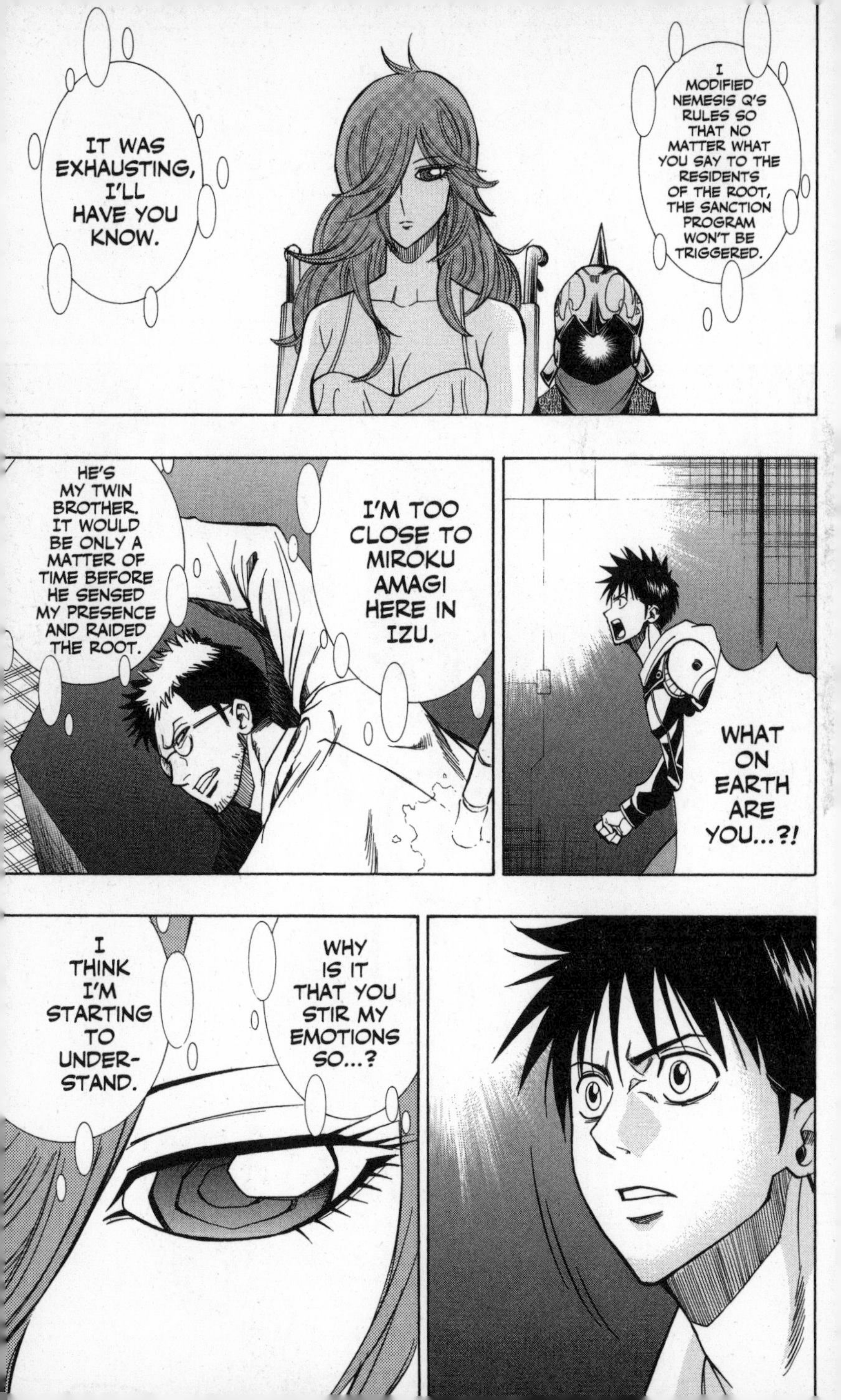
I MODIFIED NEMESIS Q'S RULES SO THAT NO MATTER WHAT YOU SAY TO THE RESIDENTS OF THE ROOT, THE SANCTION PROGRAM WON'T BE TRIGGERED.
IT WAS EXHAUSTING, I'LL HAVE YOU KNOW.
WHAT ON EARTH ARE YOU...?!
I'M TOO CLOSE TO MIROKU AMAGI HERE IN IZU.
HE'S MY TWIN BROTHER. IT WOULD BE ONLY A MATTER OF TIME BEFORE HE SENSED MY PRESENCE AND RAIDED THE ROOT.
WHY IS IT THAT YOU STIR MY EMOTIONS SO...?
I THINK I'M STARTING TO UNDER-STAND.

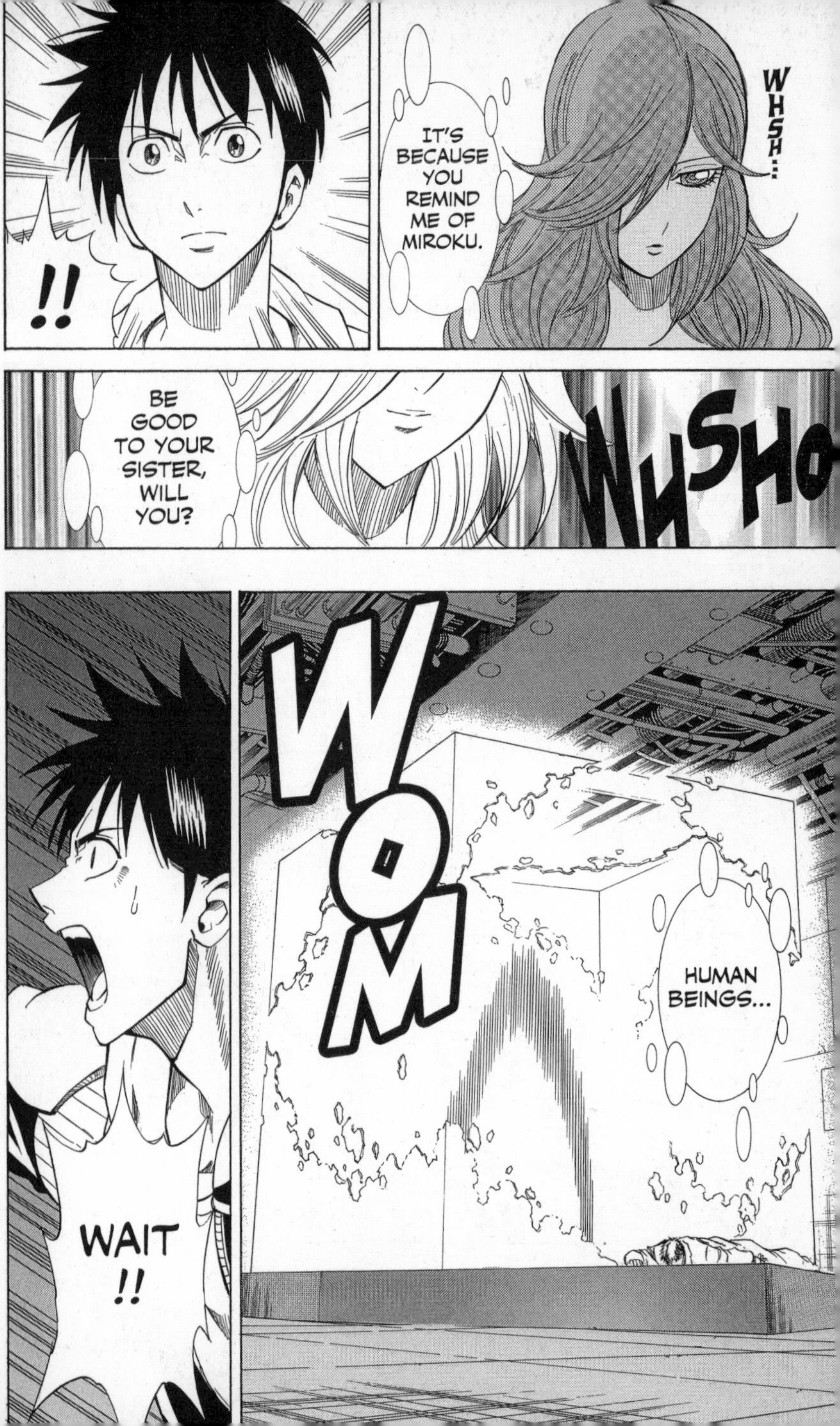
WHSH...
IT'S BECAUSE YOU REMIND ME OF MIROKU.
!!
WHSHO
BE GOOD TO YOUR SISTER, WILL YOU?
WOM
HUMAN BEINGS...
WAIT !!

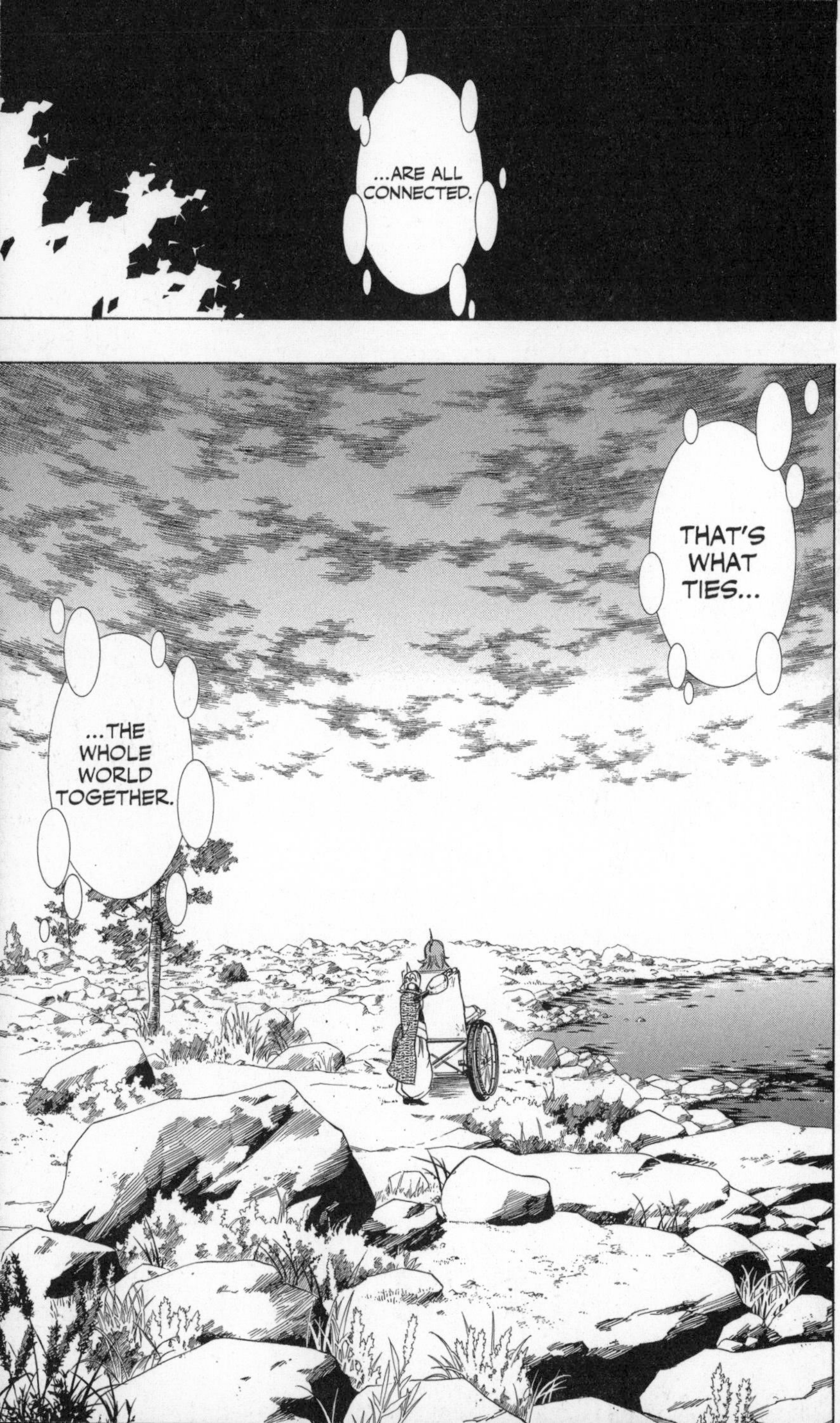
...ARE ALL CONNECTED.
THAT'S WHAT TIES...
...THE WHOLE WORLD TOGETHER.

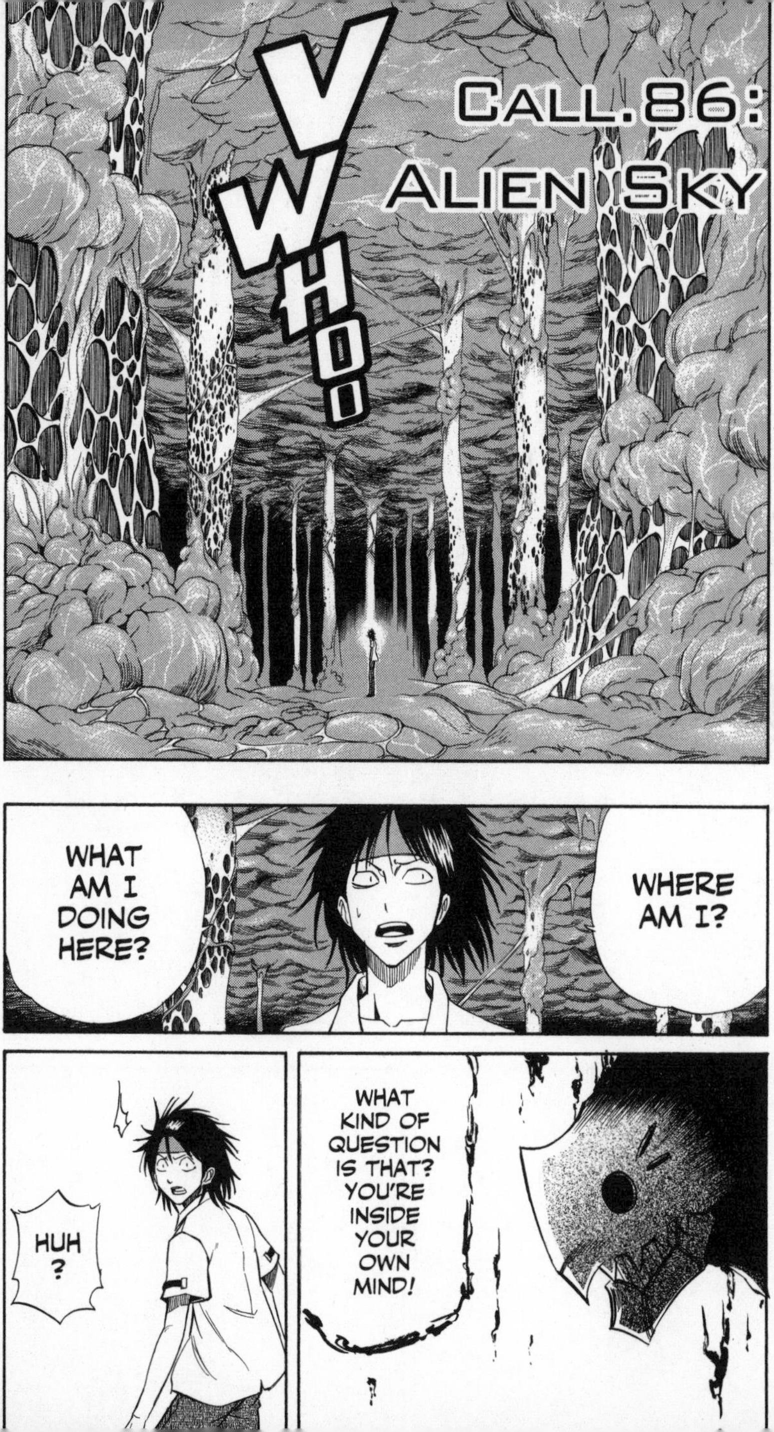
CALL. 86: ALIEN SKY
VWHOO
WHERE AM I?
WHAT AM I DOING HERE?
WHAT KIND OF QUESTION IS THAT? YOU'RE INSIDE YOUR OWN MIND!
HUH?

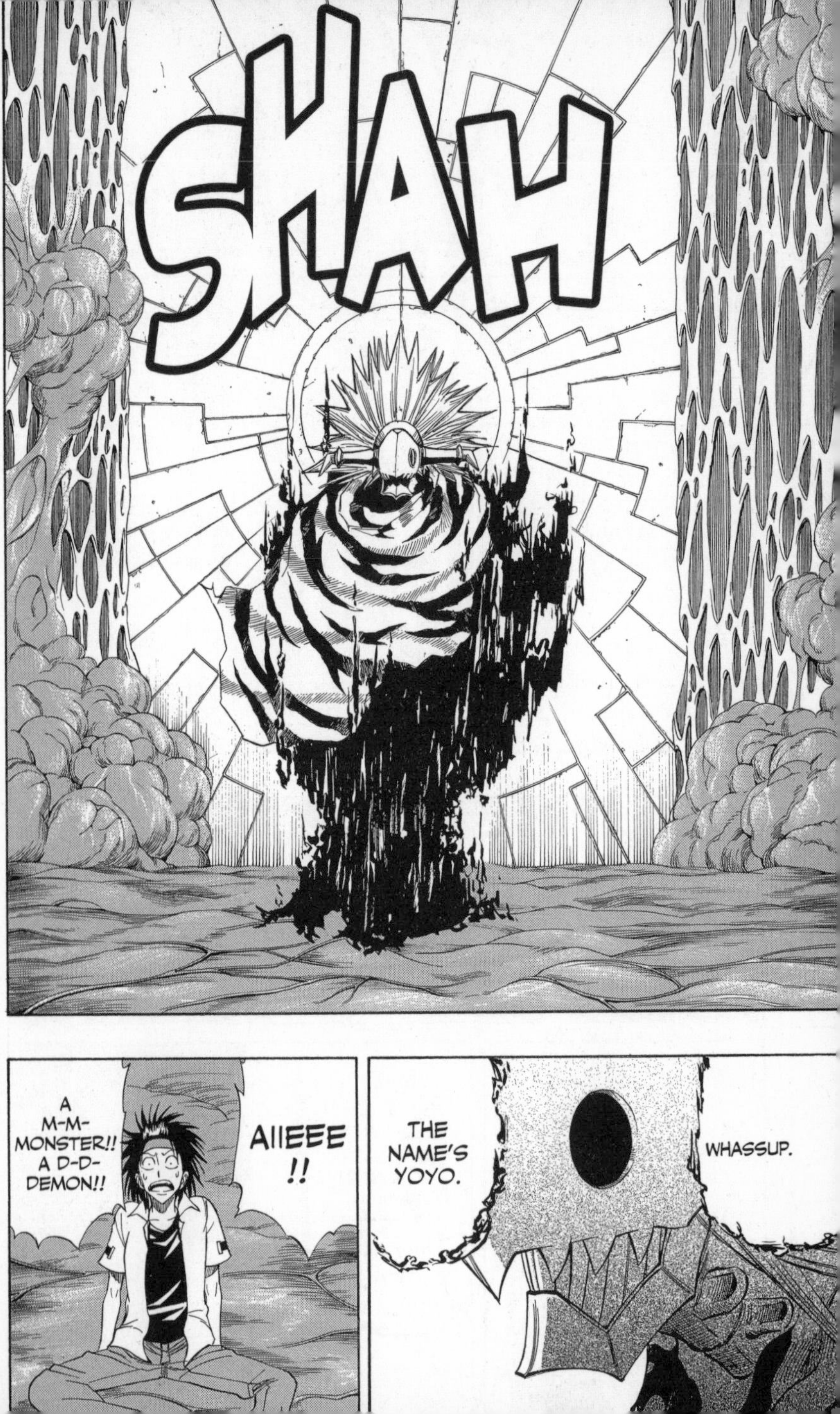
SHAH
WHASSUP.
THE NAME'S YOYO.
AIIEEE!!
A M-M-MONSTER!! A D-D-DEMON!!

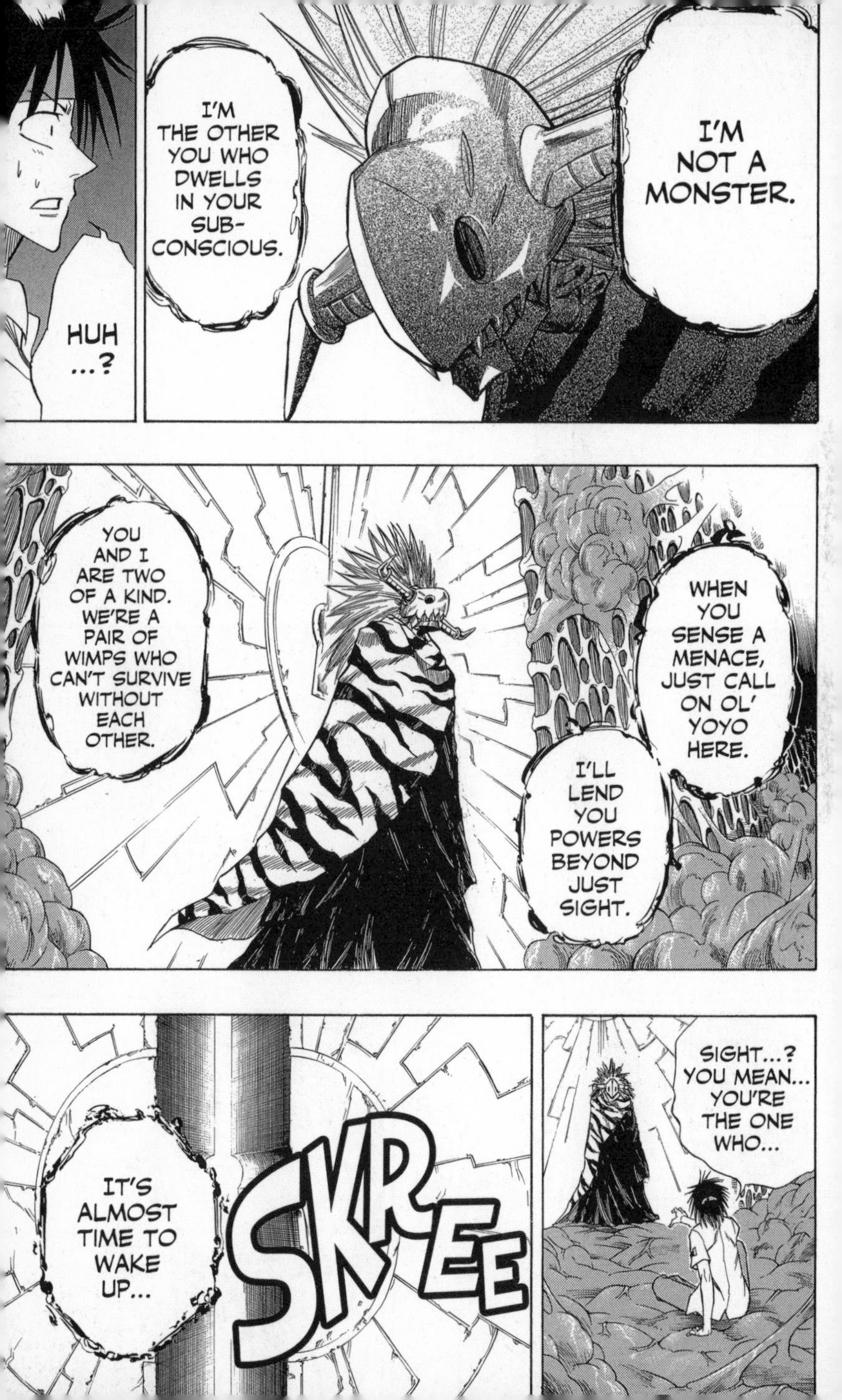
I'M NOT A MONSTER.
I'M THE OTHER YOU WHO DWELLS IN YOUR SUB-CONSCIOUS.
HUH ...?
WHEN YOU SENSE A MENACE, JUST CALL ON OL' YOYO HERE.
I'LL LEND YOU POWERS BEYOND JUST SIGHT.
YOU AND I ARE TWO OF A KIND. WE'RE A PAIR OF WIMPS WHO CAN'T SURVIVE WITHOUT EACH OTHER.
SIGHT...? YOU MEAN... YOU'RE THE ONE WHO...
SKREE
IT'S ALMOST TIME TO WAKE UP...

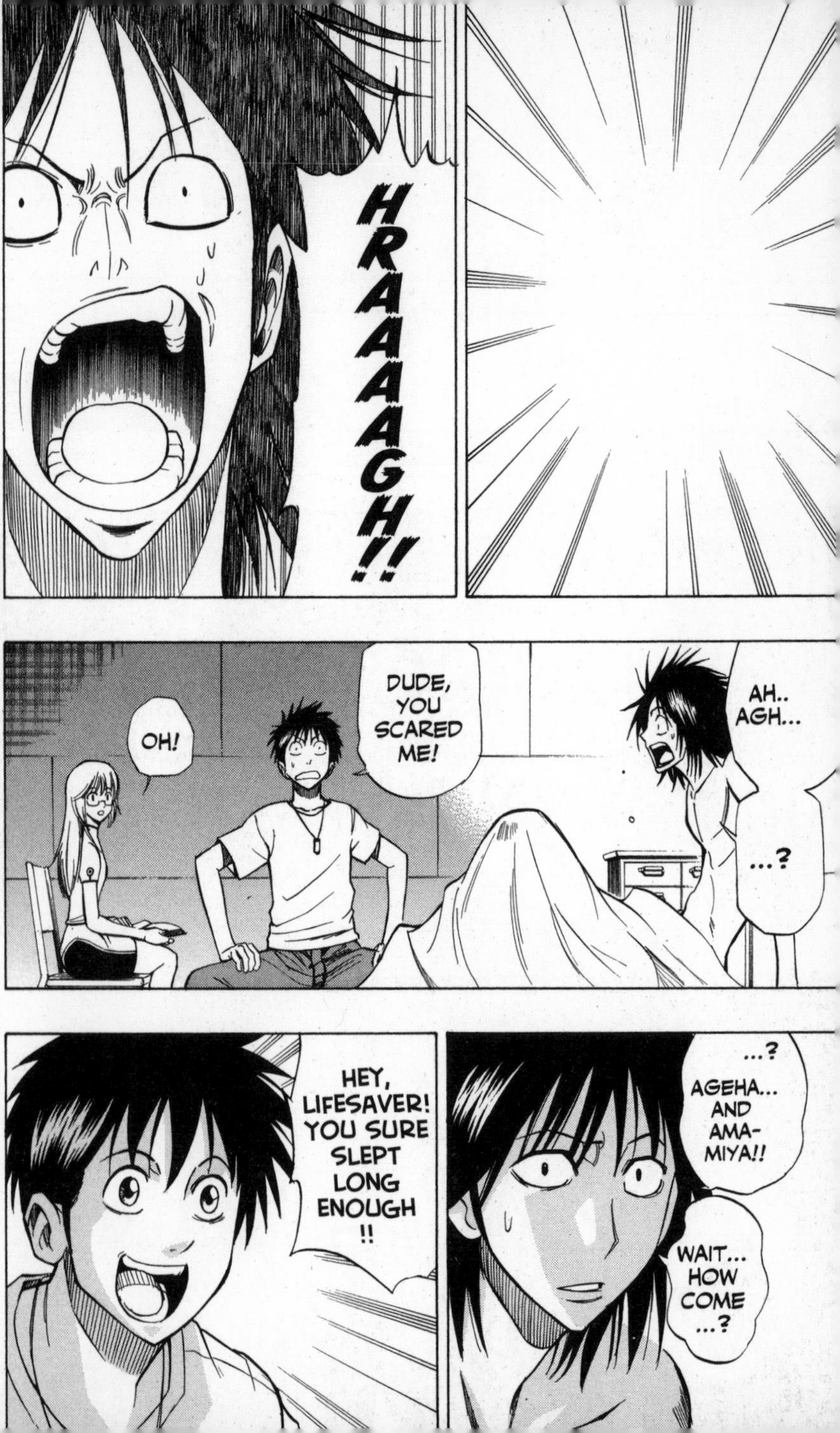
HRAAAAAGH!!
AH.. AGH...
...?
DUDE, YOU SCARED ME!
OH!
...?
AGEHA... AND AMA-MIYA!!
WAIT... HOW COME ...?
HEY, LIFESAVER! YOU SURE SLEPT LONG ENOUGH !!

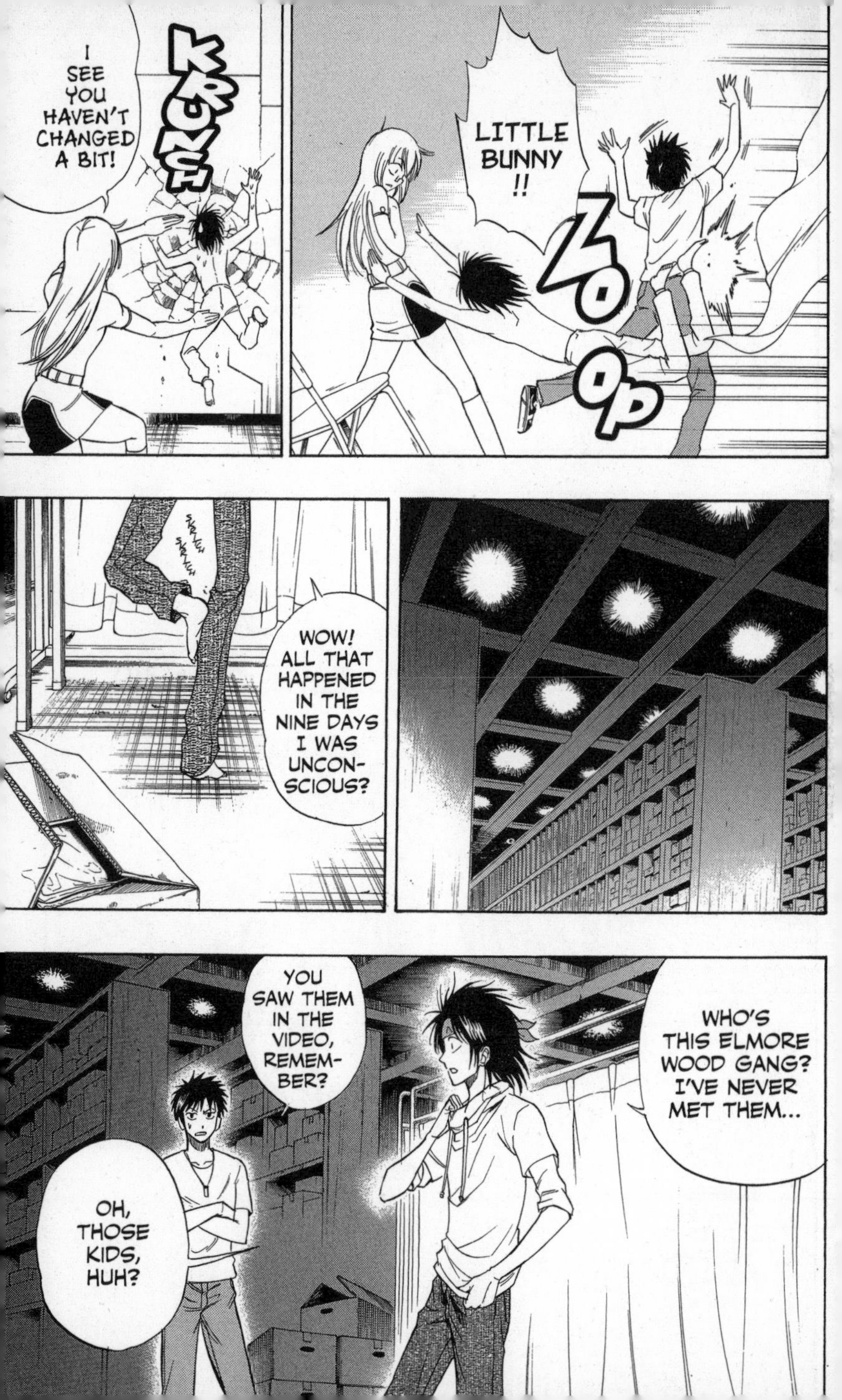
LITTLE BUNNY !!
ZOOOP
KRUNCH
I SEE YOU HAVEN'T CHANGED A BIT!
SKRITCH SKRITCH
WOW! ALL THAT HAPPENED IN THE NINE DAYS I WAS UNCON-SCIOUS?
WHO'S THIS ELMORE WOOD GANG? I'VE NEVER MET THEM...
YOU SAW THEM IN THE VIDEO, REMEM-BER?
OH, THOSE KIDS, HUH?

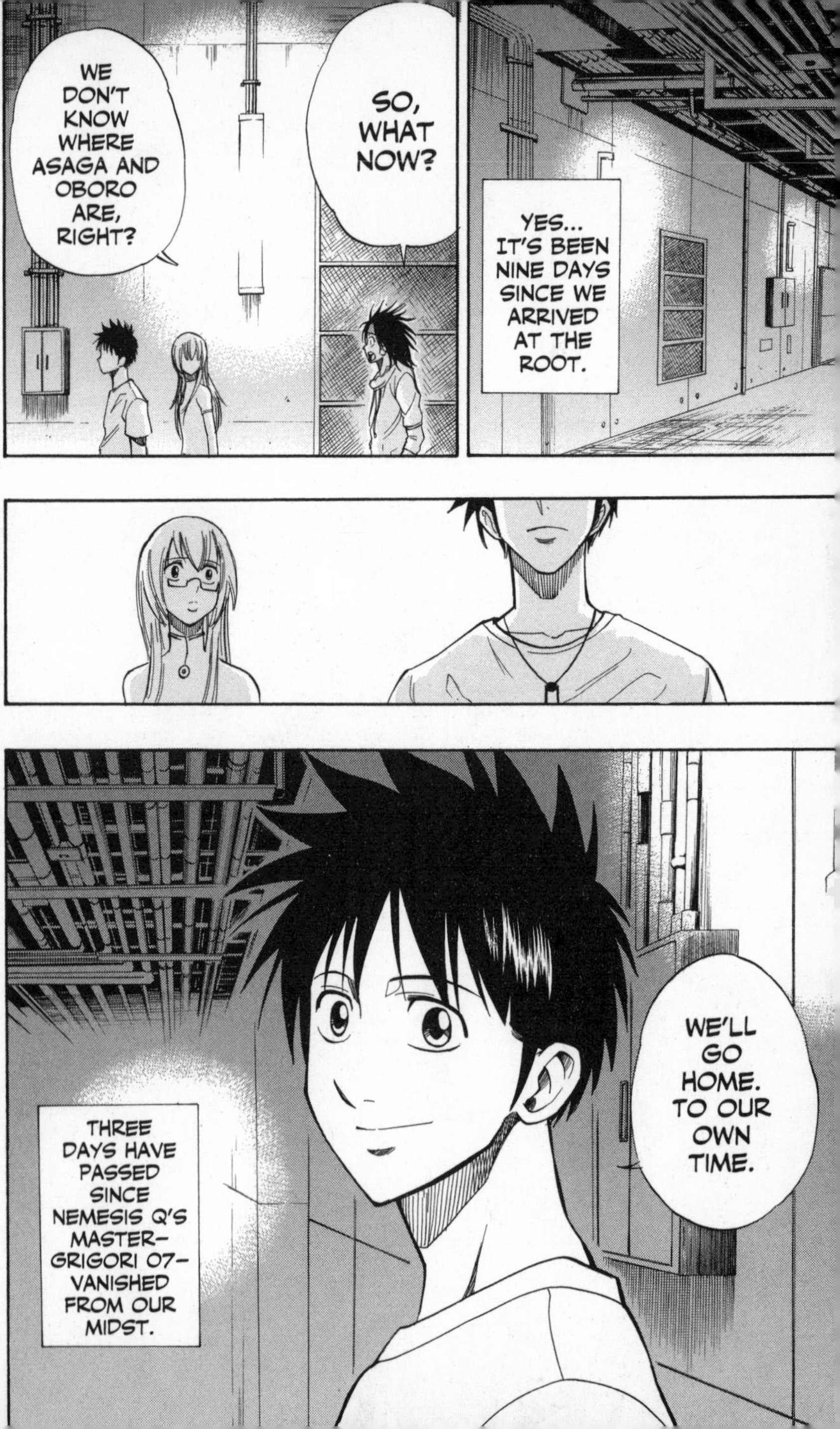
YES... IT'S BEEN NINE DAYS SINCE WE ARRIVED AT THE ROOT.
SO, WHAT NOW?
WE DON'T KNOW WHERE ASAGA AND OBORO ARE, RIGHT?
WE'LL GO HOME. TO OUR OWN TIME.
THREE DAYS HAVE PASSED SINCE NEMESIS Q'S MASTER—GRIGORI 07—VANISHED FROM OUR MIDST.

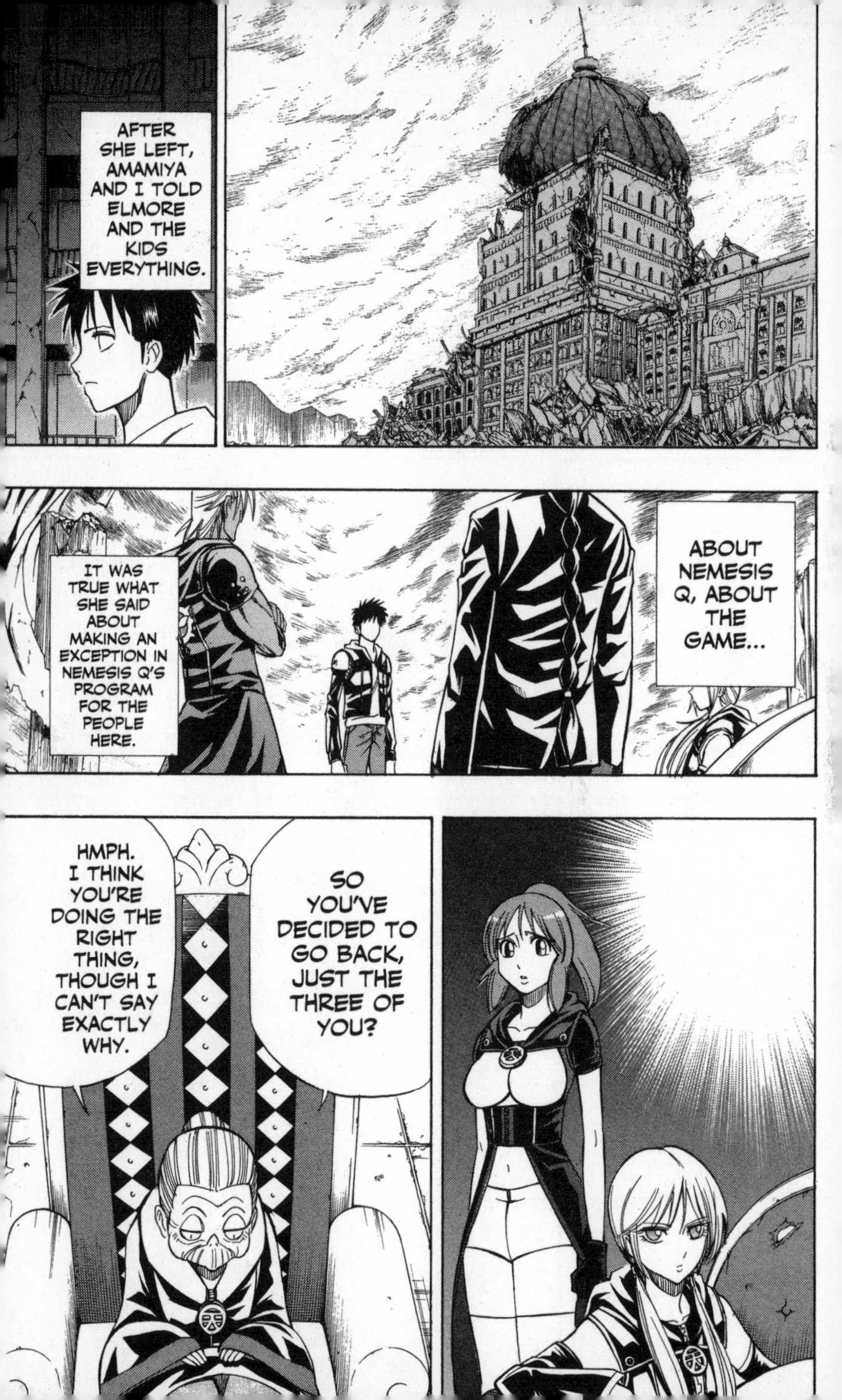
AFTER SHE LEFT, AMAMIYA AND I TOLD ELMORE AND THE KIDS EVERYTHING.
ABOUT NEMESIS Q, ABOUT THE GAME...
IT WAS TRUE WHAT SHE SAID ABOUT MAKING AN EXCEPTION IN NEMESIS Q'S PROGRAM FOR THE PEOPLE HERE.
SO YOU'VE DECIDED TO GO BACK, JUST THE THREE OF YOU?
HMPH. I THINK YOU'RE DOING THE RIGHT THING, THOUGH I CAN'T SAY EXACTLY WHY.

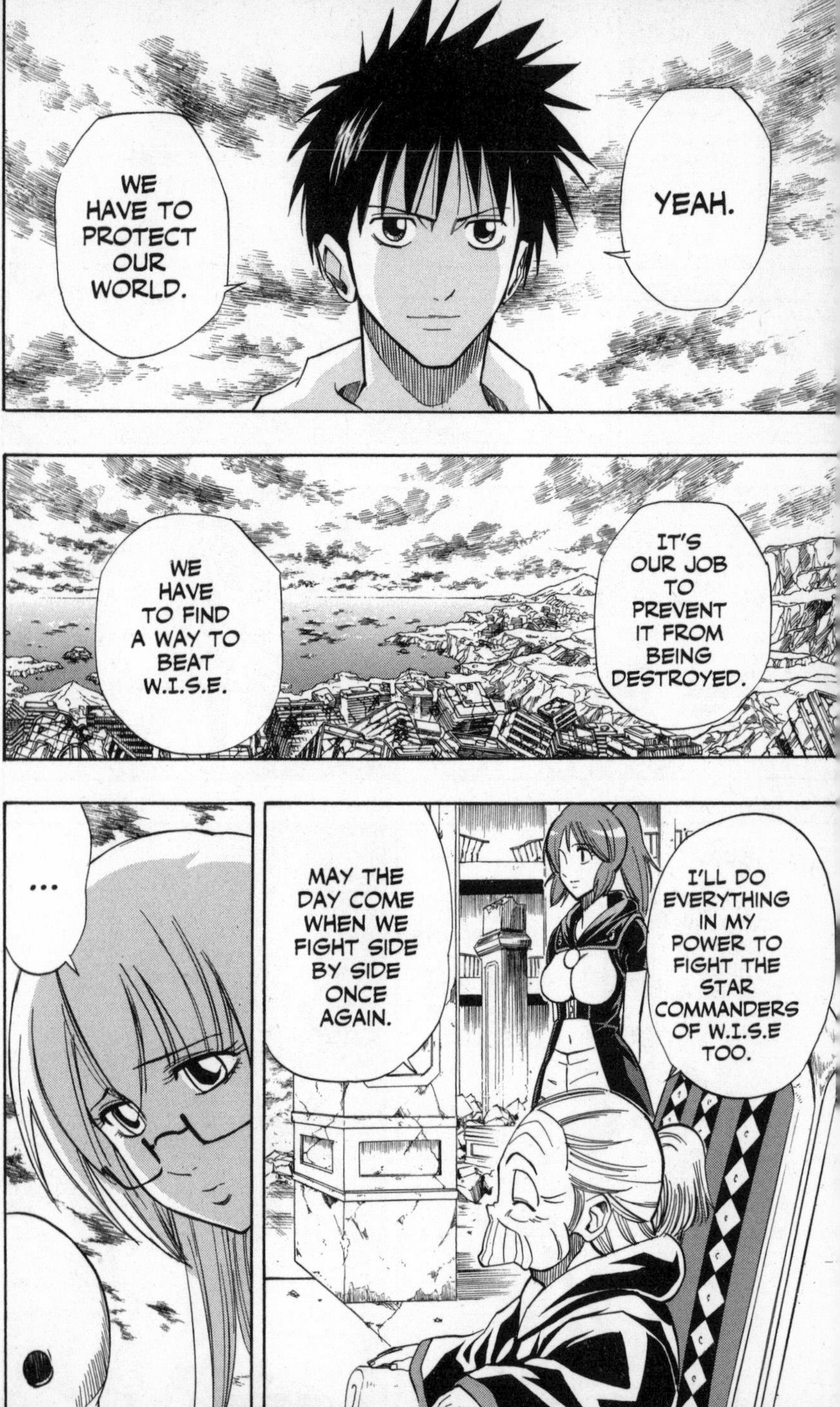
YEAH.
WE HAVE TO PROTECT OUR WORLD.
IT'S OUR JOB TO PREVENT IT FROM BEING DESTROYED.
WE HAVE TO FIND A WAY TO BEAT W.I.S.E.
I'LL DO EVERYTHING IN MY POWER TO FIGHT THE STAR COMMANDERS OF W.I.S.E TOO.
MAY THE DAY COME WHEN WE FIGHT SIDE BY SIDE ONCE AGAIN.
...

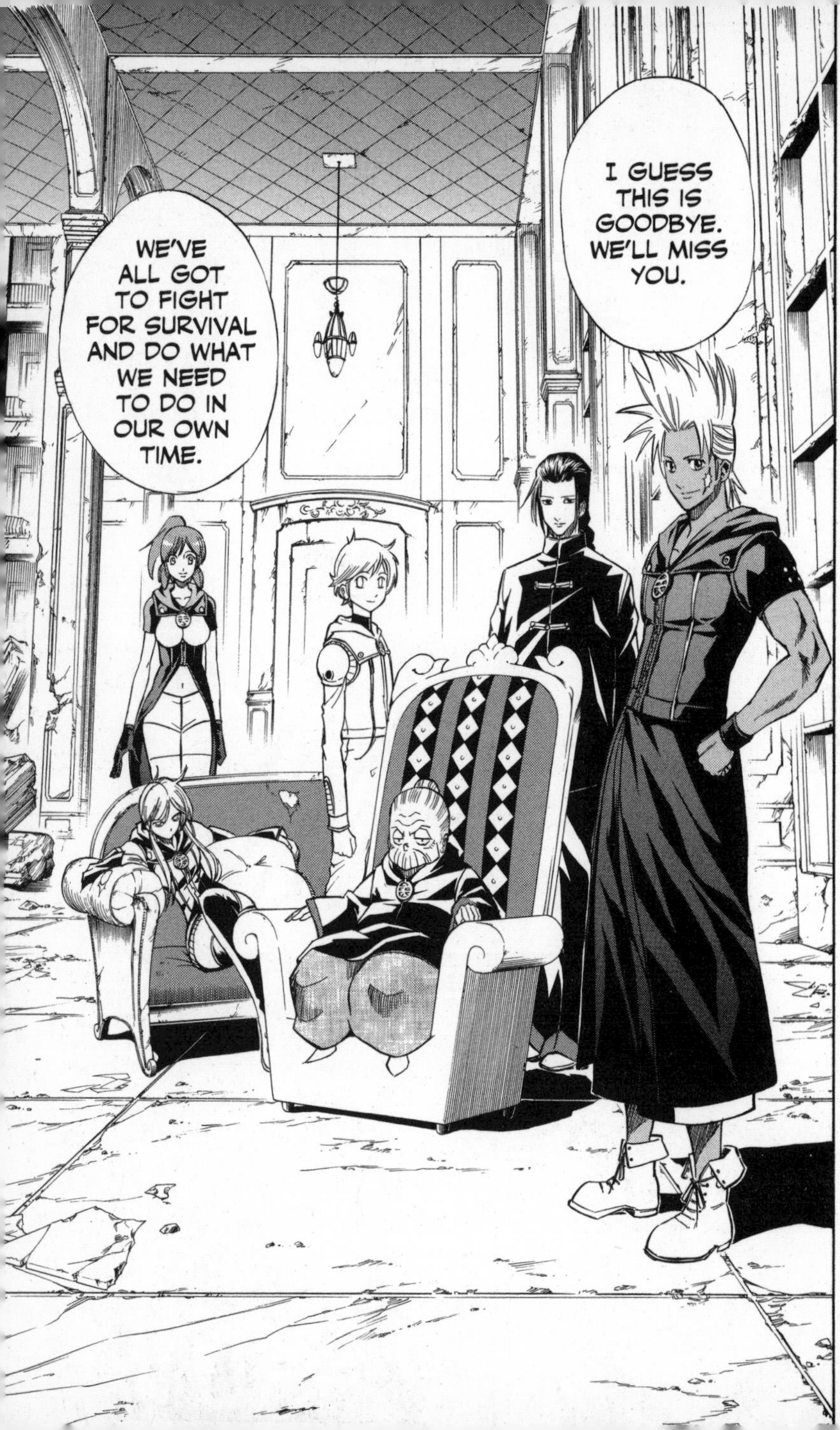
I GUESS THIS IS GOODBYE. WE'LL MISS YOU.
WE'VE ALL GOT TO FIGHT FOR SURVIVAL AND DO WHAT WE NEED TO DO IN OUR OWN TIME.

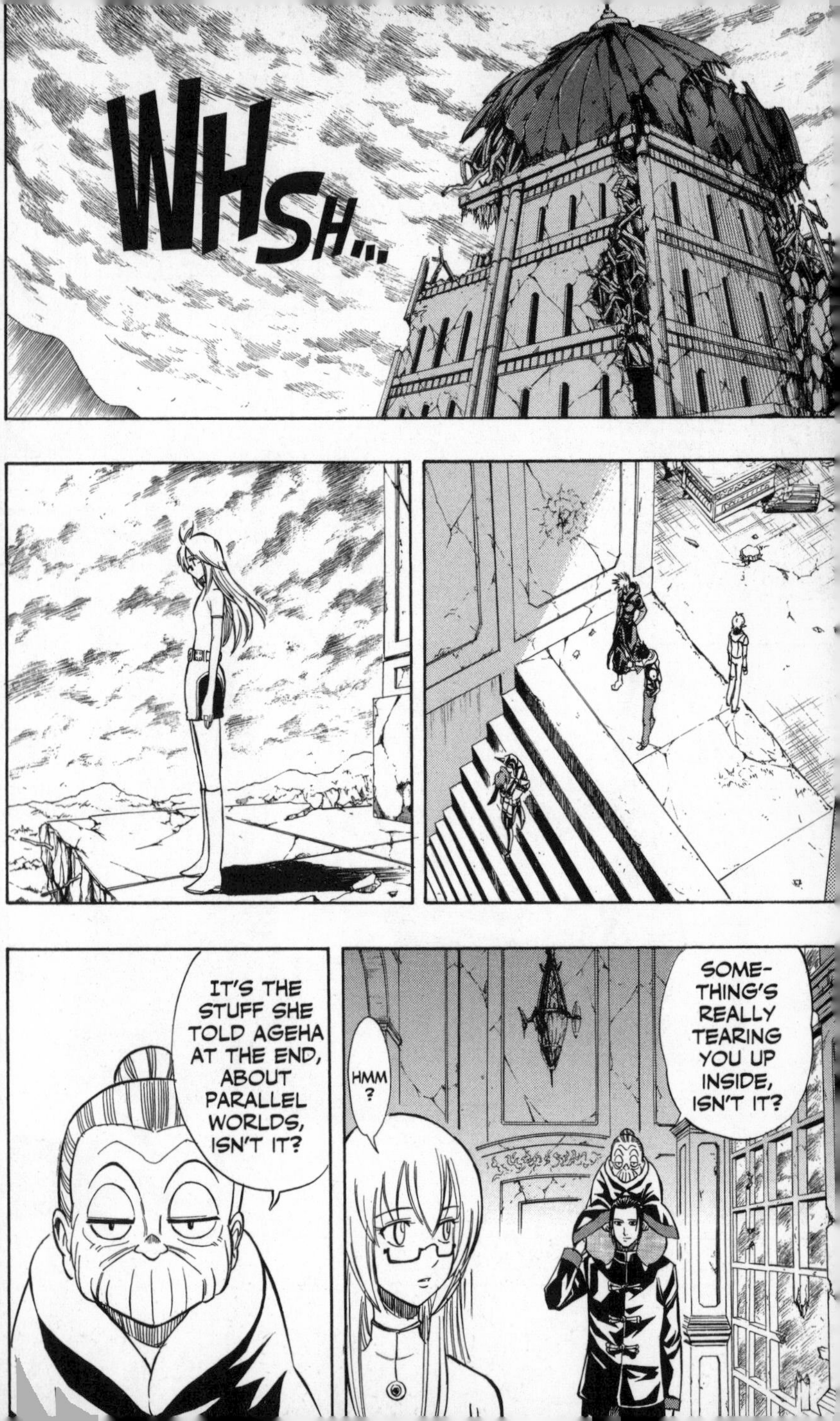
WHSH...
SOME-THING'S REALLY TEARING YOU UP INSIDE, ISN'T IT?
HMM?
IT'S THE STUFF SHE TOLD AGEHA AT THE END, ABOUT PARALLEL WORLDS, ISN'T IT?

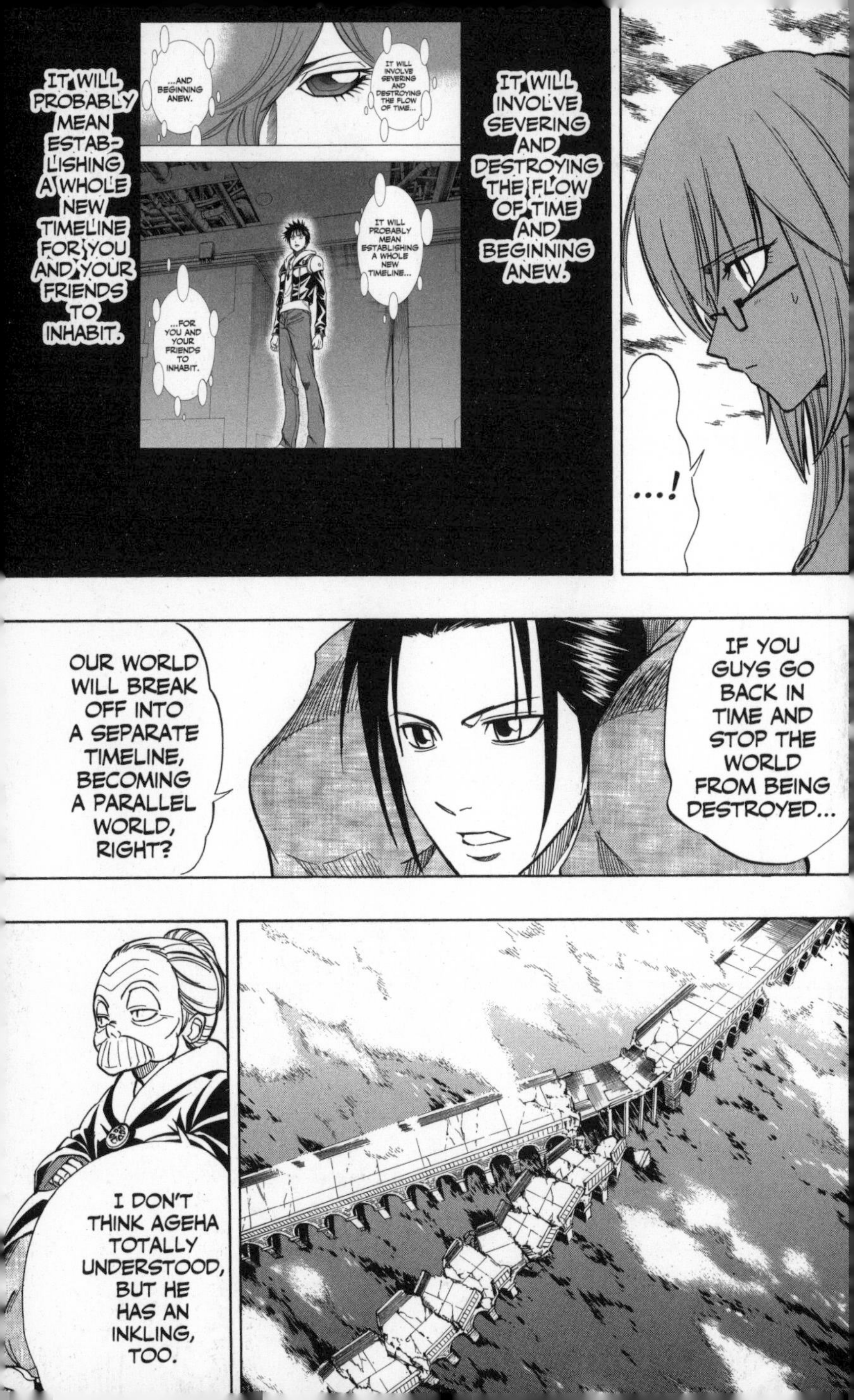
...!
IT WILL INVOLVE SEVERING AND DESTROYING THE FLOW OF TIME AND BEGINNING ANEW.
IT WILL INVOLVE SEVERING AND DESTROYING THE FLOW OF TIME...
...AND BEGINNING ANEW.
IT WILL PROBABLY MEAN ESTABLISHING A WHOLE NEW TIMELINE...
...FOR YOU AND YOUR FRIENDS TO INHABIT.
IT WILL PROBABLY MEAN ESTAB-LISHING A WHOLE NEW TIMELINE FOR YOU AND YOUR FRIENDS TO INHABIT.
IF YOU GUYS GO BACK IN TIME AND STOP THE WORLD FROM BEING DESTROYED...
OUR WORLD WILL BREAK OFF INTO A SEPARATE TIMELINE, BECOMING A PARALLEL WORLD, RIGHT?
I DON'T THINK AGEHA TOTALLY UNDERSTOOD, BUT HE HAS AN INKLING, TOO.

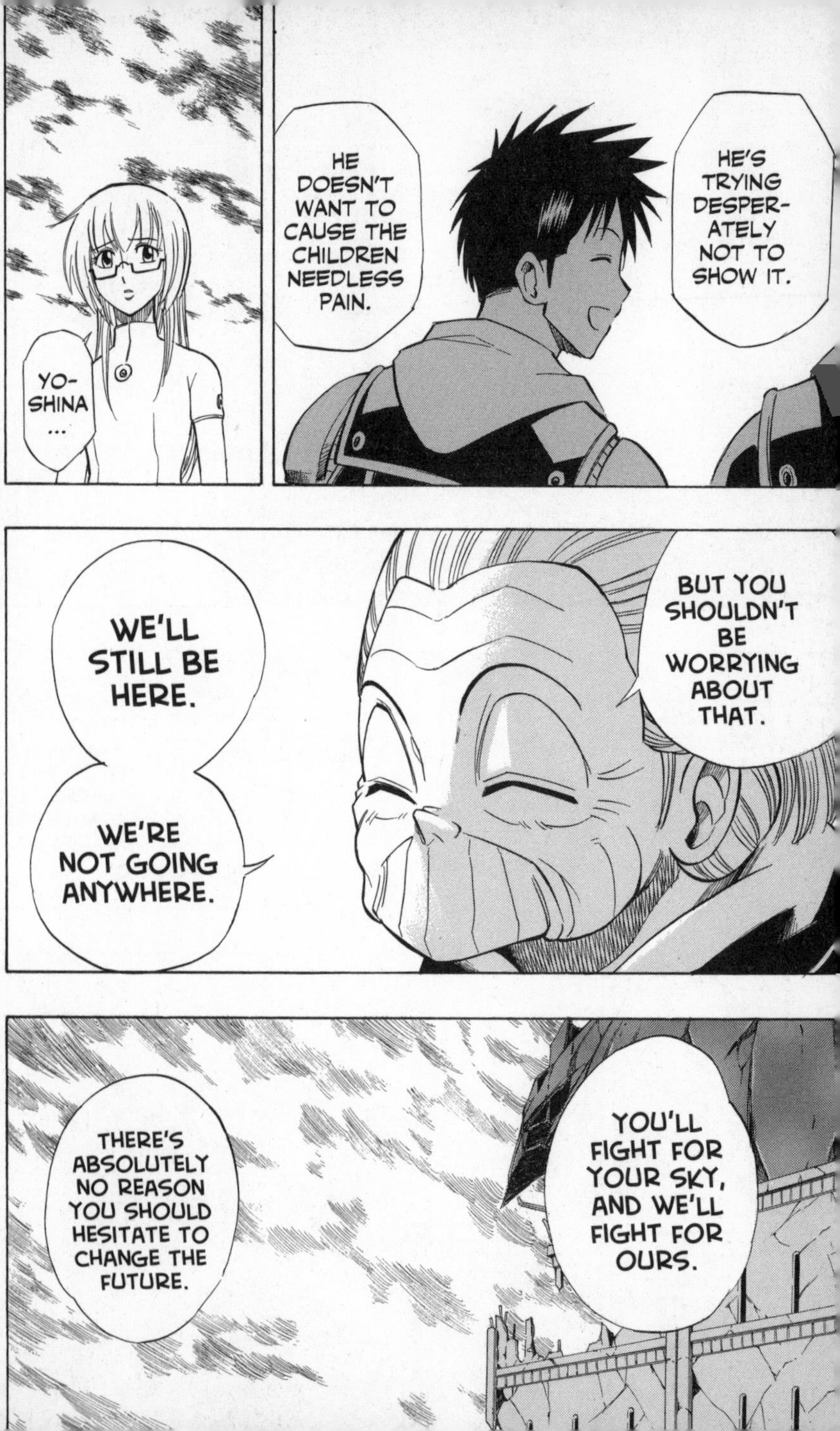
HE'S TRYING DESPERATELY NOT TO SHOW IT.
HE DOESN'T WANT TO CAUSE THE CHILDREN NEEDLESS PAIN.
YOSHINA...
BUT YOU SHOULDN'T BE WORRYING ABOUT THAT.
WE'LL STILL BE HERE.
WE'RE NOT GOING ANYWHERE.
YOU'LL FIGHT FOR YOUR SKY, AND WE'LL FIGHT FOR OURS.
THERE'S ABSOLUTELY NO REASON YOU SHOULD HESITATE TO CHANGE THE FUTURE.

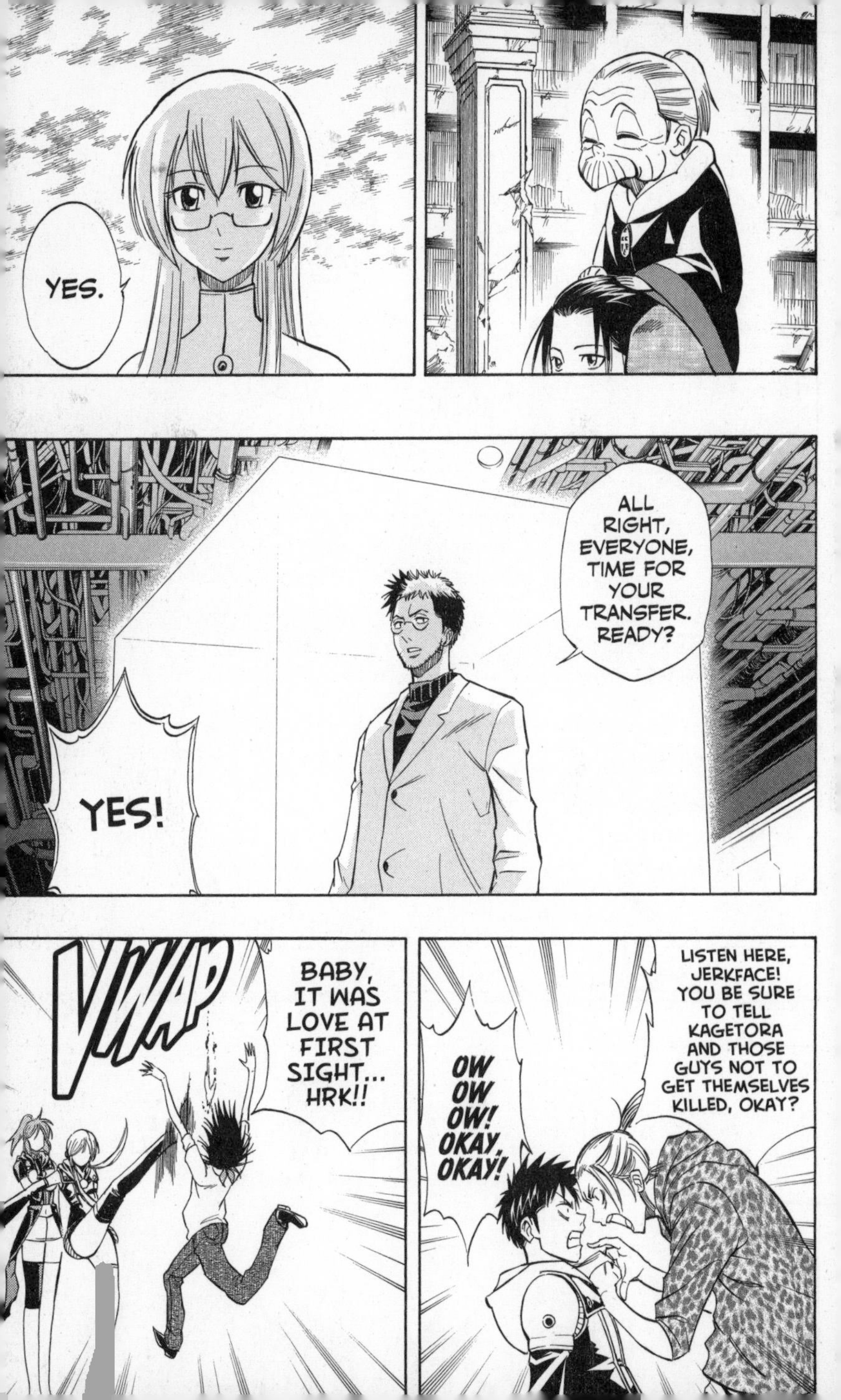
YES.
ALL RIGHT, EVERYONE, TIME FOR YOUR TRANSFER. READY?
YES!
LISTEN HERE, JERKFACE! YOU BE SURE TO TELL KAGETORA AND THOSE GUYS NOT TO GET THEMSELVES KILLED, OKAY?
OW OW OW! OKAY, OKAY!
VWAP
BABY, IT WAS LOVE AT FIRST SIGHT... HRK!!

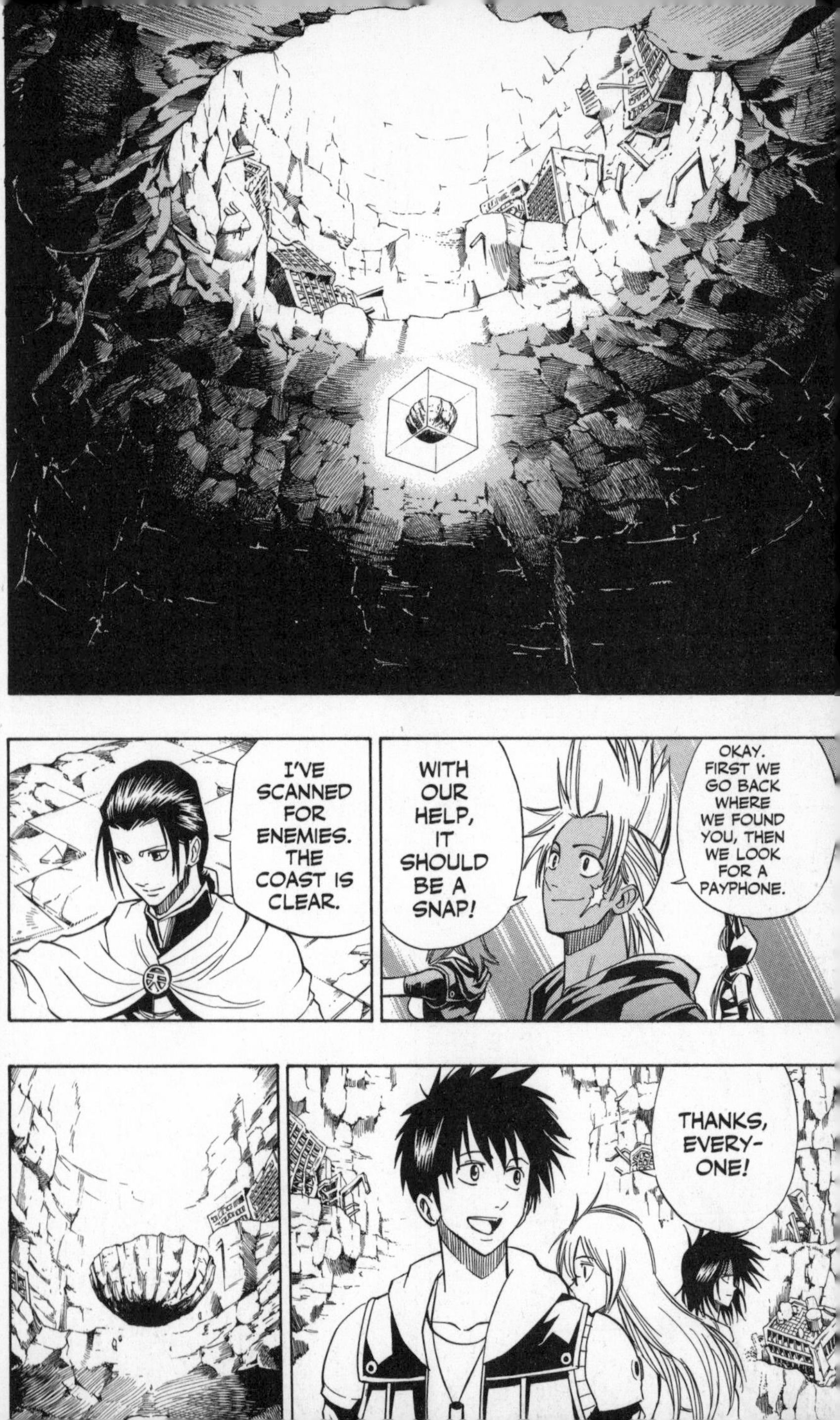
OKAY. FIRST WE GO BACK WHERE WE FOUND YOU, THEN WE LOOK FOR A PAYPHONE.
WITH OUR HELP, IT SHOULD BE A SNAP!
I'VE SCANNED FOR ENEMIES. THE COAST IS CLEAR.
THANKS, EVERY-ONE!

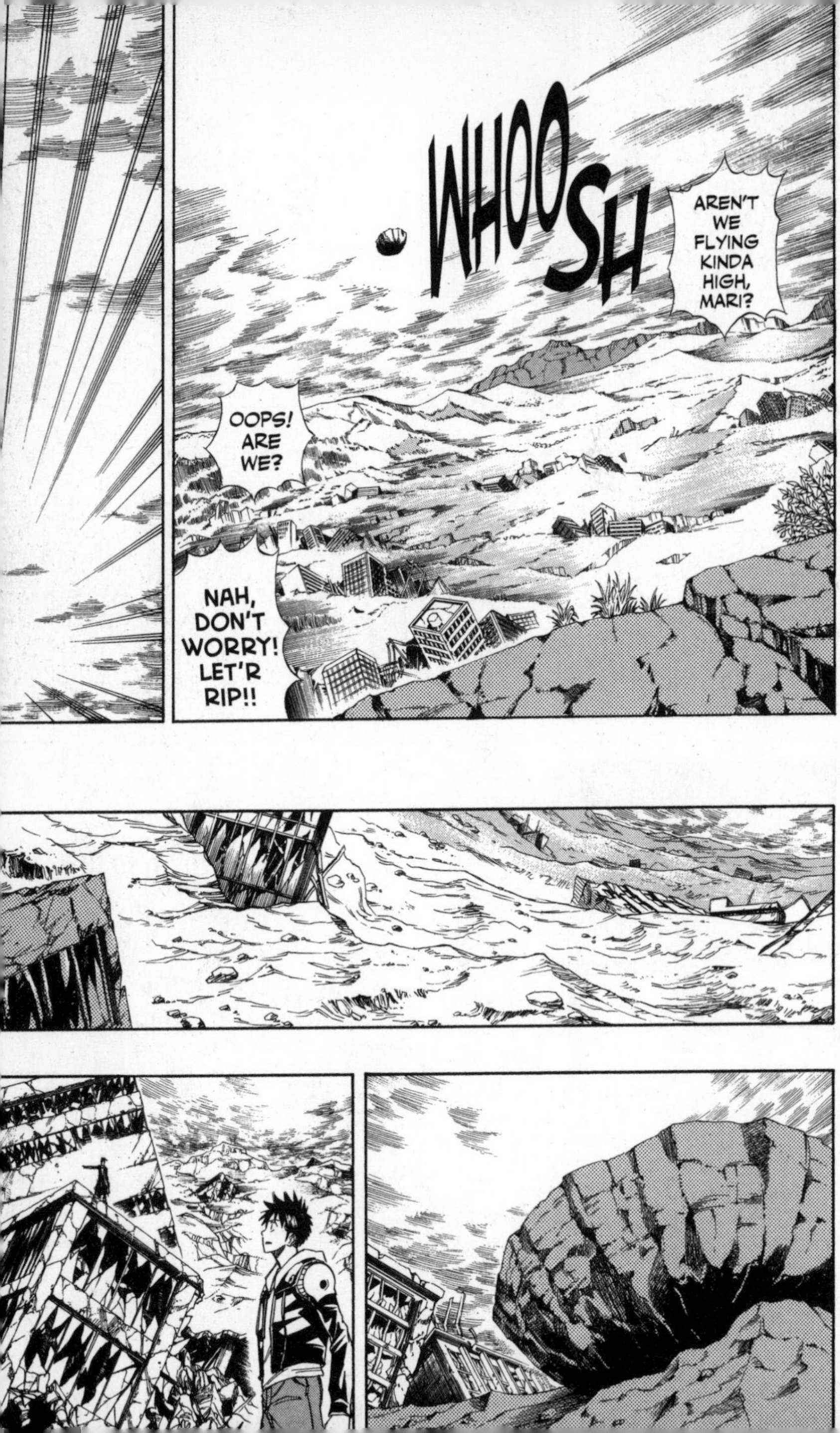

AREN'T WE FLYING KINDA HIGH, MARI?
WHOOSH
OOPS! ARE WE?
NAH, DON'T WORRY! LET'R RIP!!

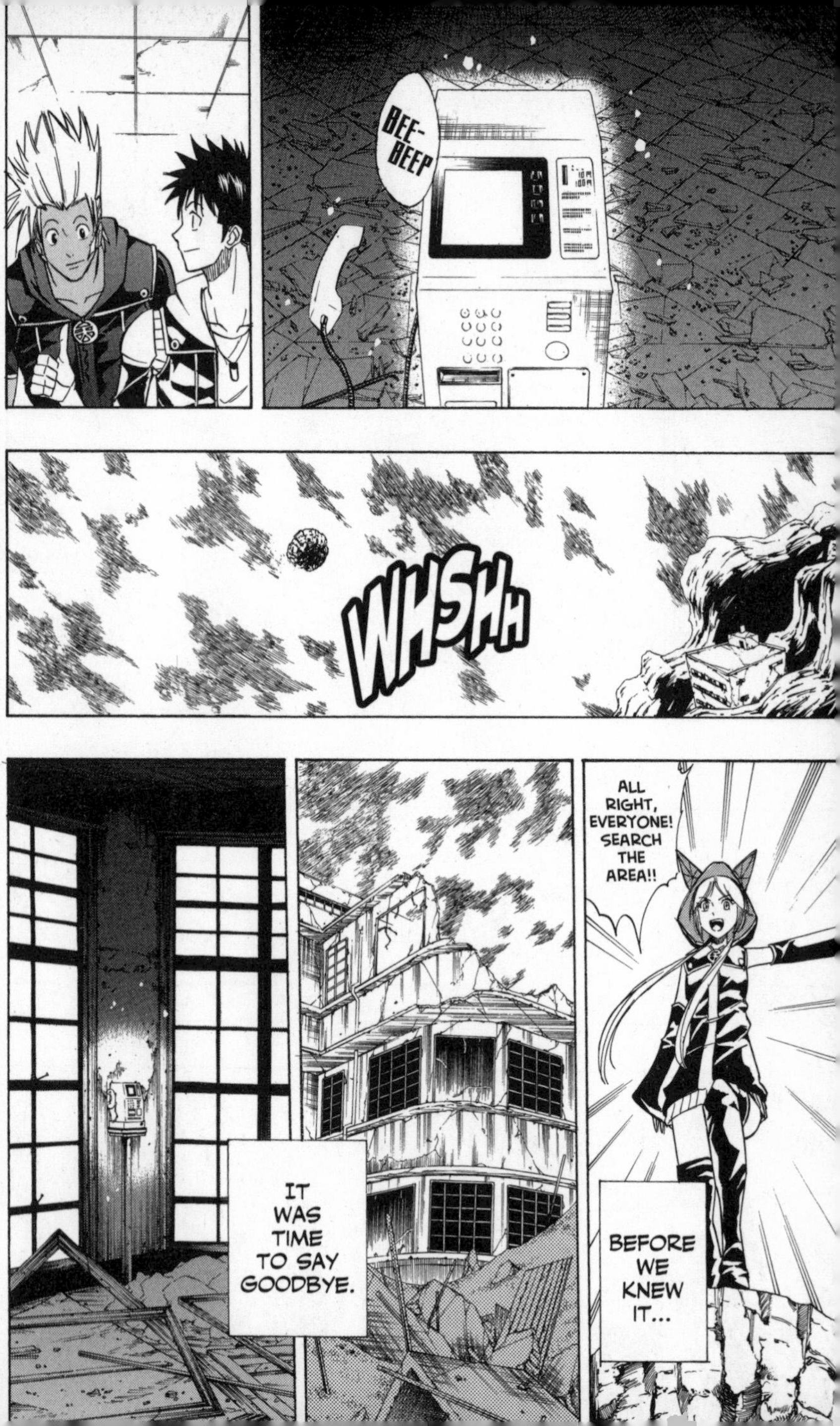
BEE-BEEP
WHSHH
ALL RIGHT, EVERYONE! SEARCH THE AREA!!
BEFORE WE KNEW IT...
IT WAS TIME TO SAY GOODBYE.

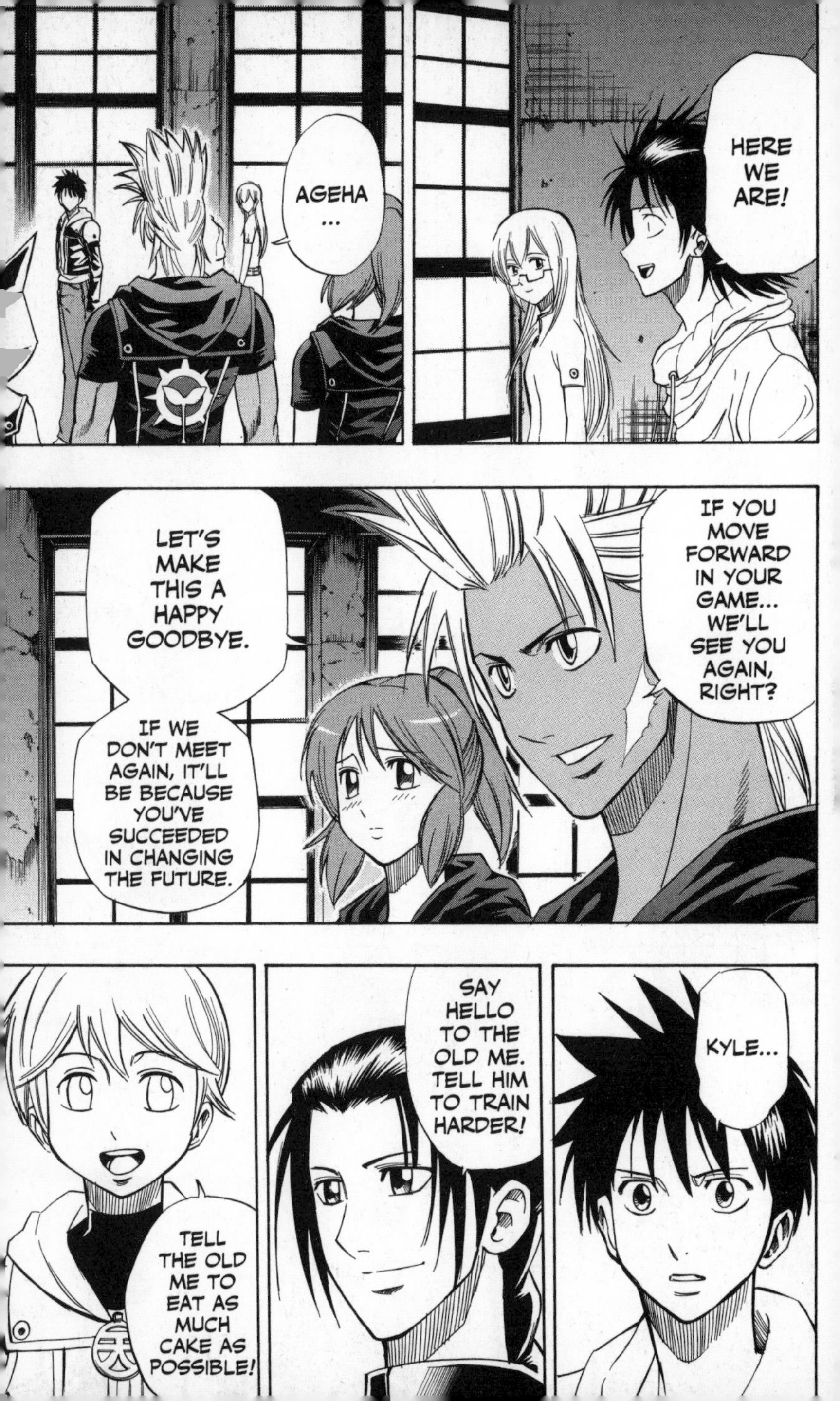
HERE WE ARE!
AGEHA ...
IF YOU MOVE FORWARD IN YOUR GAME... WE'LL SEE YOU AGAIN, RIGHT?
LET'S MAKE THIS A HAPPY GOODBYE.
IF WE DON'T MEET AGAIN, IT'LL BE BECAUSE YOU'VE SUCCEEDED IN CHANGING THE FUTURE.
KYLE...
SAY HELLO TO THE OLD ME. TELL HIM TO TRAIN HARDER!
TELL THE OLD ME TO EAT AS MUCH CAKE AS POSSIBLE!

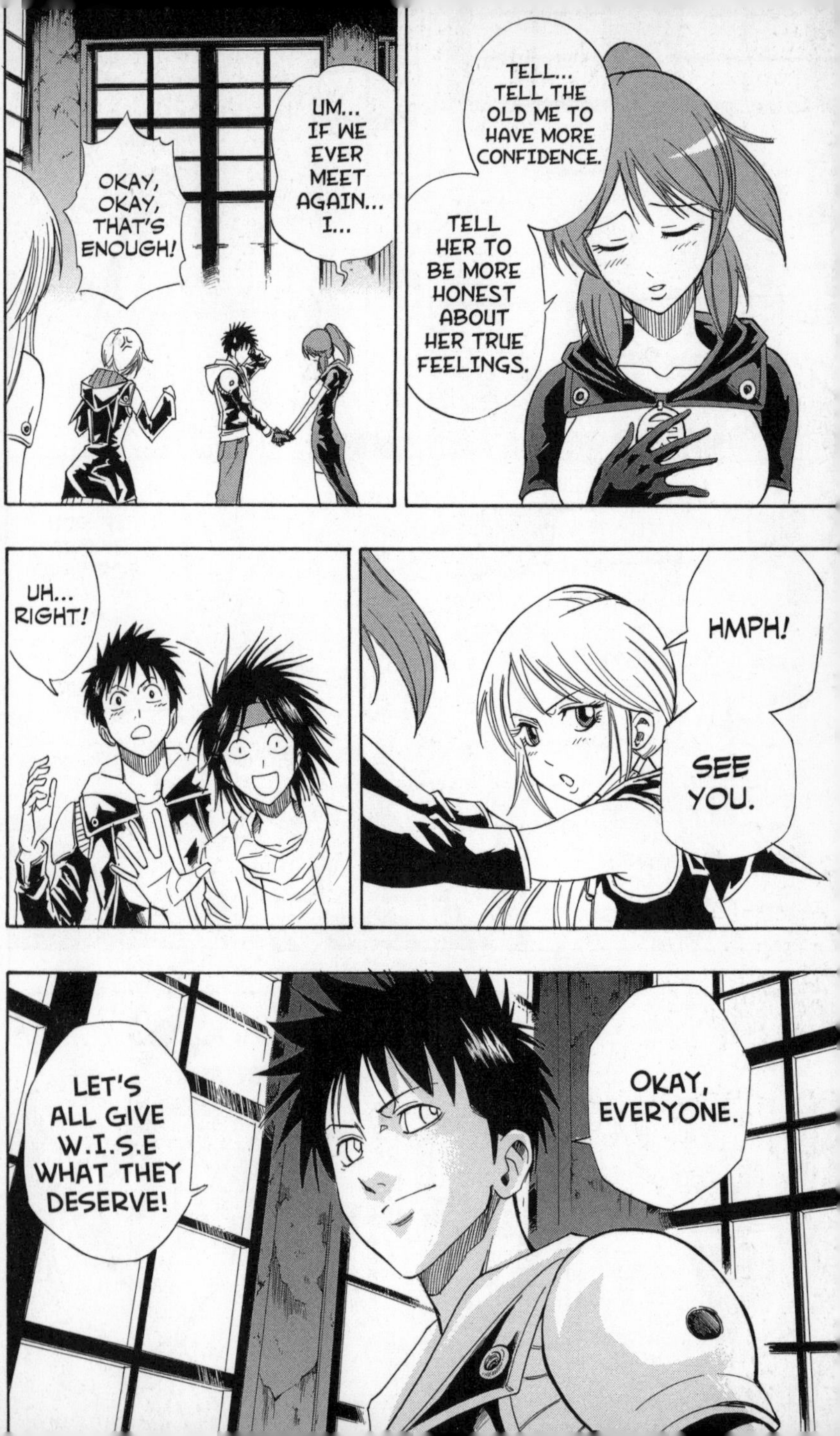
TELL... TELL THE OLD ME TO HAVE MORE CONFIDENCE.
TELL HER TO BE MORE HONEST ABOUT HER TRUE FEELINGS.
UM... IF WE EVER MEET AGAIN... I...
OKAY, OKAY, THAT'S ENOUGH!
HMPH!
SEE YOU.
UH... RIGHT!
OKAY, EVERYONE.
LET'S ALL GIVE W.I.S.E WHAT THEY DESERVE!

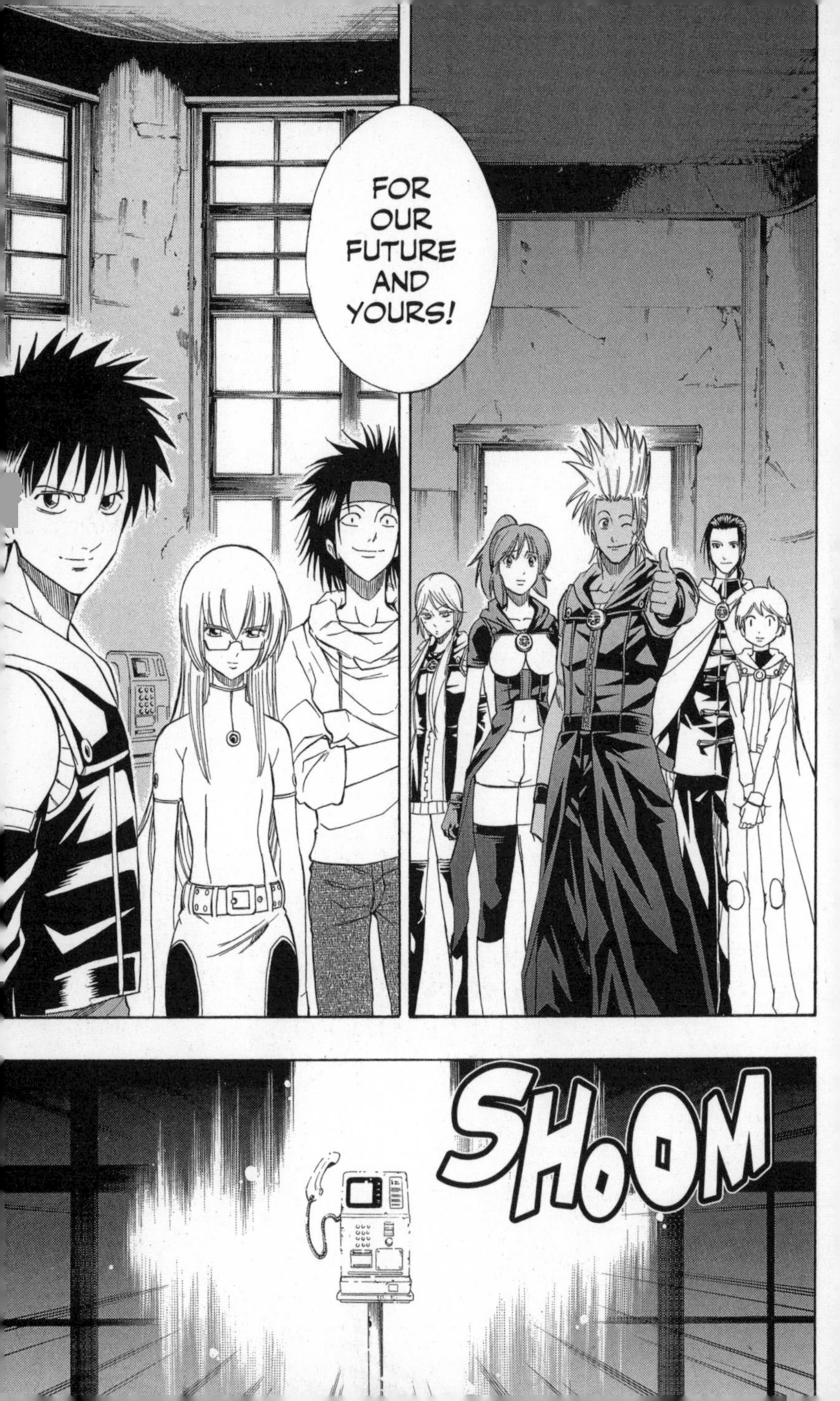
FOR OUR FUTURE AND YOURS!
SHOOM

Mutters and mumblings...

IT'S HAY FEVER SEASON, BUT I PROMISE
TO HANG IN THERE AND DO MY BEST!

CALL.87: FAMILY

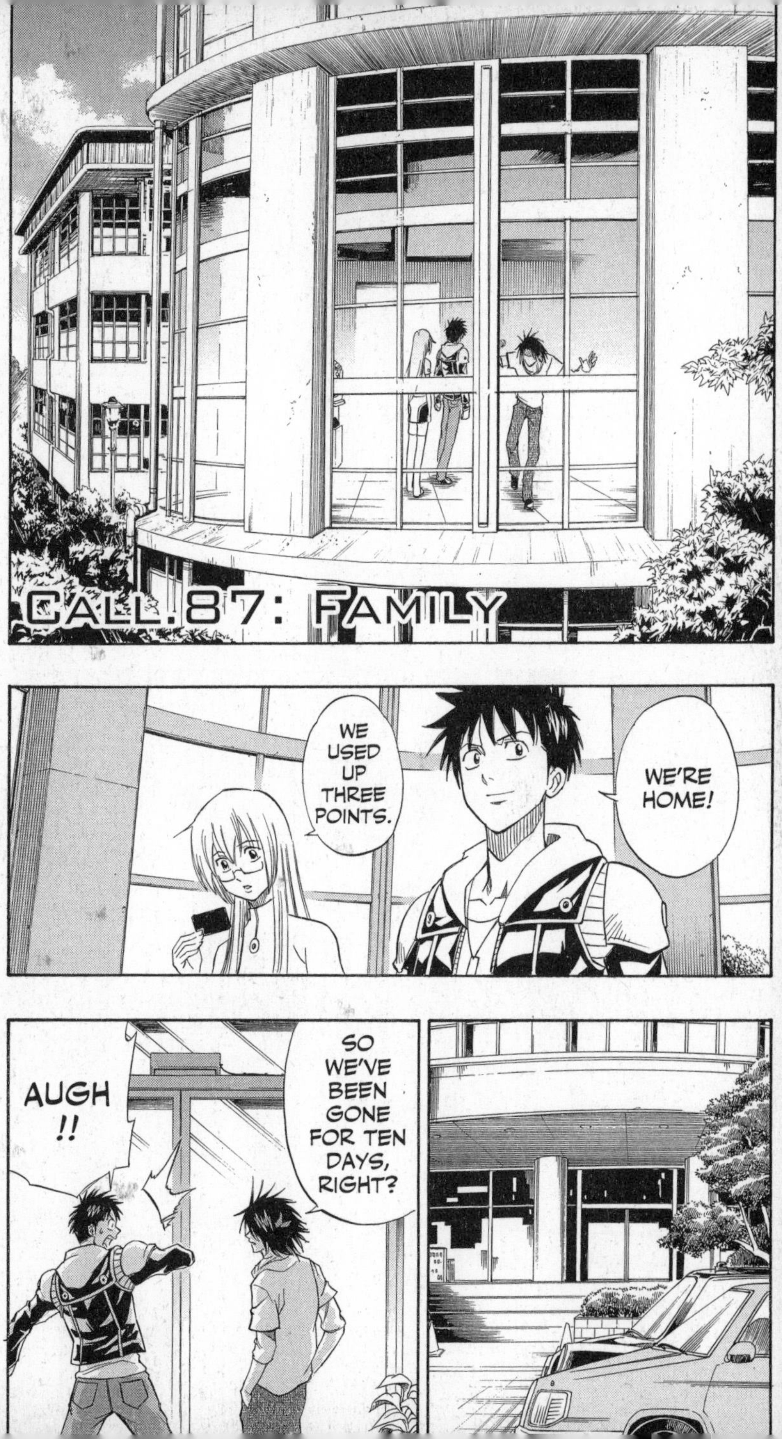

WE'RE HOME!
WE USED UP THREE POINTS.
SO WE'VE BEEN GONE FOR TEN DAYS, RIGHT?
AUGH!!

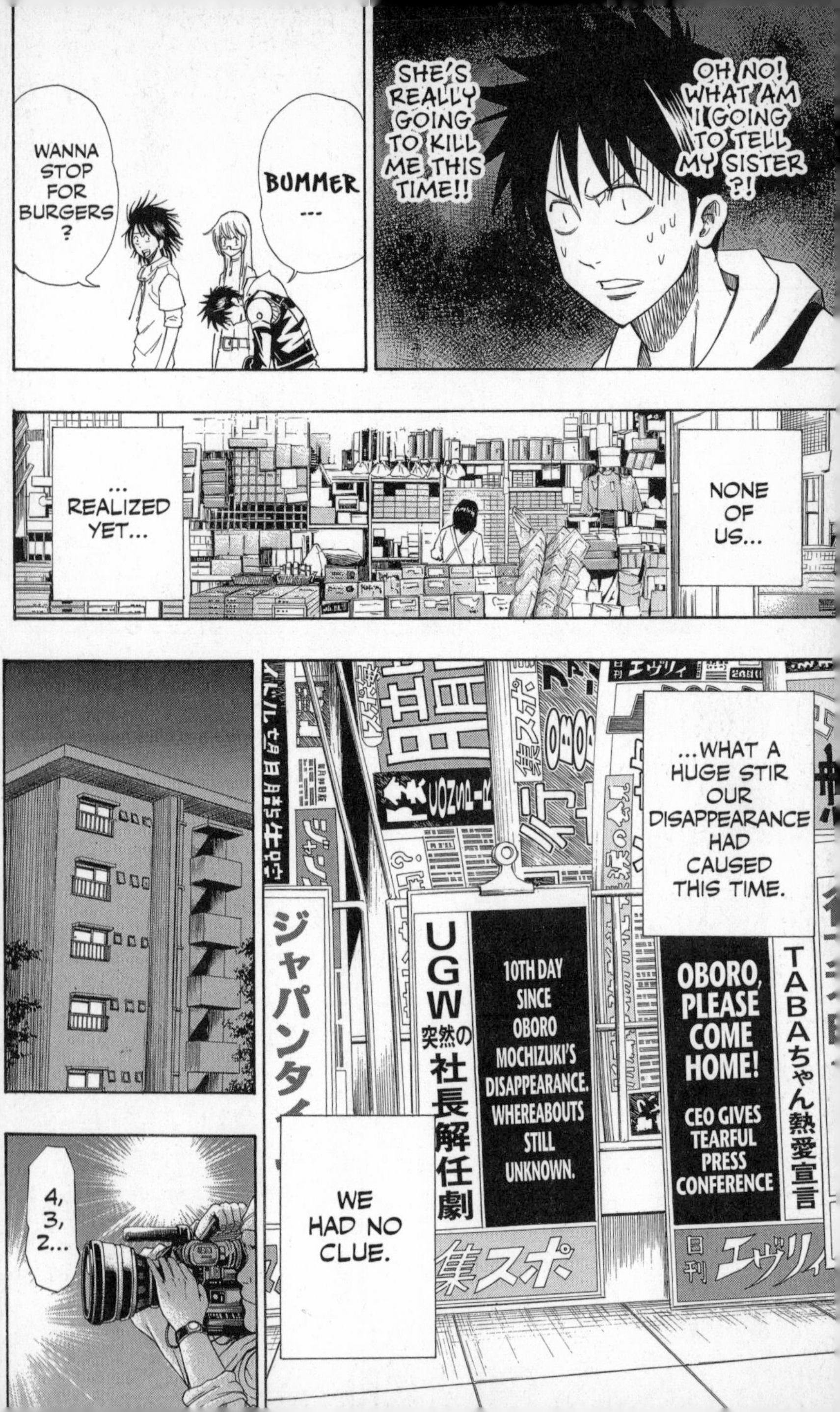
OH NO! WHAT AM I GOING TO TELL MY SISTER ?!
SHE'S REALLY GOING TO KILL ME THIS TIME!!
BUMMER ---
WANNA STOP FOR BURGERS ?
NONE OF US...
... REALIZED YET...
...WHAT A HUGE STIR OUR DISAPPEARANCE HAD CAUSED THIS TIME.
TABAちゃん熱愛宣言
OBORO, PLEASE COME HOME!
CEO GIVES TEARFUL PRESS CONFERENCE
10TH DAY SINCE OBORO MOCHIZUKI'S DISAPPEARANCE. WHEREABOUTS STILL UNKNOWN.
UGW 突然の社長解任劇
日刊エヴリィ
集スポ
WE HAD NO CLUE.
4, 3, 2...

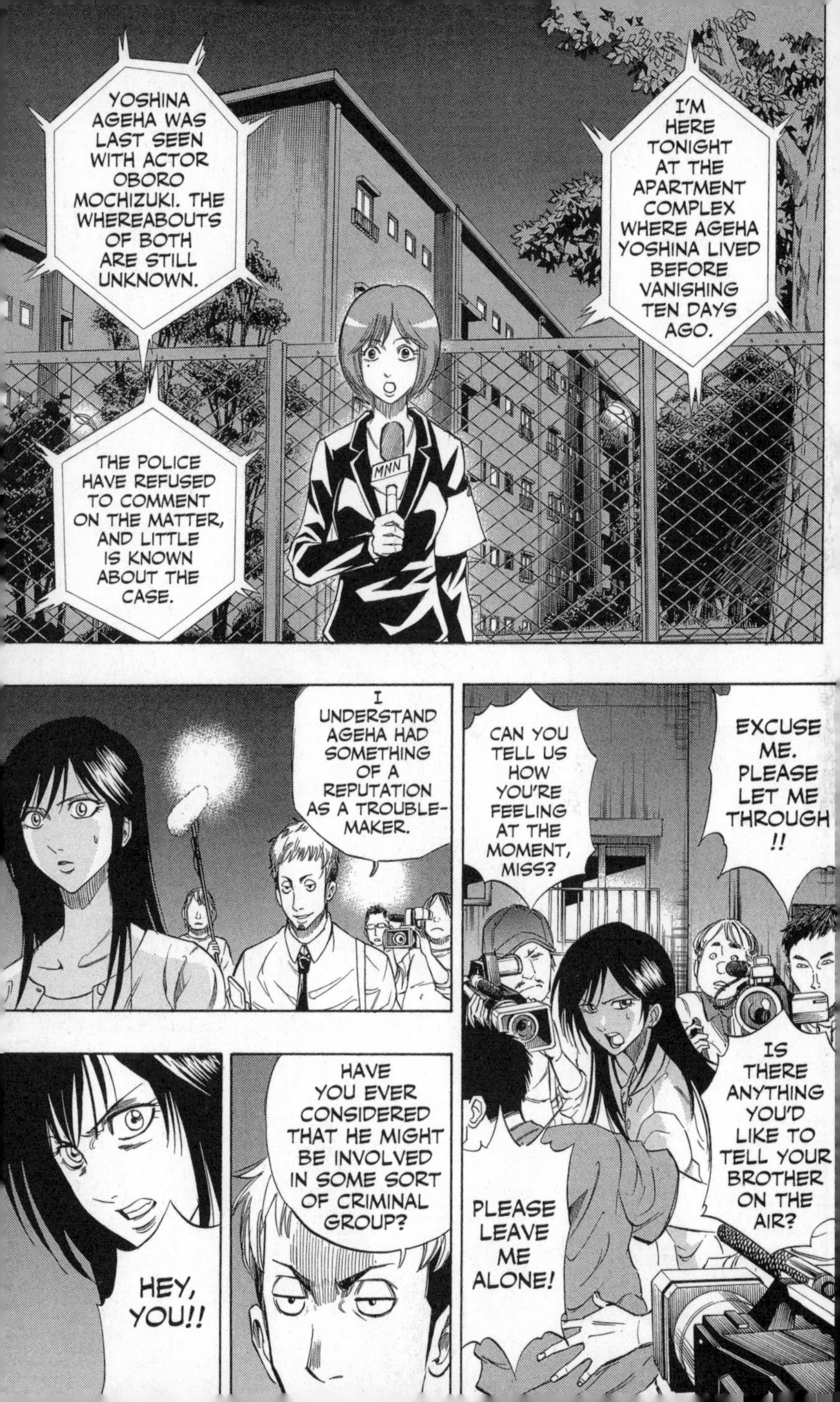

I'M HERE TONIGHT AT THE APARTMENT COMPLEX WHERE AGEHA YOSHINA LIVED BEFORE VANISHING TEN DAYS AGO.
YOSHINA AGEHA WAS LAST SEEN WITH ACTOR OBORO MOCHIZUKI. THE WHEREABOUTS OF BOTH ARE STILL UNKNOWN.
THE POLICE HAVE REFUSED TO COMMENT ON THE MATTER, AND LITTLE IS KNOWN ABOUT THE CASE.
MNN
EXCUSE ME. PLEASE LET ME THROUGH!!
CAN YOU TELL US HOW YOU'RE FEELING AT THE MOMENT, MISS?
IS THERE ANYTHING YOU'D LIKE TO TELL YOUR BROTHER ON THE AIR?
PLEASE LEAVE ME ALONE!
I UNDERSTAND AGEHA HAD SOMETHING OF A REPUTATION AS A TROUBLE-MAKER.
HAVE YOU EVER CONSIDERED THAT HE MIGHT BE INVOLVED IN SOME SORT OF CRIMINAL GROUP?
HEY, YOU!!

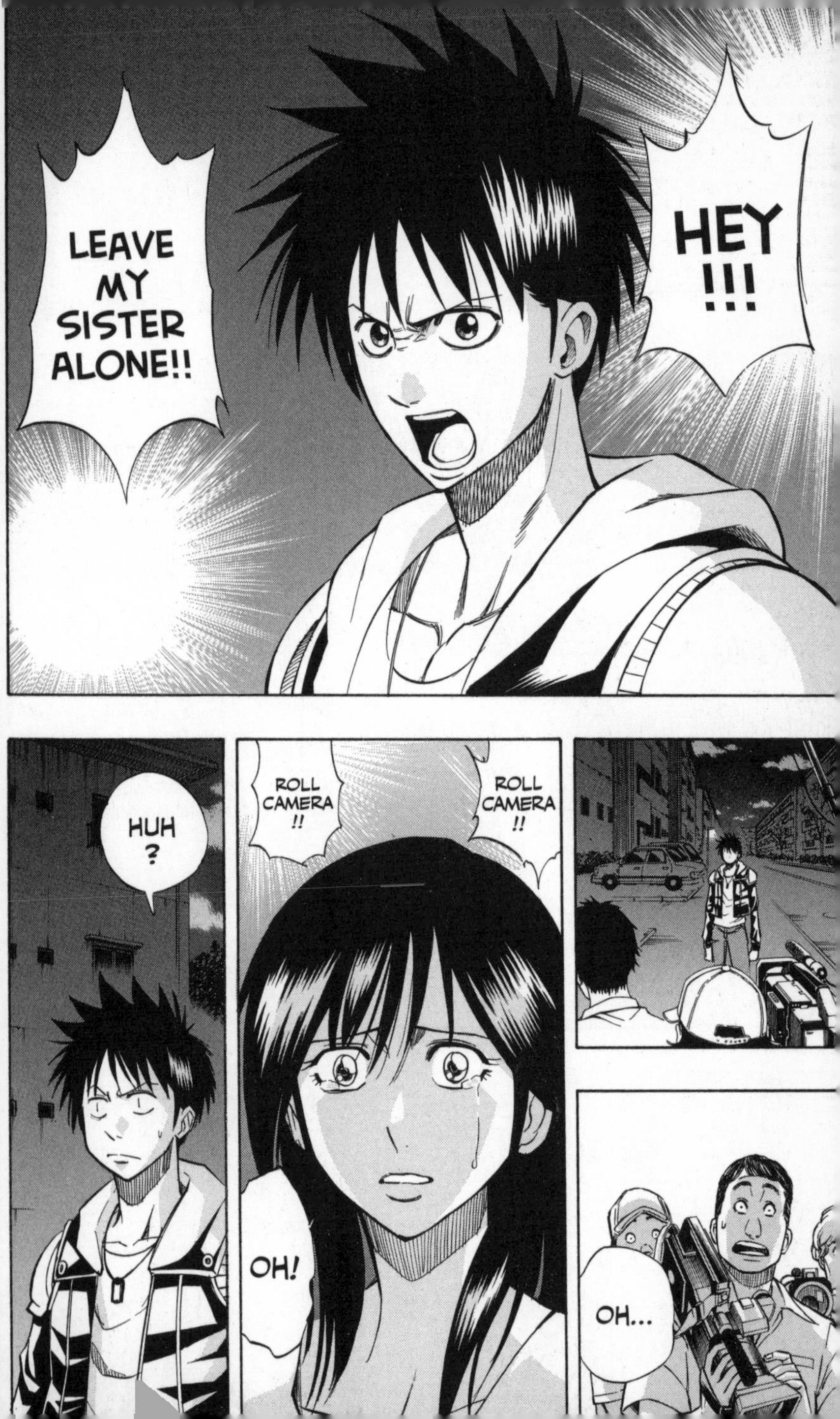
HEY !!!
LEAVE MY SISTER ALONE!!
OH...
ROLL CAMERA !!
ROLL CAMERA !!
OH!
HUH ?

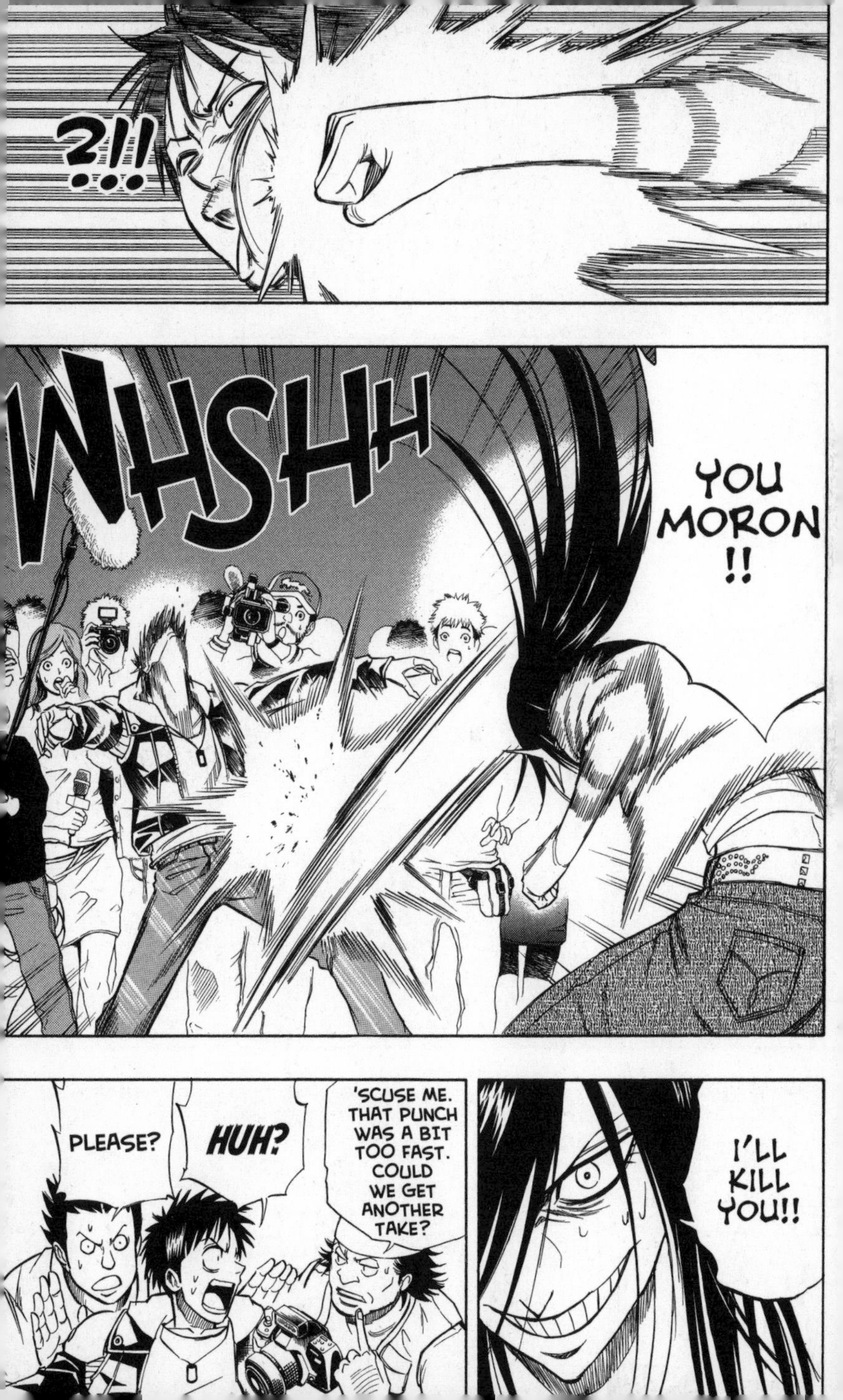
?!!...
YOU MORON!!
WHSHH
I'LL KILL YOU!!
'SCUSE ME. THAT PUNCH WAS A BIT TOO FAST. COULD WE GET ANOTHER TAKE?
HUH?
PLEASE?

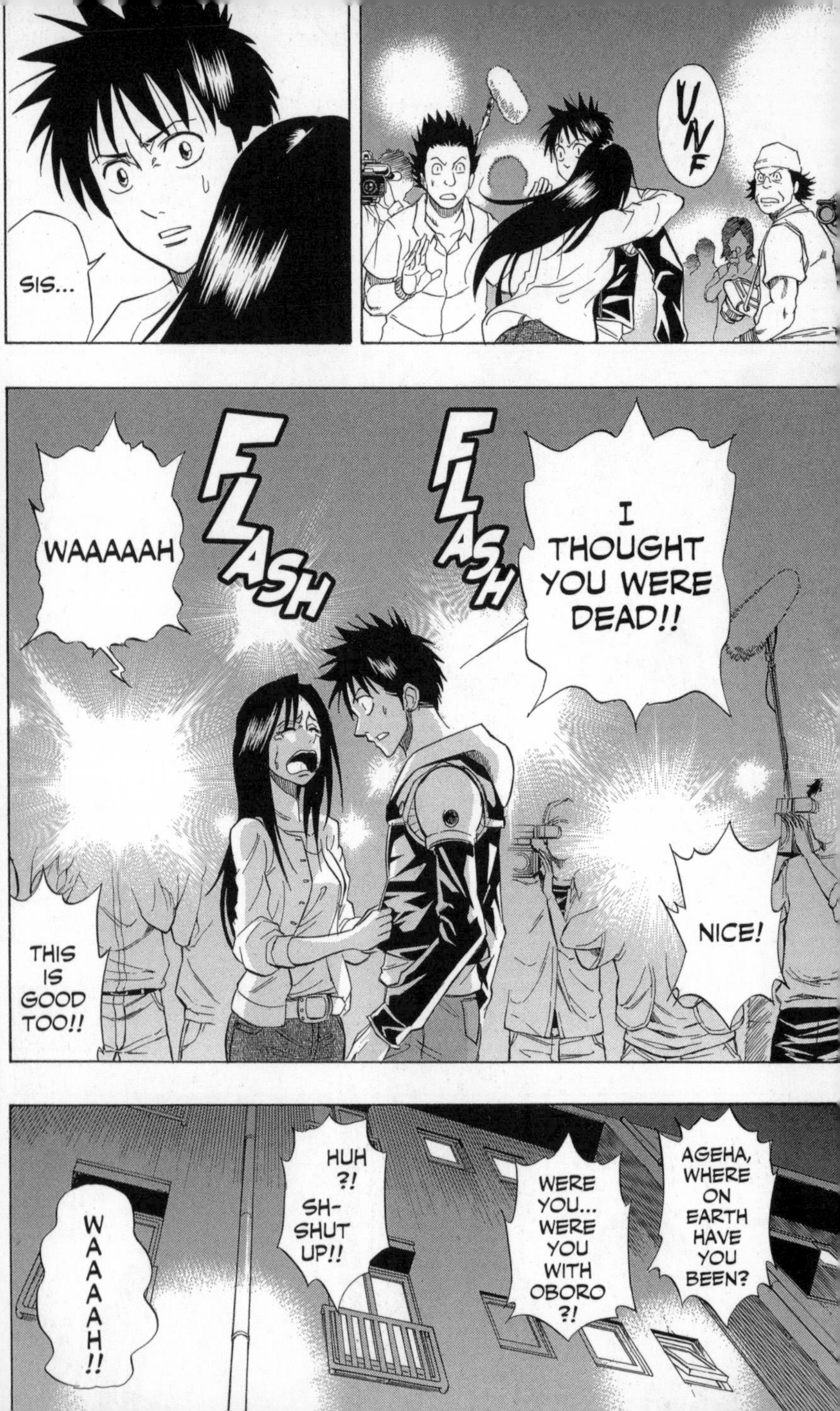
UNF
SIS...
I THOUGHT YOU WERE DEAD!!
FLASH
FLASH
WAAAAAH
NICE!
THIS IS GOOD TOO!!
AGEHA, WHERE ON EARTH HAVE YOU BEEN?
WERE YOU... WERE YOU WITH OBORO?!
HUH?! SH-SHUT UP!!
WAAAAAH!!

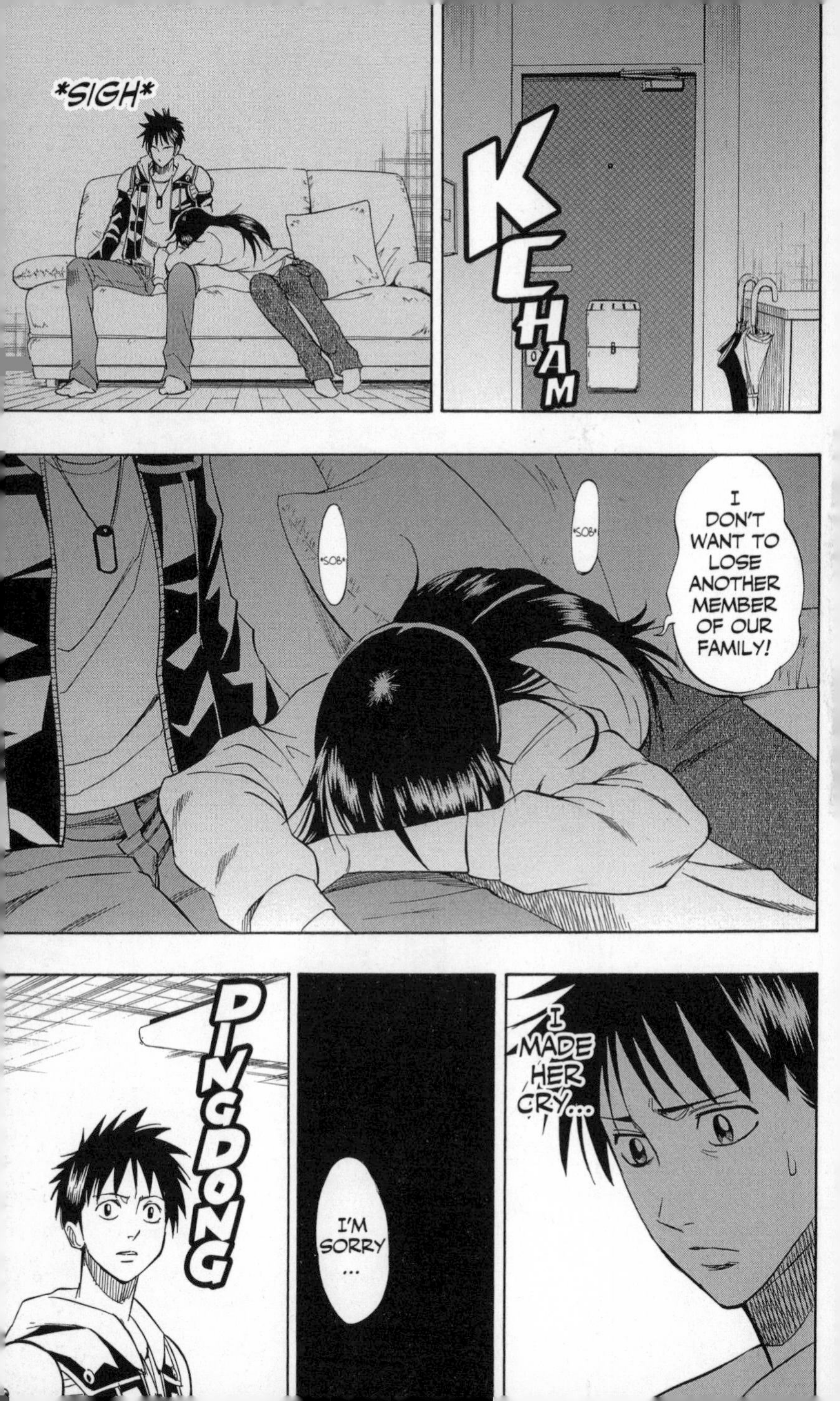
KCHAM
SIGH
I DON'T WANT TO LOSE ANOTHER MEMBER OF OUR FAMILY!
SOB
SOB
I MADE HER CRY...
I'M SORRY...
DINGDONG

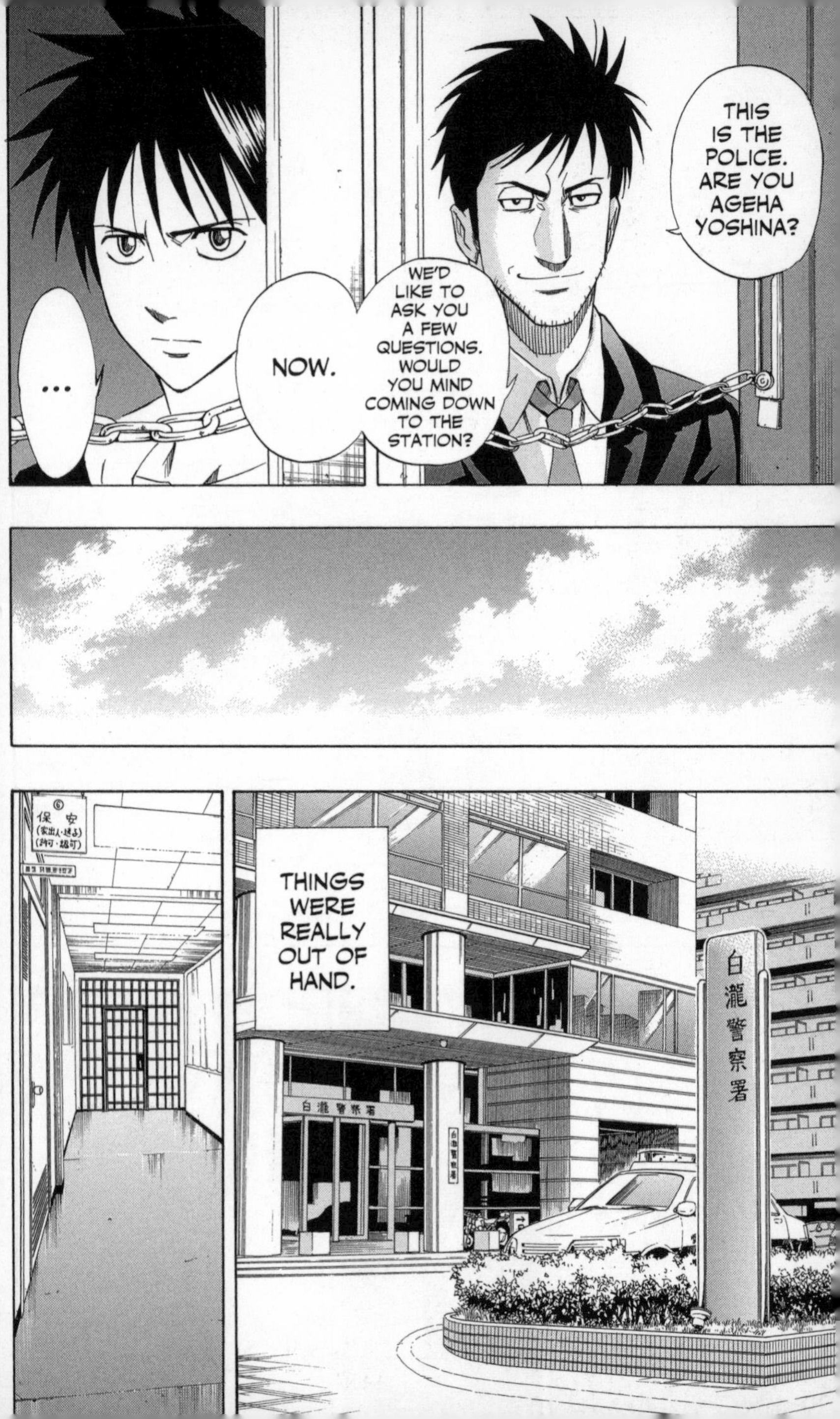
THIS IS THE POLICE. ARE YOU AGEHA YOSHINA?
WE'D LIKE TO ASK YOU A FEW QUESTIONS. WOULD YOU MIND COMING DOWN TO THE STATION?
NOW.
...
THINGS WERE REALLY OUT OF HAND.
白瀧警察署
白瀧警察署
保安

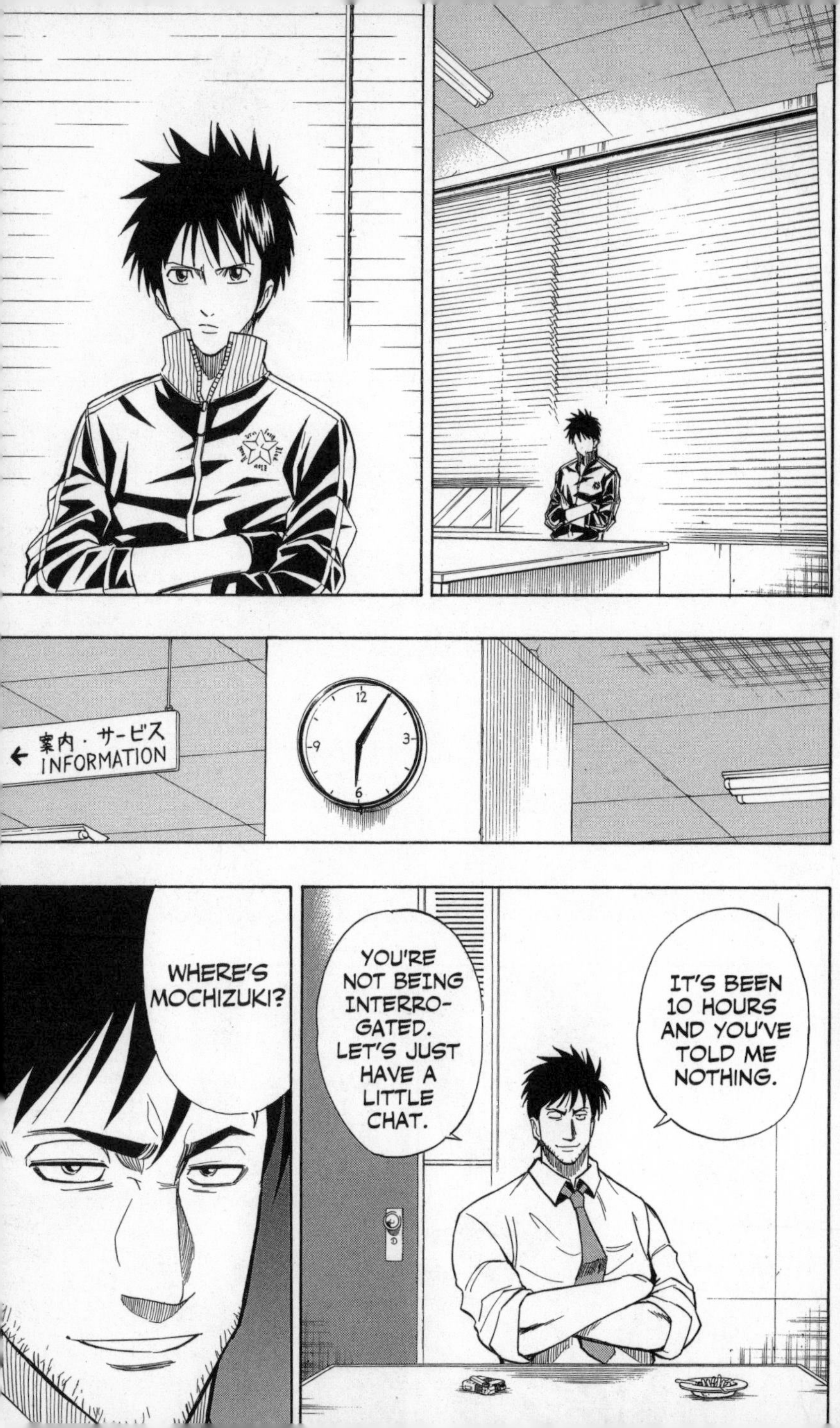

案内・サービス
INFORMATION
IT'S BEEN 10 HOURS AND YOU'VE TOLD ME NOTHING.
YOU'RE NOT BEING INTERROGATED. LET'S JUST HAVE A LITTLE CHAT.
WHERE'S MOCHIZUKI?

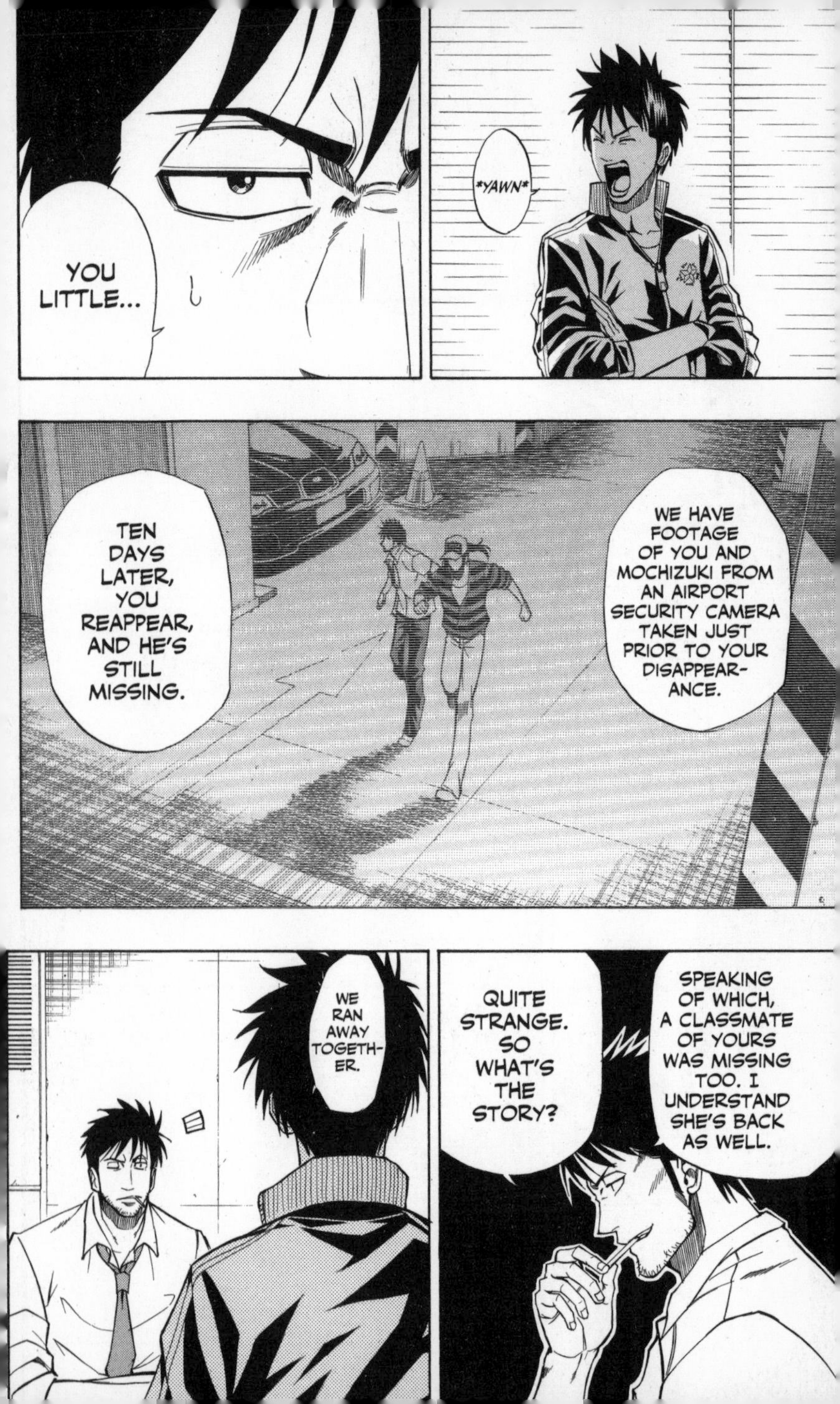
YAWN
YOU LITTLE...
WE HAVE FOOTAGE OF YOU AND MOCHIZUKI FROM AN AIRPORT SECURITY CAMERA TAKEN JUST PRIOR TO YOUR DISAPPEAR-ANCE.
TEN DAYS LATER, YOU REAPPEAR, AND HE'S STILL MISSING.
SPEAKING OF WHICH, A CLASSMATE OF YOURS WAS MISSING TOO. I UNDERSTAND SHE'S BACK AS WELL.
QUITE STRANGE. SO WHAT'S THE STORY?
WE RAN AWAY TOGETH-ER.

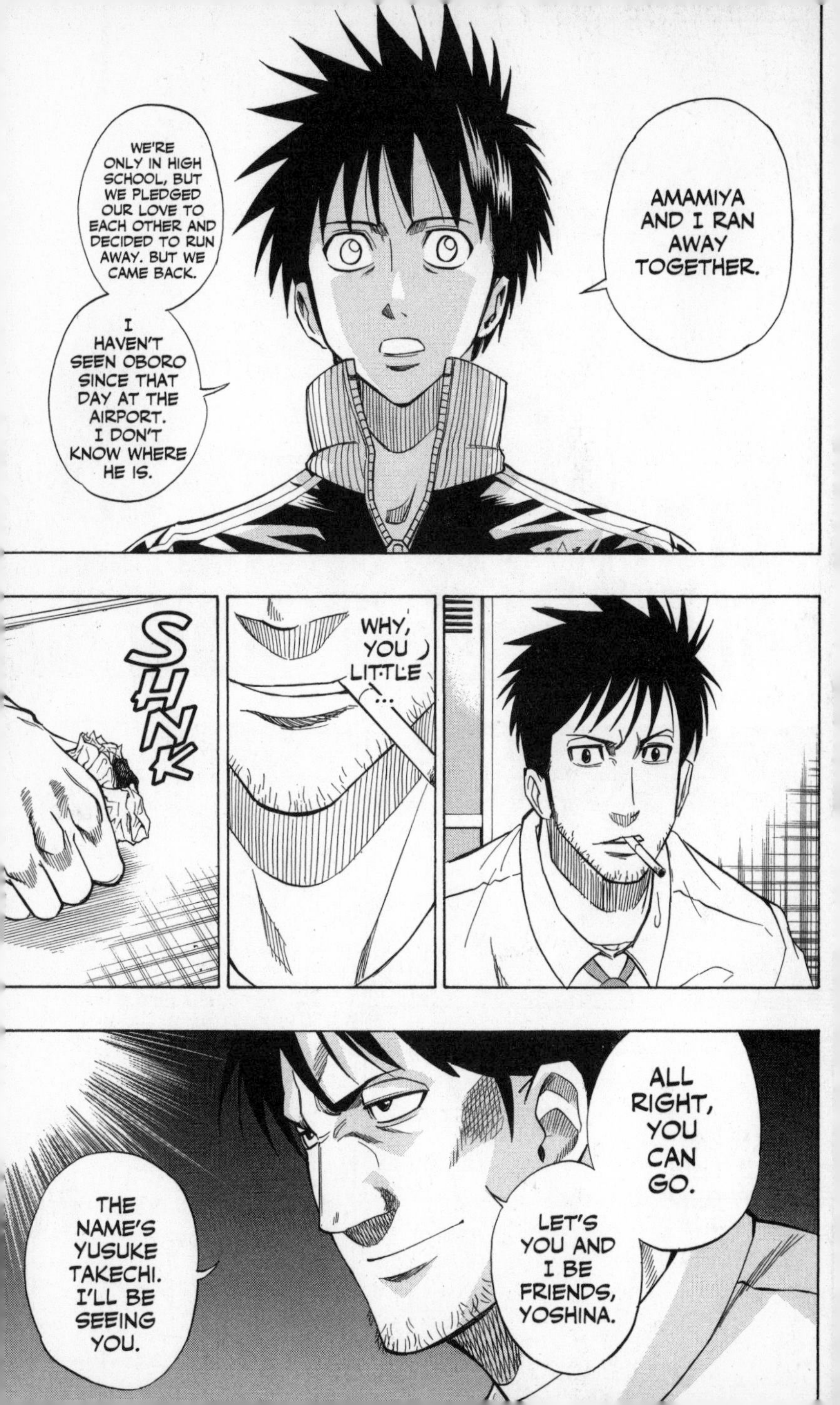
AMAMIYA AND I RAN AWAY TOGETHER.
WE'RE ONLY IN HIGH SCHOOL, BUT WE PLEDGED OUR LOVE TO EACH OTHER AND DECIDED TO RUN AWAY. BUT WE CAME BACK.
I HAVEN'T SEEN OBORO SINCE THAT DAY AT THE AIRPORT. I DON'T KNOW WHERE HE IS.
WHY, YOU LITTLE...
SHNK
ALL RIGHT, YOU CAN GO.
LET'S YOU AND I BE FRIENDS, YOSHINA.
THE NAME'S YUSUKE TAKECHI. I'LL BE SEEING YOU.

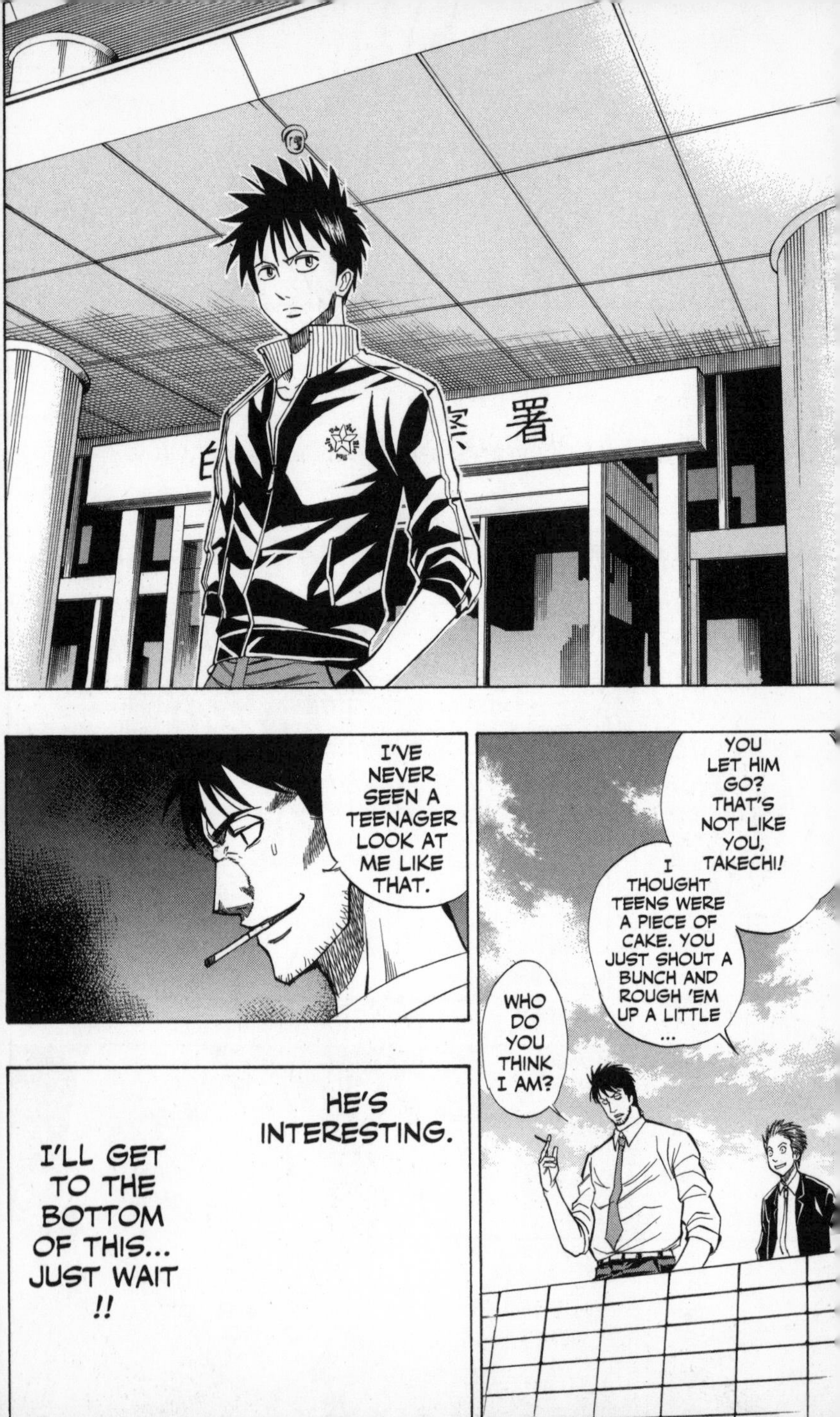
YOU LET HIM GO? THAT'S NOT LIKE YOU, TAKECHI!
I THOUGHT TEENS WERE A PIECE OF CAKE. YOU JUST SHOUT A BUNCH AND ROUGH 'EM UP A LITTLE ...
WHO DO YOU THINK I AM?
I'VE NEVER SEEN A TEENAGER LOOK AT ME LIKE THAT.
HE'S INTERESTING.
I'LL GET TO THE BOTTOM OF THIS... JUST WAIT !!

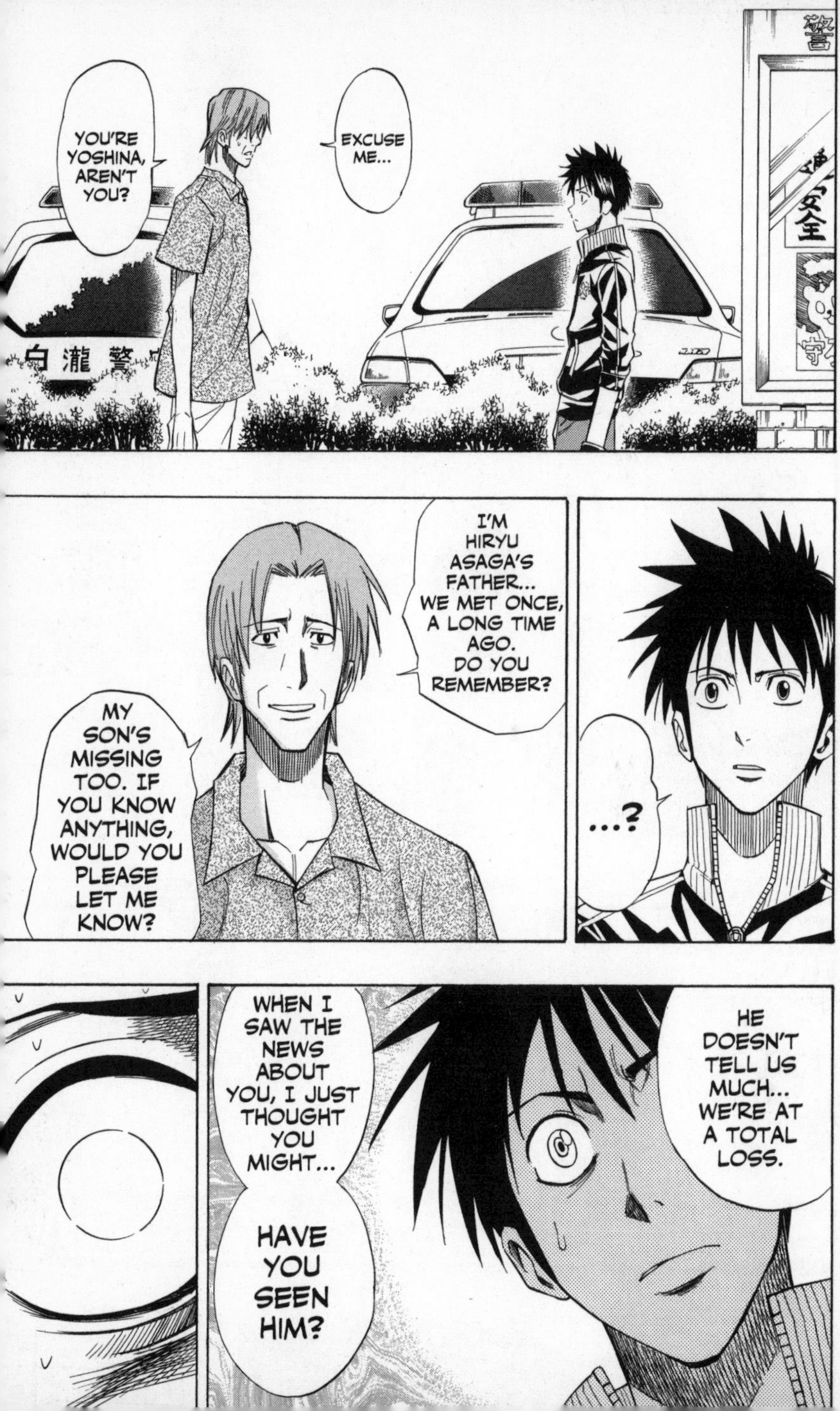
EXCUSE ME...
YOU'RE YOSHINA, AREN'T YOU?
...?
I'M HIRYU ASAGA'S FATHER... WE MET ONCE, A LONG TIME AGO. DO YOU REMEMBER?
MY SON'S MISSING TOO. IF YOU KNOW ANYTHING, WOULD YOU PLEASE LET ME KNOW?
HE DOESN'T TELL US MUCH... WE'RE AT A TOTAL LOSS.
WHEN I SAW THE NEWS ABOUT YOU, I JUST THOUGHT YOU MIGHT...
HAVE YOU SEEN HIM?

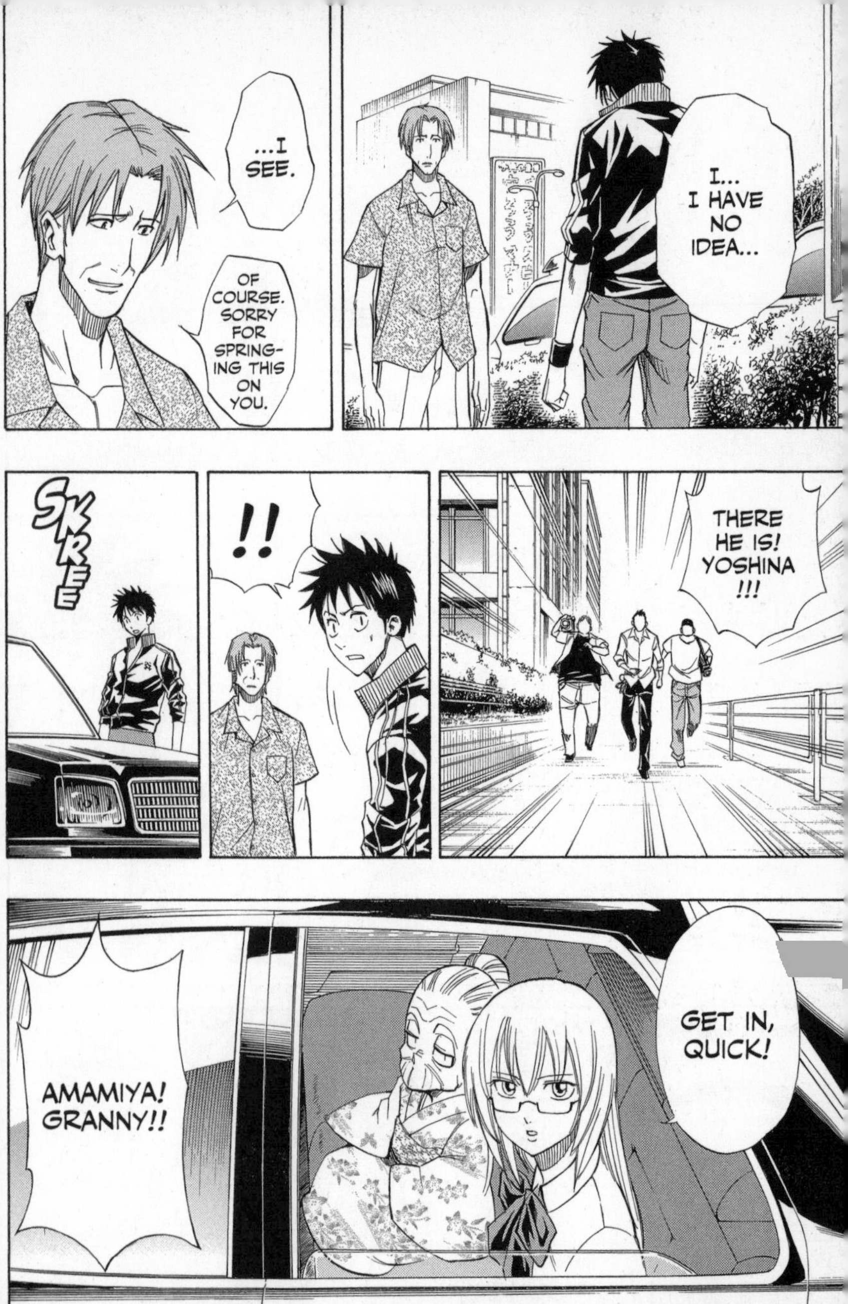
I... I HAVE NO IDEA...
...I SEE.
OF COURSE. SORRY FOR SPRINGING THIS ON YOU.
THERE HE IS! YOSHINA!!!
!!
SKREE
GET IN, QUICK!
AMAMIYA! GRANNY!!

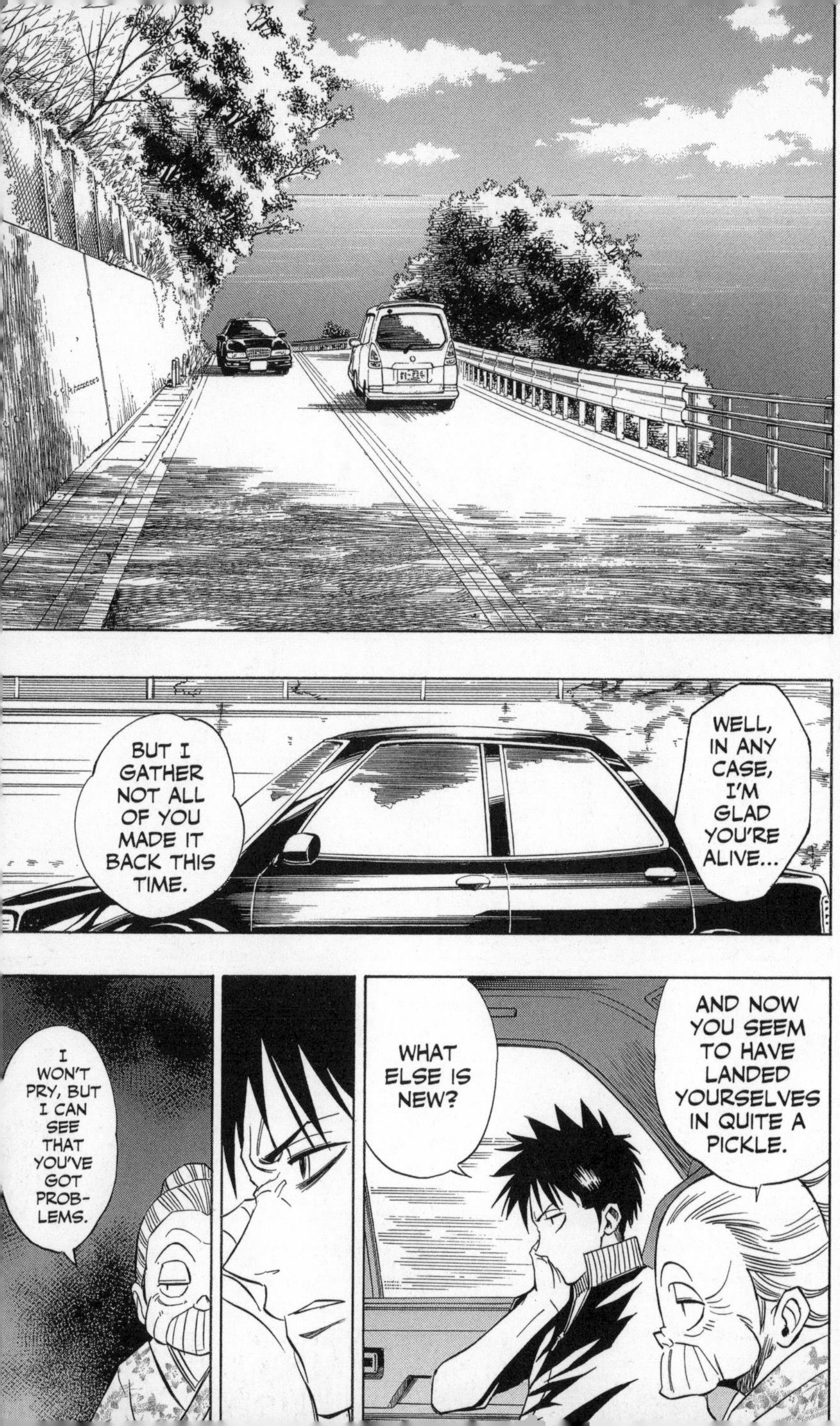
WELL, IN ANY CASE, I'M GLAD YOU'RE ALIVE...
BUT I GATHER NOT ALL OF YOU MADE IT BACK THIS TIME.
AND NOW YOU SEEM TO HAVE LANDED YOURSELVES IN QUITE A PICKLE.
WHAT ELSE IS NEW?
I WON'T PRY, BUT I CAN SEE THAT YOU'VE GOT PROB-LEMS.

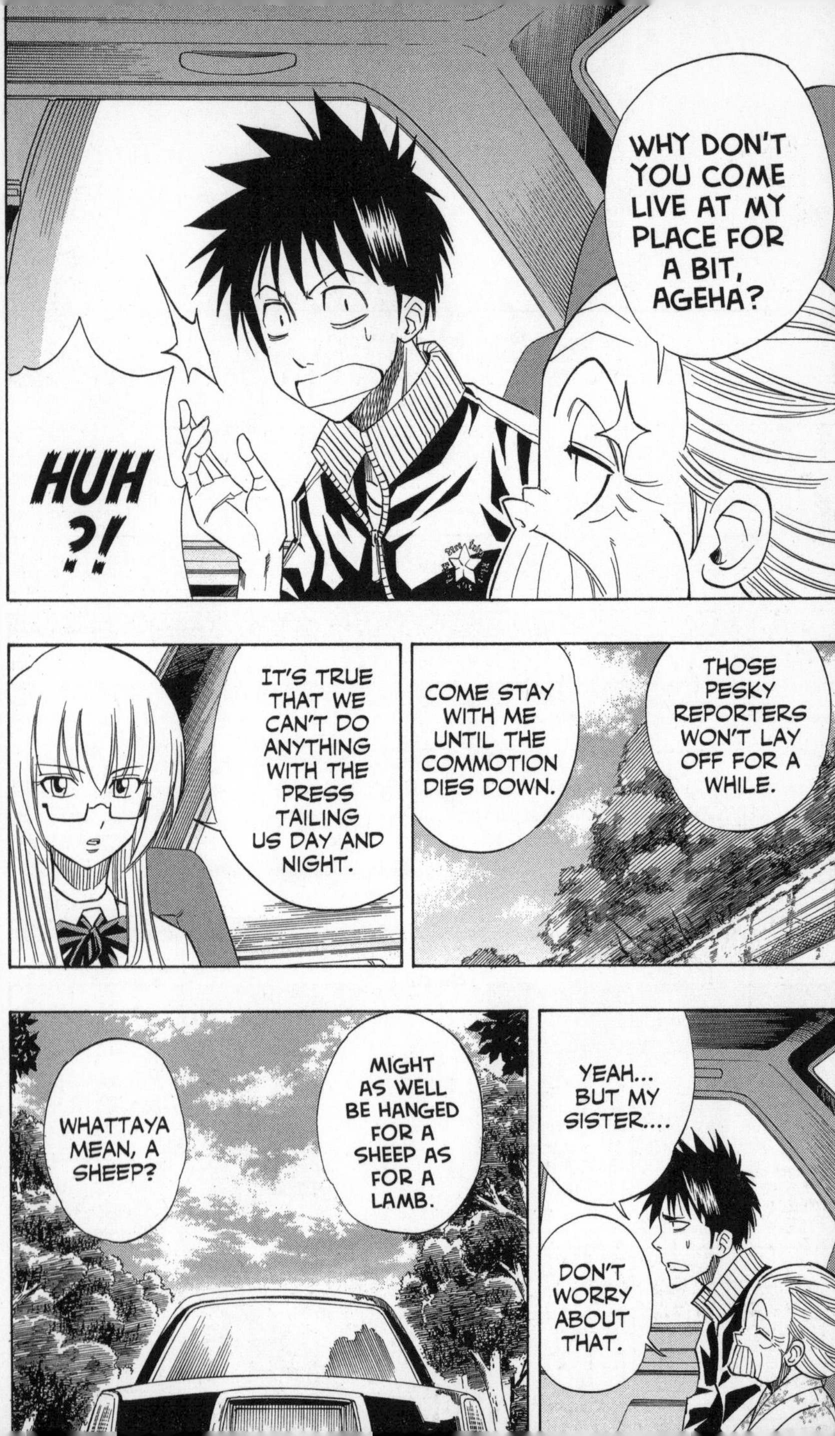
WHY DON'T YOU COME LIVE AT MY PLACE FOR A BIT, AGEHA?
HUH ?!
THOSE PESKY REPORTERS WON'T LAY OFF FOR A WHILE.
COME STAY WITH ME UNTIL THE COMMOTION DIES DOWN.
IT'S TRUE THAT WE CAN'T DO ANYTHING WITH THE PRESS TAILING US DAY AND NIGHT.
YEAH... BUT MY SISTER....
DON'T WORRY ABOUT THAT.
MIGHT AS WELL BE HANGED FOR A SHEEP AS FOR A LAMB.
WHATTAYA MEAN, A SHEEP?

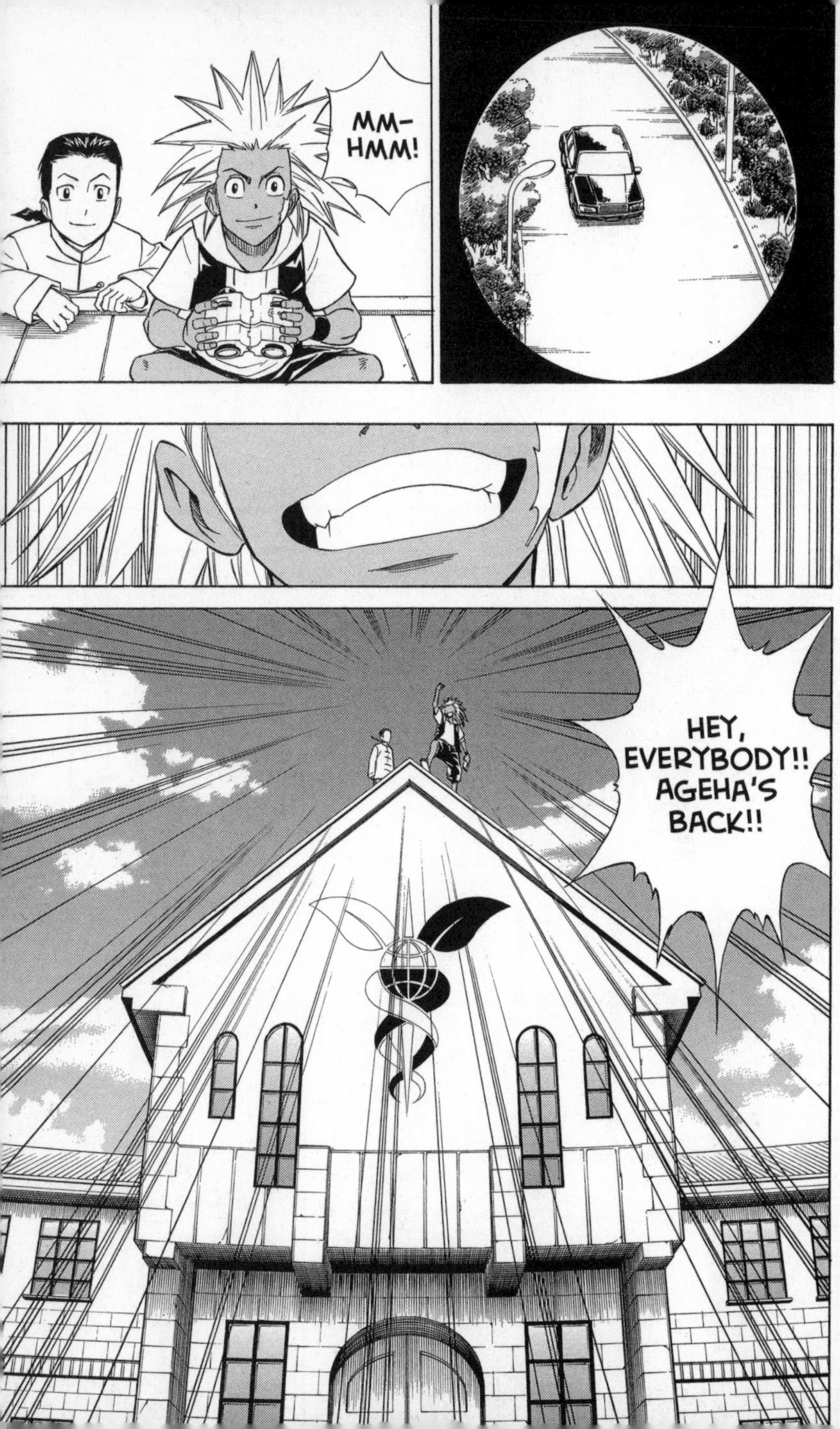
MM-HMM!
HEY, EVERYBODY!! AGEHA'S BACK!!

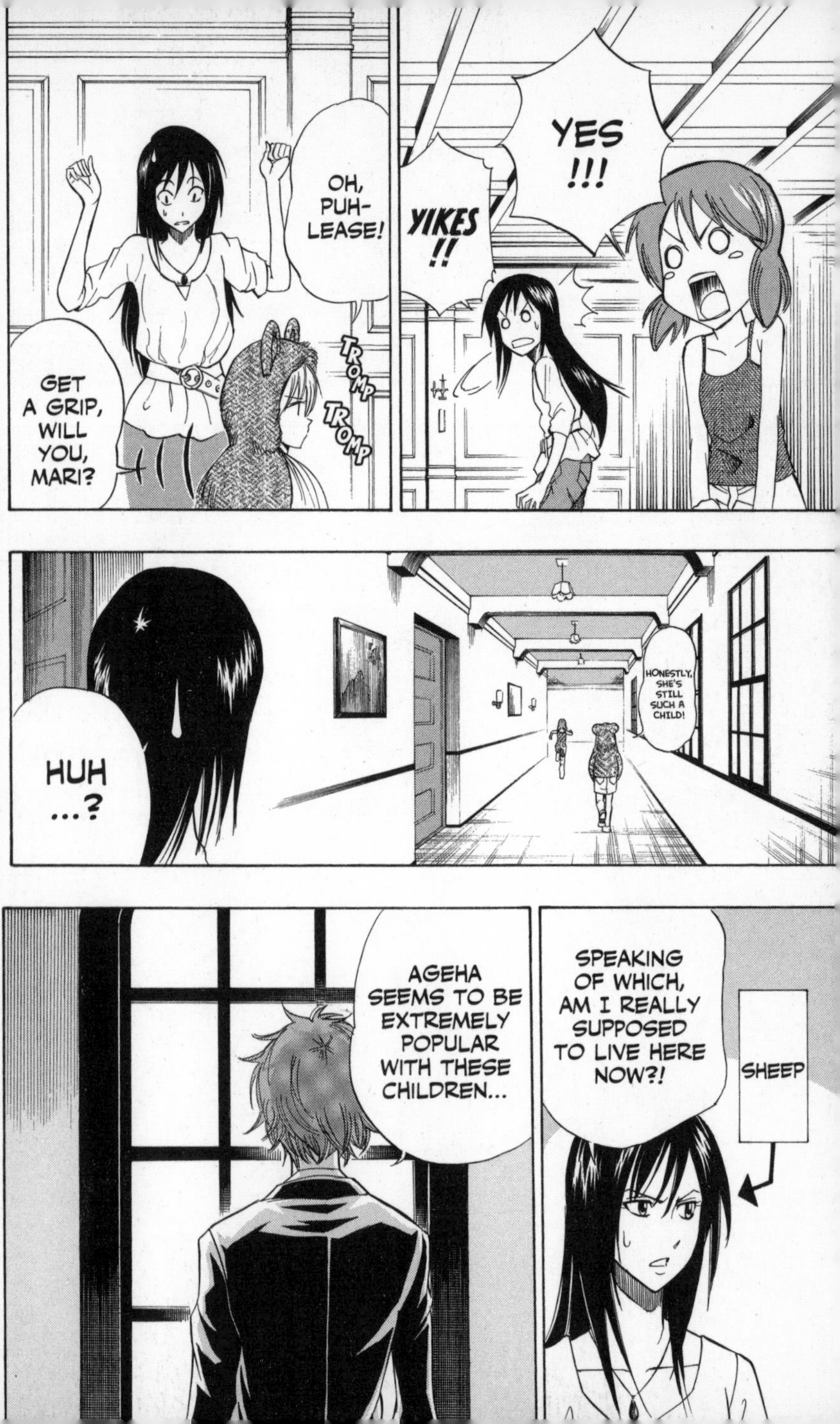
YES !!!
YIKES !!
OH, PUH-LEASE!
TROMP
TROMP
GET A GRIP, WILL YOU, MARI?
HONESTLY, SHE'S STILL SUCH A CHILD!
HUH ...?
SPEAKING OF WHICH, AM I REALLY SUPPOSED TO LIVE HERE NOW?!
SHEEP
AGEHA SEEMS TO BE EXTREMELY POPULAR WITH THESE CHILDREN...

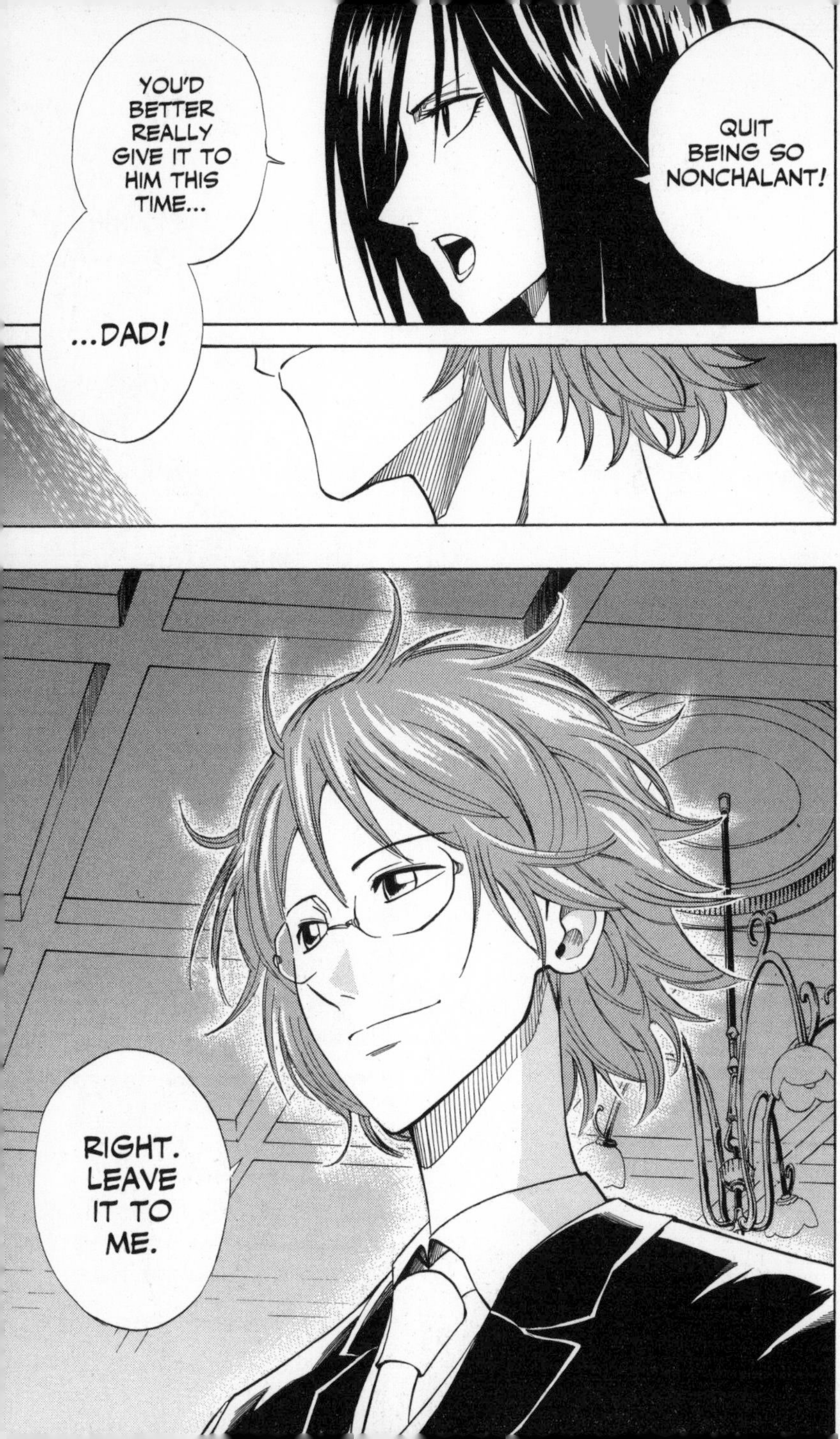
QUIT BEING SO NONCHALANT!
YOU'D BETTER REALLY GIVE IT TO HIM THIS TIME...
...DAD!
RIGHT. LEAVE IT TO ME.

A PARTY FOR EVERYONE

AFTER WE EAT CAKE, LET'S ALL PLAY MARIO BROTHERS!
I RESERVED A KARAOKE BOX TOO!
RIGHT ON! PARTY ALL NIGHT!
TA-DAAA
THIS IS FOR YOU.
HERE WE GO. I'VE DREAMED OF THIS SINCE CHILDHOOD.
WAP
DOES THIS MEAN WE'RE GONNA BE TREATED LIKE SLAVES NEXT YEAR TOO?
JINGLE JINGLE

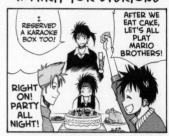

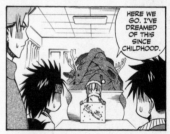

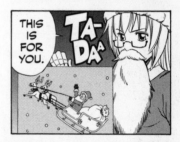

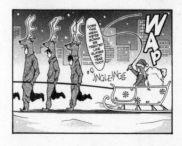

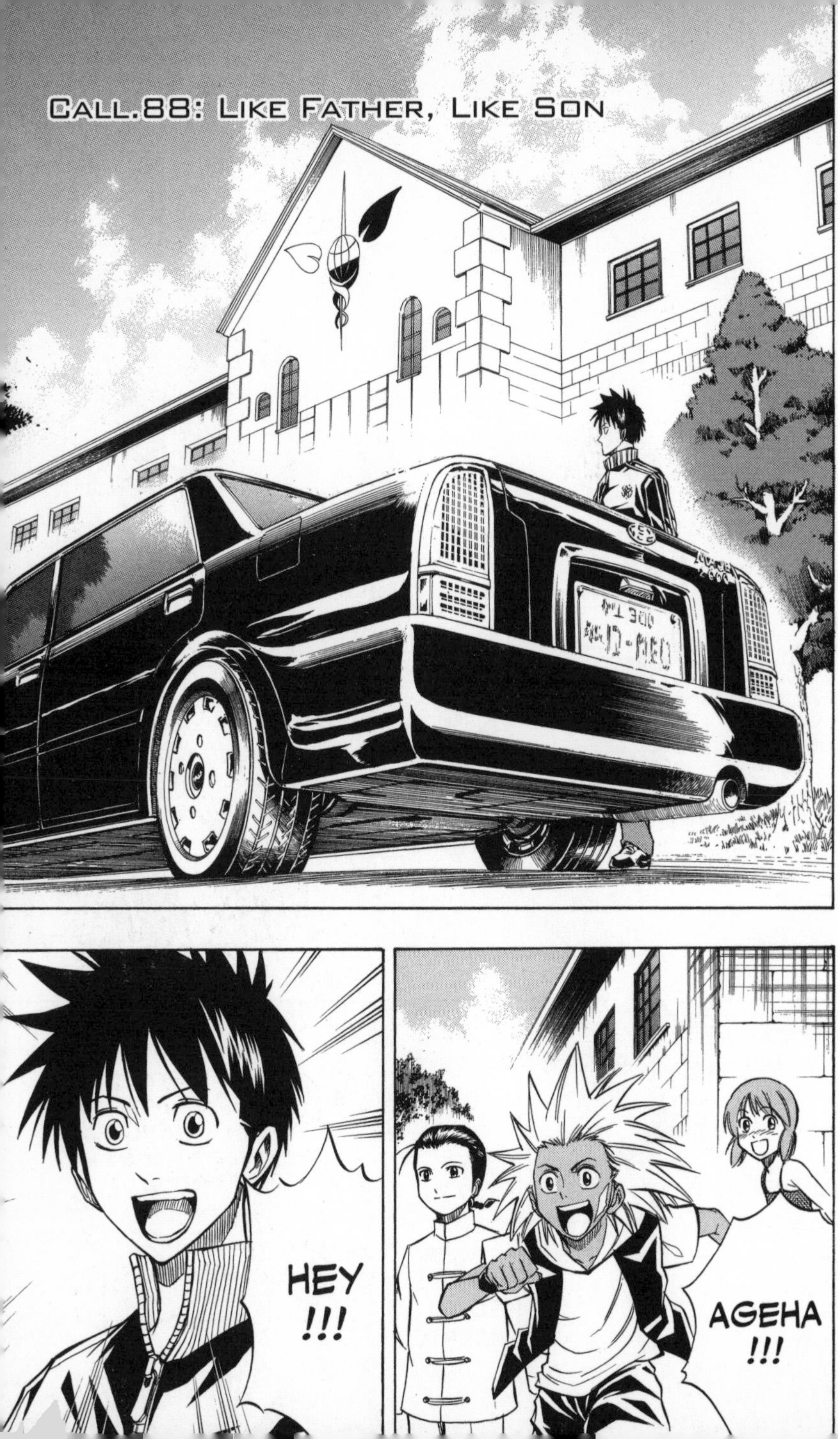
Call.88: Like Father, Like Son
AGEHA !!!
HEY !!!

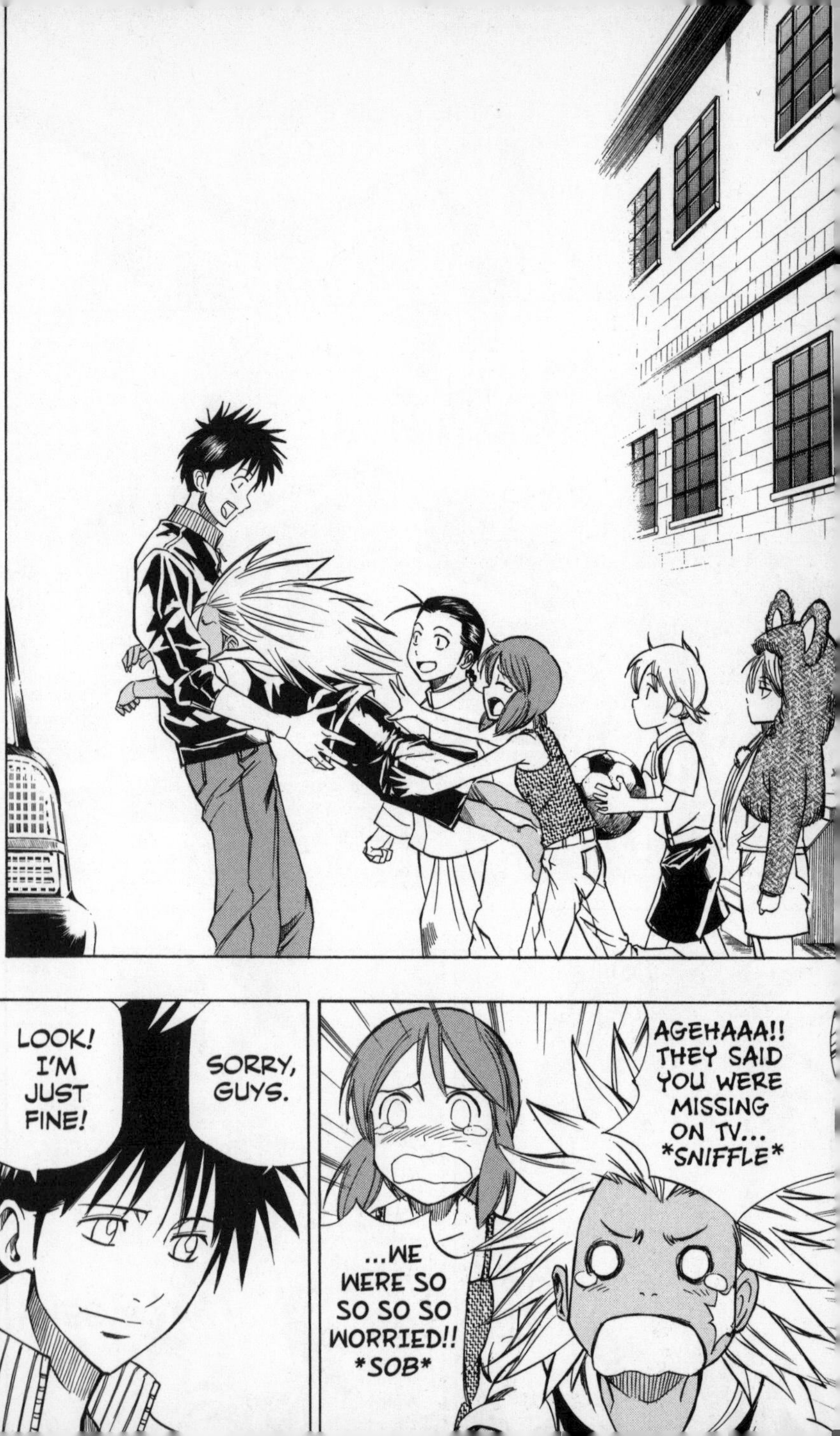
AGEHAAA!! THEY SAID YOU WERE MISSING ON TV... *SNIFFLE*
...WE WERE SO SO SO SO WORRIED!! *SOB*
SORRY, GUYS.
LOOK! I'M JUST FINE!

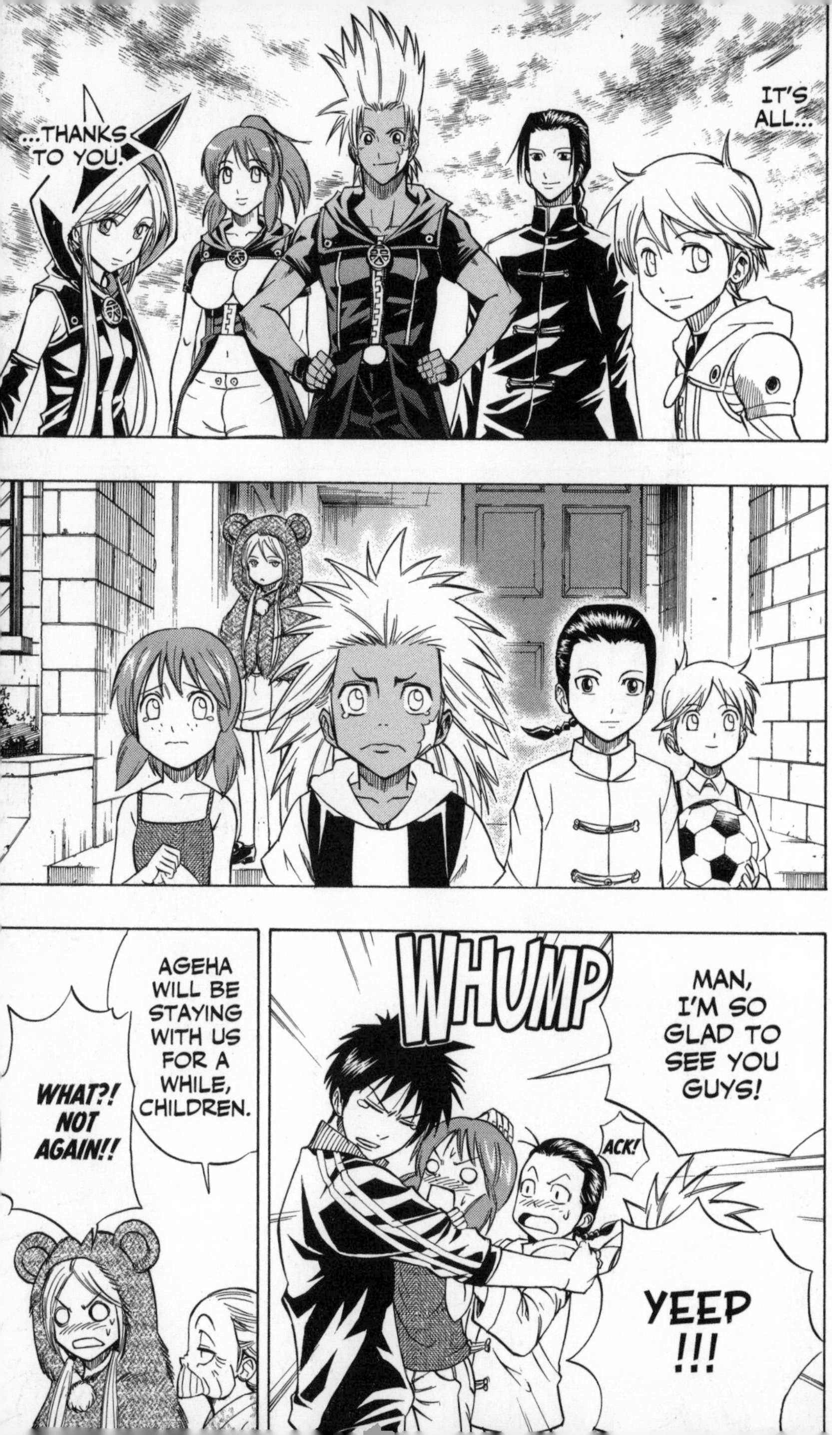

IT'S ALL...
...THANKS TO YOU.
MAN, I'M SO GLAD TO SEE YOU GUYS!
WHUMP
ACK!
YEEP!!!
AGEHA WILL BE STAYING WITH US FOR A WHILE, CHILDREN.
WHAT?! NOT AGAIN!!

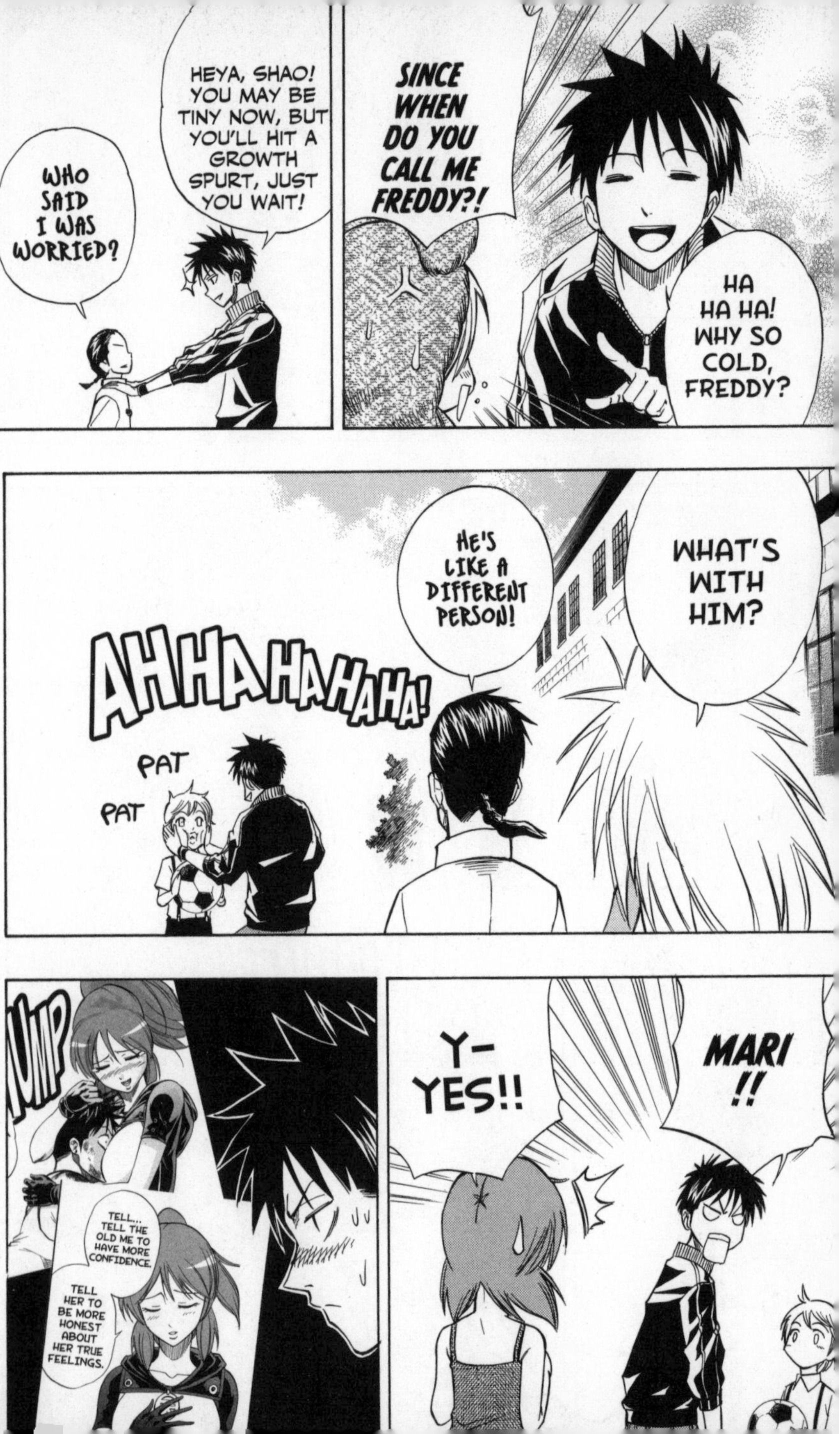
HA HA HA! WHY SO COLD, FREDDY?
SINCE WHEN DO YOU CALL ME FREDDY?!
HEYA, SHAO! YOU MAY BE TINY NOW, BUT YOU'LL HIT A GROWTH SPURT, JUST YOU WAIT!
WHO SAID I WAS WORRIED?
WHAT'S WITH HIM?
HE'S LIKE A DIFFERENT PERSON!
AHHAHAHAHA!
PAT
PAT
MARI!!
Y-YES!!
TELL... TELL THE OLD ME TO HAVE MORE CONFIDENCE.
TELL HER TO BE MORE HONEST ABOUT HER TRUE FEELINGS.

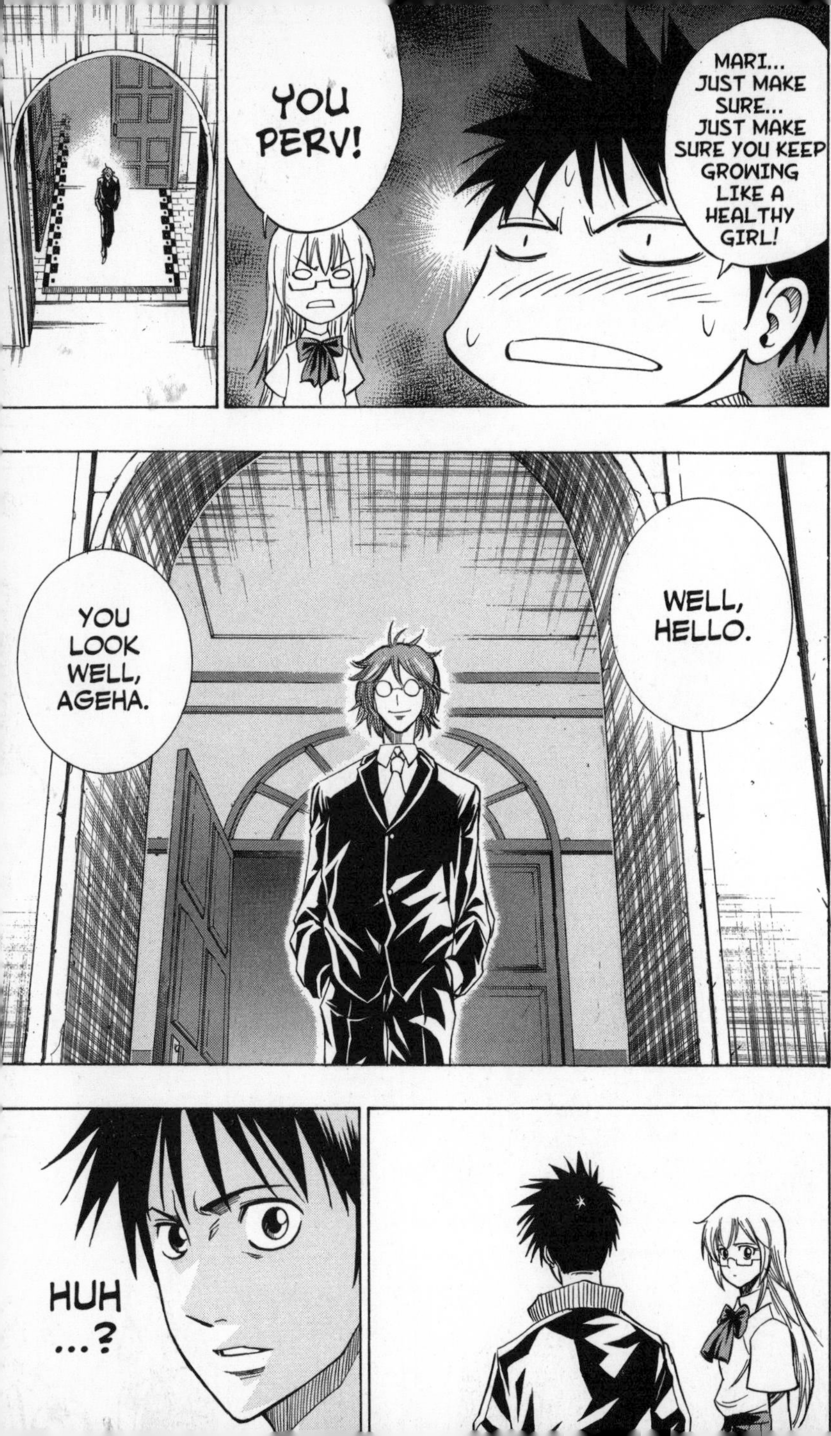

MARI... JUST MAKE SURE... JUST MAKE SURE YOU KEEP GROWING LIKE A HEALTHY GIRL!
YOU PERV!
WELL, HELLO.
YOU LOOK WELL, AGEHA.
HUH ...?

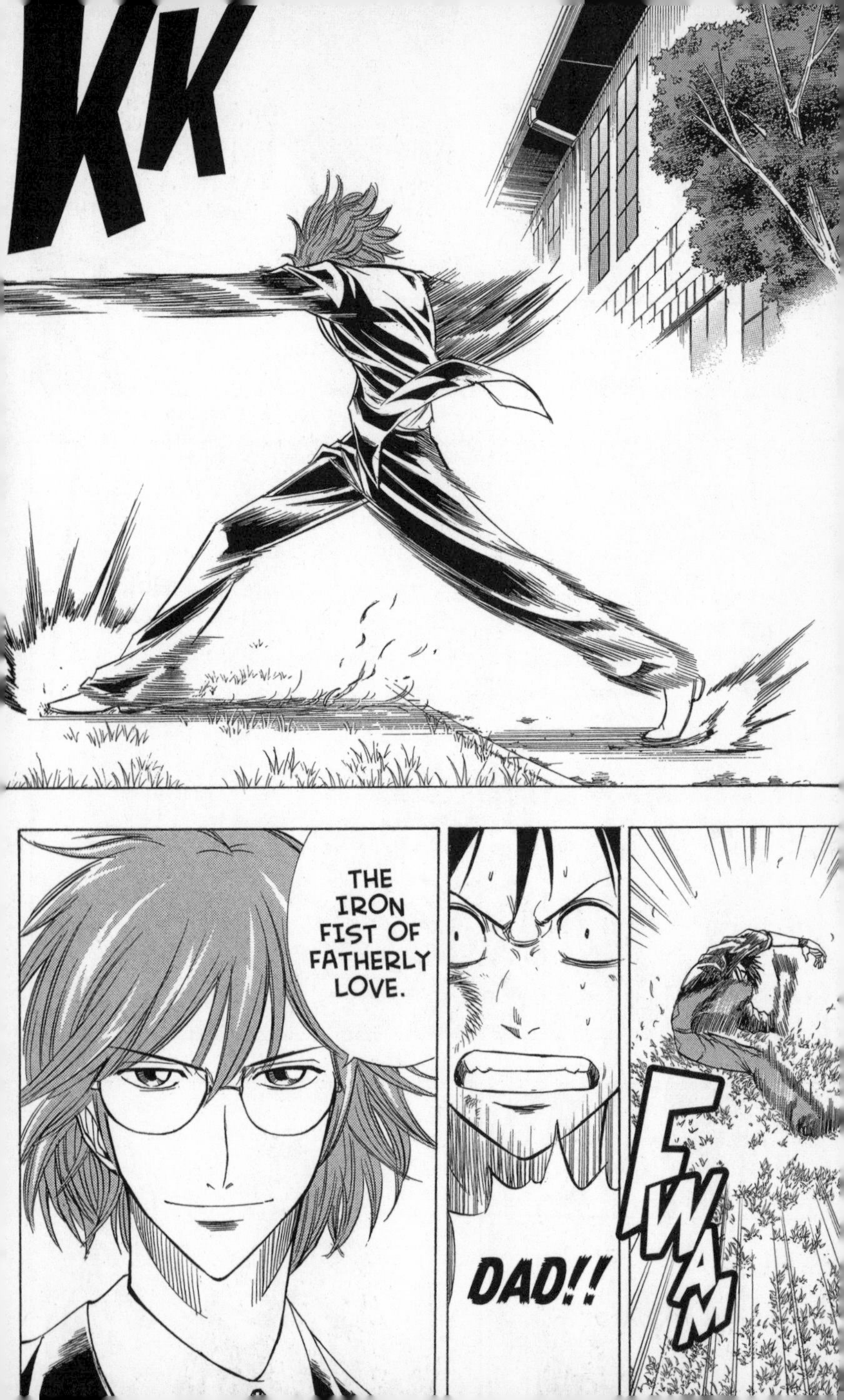
KK
FWAM
DAD!!
THE IRON FIST OF FATHERLY LOVE.

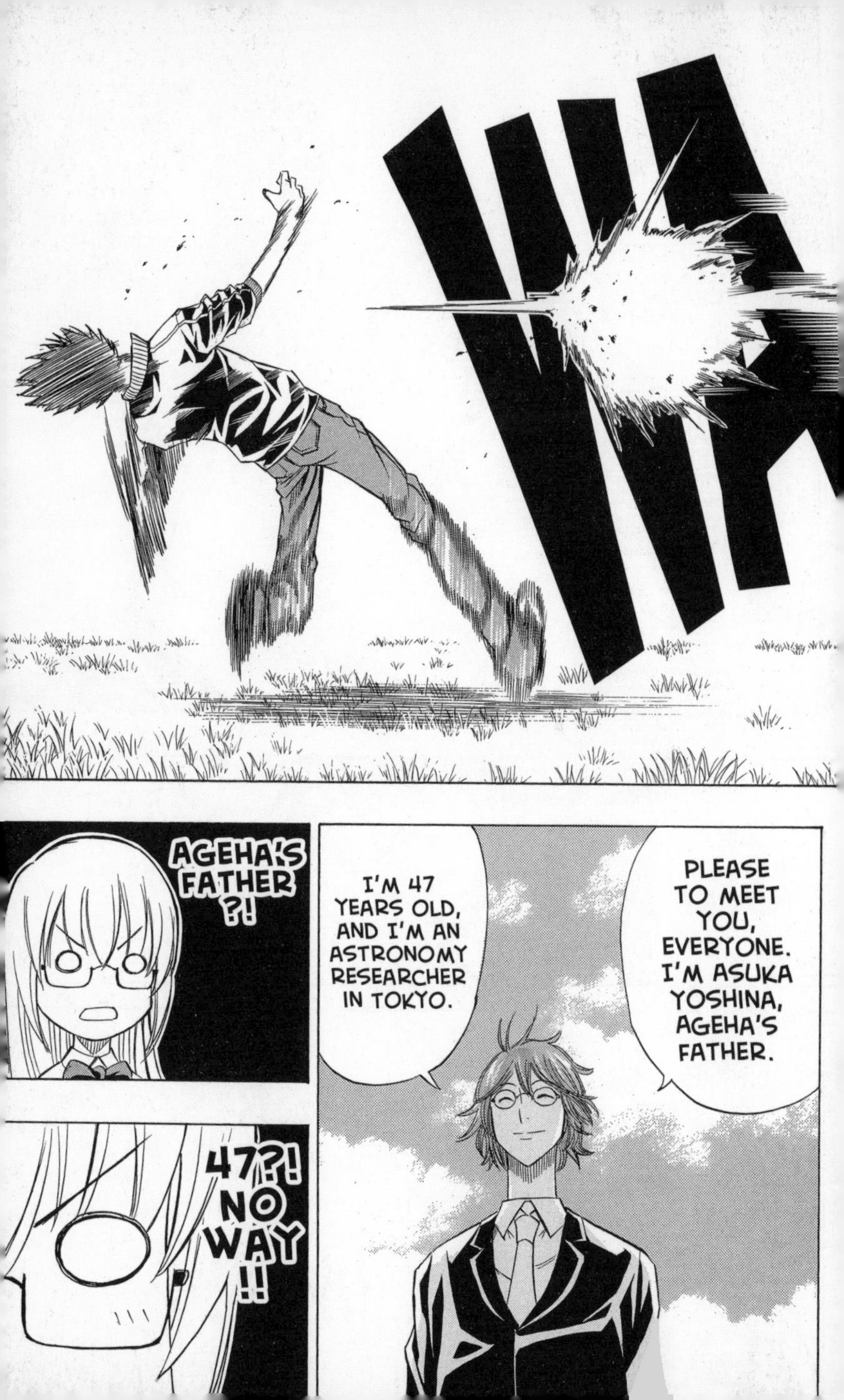
PLEASE TO MEET YOU, EVERYONE. I'M ASUKA YOSHINA, AGEHA'S FATHER.
I'M 47 YEARS OLD, AND I'M AN ASTRONOMY RESEARCHER IN TOKYO.
AGEHA'S FATHER ?!
47?! NO WAY !!

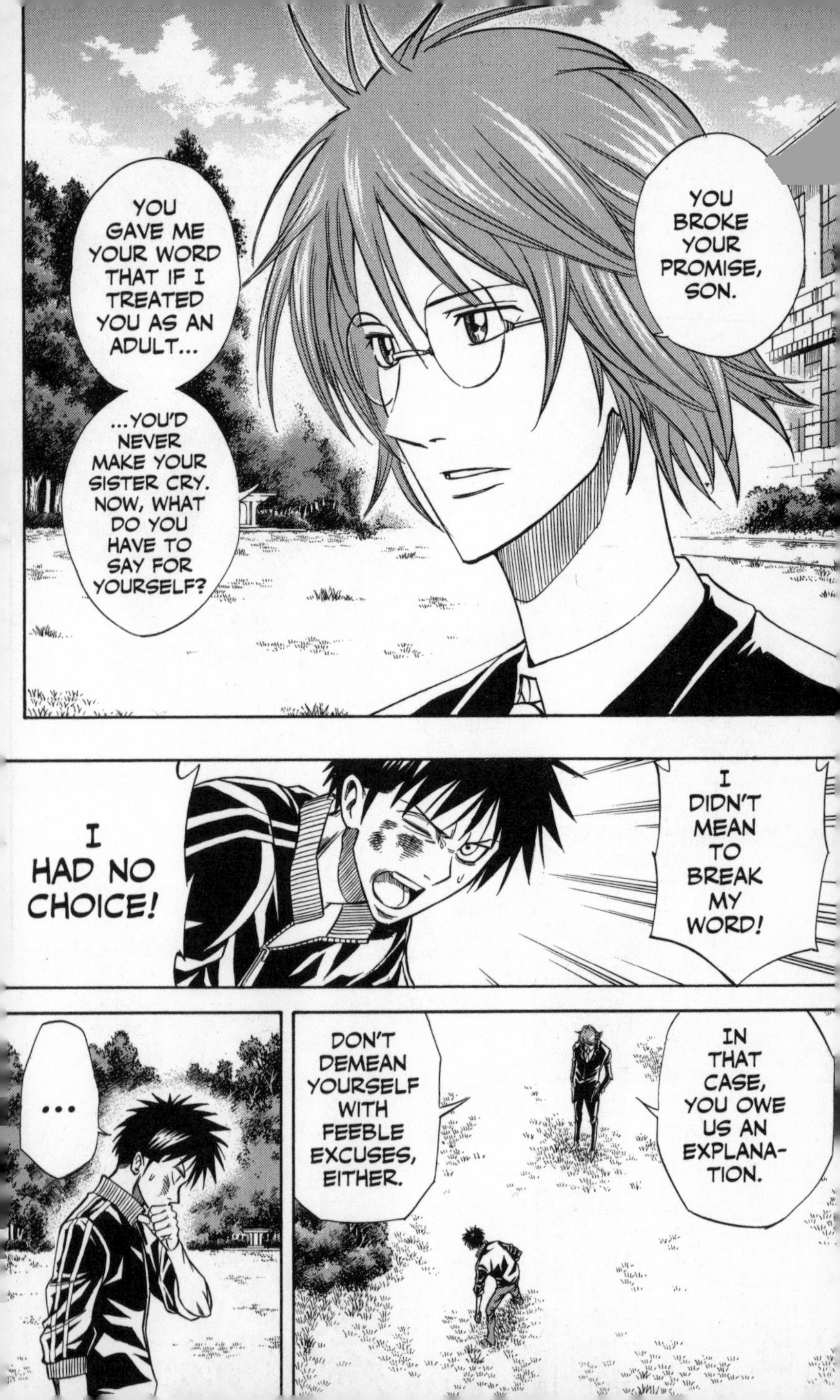
YOU BROKE YOUR PROMISE, SON.
YOU GAVE ME YOUR WORD THAT IF I TREATED YOU AS AN ADULT...
...YOU'D NEVER MAKE YOUR SISTER CRY. NOW, WHAT DO YOU HAVE TO SAY FOR YOURSELF?
I DIDN'T MEAN TO BREAK MY WORD!
I HAD NO CHOICE!
IN THAT CASE, YOU OWE US AN EXPLANA-TION.
DON'T DEMEAN YOURSELF WITH FEEBLE EXCUSES, EITHER.
...

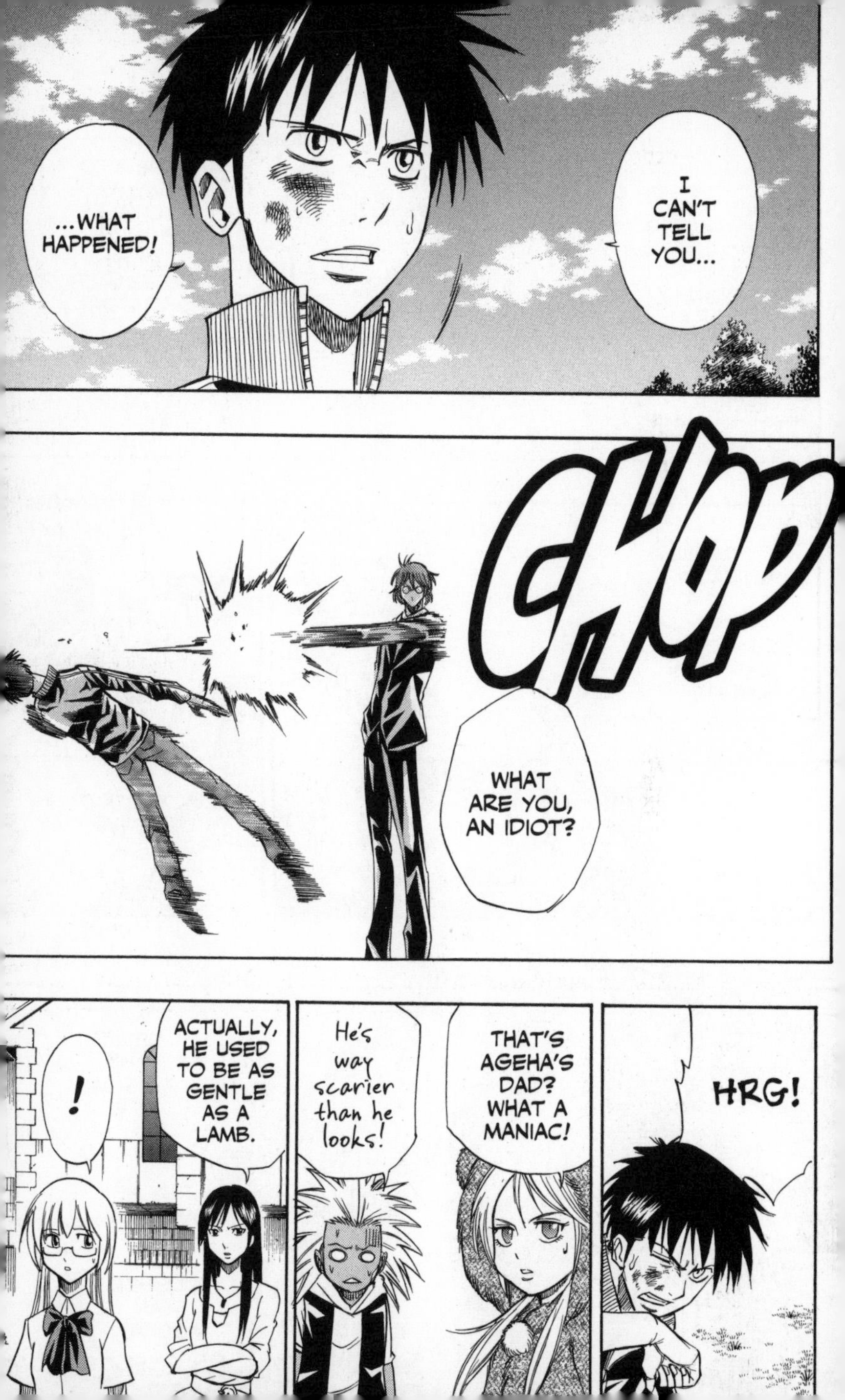
I CAN'T TELL YOU...
...WHAT HAPPENED!
CHOP
WHAT ARE YOU, AN IDIOT?
HRG!
THAT'S AGEHA'S DAD? WHAT A MANIAC!
He's way scarier than he looks!
ACTUALLY, HE USED TO BE AS GENTLE AS A LAMB.
!

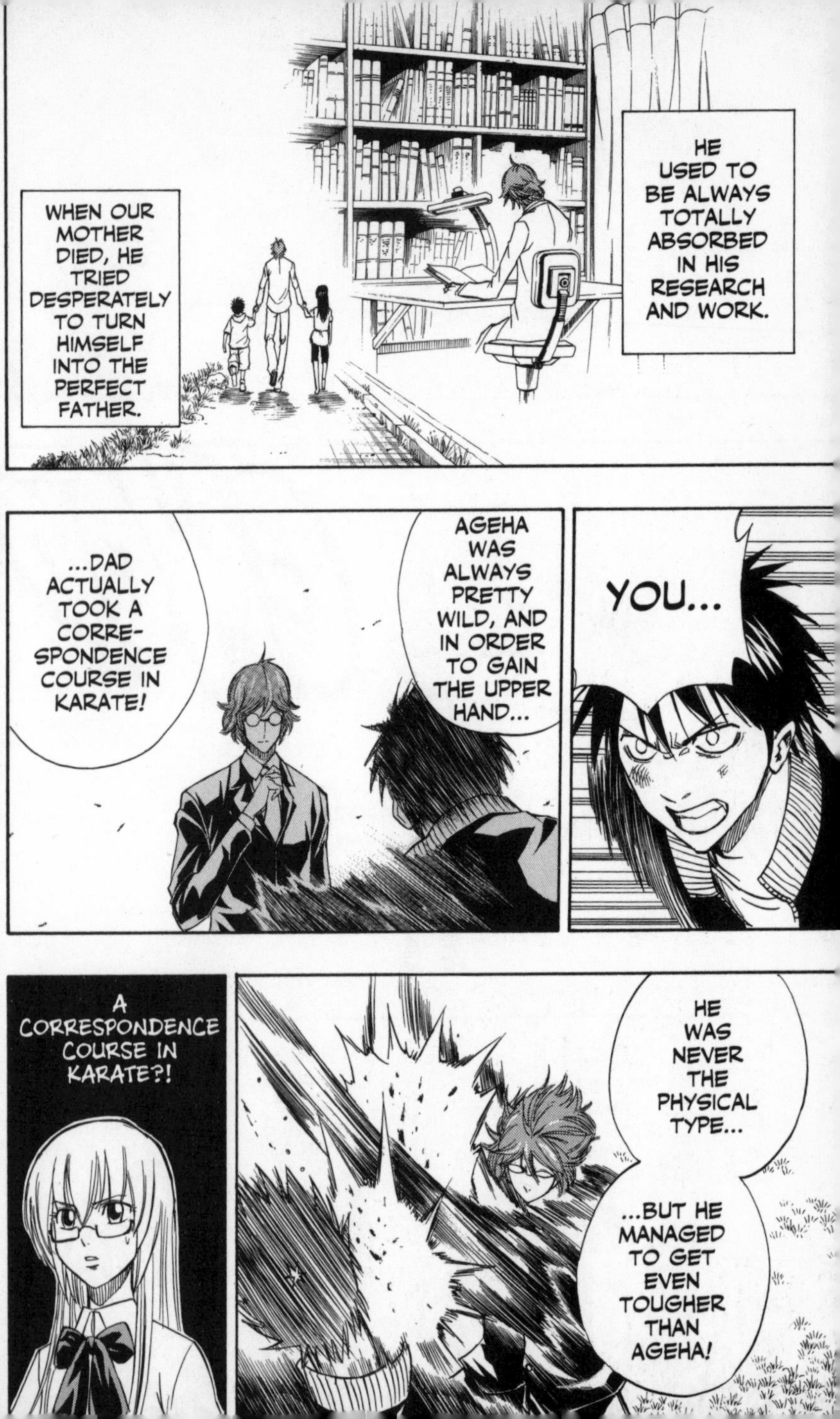
HE USED TO BE ALWAYS TOTALLY ABSORBED IN HIS RESEARCH AND WORK.
WHEN OUR MOTHER DIED, HE TRIED DESPERATELY TO TURN HIMSELF INTO THE PERFECT FATHER.
YOU...
AGEHA WAS ALWAYS PRETTY WILD, AND IN ORDER TO GAIN THE UPPER HAND...
...DAD ACTUALLY TOOK A CORRE-SPONDENCE COURSE IN KARATE!
HE WAS NEVER THE PHYSICAL TYPE...
...BUT HE MANAGED TO GET EVEN TOUGHER THAN AGEHA!
A CORRESPONDENCE COURSE IN KARATE?!

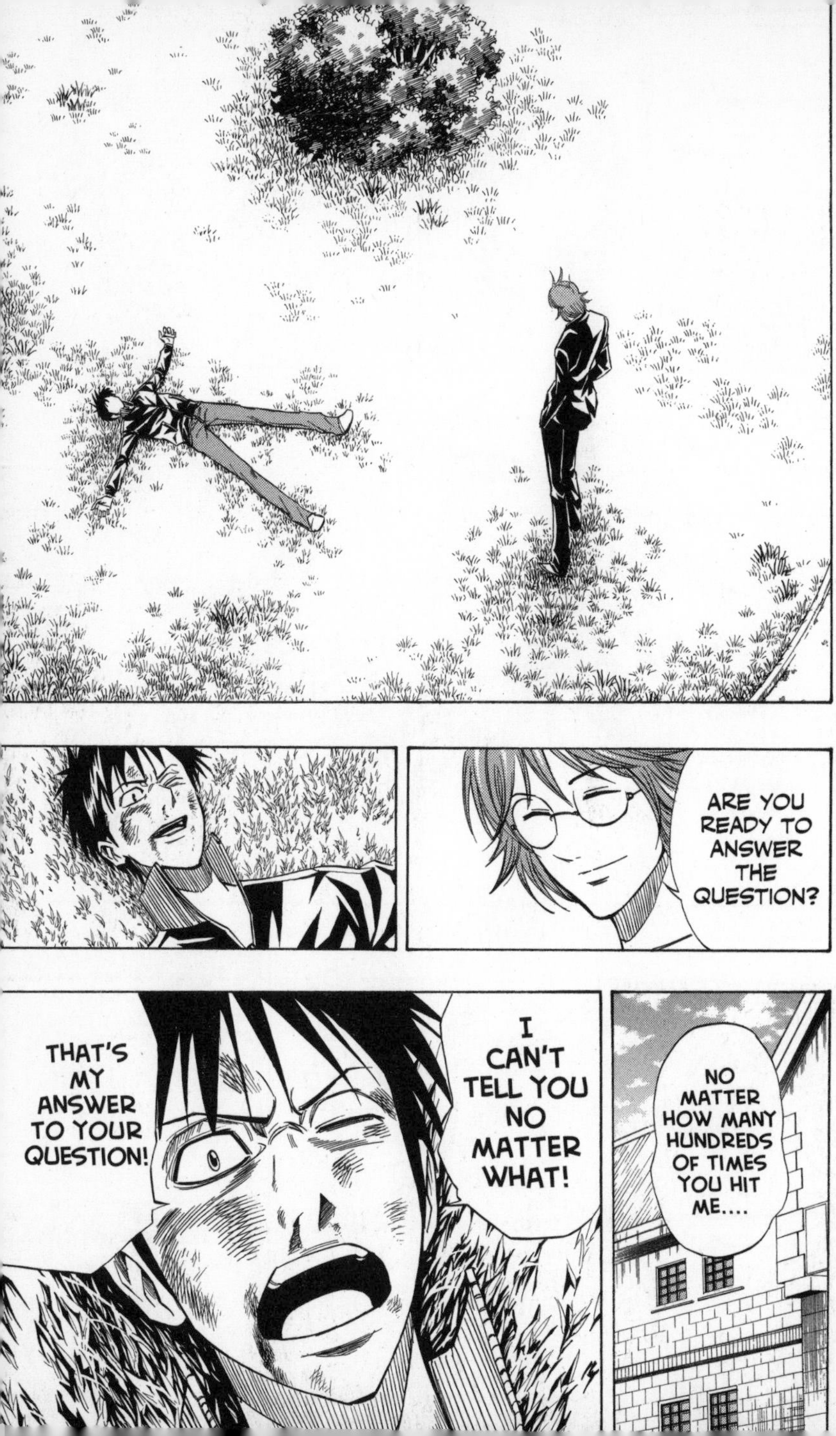
ARE YOU READY TO ANSWER THE QUESTION?
NO MATTER HOW MANY HUNDREDS OF TIMES YOU HIT ME....
I CAN'T TELL YOU NO MATTER WHAT!
THAT'S MY ANSWER TO YOUR QUESTION!

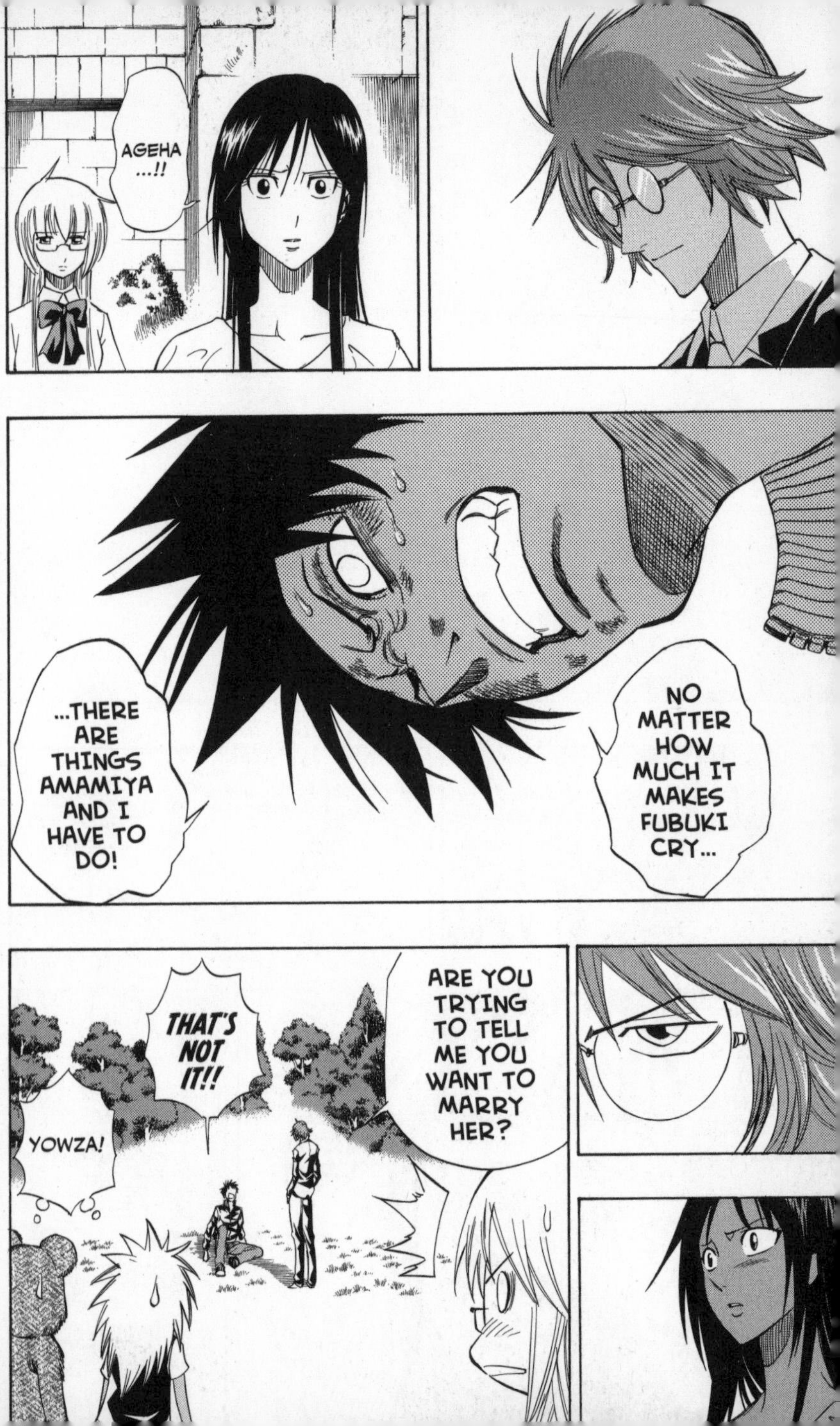
AGEHA ...!!
NO MATTER HOW MUCH IT MAKES FUBUKI CRY...
...THERE ARE THINGS AMAMIYA AND I HAVE TO DO!
ARE YOU TRYING TO TELL ME YOU WANT TO MARRY HER?
THAT'S NOT IT!!
YOWZA!

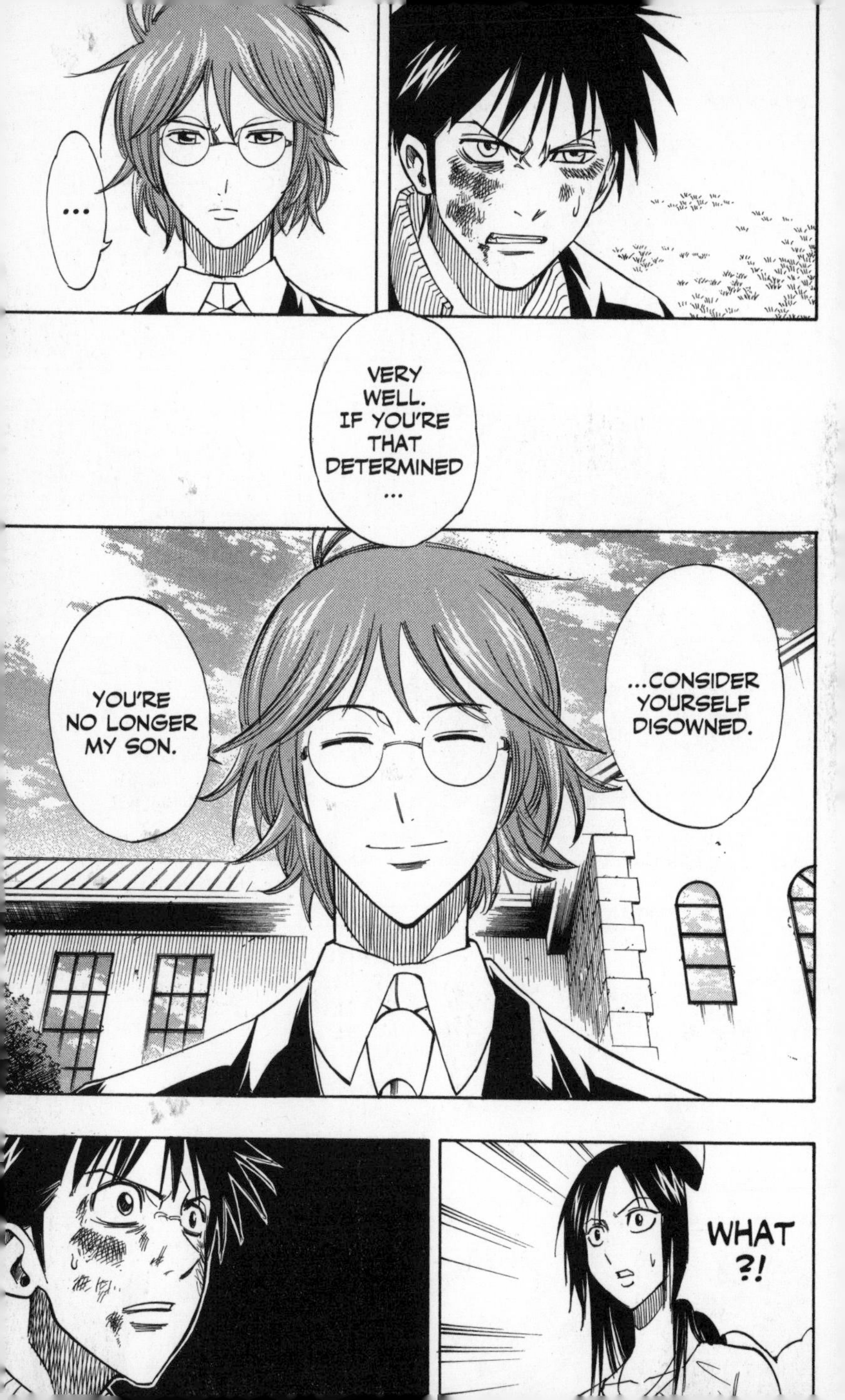
...
VERY WELL. IF YOU'RE THAT DETERMINED ...
...CONSIDER YOURSELF DISOWNED.
YOU'RE NO LONGER MY SON.
WHAT ?!

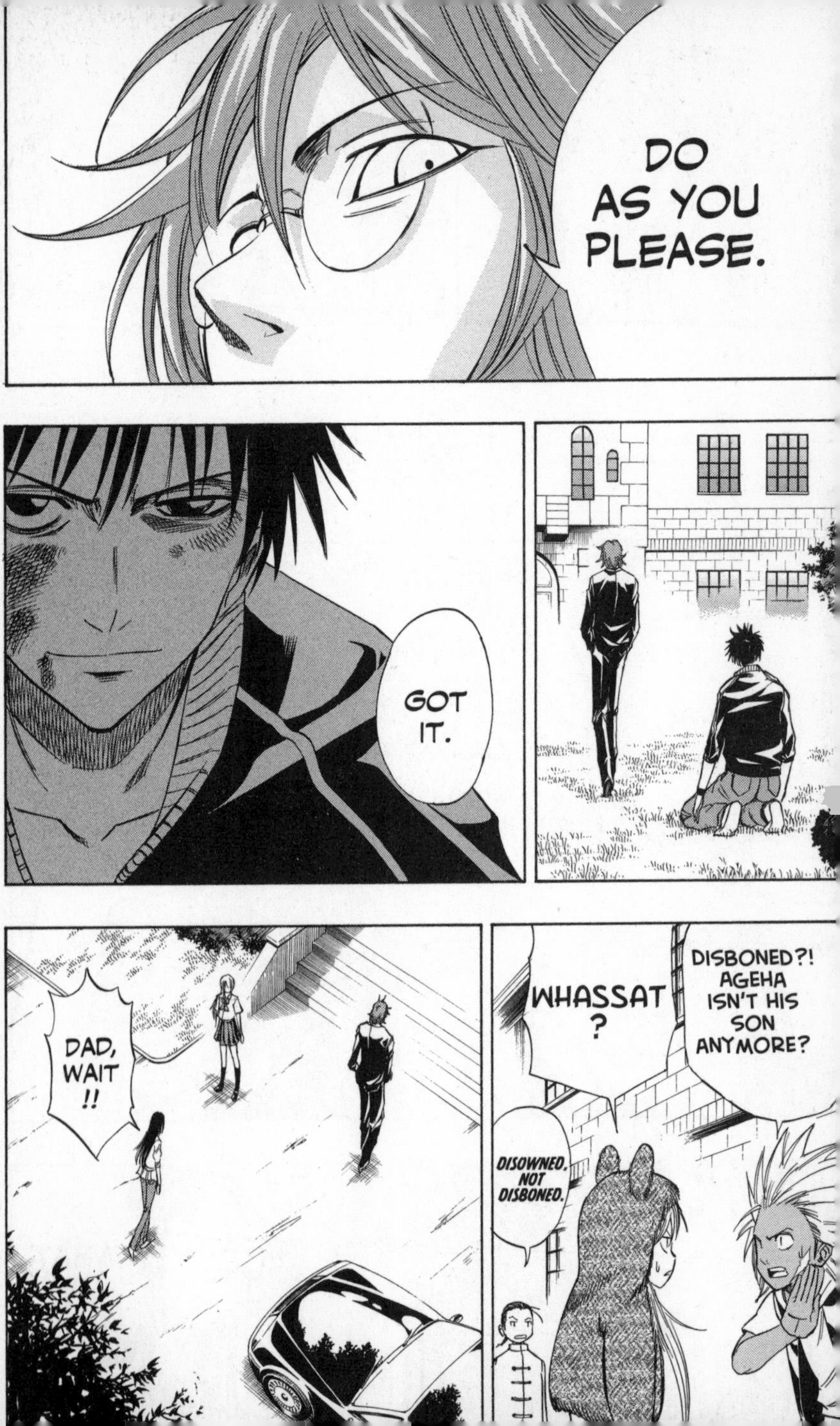
DO AS YOU PLEASE.
GOT IT.
DISBONED?! AGEHA ISN'T HIS SON ANYMORE?
WHASSAT?
DISOWNED, NOT DISBONED.
DAD, WAIT!!

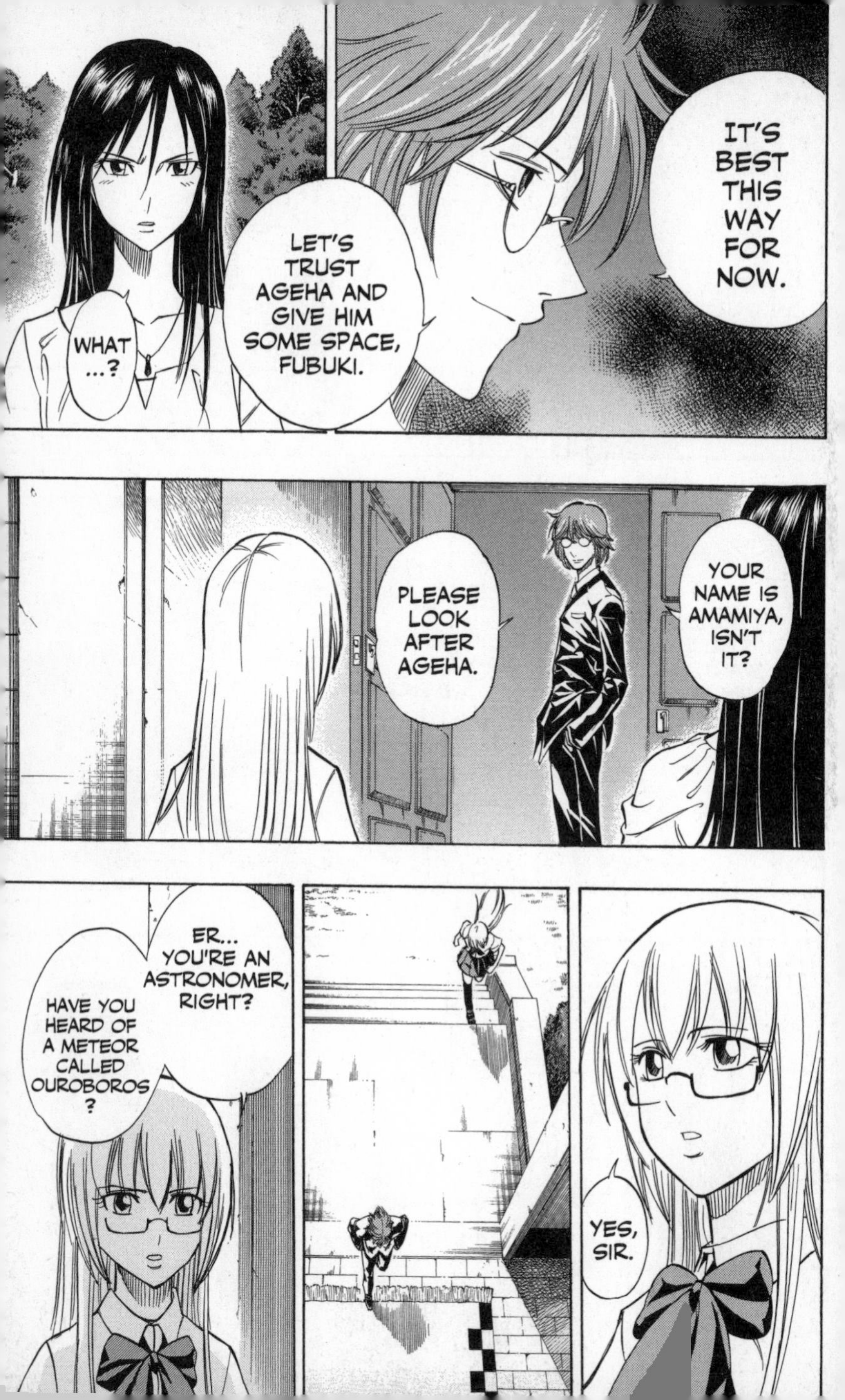
IT'S BEST THIS WAY FOR NOW.
LET'S TRUST AGEHA AND GIVE HIM SOME SPACE, FUBUKI.
WHAT...?
YOUR NAME IS AMAMIYA, ISN'T IT?
PLEASE LOOK AFTER AGEHA.
YES, SIR.
ER... YOU'RE AN ASTRONOMER, RIGHT?
HAVE YOU HEARD OF A METEOR CALLED OUROBOROS?

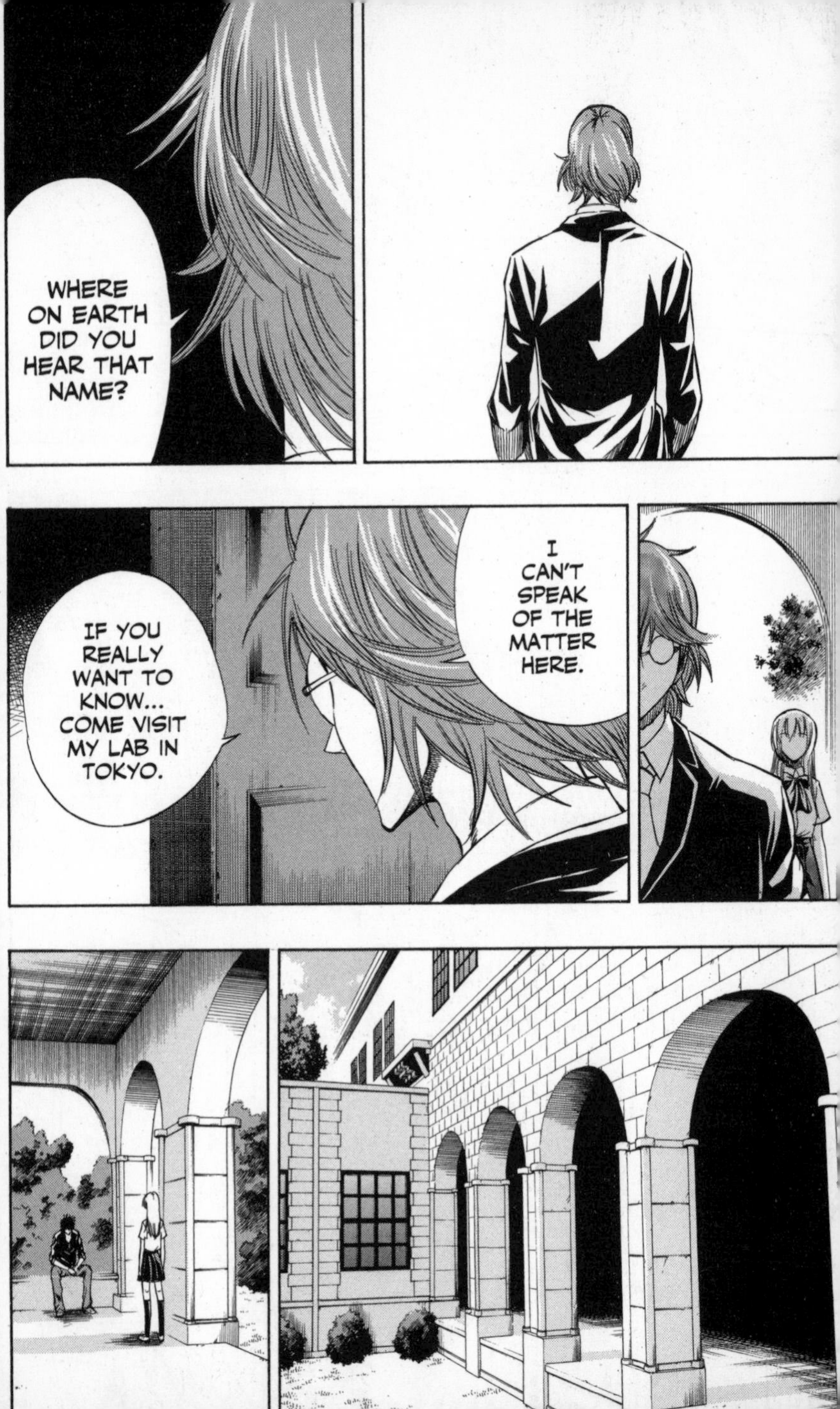
WHERE ON EARTH DID YOU HEAR THAT NAME?
I CAN'T SPEAK OF THE MATTER HERE.
IF YOU REALLY WANT TO KNOW... COME VISIT MY LAB IN TOKYO.

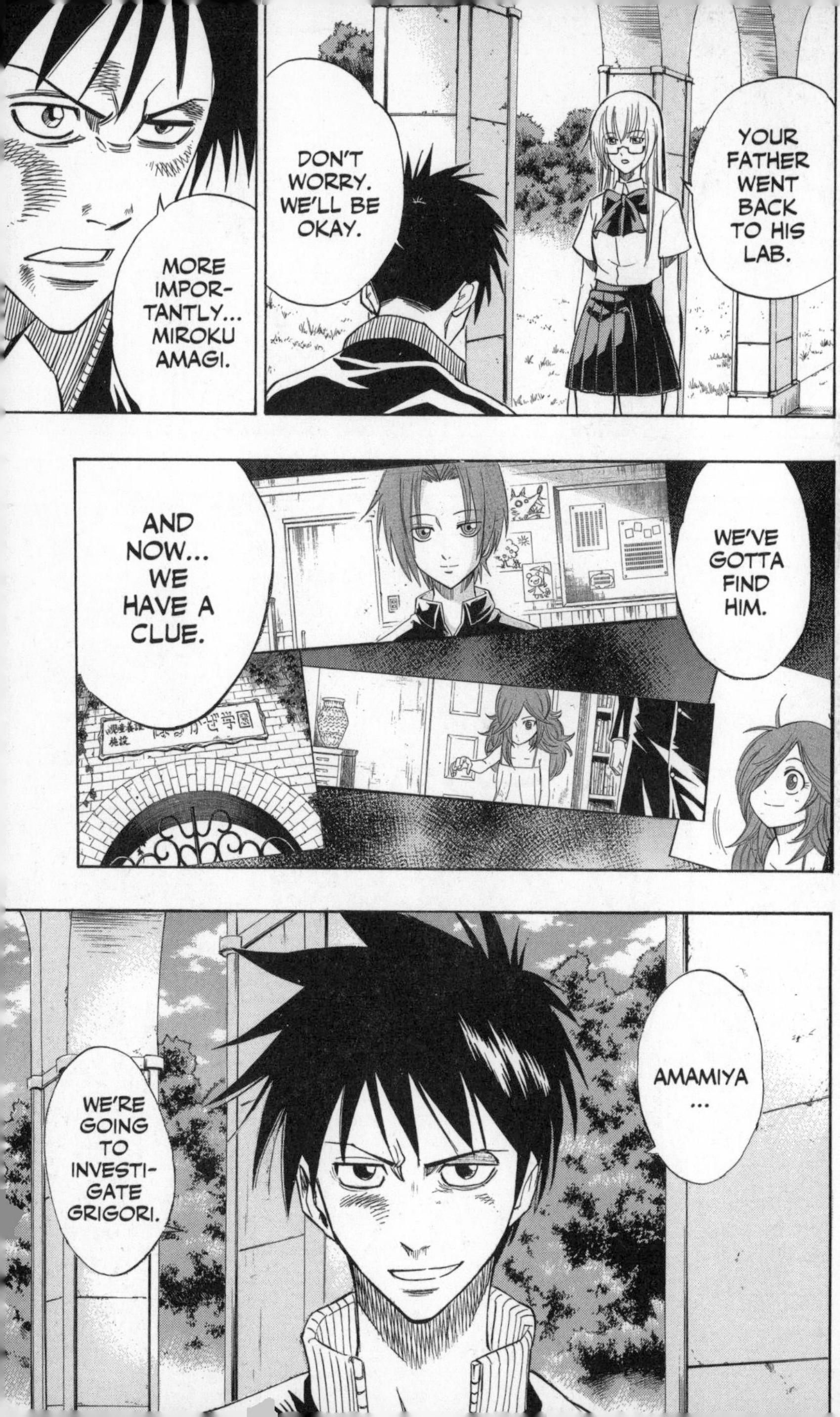
YOUR FATHER WENT BACK TO HIS LAB.
DON'T WORRY. WE'LL BE OKAY.
MORE IMPORTANTLY... MIROKU AMAGI.
WE'VE GOTTA FIND HIM.
AND NOW... WE HAVE A CLUE.
AMAMIYA ...
WE'RE GOING TO INVESTIGATE GRIGORI.

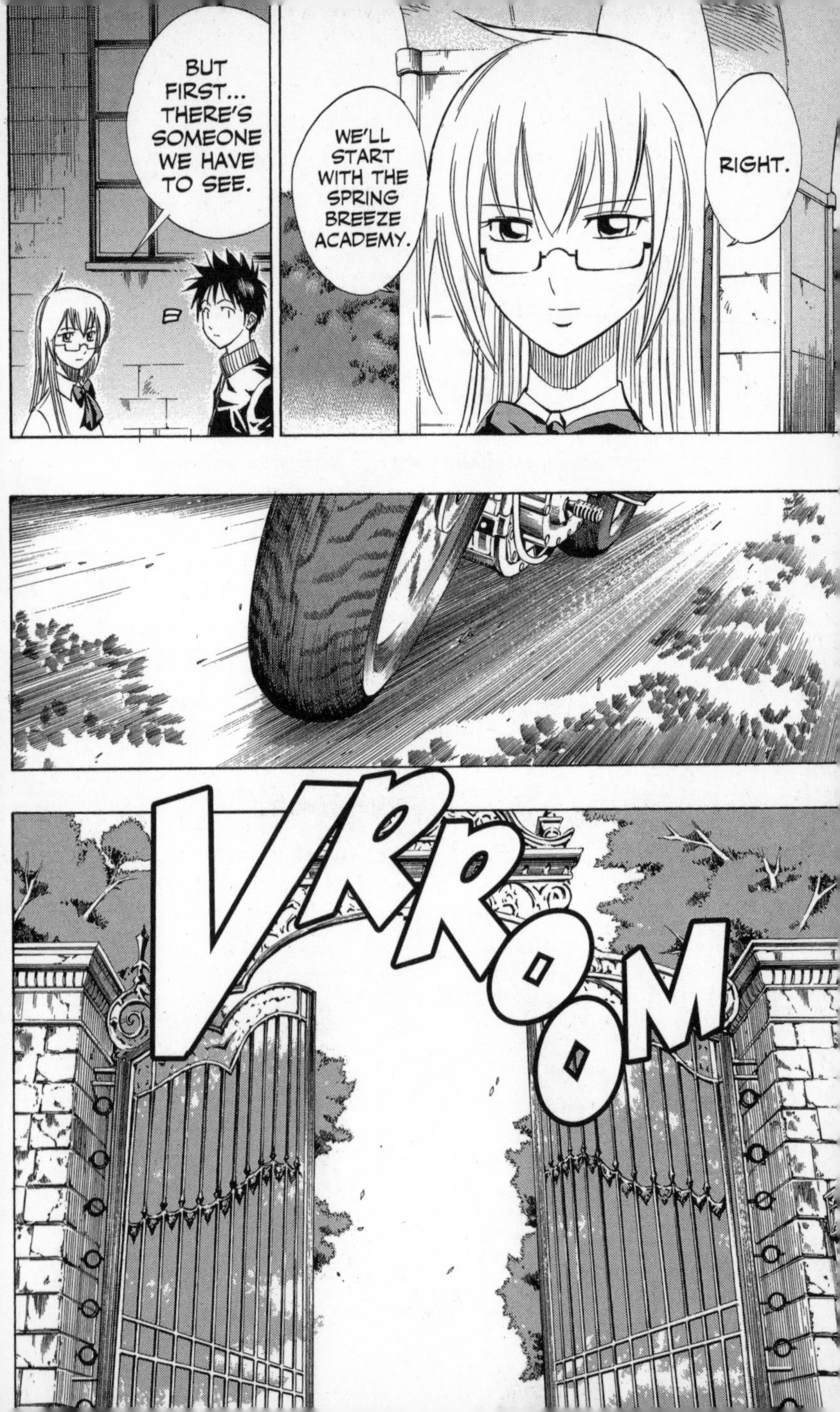
RIGHT.
WE'LL START WITH THE SPRING BREEZE ACADEMY.
BUT FIRST... THERE'S SOMEONE WE HAVE TO SEE.
VRROOM

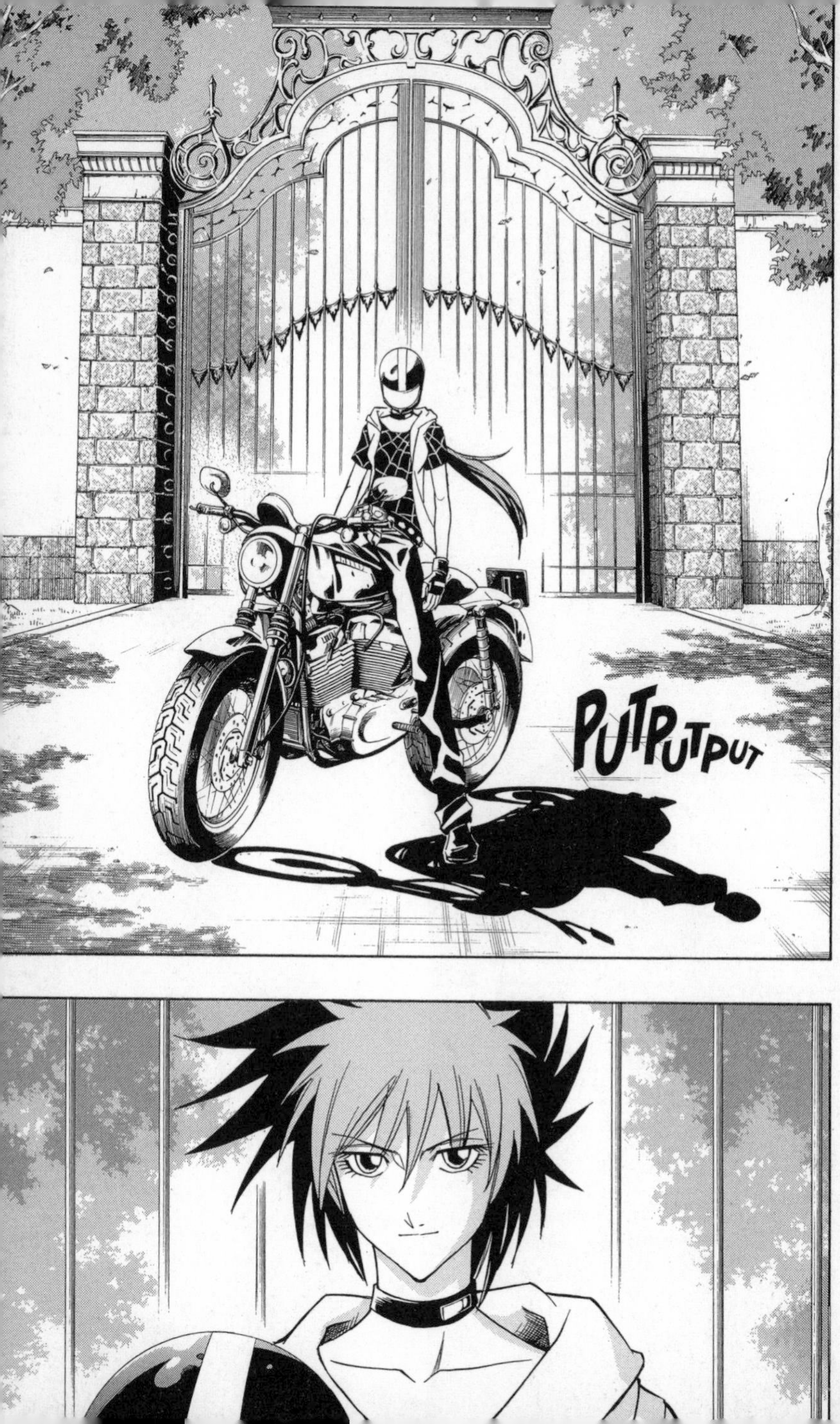
PUTPUTPUT

PSYREN 10

Afterword

THANK YOU FOR READING VOLUME 10!

THE SERIES HAS BEEN GOING FOR THREE YEARS NOW, AND THIS IS THE 10TH TANKO VOLUME!

WHEN I GO BACK AND REREAD VOLUME 1, I REALLY NOTICE HOW MUCH THE ILLUSTRATIONS HAVE CHANGED.

PEOPLE OFTEN ASK ME HOW LONG I INTEND TO KEEP THE STORY GOING.

I REALLY DON'T KNOW.
FOR NOW, I PROMISE TO WORK HARD AND KEEP MY EYES ON THE GOAL!

TOSHIAKI IWASHIRO
FEBRUARY 2010

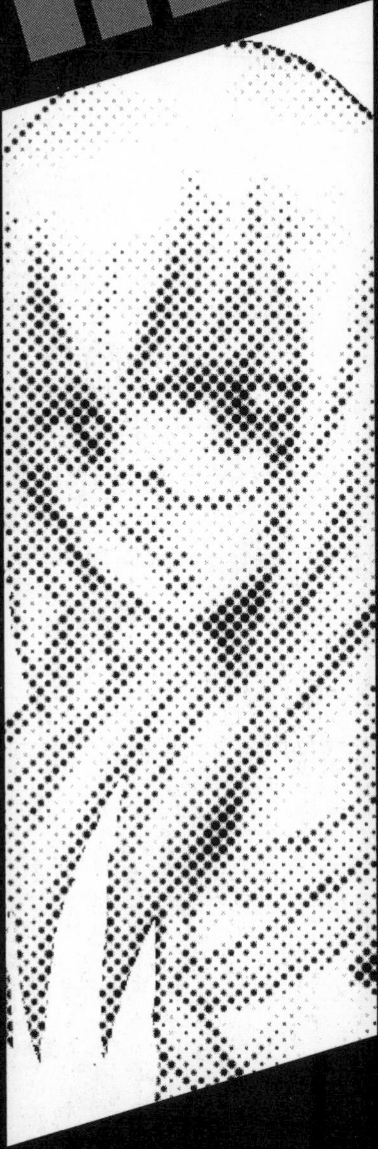

Call.89: Amamiya

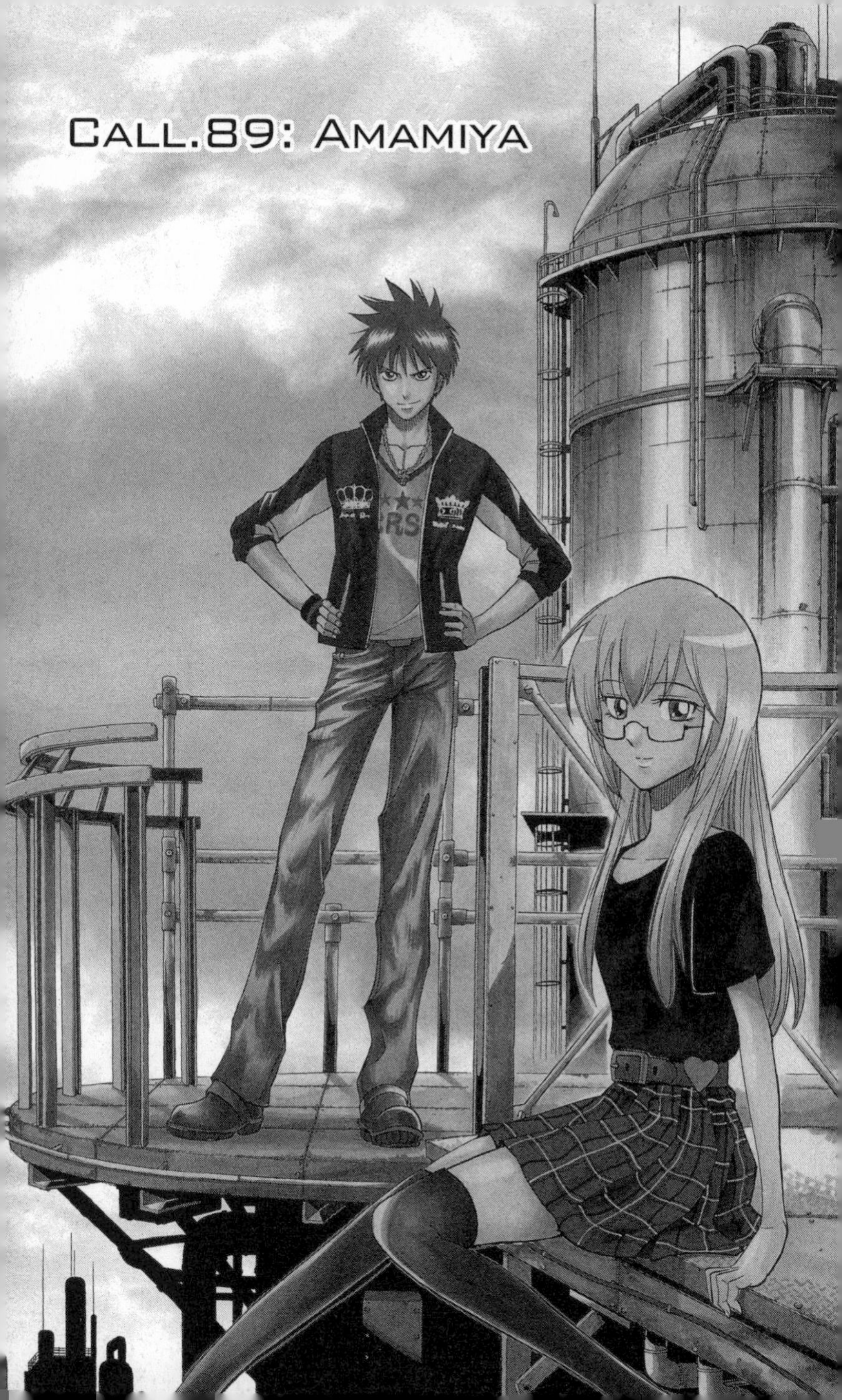

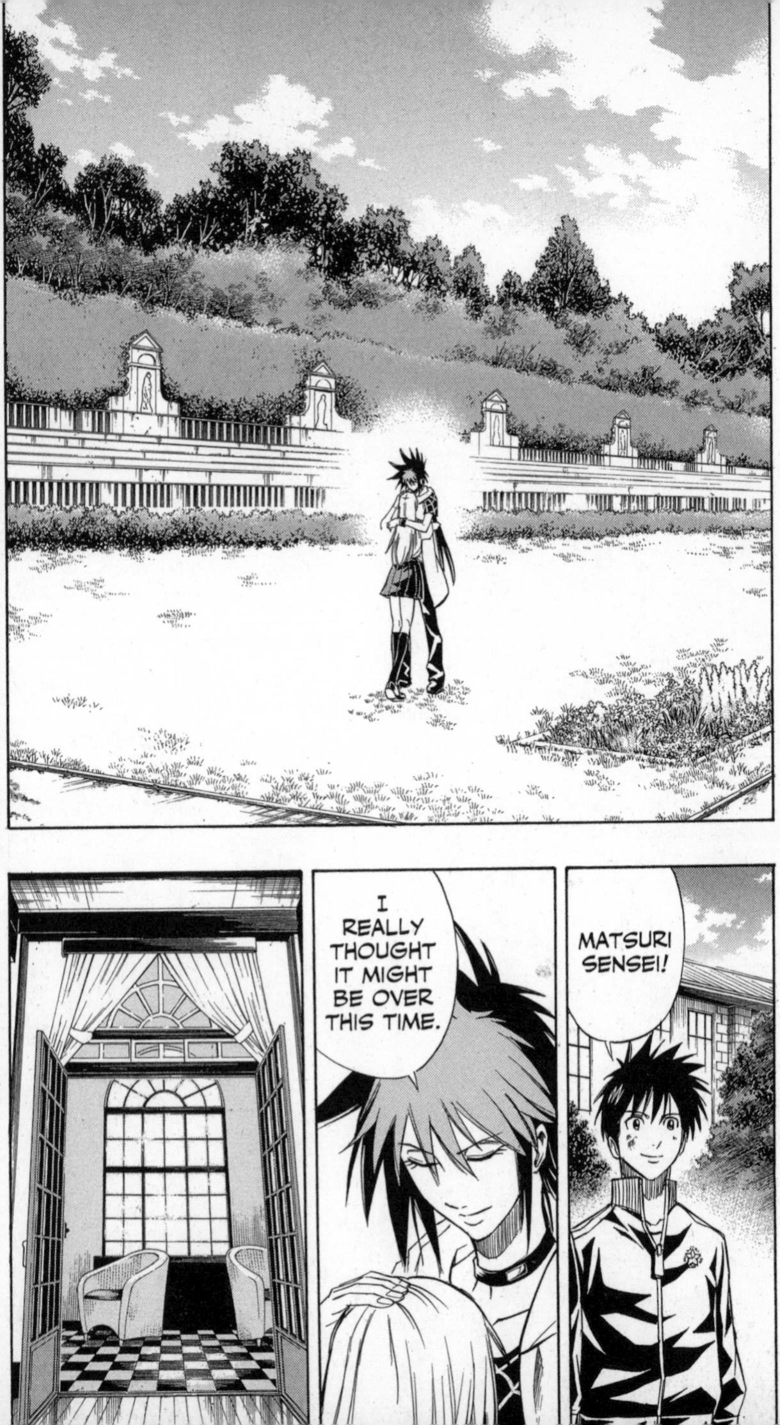
MATSURI SENSEI!
I REALLY THOUGHT IT MIGHT BE OVER THIS TIME.

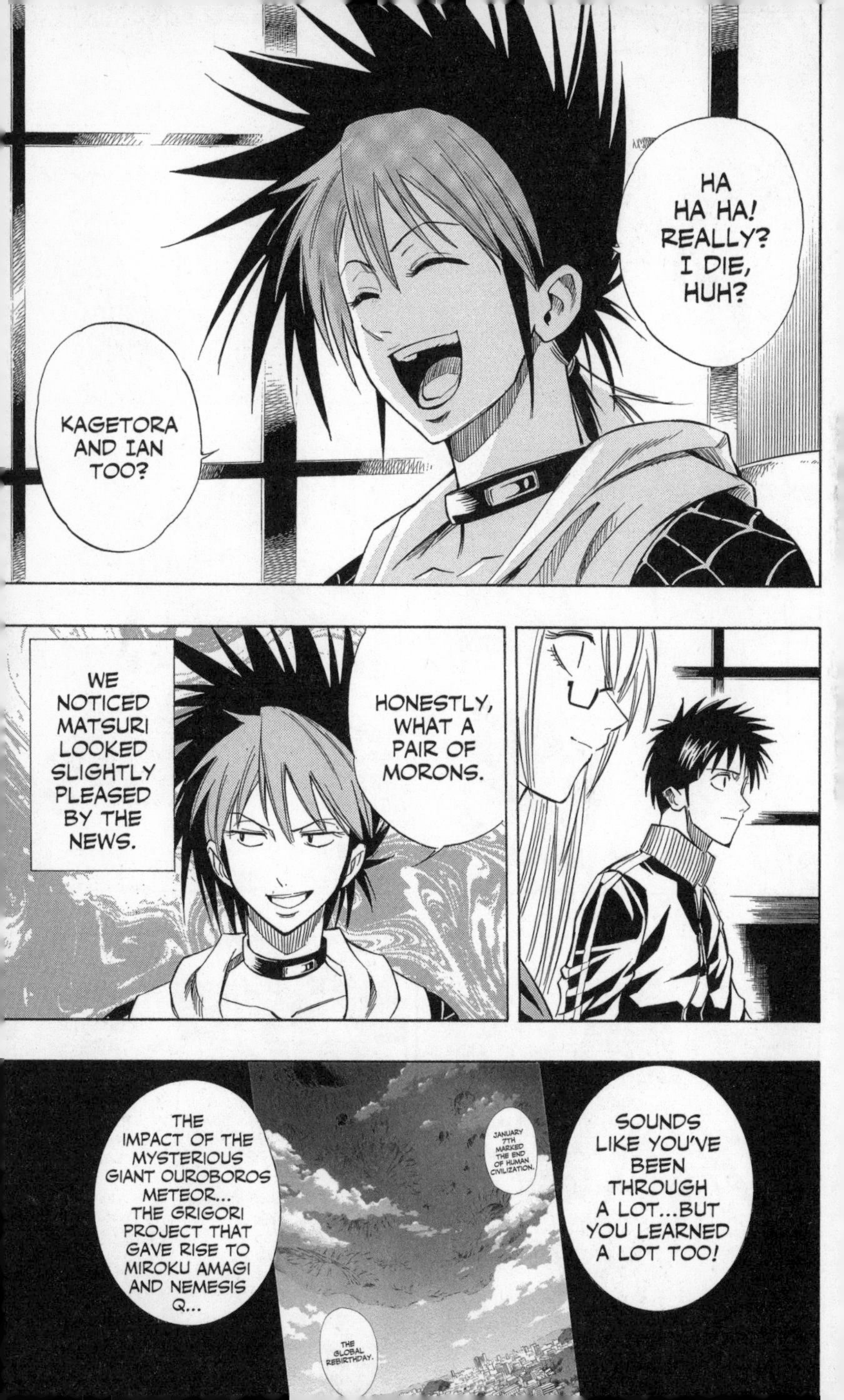
HA HA HA! REALLY? I DIE, HUH?
KAGETORA AND IAN TOO?
HONESTLY, WHAT A PAIR OF MORONS.
WE NOTICED MATSURI LOOKED SLIGHTLY PLEASED BY THE NEWS.
SOUNDS LIKE YOU'VE BEEN THROUGH A LOT...BUT YOU LEARNED A LOT TOO!
JANUARY 7TH MARKED THE END OF HUMAN CIVILIZATION.
THE IMPACT OF THE MYSTERIOUS GIANT OUROBOROS METEOR... THE GRIGORI PROJECT THAT GAVE RISE TO MIROKU AMAGI AND NEMESIS Q...
THE GLOBAL REBIRTHDAY.

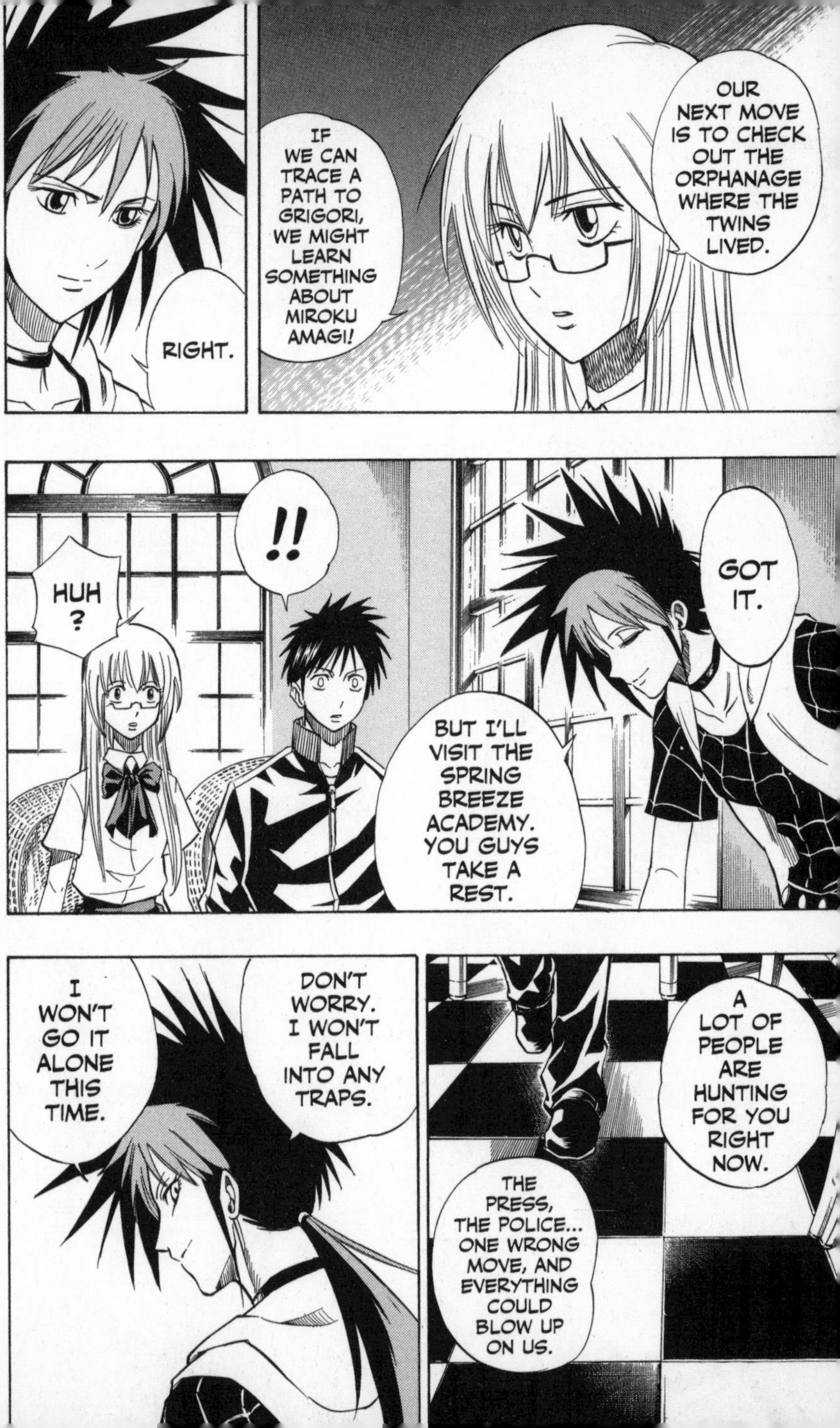
OUR NEXT MOVE IS TO CHECK OUT THE ORPHANAGE WHERE THE TWINS LIVED.
IF WE CAN TRACE A PATH TO GRIGORI, WE MIGHT LEARN SOMETHING ABOUT MIROKU AMAGI!
RIGHT.
GOT IT.
BUT I'LL VISIT THE SPRING BREEZE ACADEMY. YOU GUYS TAKE A REST.
!!
HUH?
A LOT OF PEOPLE ARE HUNTING FOR YOU RIGHT NOW.
THE PRESS, THE POLICE... ONE WRONG MOVE, AND EVERYTHING COULD BLOW UP ON US.
DON'T WORRY. I WON'T FALL INTO ANY TRAPS.
I WON'T GO IT ALONE THIS TIME.

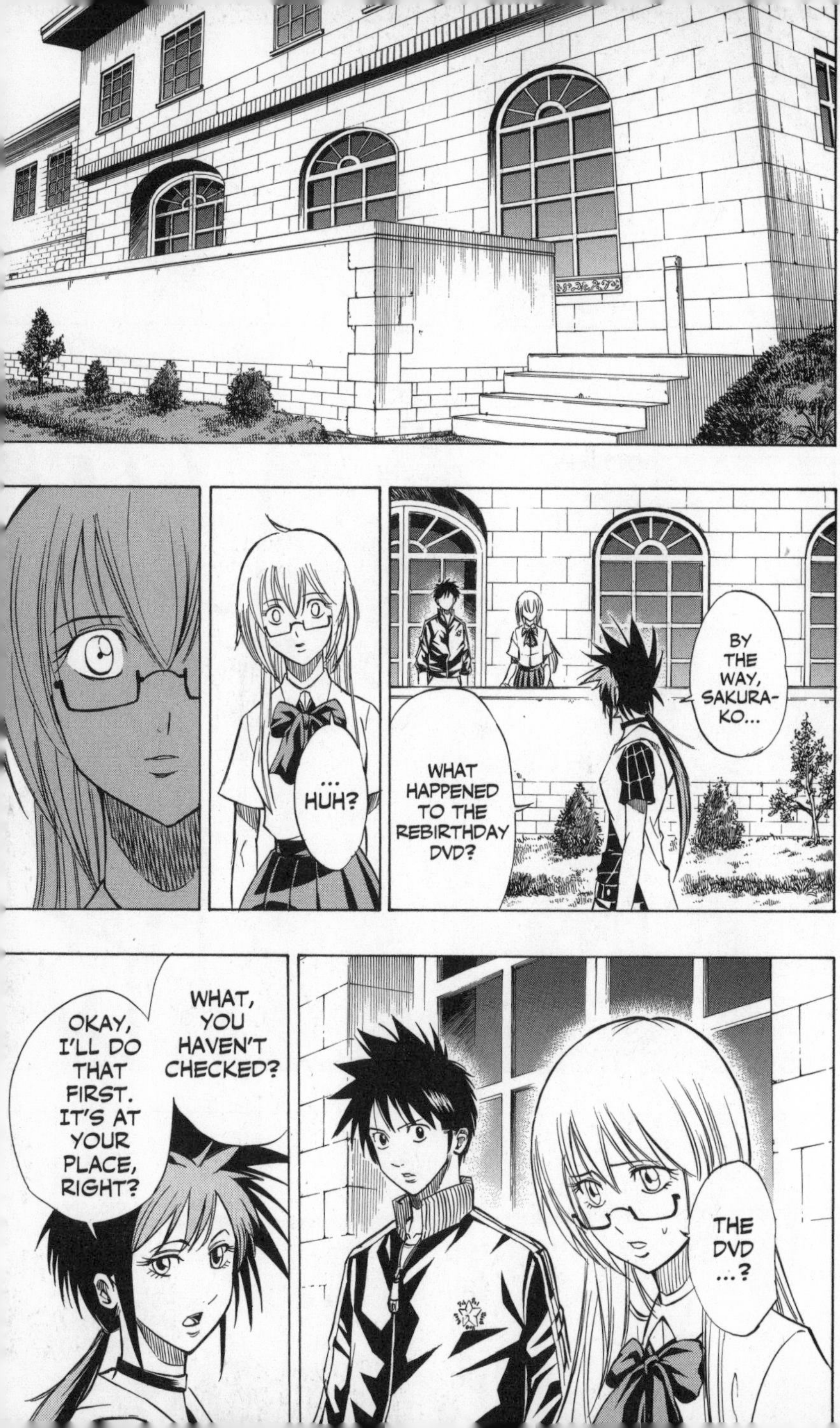
BY THE WAY, SAKURA-KO...
WHAT HAPPENED TO THE REBIRTHDAY DVD?
... HUH?
THE DVD ...?
WHAT, YOU HAVEN'T CHECKED?
OKAY, I'LL DO THAT FIRST. IT'S AT YOUR PLACE, RIGHT?

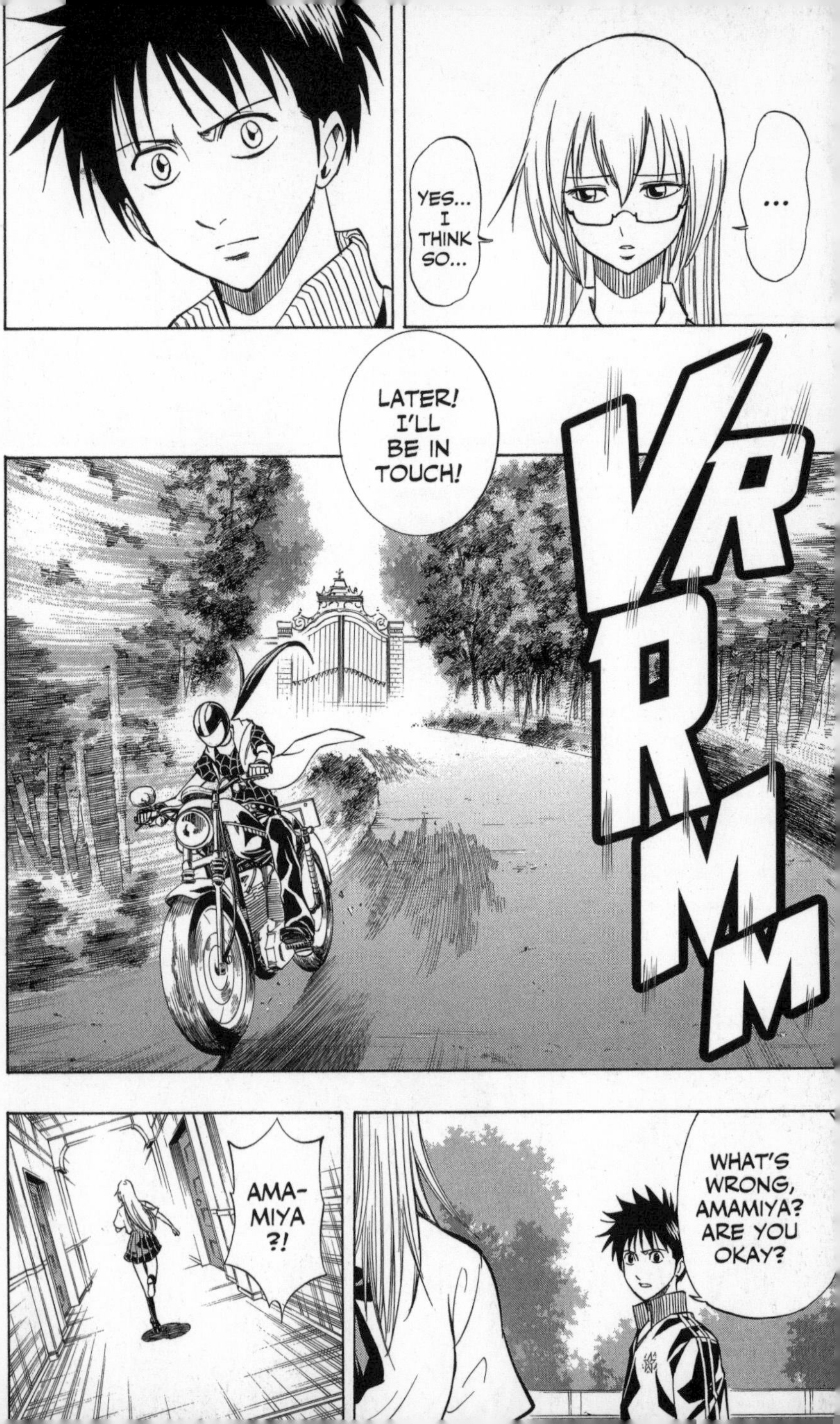
...
YES... I THINK SO...
LATER! I'LL BE IN TOUCH!
VRRMM
WHAT'S WRONG, AMAMIYA? ARE YOU OKAY?
AMA-MIYA?!

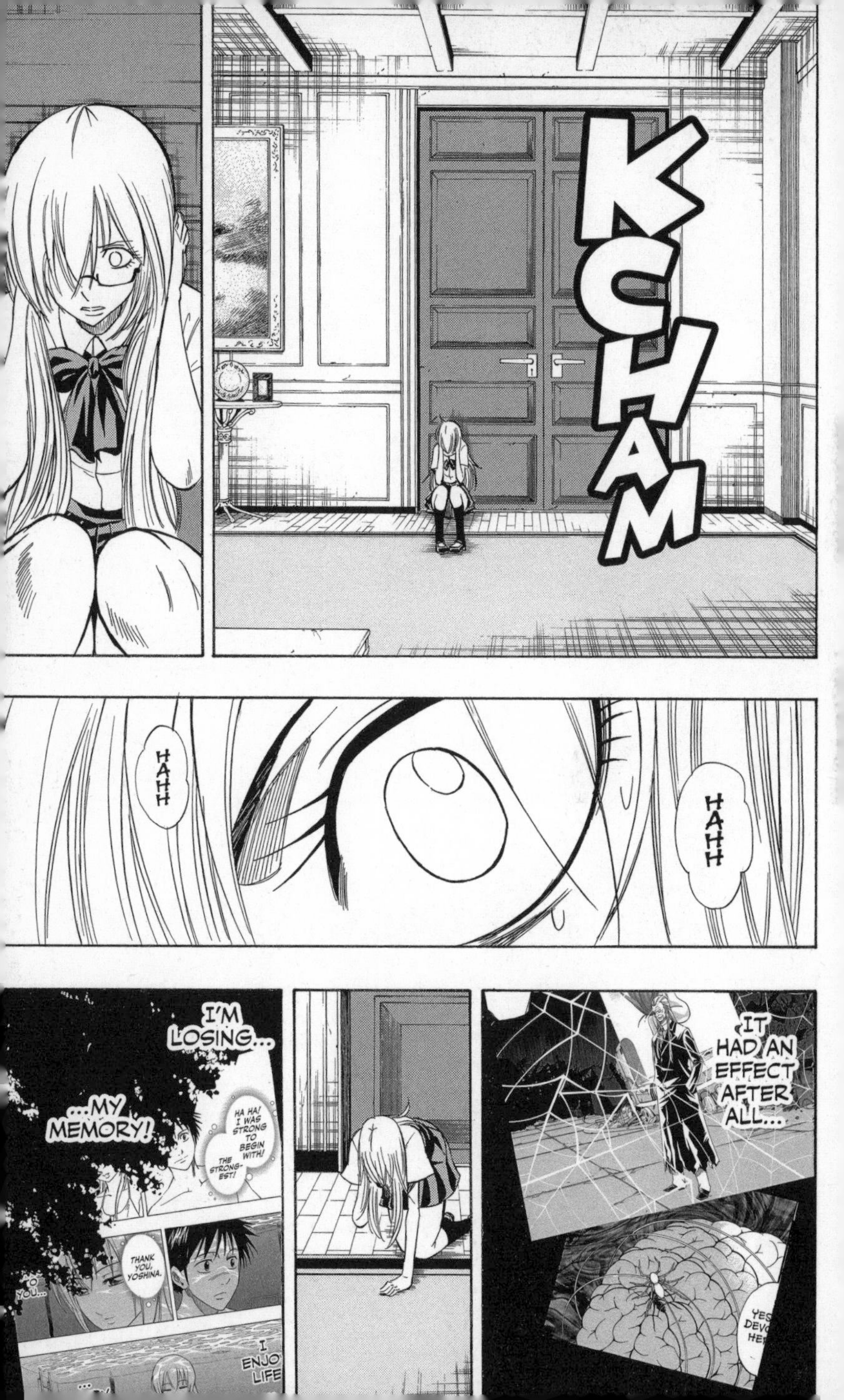
KCHAM
HAHH
HAHH
IT HAD AN EFFECT AFTER ALL...
I'M LOSING...
...MY MEMORY!
HA HA! I WAS STRONG TO BEGIN WITH!
THE STRONG-EST!
THANK YOU, YOSHINA.

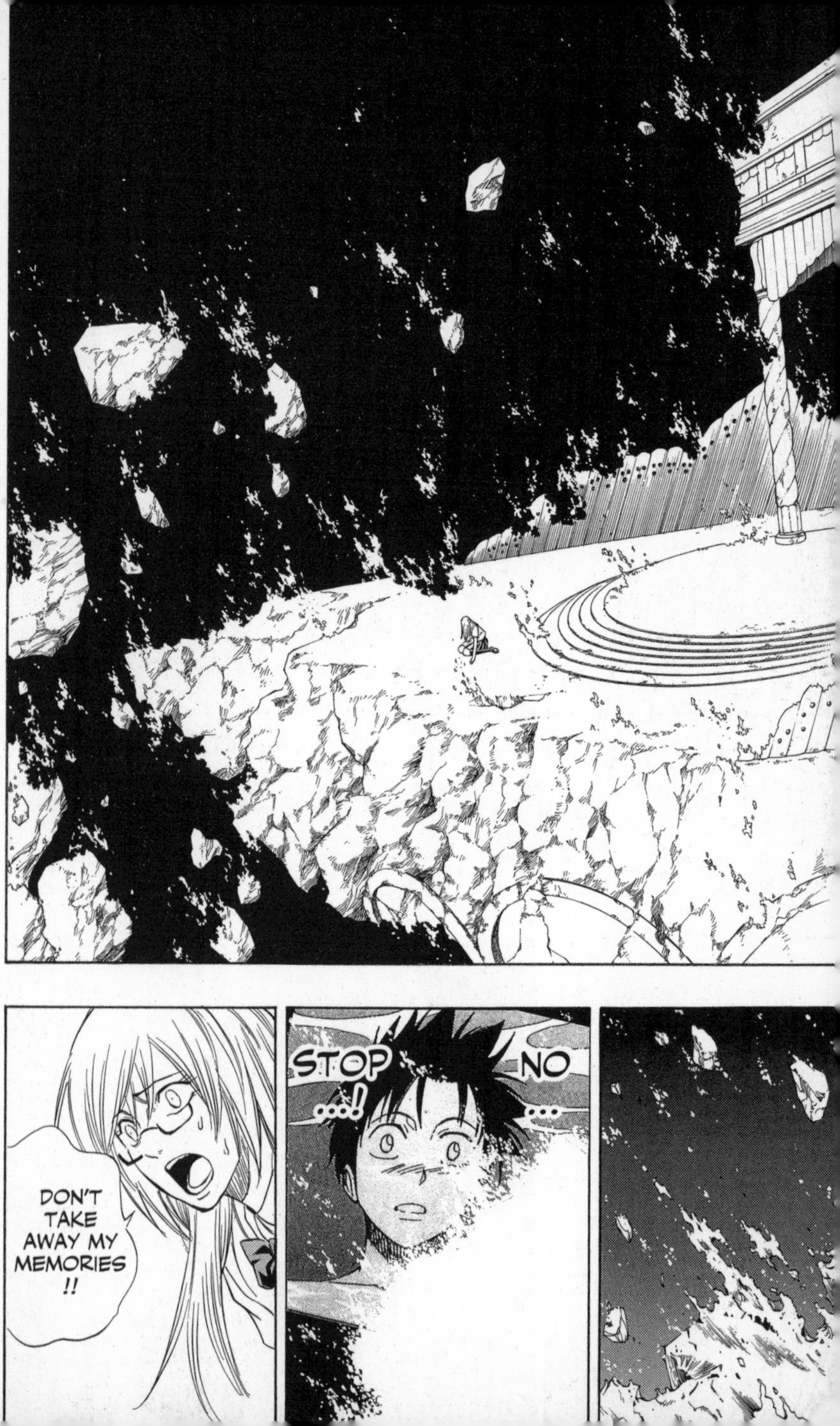
NO ...
STOP ...!
DON'T TAKE AWAY MY MEMORIES !!

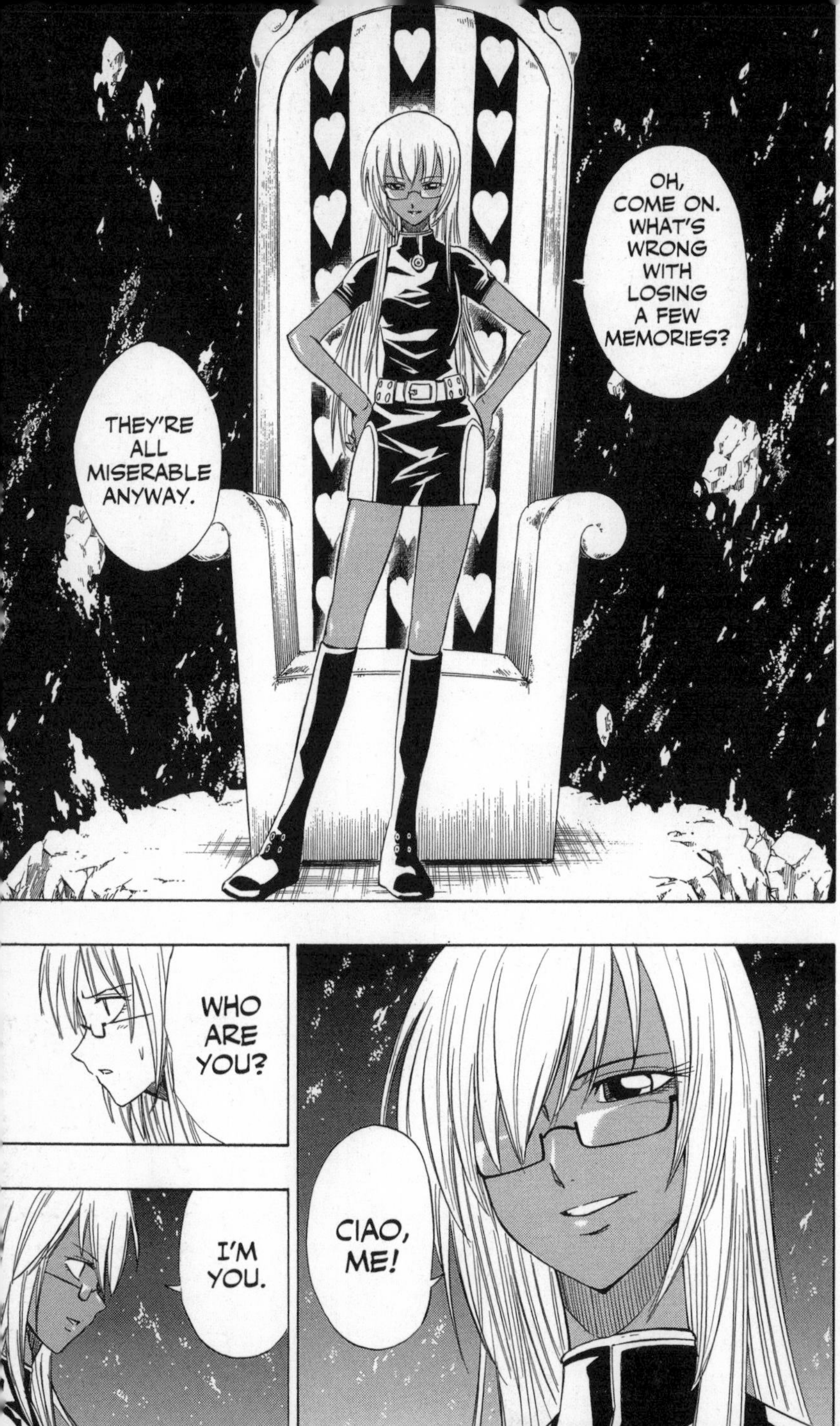
OH, COME ON. WHAT'S WRONG WITH LOSING A FEW MEMORIES?
THEY'RE ALL MISERABLE ANYWAY.
CIAO, ME!
WHO ARE YOU?
I'M YOU.

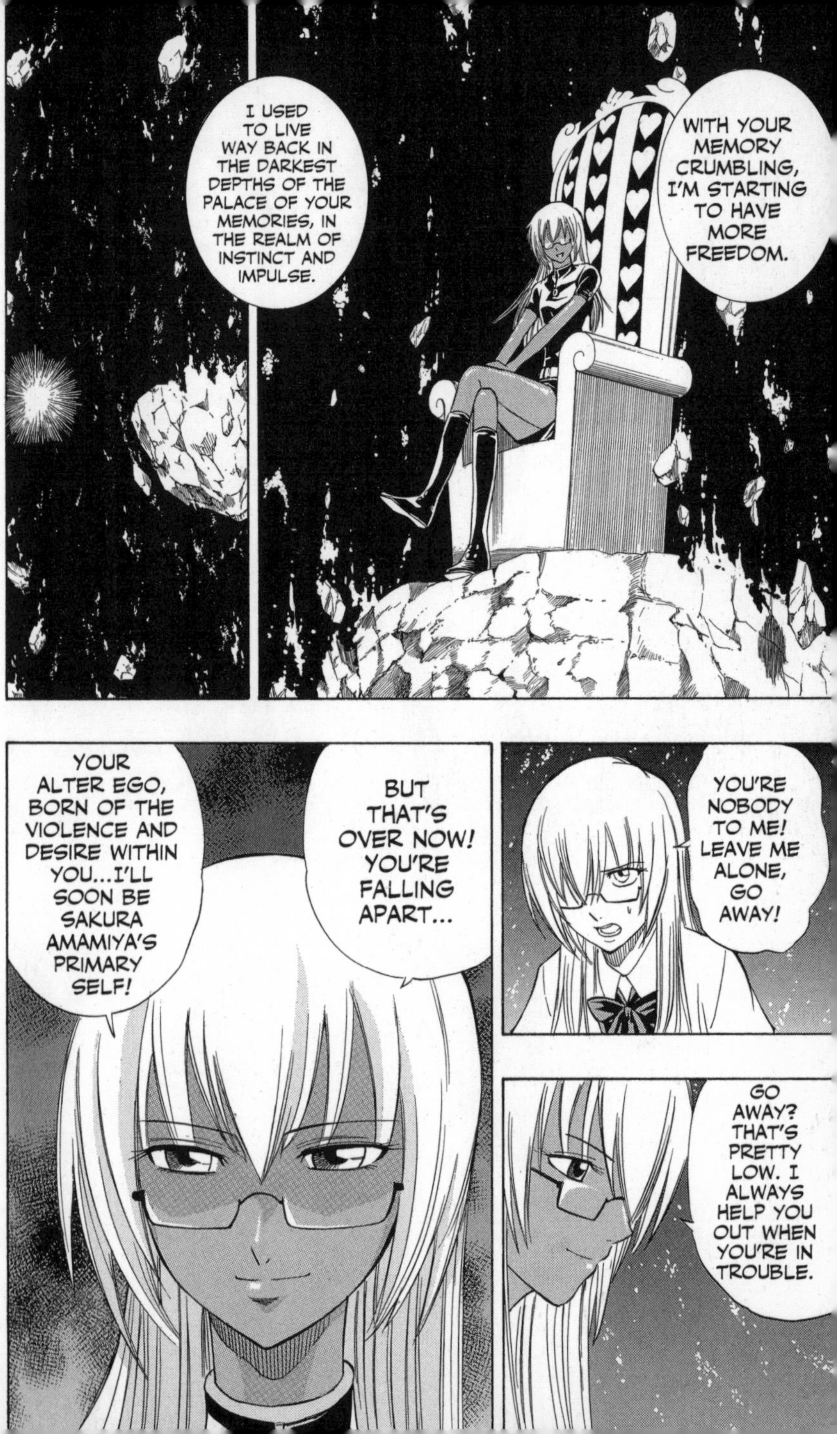
WITH YOUR MEMORY CRUMBLING, I'M STARTING TO HAVE MORE FREEDOM.
I USED TO LIVE WAY BACK IN THE DARKEST DEPTHS OF THE PALACE OF YOUR MEMORIES, IN THE REALM OF INSTINCT AND IMPULSE.
YOU'RE NOBODY TO ME! LEAVE ME ALONE, GO AWAY!
GO AWAY? THAT'S PRETTY LOW. I ALWAYS HELP YOU OUT WHEN YOU'RE IN TROUBLE.
BUT THAT'S OVER NOW! YOU'RE FALLING APART...
YOUR ALTER EGO, BORN OF THE VIOLENCE AND DESIRE WITHIN YOU...I'LL SOON BE SAKURA AMAMIYA'S PRIMARY SELF!

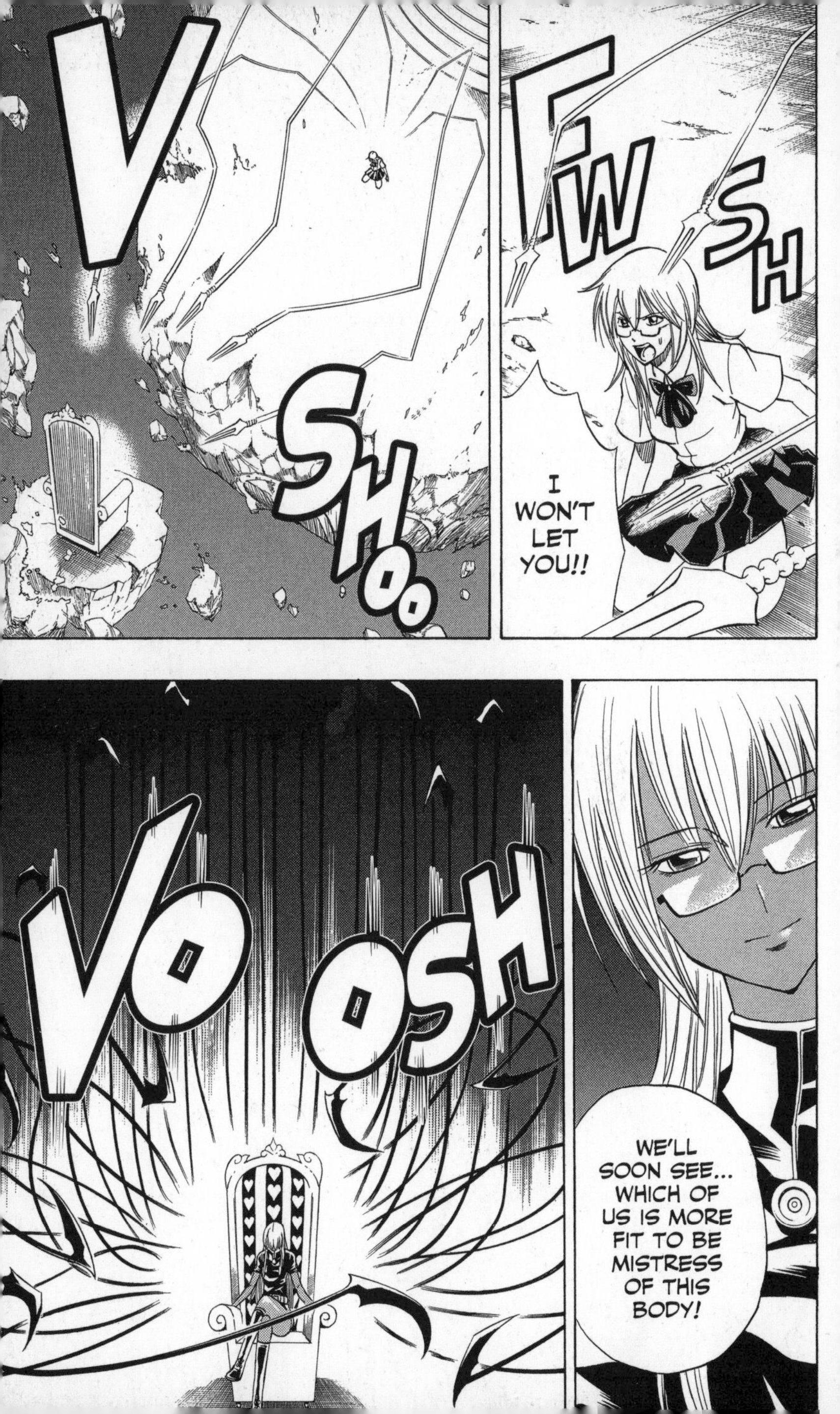
FWSH
I WON'T LET YOU!!
VSHOO
WE'LL SOON SEE... WHICH OF US IS MORE FIT TO BE MISTRESS OF THIS BODY!
VOOSH

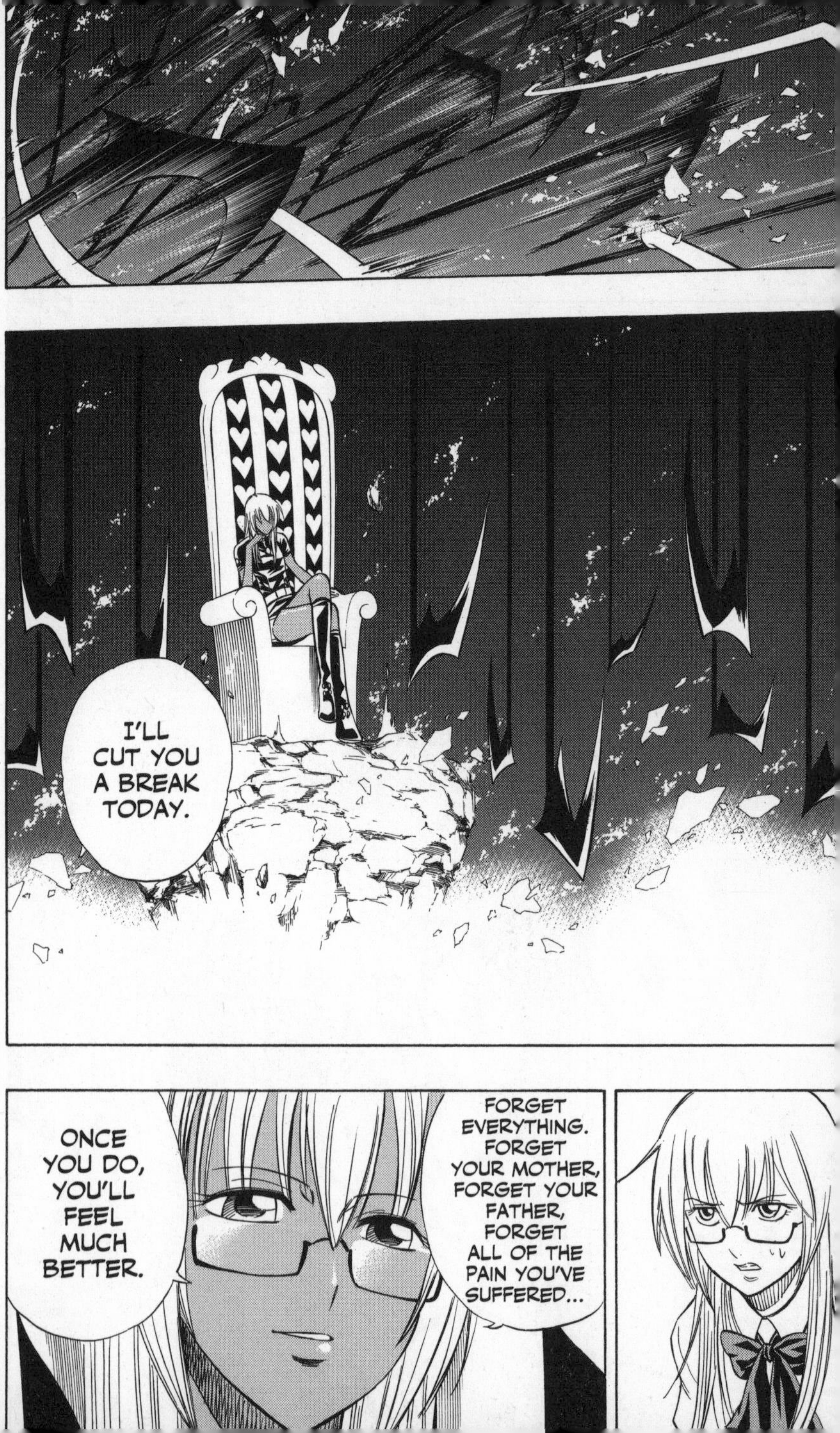
I'LL CUT YOU A BREAK TODAY.
FORGET EVERYTHING. FORGET YOUR MOTHER, FORGET YOUR FATHER, FORGET ALL OF THE PAIN YOU'VE SUFFERED...
ONCE YOU DO, YOU'LL FEEL MUCH BETTER.

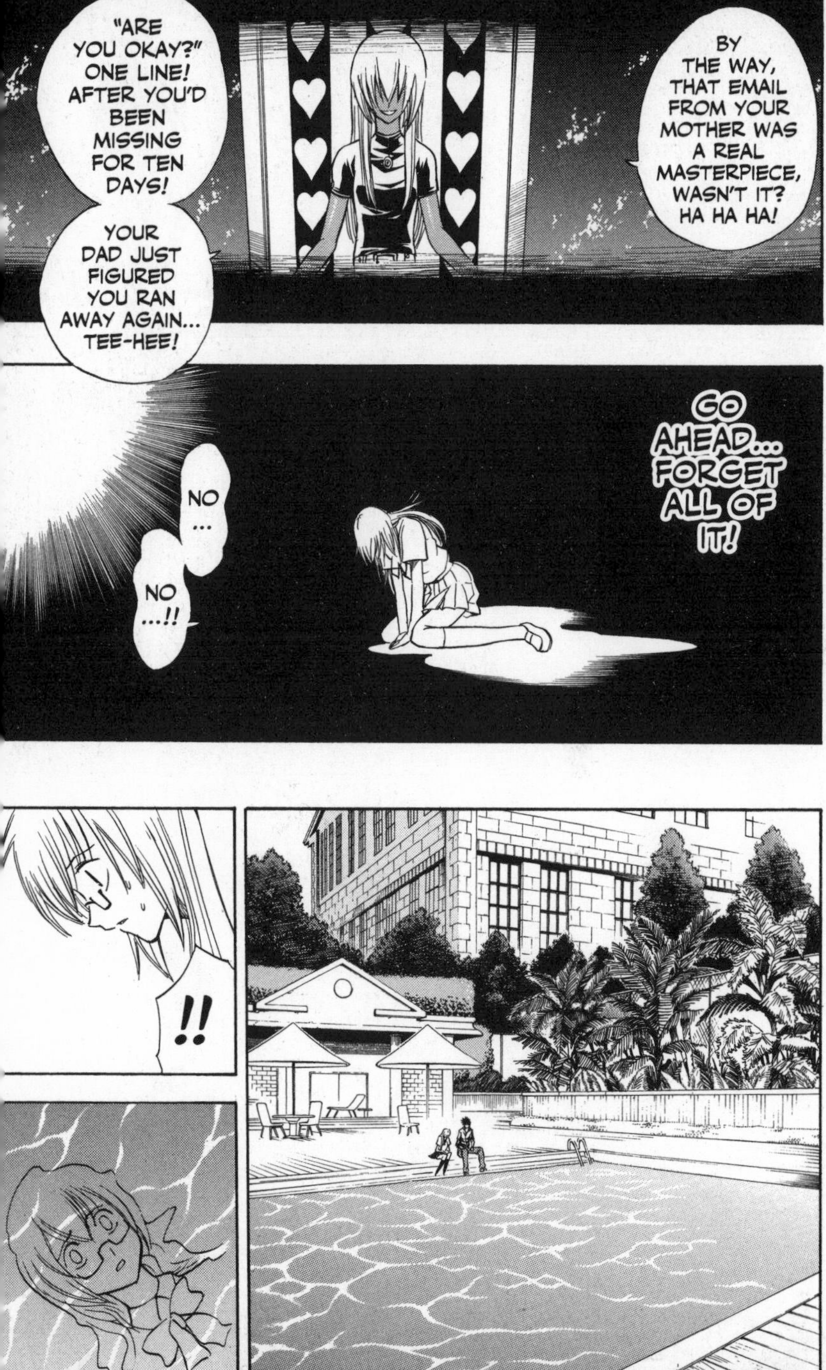
BY THE WAY, THAT EMAIL FROM YOUR MOTHER WAS A REAL MASTERPIECE, WASN'T IT? HA HA HA!
"ARE YOU OKAY?" ONE LINE! AFTER YOU'D BEEN MISSING FOR TEN DAYS!
YOUR DAD JUST FIGURED YOU RAN AWAY AGAIN... TEE-HEE!
GO AHEAD... FORGET ALL OF IT!
NO ...
NO ...!!
!!

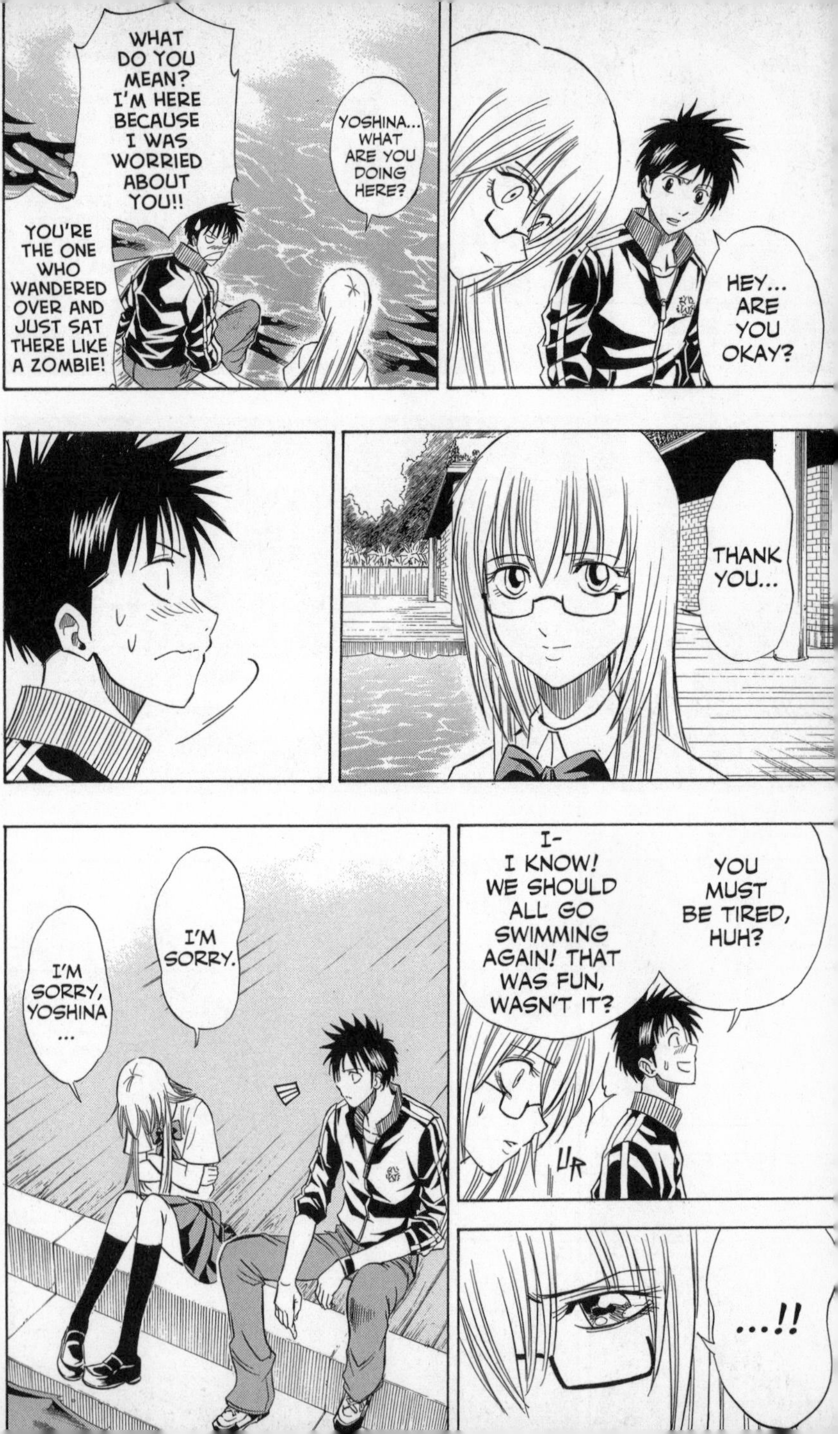
HEY... ARE YOU OKAY?
YOSHINA... WHAT ARE YOU DOING HERE?
WHAT DO YOU MEAN? I'M HERE BECAUSE I WAS WORRIED ABOUT YOU!!
YOU'RE THE ONE WHO WANDERED OVER AND JUST SAT THERE LIKE A ZOMBIE!
THANK YOU...
YOU MUST BE TIRED, HUH?
I- I KNOW! WE SHOULD ALL GO SWIMMING AGAIN! THAT WAS FUN, WASN'T IT?
UR
...!!
I'M SORRY.
I'M SORRY, YOSHINA ...

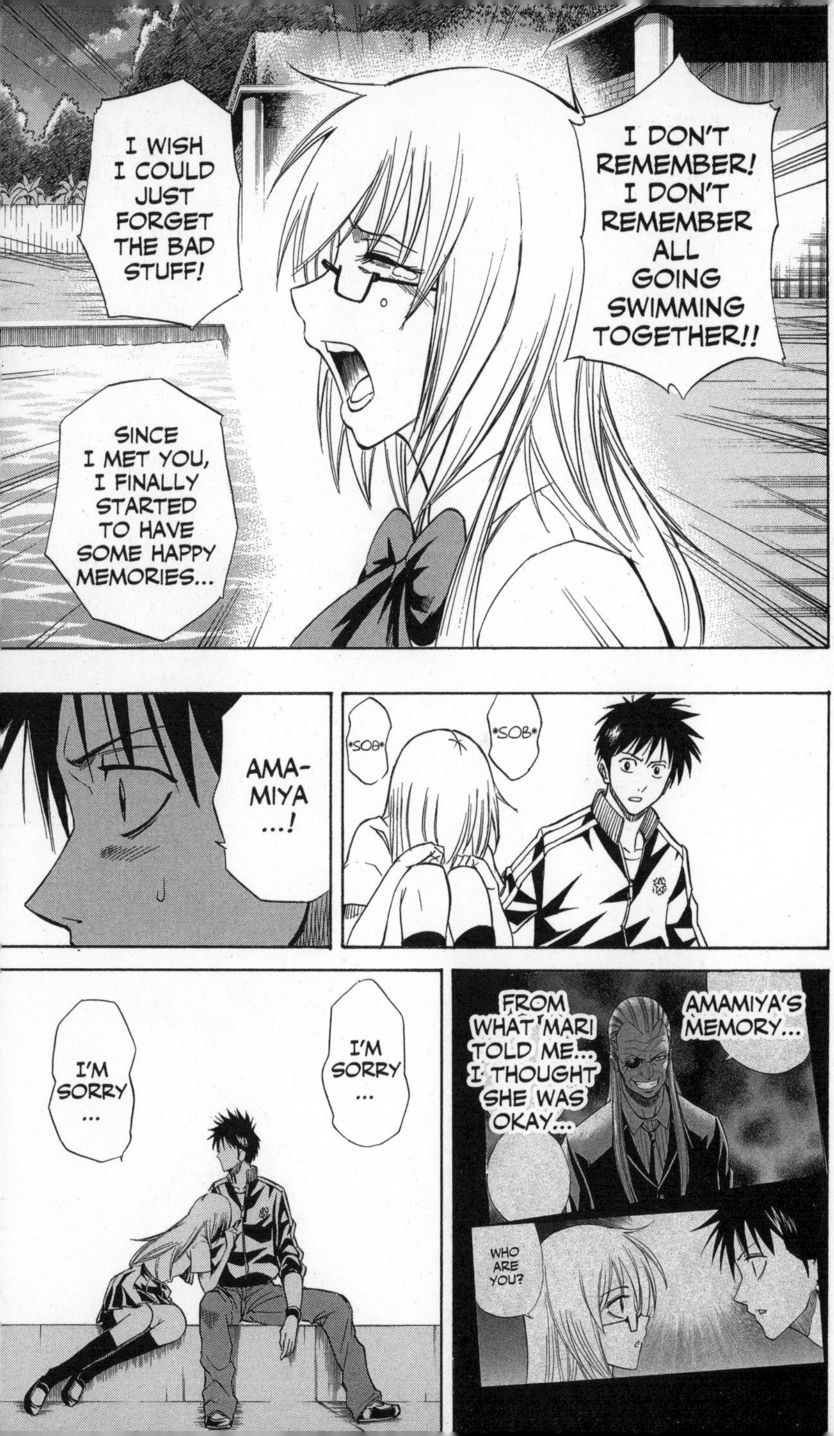
I DON'T REMEMBER! I DON'T REMEMBER ALL GOING SWIMMING TOGETHER!!
I WISH I COULD JUST FORGET THE BAD STUFF!
SINCE I MET YOU, I FINALLY STARTED TO HAVE SOME HAPPY MEMORIES...
SOB
SOB
AMA-MIYA ...!
AMAMIYA'S MEMORY...
FROM WHAT MARI TOLD ME... I THOUGHT SHE WAS OKAY...
WHO ARE YOU?
I'M SORRY ...
I'M SORRY ...

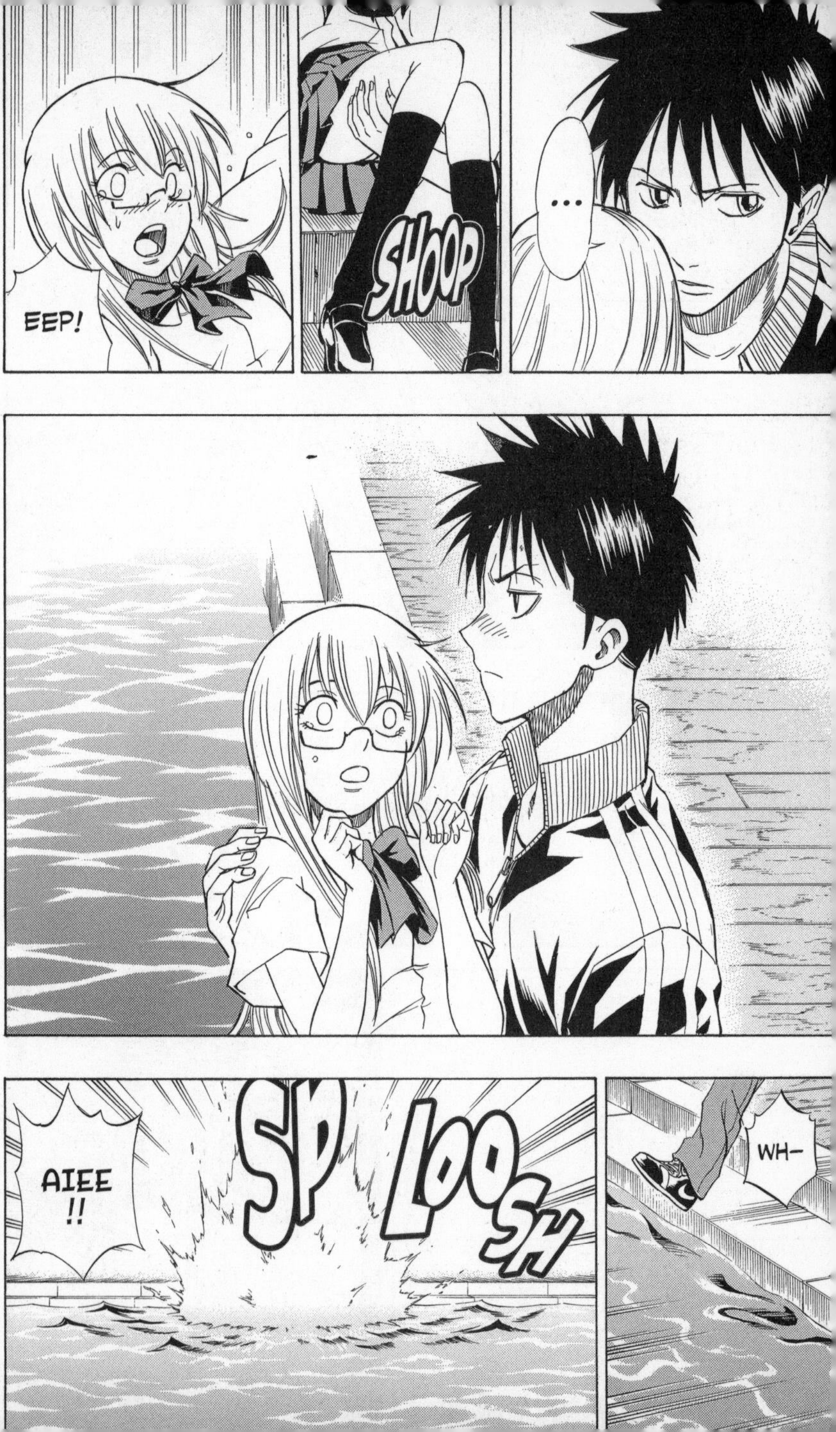
...
SHOOP
EEP!
WH–
AIEE !!
SPLOOSH

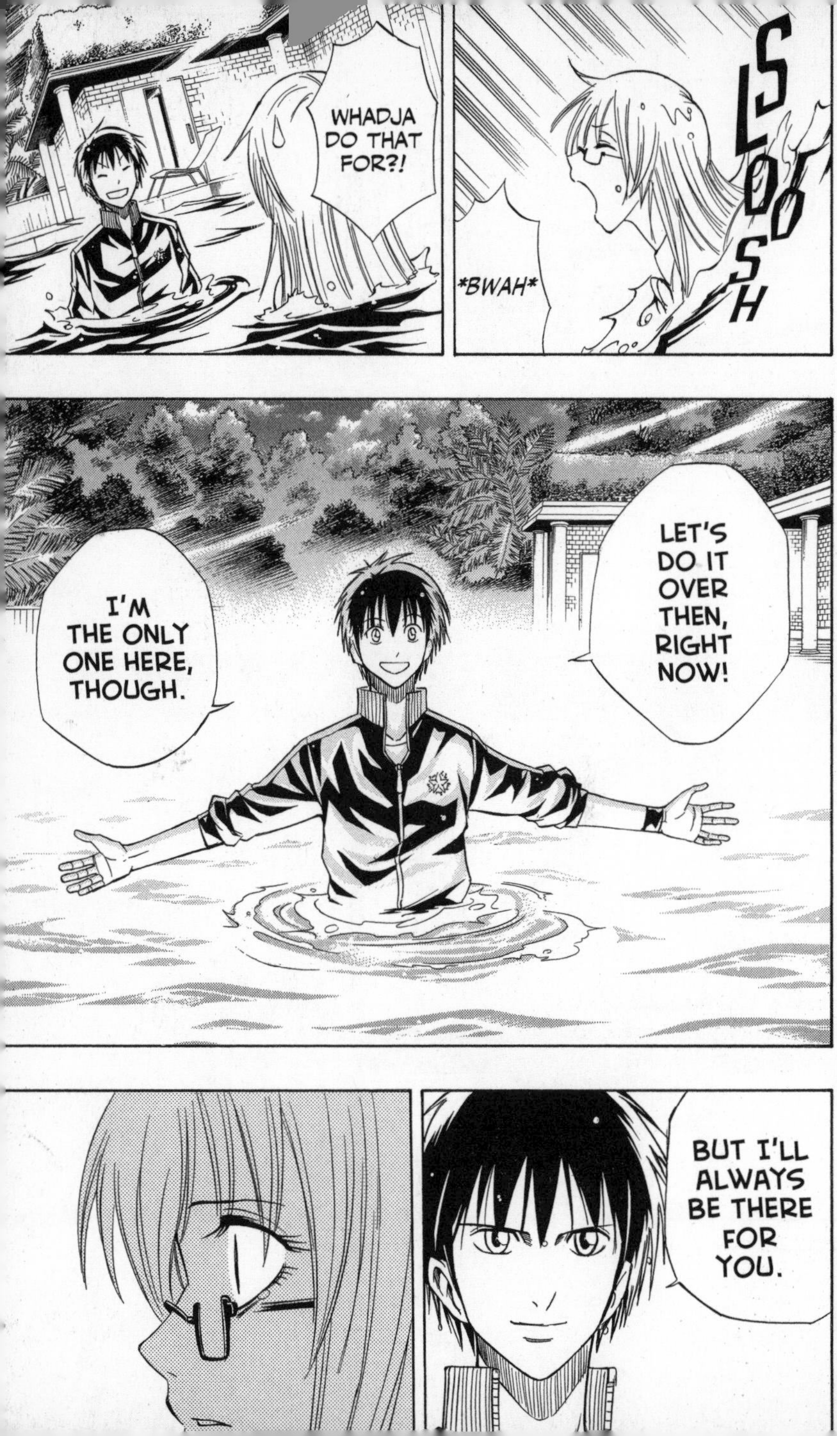
SLOOSH
BWAH
WHADJA DO THAT FOR?!
LET'S DO IT OVER THEN, RIGHT NOW!
I'M THE ONLY ONE HERE, THOUGH.
BUT I'LL ALWAYS BE THERE FOR YOU.

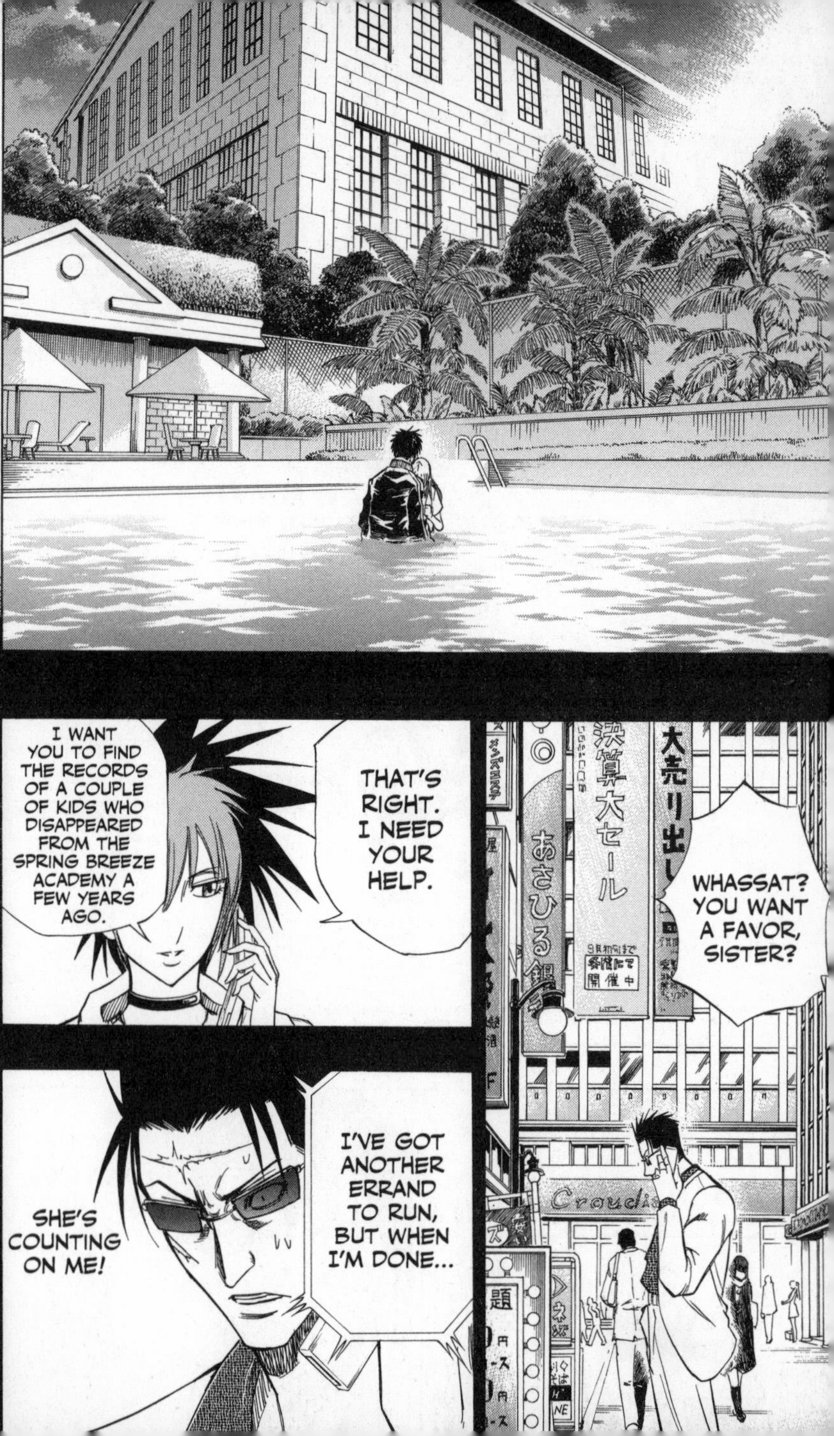

決算大セール
大売り出し
WHASSAT? YOU WANT A FAVOR, SISTER?
THAT'S RIGHT. I NEED YOUR HELP.
I WANT YOU TO FIND THE RECORDS OF A COUPLE OF KIDS WHO DISAPPEARED FROM THE SPRING BREEZE ACADEMY A FEW YEARS AGO.
I'VE GOT ANOTHER ERRAND TO RUN, BUT WHEN I'M DONE...
SHE'S COUNTING ON ME!

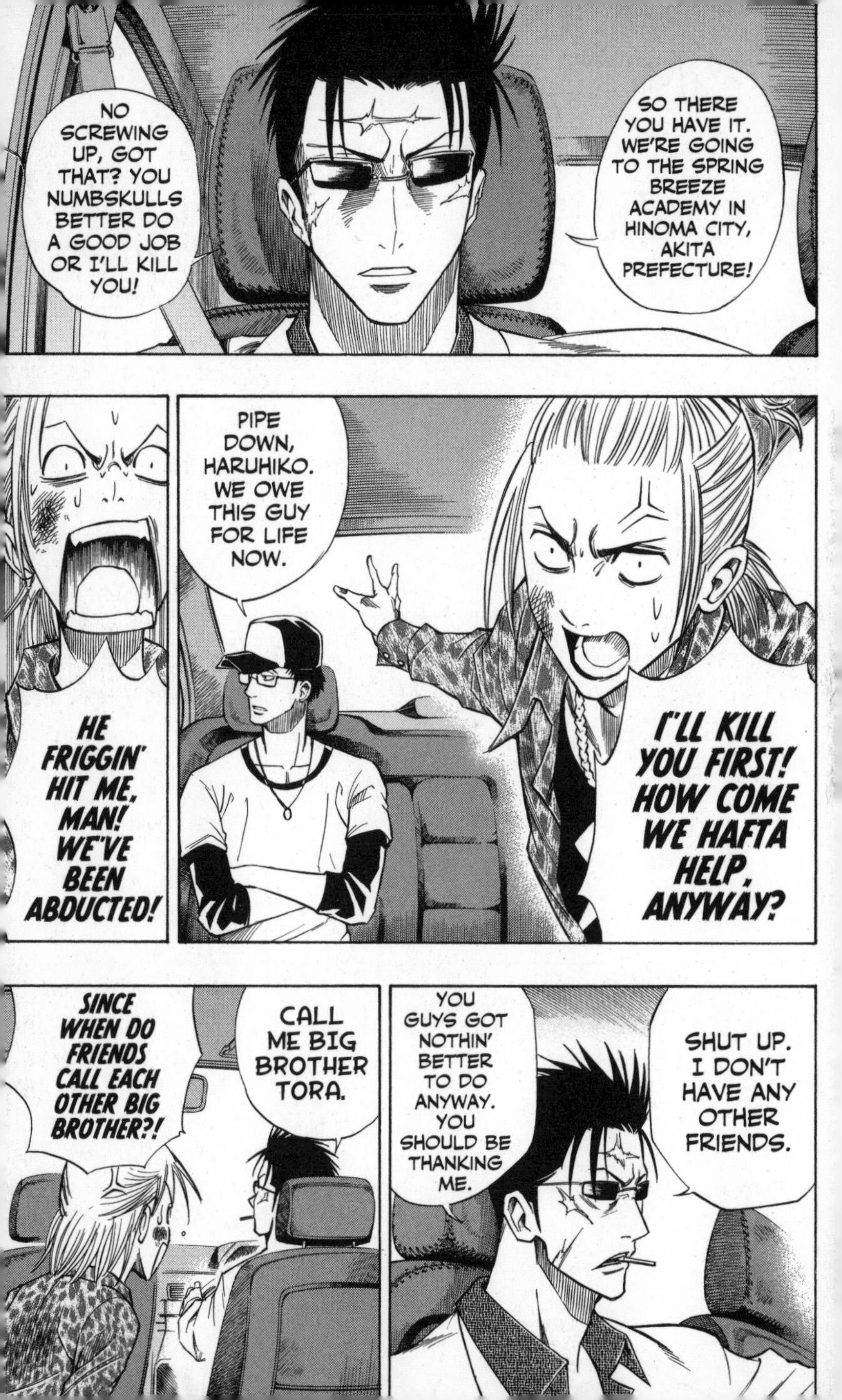

SO THERE YOU HAVE IT. WE'RE GOING TO THE SPRING BREEZE ACADEMY IN HINOMA CITY, AKITA PREFECTURE!
NO SCREWING UP, GOT THAT? YOU NUMBSKULLS BETTER DO A GOOD JOB OR I'LL KILL YOU!
I'LL KILL YOU FIRST! HOW COME WE HAFTA HELP, ANYWAY?
PIPE DOWN, HARUHIKO. WE OWE THIS GUY FOR LIFE NOW.
HE FRIGGIN' HIT ME, MAN! WE'VE BEEN ABDUCTED!
YOU GUYS GOT NOTHIN' BETTER TO DO ANYWAY. YOU SHOULD BE THANKING ME.
SHUT UP. I DON'T HAVE ANY OTHER FRIENDS.
CALL ME BIG BROTHER TORA.
SINCE WHEN DO FRIENDS CALL EACH OTHER BIG BROTHER?!

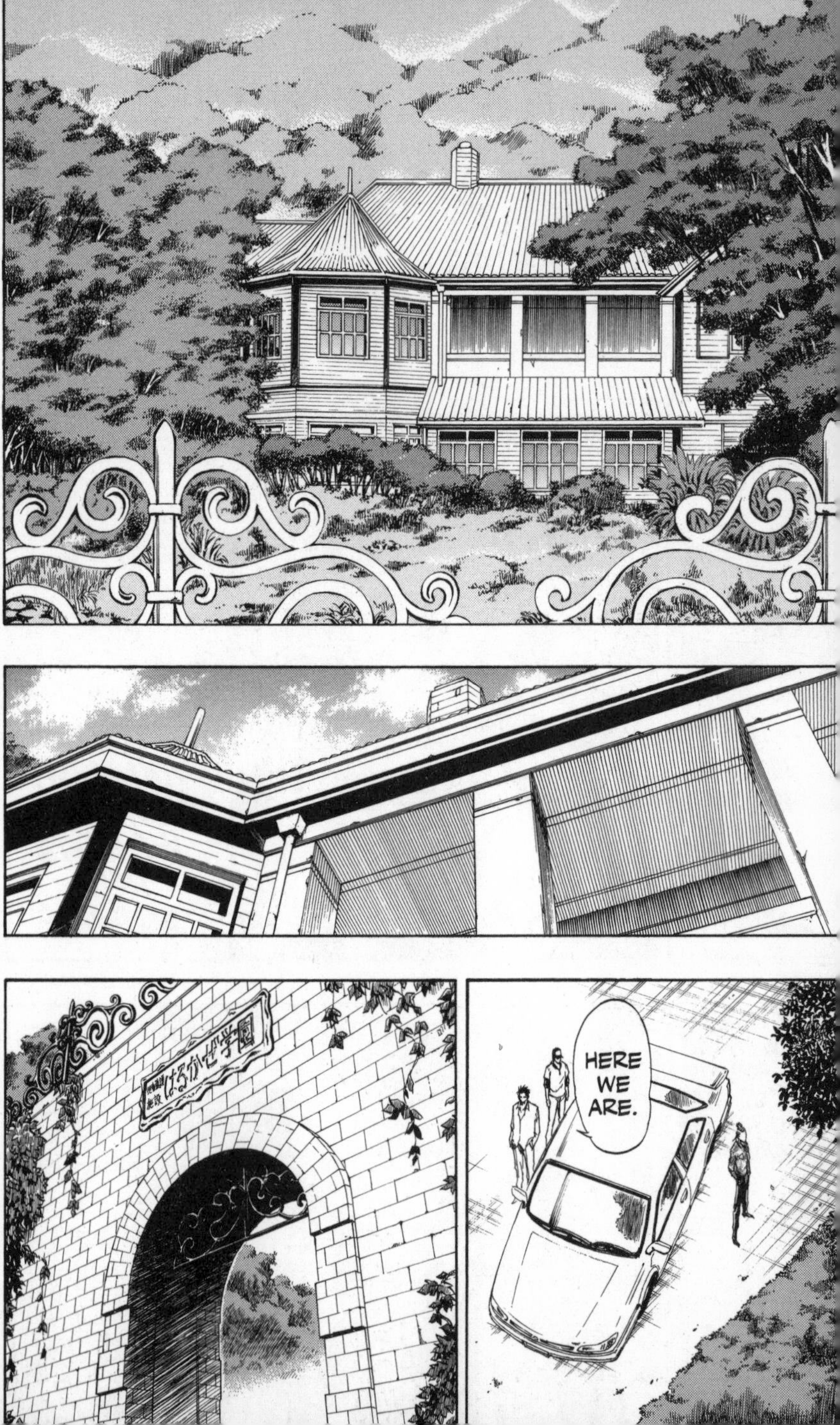
HERE WE ARE.
はるかぜ学園

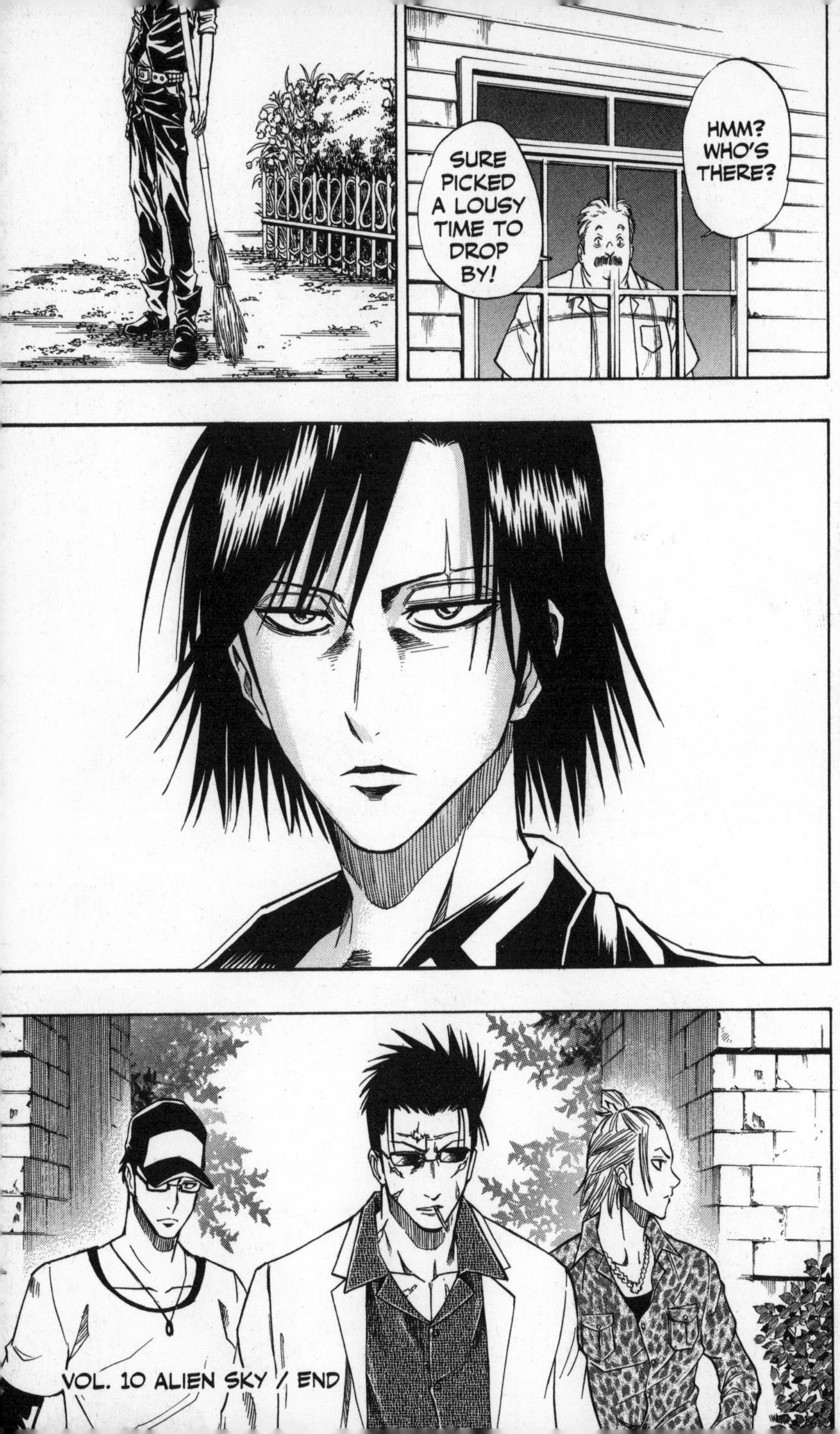
HMM? WHO'S THERE?
SURE PICKED A LOUSY TIME TO DROP BY!
VOL. 10 ALIEN SKY / END

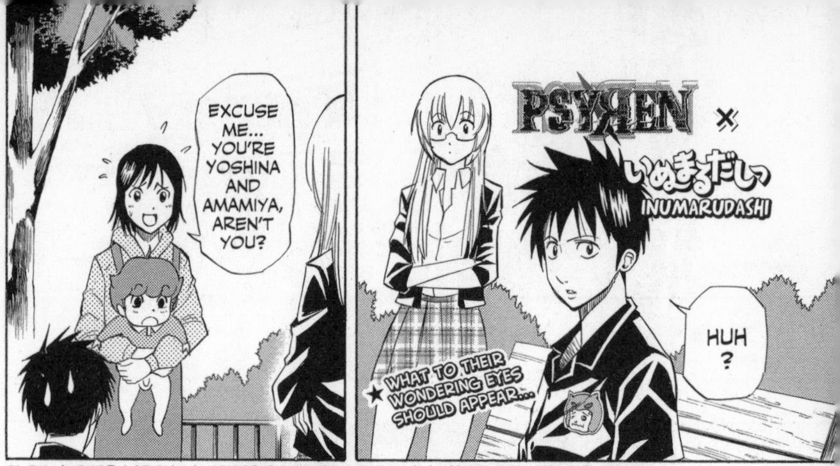
PSYREN ×
いぬまるだしっ
INUMARUDASHI
HUH?
★ WHAT TO THEIR WONDERING EYES SHOULD APPEAR...
EXCUSE ME... YOU'RE YOSHINA AND AMAMIYA, AREN'T YOU?

PLOT: A STORY ABOUT A YOUNG BOY WHO LETS IT ALL HANG OUT WHILE PLAYING GAMES AND HAVING FUN. NO TIME TRAVEL INVOLVED.

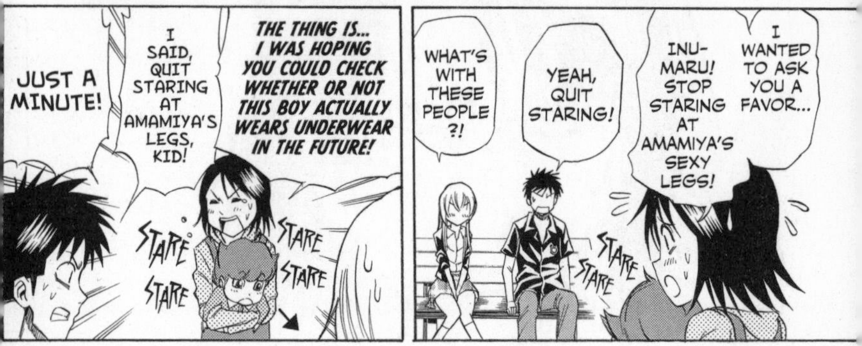
I WANTED TO ASK YOU A FAVOR...
INU-MARU! STOP STARING AT AMAMIYA'S SEXY LEGS!
YEAH, QUIT STARING!
WHAT'S WITH THESE PEOPLE?!
STARE STARE
THE THING IS... I WAS HOPING YOU COULD CHECK WHETHER OR NOT THIS BOY ACTUALLY WEARS UNDERWEAR IN THE FUTURE!
I SAID, QUIT STARING AT AMAMIYA'S LEGS, KID!
JUST A MINUTE!
STARE STARE
STARE STARE

TOSHIAKI IWASHIRO & KOJI OISHI

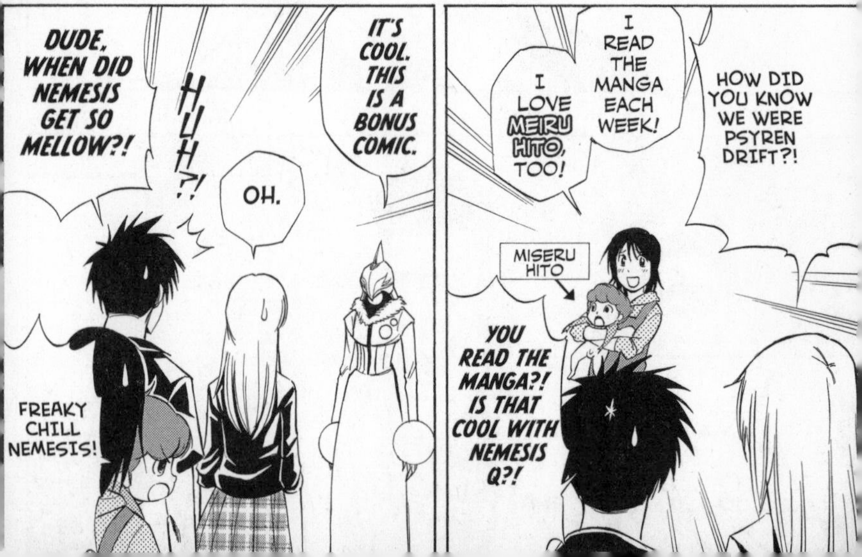
HOW DID YOU KNOW WE WERE PSYREN DRIFT?!
I READ THE MANGA EACH WEEK!
I LOVE MEIRU HITO, TOO!
MISERU HITO
YOU READ THE MANGA?! IS THAT COOL WITH NEMESIS Q?!
IT'S COOL. THIS IS A BONUS COMIC.
OH.
HUH?!
DUDE, WHEN DID NEMESIS GET SO MELLOW?!
FREAKY CHILL NEMESIS!

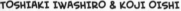

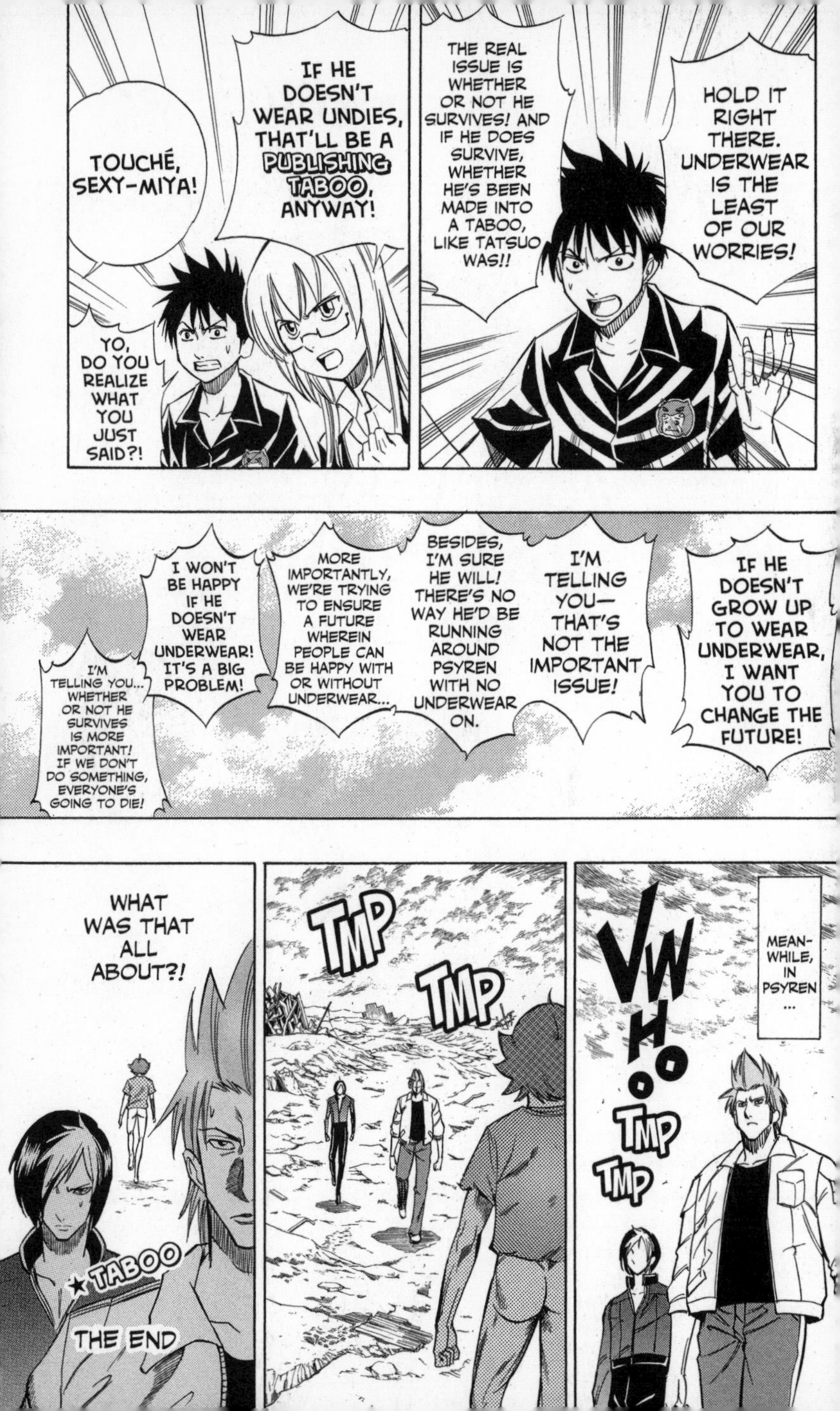
HOLD IT RIGHT THERE. UNDERWEAR IS THE LEAST OF OUR WORRIES!
THE REAL ISSUE IS WHETHER OR NOT HE SURVIVES! AND IF HE DOES SURVIVE, WHETHER HE'S BEEN MADE INTO A TABOO, LIKE TATSUO WAS!!
IF HE DOESN'T WEAR UNDIES, THAT'LL BE A PUBLISHING TABOO, ANYWAY!
TOUCHÉ, SEXY-MIYA!
YO, DO YOU REALIZE WHAT YOU JUST SAID?!
IF HE DOESN'T GROW UP TO WEAR UNDERWEAR, I WANT YOU TO CHANGE THE FUTURE!
I'M TELLING YOU— THAT'S NOT THE IMPORTANT ISSUE!
BESIDES, I'M SURE HE WILL! THERE'S NO WAY HE'D BE RUNNING AROUND PSYREN WITH NO UNDERWEAR ON.
MORE IMPORTANTLY, WE'RE TRYING TO ENSURE A FUTURE WHEREIN PEOPLE CAN BE HAPPY WITH OR WITHOUT UNDERWEAR...
I WON'T BE HAPPY IF HE DOESN'T WEAR UNDERWEAR! IT'S A BIG PROBLEM!
I'M TELLING YOU... WHETHER OR NOT HE SURVIVES IS MORE IMPORTANT! IF WE DON'T DO SOMETHING, EVERYONE'S GOING TO DIE!
MEAN-WHILE, IN PSYREN...
VWHOOO
TMP
TMP
TMP
TMP
WHAT WAS THAT ALL ABOUT?!
★TABOO
THE END

IN THE NEXT VOLUME...

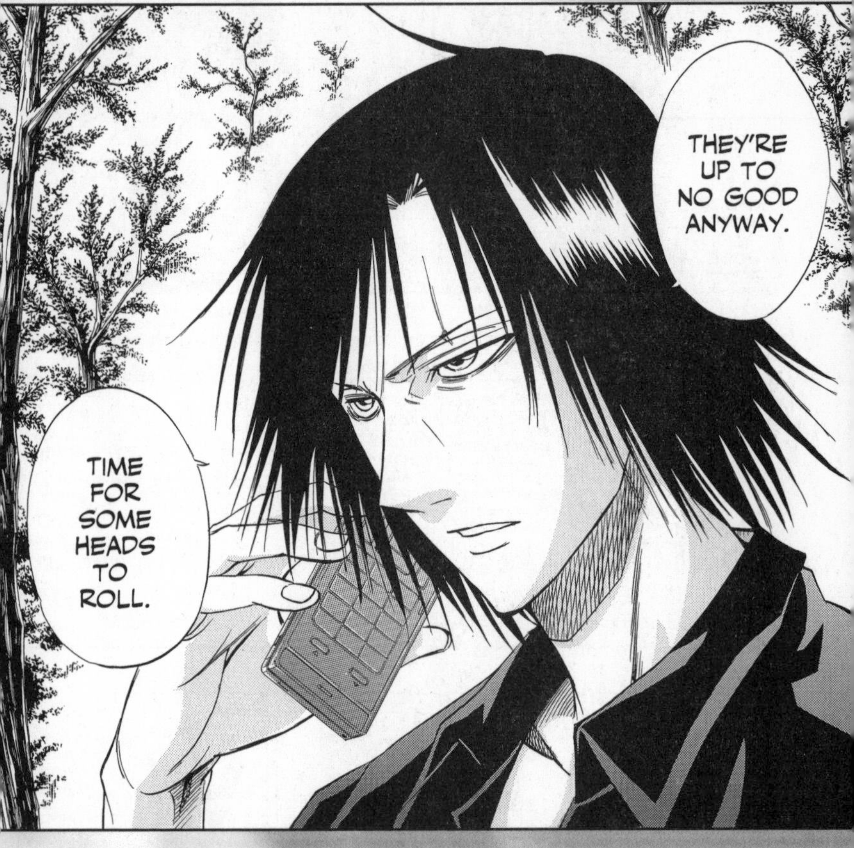
THEY'RE UP TO NO GOOD ANYWAY.
TIME FOR SOME HEADS TO ROLL.

THE TWO TEST SUBJECTS

Ageha's friend Kagetora and his team head to Spring Breeze Academy to look for information about Miroku Amagi, the man destined to end the world. Once there Kagetora clashes with Junas, Star Commander of the shadowy group know as W.I.S.E, and Miroku takes on a powerful psionist whom Miroku hopes to recruit for his new world order.

Available JULY 2013!

You're Reading in the Wrong Direction!!

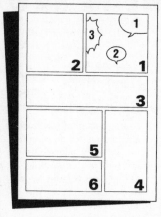

Whoops! Guess what? You're starting at the wrong end of the comic!

…It's true! In keeping with the original Japanese format, **Psyren** is meant to be read from right to left, starting in the upper-right corner.

Unlike English, which is read from left to right, Japanese is read from right to left, meaning that action, sound effects and word-balloon order are completely reversed—something which can make readers unfamiliar with Japanese feel pretty backwards themselves. For this reason, manga or Japanese comics published in the U.S. in English have sometimes been published "flopped"—that is, printed in exact reverse order, as though seen from the other side of a mirror.

By flopping pages, U.S. publishers can avoid confusing readers, but the compromise is not without its downside. For one thing, a character in a flopped manga series who once wore in the original Japanese version a T-shirt emblazoned with "M A Y" (as in "the merry month of") now wears one which reads "Y A M"! Additionally, many manga creators in Japan are themselves unhappy with the process, as some feel the mirror-imaging of their art changes their original intentions.

We are proud to bring you Toshiaki Iwashiro's **Psyren** in the original unflopped format. For now, though, turn to the other side of the book and let the fun begin…!

—Editor